Reading the
New Testament

An Introduction

by

Pheme Perkins

PAULIST PRESS
New York, N.Y./Mahwah, N.J.

The Publisher gratefully acknowledges permission to adapt illustrations found in chapter ten, "The Asclepion at Corinth," after J. Murphy-O'Connor's figure in *St. Paul's Corinth*, © 1983, Michael Glazier, Inc., Wilmington, Delaware; in chapter eleven, "The Upper Square at Ephesus," and in chapter fifteen, "Asclepion at Messene," after Christian Habicht's *Pausanias' Guide to Ancient Greece*, figures 3 and 8a, © 1985, the Regents of the University of California.

Cover art and design by Gloria Claudia Ortiz.
Book design by Theresa M. Sparacio.

Library of Congress Cataloging-in-Publication Data

Perkins, Pheme.
    Reading the New Testament.

    Bibliography: p.
    Includes index.
    1. Bible. N.T.—Introductions. I. Title.
BS2330.2.P45   1987   225.6'1   87-29065
ISBN 0-8091-2939-6 (pbk.)

Published by Paulist Press
997 Macarthur Boulevard
Mahwah, New Jersey 07430

Printed and bound in the
United States of America

CONTENTS

Chapter 1

WHY STUDY THE BIBLE?

What Is the New Testament?

Many people would find it difficult to answer the question, "What is the New Testament?" Sometimes students say, "What they read in church," or "the story of Jesus." You will see twenty-seven different writings listed in the table of contents. What holds the whole collection together? They are not twenty-seven chapters in a single book. The most general answer you could give would be to speak of a common belief shared by all the writers: Jesus of Nazareth represents a decisive turning point in God's relationship to humanity. Or, to put it in the words of Acts 4:12, "There is salvation in no one else, for there is no other name under heaven, given to human beings by which we must be saved."

This common belief in Jesus Christ is expressed in many different ways in the New Testament. We will constantly be asking ourselves how each way of expressing the message speaks to the situation of Christians in an author's audience. The New Testament provides us with a window into the emergence of Christianity.

You may also have noticed that the NT writings are arranged in groups. The four gospels are grouped together at the beginning. That meant separating the gospel written by Luke from Acts, which he considered to be the second part of the work he had begun in the gospel. Then we have fourteen letters that were either written by Paul or were attributed to his authorship. The last, Hebrews, does not really belong in the group, since it does not claim any connection with the Pauline tradition. The others, whether by Paul or by disciples writing in Paul's name, are divided into two groups, each in descending order of length. The first group comprises letters addressed to churches. The second comprises those addressed to individuals. Then we have a group of seven letters that

1

were attributed to other apostolic figures: James, Peter, John and Jude. Finally, Revelation, a prophetic vision of the end of this world with the great victory of Jesus and his "holy ones," brings the collection to its close.

Dating Books in the New Testament

Unlike modern books, most ancient writings do not carry dates. Clearly, any book must be written after events to which it refers and sometime before it is used by another writer or before the date of our earliest manuscript fragments. Sometimes, like the book of Daniel, which seems to have been written around 167 B.C., a book may "pretend" to be written in an earlier time. Daniel is set in the Babylonian captivity of the sixth century B.C. But even distinguishing when a work was composed from the fictive time in which it is set does not tell the whole story. Daniel chs. 1–6 contain a number of stories about Jewish courtiers and their dealings with Babylonian kings. Scholars think that some of these stories actually originated several hundred years before they were taken over by the author of Daniel.

To even guess at when a biblical book was written, we have to answer a number of questions. First, does the book refer to any historical persons or events for which we can give dates on the basis of other historical information that we have? Second, is the book itself taken up and used by later writers? Third, how does the date suggested by such clues compare with the setting implied by the narrative? Has the author chosen to write as though living at some other time or place? Fourth, what about the possible dates of stories or traditions being used within a book? Has the author used older traditions or even earlier written materials that we can identify. (Lk 1:1 claims familiarity with a number of earlier accounts, for example.) Fifth, can we isolate possible time and place of origin for any of the traditions being used?

We can only estimate when particular writings were composed. What follows is a very rough, "best guess" chronology. Some of the guesses can be established with more certainty than others. Any commentary on a particular writing will discuss the problems of dating and some of the alternatives proposed by scholars.

The Contents of the New Testament

I. Gospels and Acts

(1) *Matthew* (ca. A.D. 85–90). This gospel makes use of Mk as well as other traditions about Jesus and collections of Jesus' sayings. It was com-

posed in Greek as the reference to Daniel as "the prophet" in 24:15 implies. (It is only in the Greek translation of the OT that Dan is included among the prophets.) Mt also contains special material which suggests a Palestinian origin such as the references to the "towns of Israel" (10:23; 2:20–21, "land of Israel"). Many scholars think that the community which formed the basis of the Matthean church had come from Palestine and settled in Syria. Mt 4:24 has the only reference in the gospels to Jesus' fame spreading "throughout all Syria." The community may have been predominantly Christians of Jewish background, since non-Jews (Gentiles) are referred to as outsiders (5:47; 6:7,32; 10:5–6,17–18; 18:17). The community continues to reverence the Jewish law (5:18–19; 23:2).

(2) *Mark* (ca. A.D. 68–70). Our earliest gospel, Mk has been used by both Mt and Lk. Mk emphasizes the need for Christians to expect suffering. Mk 13:9–10 speaks of persecution by Jews and "governors and kings." Many scholars think that the crisis of suffering should be linked to Nero's execution of Christians at Rome ca. A.D. 62, which claimed the lives of both Peter and Paul. Others think that Mk is referring to the sufferings of Christians in Palestine during the Jewish revolt against Rome (A.D. 66–70). Mk 13 collects a number of prophecies about the coming destruction of the temple and Jerusalem, and Mk 16:7 focuses our attention on Galilee as the place where Jesus' frightened disciples are to see him again. The Marcan community is predominantly Gentile. Explanations for Jewish customs are given (e.g. Mk 7:3–4,11c,19c). Freedom from Jewish sabbath rules and purity regulations applies to all Christians (e.g. 2:27–28; 7:3,8,19).

(3) *Luke* (ca. A.D. 85). When Lk repeats the prophecies of the destruction of Jerusalem from Mk, Lk makes sure that they reflect details of Titus' siege of Jerusalem (cp. Mk 13:2 and Lk 21:5; Mk 13:14 and Lk 21:10; as well as the sayings about Jerusalem in Lk 13:35a and 19:43–44). Lk 1:2 clearly separates the author from the generation of persons who were "eyewitnesses" to the ministry of Jesus. Lk's uncertainty about Palestinian geography suggests that he could not have been from that part of the world. The quality of his writing points to education beyond the elementary level. Lk shows familiarity with the Greek Old Testament and with Hellenistic literary techniques. Lk tries to locate the emergence of Christianity within the context of the larger Graeco-Roman world. Some exegetes identify Lk with the "fellow worker" in the Pauline mission (Phlm 24; Col 4:14 [basis for the later story that Lk was a physician] and 2 Tim 4:11).

(4) *John* (ca. A.D. 90). Johannine traditions about Jesus are quite different from what we find in the synoptic gospels (= Mt, Mk and Lk). They do show points of contact with Marcan and Lucan material, which suggests that the Johannine traditions represent an independent line of develop-

ment of the Jesus tradition. Jn alludes to expulsion of Christians from Jewish synagogues (9:22; 16:2a). Many scholars link that event with the addition of a curse against Jewish Christians to the benedictions of the synagogue liturgy around A.D. 90. Our earliest fragments of Jn come from the first quarter of the second century. The gospel's author is unknown, though its traditions are attributed to an anonymous figure in the narrative, "the beloved disciple." This disciple is not one of the twelve. He only appears in the story during Jesus' last days in Jerusalem, at the cross (Jn 19:35) and in the resurrection stories (21:24). He may have been the founder of the Johannine community. Jn 21:23 hints that unlike Peter he did not die a martyr but lived to a considerable age. He may have been responsible for the unique symbolic language that we find in the gospel.

(5) *Acts* (ca. A.D. 95). Acts 1:1–5 identifies the book as a continuation of Luke's gospel. The introduction summarizes the gospel story and prepares the reader for the new stage that begins with Pentecost. Acts does not appear to have been intended to be a "history" of the earliest years of the church. The events mentioned do not extend beyond Paul's imprisonment at Jerusalem and subsequent removal to Rome for trial (ca. A.D. 57–60). The story of Peter and the other apostles is dropped when the narrative shifts to Paul's journeys. We never learn about the martyrdom of either of these famous apostles.

II. Pauline Letters

(6) *Romans* (ca. A.D. 55–58). Paul wrote this letter to the Christians in Rome as he was winding up his missionary activity in Asia Minor and Greece. After delivering a collection from those churches for the poor in Jerusalem, he hoped to visit Rome and receive aid from Christians there to begin a missionary effort in Spain (Rom 15:22–32). Chapter 16 contains greetings to fellow workers who had been active in Paul's mission in Asia Minor and Greece.

(7) *1 Corinthians* (ca. A.D. 53/54). Paul had spent eighteen months working in Corinth (ca. A.D. 50/52) and had founded the church in this important commercial city. He has received a letter from Christians there as well as various reports about problems at Corinth. He expects that 1 Cor will arrive before his associate Timothy comes to Corinth. He urges the Corinthians to give Timothy a warm welcome and to set aside money for the poor. Paul himself expects to travel through Macedonia to Corinth for a visit (1 Cor 16:1–11).

(8) *2 Corinthians* (ca. A.D. 55/56). This is a very complex letter, since it appears to be made up of three or four different letters that Paul sent to Corinth. The visit mentioned in 1 Cor had been a disaster. Paul had been

humiliated by someone in the Corinthian church (2 Cor 2:5–8). His apostleship was being challenged as "weak" and lacking in power by traveling missionaries who had come to Corinth and won a following among the Corinthians (2 Cor 10:10–11; 11:4–6). Paul had apparently cancelled another visit to Corinth and had written a very sharp letter of rebuke (2 Cor 1:23–2:4). 2 Cor 1–7 gives thanks that the rift between Paul and the Corinthians has been healed through the work of Titus. But 2 Cor 10–13 is written in such a painful tone that many think these chapters were copied from the earlier "tearful letter." 2 Cor 8–9 deals with a different subject entirely, the collection for the poor at Jerusalem. These chapters may be a single letter of appeal or a combination of two letters, one to Corinth and one to the Christians elsewhere in the province of Achaia.

(9) *Galatians* (ca. A.D. 55). Paul tells us that he founded this church when he became ill on a journey through Galatia (Gal 4:13). His letter does not mention any plans for a future visit to the church there, so some scholars think that Gal was written toward the end of Paul's missionary work. Paul is confronting a serious problem. When he had converted the Gentiles of this region to Christianity, he did not require that they adopt any Jewish customs. Now others are telling them that they should also adopt Jewish ways. They should show loyalty to the covenant between God and the Jewish people by being circumcised, keeping certain Jewish holidays and observing some Jewish dietary restrictions. Some people may have said that Paul had violated the agreements he had made with Peter and James in Jerusalem by not imposing such requirements. Paul is furious. He retells the story of his conversion and his early association with the Jerusalem church (Gal 1:11–2:14). He insists that they all agreed that Gentile converts would be free from the obligations of the Jewish law but that Paul would take up a collection among the Gentiles to be brought to Jerusalem for the poor.

(10) *Ephesians* (date uncertain). This letter appears to have been written sometime after Paul's death in Rome. Phrases in the letter echo another letter, Colossians. Eph develops some of Paul's themes about the church as the body of Christ and praises the apostle as the one to whom God had given special insight into the plan for bringing Gentiles to salvation. The second half of Eph reminds the audience that they have to live lives of holiness, putting aside all the immorality of the "pagan/Gentile" world around them.

(11) *Philippians* (ca. A.D. 52/54). Paul is writing from prison. The letter will be taken back to Philippi by Epaphroditus who had brought Paul money from the Philippian church and had fallen seriously ill (2:25–30). Older books sometimes presume that the mention of "Caesar's household" (4:22) means that this letter was written when Paul was jailed in Rome be-

fore his death. However, most scholars now reject that view. Paul really expects to be released (1:25f), and there is an exchange of news between Paul and the Philippians that would not be possible if Paul were in Rome. Paul was jailed on a number of occasions (e.g. 1 Cor 15:32; 2 Cor 11:23; 2 Cor 1:8–11). There was a cohort of the imperial guard in Ephesus, so it seems plausible that this letter was written from an imprisonment in Ephesus.

(12) *Colossians* (ca. A.D. 62/70). There are enough differences in phrasing and expression between this letter and others by Paul to lead scholars to think that Paul did not compose it. Its opening says that the church at Colossae was founded by Epaphras, not Paul (1:6–7) and that neither they nor the Christians in Laodicea have ever seen Paul (2:1). However, these churches are being troubled by false preachers who apparently want to combine Christ with elements of Jewish mysticism and perhaps even pagan philosophy. This letter has been sent in Paul's name to encourage Christians not to be led astray but to hold fast to what they have learned about Christ. Greetings are sent to Christians in the area from others who have been working in the Pauline mission.

(13) *1 Thessalonians* (ca. A.D. 51). This appears to be one of the earliest of Paul's letters. He had been worried about the newly founded church in Thessalonica, the capital of the province, and had sent Timothy from Athens to check on the church. Timothy has brought back a glowing report of the faith and love among the Thessalonians. He also reported that the Thessalonians were troubled by the death of Christians in their church. Paul sends them this letter of encouragement.

(14) *2 Thessalonians* (date uncertain). Again, the language about judgment of this letter is not typical of Paul elsewhere and the opening verses appear to be an attempt to compose something that will reflect 1 Thessalonians. 2 Thess 2:2 refers to a letter that claims to be by Paul which had led Christians to think the day of judgment was around the corner. The author, writing in Paul's name, wants to tell them not to accept such teaching. The end of the world will come only when God decides. In the meantime Christians are to follow the example Paul had set, working hard to earn a living and continuing in love of one another.

(15–17) *1 and 2 Timothy, Titus* (ca. A.D. 100/110). Timothy and Titus were very important associates of Paul. He often sent them on missions to churches that he was unable to visit. These letters, called the "pastoral epistles," are written as though Paul was writing from his prison cell in Rome. But they reflect a different situation than that in the Pauline letters of the 50's and 60's. In these letters, Timothy and Titus are the models for those persons who are to be "bishops," people who will lead the local churches and keep them from falling prey to all the different opinions about Christianity that are circulating, especially now that the apostles are no longer around to resolve the problems. Thus, these letters want to guard the tradition of the Pauline churches for the future.

(18) *Philemon* (ca. A.D. 52/54). Another letter from an imprisonment (also Ephesus?) that Paul expects will soon be over (v. 22). It is addressed to Philemon, one of Paul's converts. Philemon's slave, Onesimus, had run away and wound up in jail where Paul had converted him to Christianity. Paul is now sending the slave back to his master. He wants Philemon to receive the runaway back as a "beloved Christian brother," not as a runaway who deserves punishment.

III. Other "Apostolic Letters"

(19) *Hebrews* (ca. A.D. 90). This writing is an extended homily, which has been transmitted with a conclusion that might be found at the end of a letter (13:20–25). The author presumes that his audience have been Christians for some time and are in danger of growing lukewarm in their faith or even abandoning it altogether. Heb has no connection with Paul in theology and is composed in a very polished Greek quite unlike the apostle. But because it mentions that Timothy has been released from prison (13:23), the letter was sometimes spoken of as though Paul had written it.

(20) *James* (ca. A.D. 65–85). Although it claims to be by "James," the leader of Jewish Christians at Jerusalem, the careful Greek style of this work makes its composition by one of Jesus' Galilean relatives unlikely. However, it does represent the ethics of Jewish Christianity. Like Hebrews, Jas is really not a letter but a sermon for the faithful. It has been transmitted with a brief letter of introduction to establish James as the authority behind it.

(21) *1 Peter* (ca. A.D. 90). This letter was written in the name of Peter from Christians at Rome to those in rural churches of Asia Minor. Its conclusion mentions Silvanus, a frequent associate of Paul in Asia Minor, and Mark, who was originally part of Paul's mission and had then worked with Barnabas. Some think that they may have been responsible for sending this letter. The Christians are suffering harassment and persecution from their "pagan" neighbors because they have become Christians. The author wants to encourage them to live in holiness so that the people who are tormenting them will see what God has done in turning them from their former sinful ways to lives of goodness (2:11–12; 3:14–16; 4:4–5).

(22) *2 Peter* (ca. A.D. 110). This letter appears to be one of the latest in the New Testament. It incorporates material from Jude. Apparently, some people using material from Paul's letters (3:16) have been telling Christians that there will be no day of judgment. The author defends the traditional view that Christ will come again in glory, and he refers to the gospel story of the transfiguration (1:16–21) to prove the truth of that belief.

(23–24) *1 and 2 John* (ca. A.D. 100). 1 Jn is really a treatise defending the interpretation of the Johannine tradition held by the author and those persons who remain in fellowship with him (1:1–4). Other Christians have apparently broken off from the Johannine fellowship and started their own groups. 2 Jn is a brief note to Johannine Christians in another church warning them not to have anything to do with the Christians who have broken away.

(25) *3 John* (ca. A.D. 100). A brief personal note from the elder who wrote 2 Jn to a man named Gaius. Diotrephes, the leader of a Christian group in the area where Gaius lives, had begun to refuse hospitality to missionaries who came from the elder's church and was telling others to do the same. The elder hopes that Gaius will offer the missionaries hospitality, and he includes words of recommendation for Demetrius, who is carrying the letter.

(26) *Jude* (date uncertain). This is a brief piece which invokes the certainty of divine judgment against some who are said to lead the community astray. Its claims are defended by references to apocryphal Jewish traditions attached to Moses and Enoch.

(27) *Revelation* (ca. A.D. 95). The author of Rev tells us that he is a Christian prophet named John. He had been exiled to an island called Patmos for preaching the gospel (Rev 1:9–10). You will notice that John is a very common name. This Christian prophet is not the same as Jesus' disciples named John or as the John to whom the fourth gospel is attributed. Rev is like the book of Daniel in the Old Testament in that it contains symbolic visions about the end of the world. These visions describe political powers (in Rev the Roman empire and its rulers) in cryptic symbols. The visions are interpreted by angelic figures, and they also describe the future glory of those who have remained faithful to God. However, Rev is also influenced by the important Christian practice of sending apostolic letters to churches to instruct them about how they are to remain faithful. Therefore, the author begins with letters from the heavenly Jesus to the seven leading churches of Asia Minor (chs. 2 and 3). Scholars are able to tell from the symbolic visions that the author was living in the time of the emperor Domitian around A.D. 95.

The Bible as Classic and as Canon

You can see from the survey of the NT books that it contains a number of different types of writing spread over a period of about sixty years. As the church continued to grow in the second and third centuries, these writings took on a special importance. They became a Christian scripture which could be used alongside the scripture which the Christians had received from their Jewish origins, the Greek translation of the Old Testament. In fact, Christians found that they had to refer back to these books from the first century in order to decide new questions about what Christianity meant.

Early Christian writings from the first and second century were not limited to those contained in our New Testament. Collections of Jesus' sayings and miracles were in circulation from an early time. Others attempted to retell the story of Jesus' life or stories of the various apostles. A whole group of writings sprang up that claimed to give secret teachings transmitted to the apostles by the risen Jesus.

Doctrinal controversies and confusion over the authority of these various writings played an important role in the move to develop some list of authoritative Christian writings. We speak of this authoritative collection as "canon." Although most of the writings we find in our New Testament were accepted as canonical in many churches by the end of the second century A.D., divergence over the authority of writings like Rev, Heb and some of the later epistles continued for several centuries. The Syrian churches continued to use a harmonization of the gospels by Tatian known as the *Diatesseron* until into the fifth century. Thus, we should remember that what we speak of as New Testament owes its authority to its gradual acceptance in broad areas of the church.

In addition to its authority as "canon," the Bible has also played an important role in shaping Western culture, in music, art and literature as well as in the general ethical norms that our culture has taken from its Judaeo-Christian roots. Some scholars have described this function of the Bible as that of the "classic." Any work which a culture endows with such authority plays a special role in revealing who we are as a people. Through the classics we begin to sense the mysteries of the world and of human life that are only expressed in the great works of art, music, literature and philosophy. We are challenged to go beyond the narrow world in which we live and ask about the overall shape of reality. We are confronted with the tragedies of human life that seem beyond our control. And we discover ways in which the human spirit can reach beyond the boundaries that often seem to limit.

Because the Bible is a "classic" in our culture, its "truth" is not limited to the religious doctrines and practices that believing Christians derive from the Bible. The Bible belongs with the other great works as part of the heritage of everyone who lives in our culture, believer and unbeliever alike. The Bible's vision of the world, the place of humans in it and the values and tragedies that shape human life deserve to be set over against the other great visions that have entered into our tradition.

Of course, study of the Bible as "classic" will never be enough for the Christian believer. That study can never evaluate the faith claims made in the Bible. It can never say to the person that one must shape one's life in accord with the biblical vision. But the Christian has taken upon herself or himself the obligation to live out the biblical vision in a community with others who are also heirs to the faith tradition of the Bible. As we shall see, the Bible contains a diversity of insights and traditions. The global Christian community is equally pluralistic. Christians do not all agree about how the Bible's message is to be incarnated in the lives of believers today. Their different denominations have different theological and liturgical traditions. These differences also exercise an important influence on the interpretation of the Bible. But in our time, one of the unifying factors in Christian experience has been the shared task of historical study of the Bible. We find a source of Christian unity in the faith that we seek to share with our biblical ancestors.

Language, Text and Translation

Sometimes people go around quoting the Bible in English as though those were words directly spoken by God. However, God's revelation comes to us through human beings seeking to understand God's will within their own culture and language. Jesus lived in a country in which four different languages could be found: Hebrew, Aramaic, Greek and Latin. Aramaic was the common language of the people. Dialects of Aramaic were spoken across the Middle East from the Mediterranean to India. But after the conquest of the Near East and Egypt by Alexander the Great in the second half of the fourth century B.C., Greek became the dominant official language of government and commerce.

Although Aramaic and then Greek were the most important, universal languages in this period, many Jews continued to learn the Hebrew of their ancestors and of most of the Old Testament. For those Jews who no longer understood Hebrew, we find translations of the Old Testament into Greek and into Aramaic. The latter are called targums. Some are almost direct translations. Others are more like paraphrases of the Old Testament text in Aramaic. They provide us with fascinating glimpses into the legends and traditions that Jews of this period associated with the biblical figures.

In 63 B.C. the Roman general Pompey marched into Jerusalem and the period of direct Roman presence in this area of the world begins. The Roman military brought Latin along as its official language. But since many educated Romans knew Greek and were fond of "things Greek," Latin remained limited to the special concerns of Roman officialdom.

Naturally, the languages used among the people of this region—Hebrew, Aramaic and Greek—did not retain their classical form. Not only do they show a process of development typical of any language spoken over centuries, but they also influenced one another. Sometimes earlier scholars called expressions in the Greek of the New Testament examples of translation from Aramaic which should have been identified as peculiarities of Greek spoken by persons in an Aramaic-speaking environment. Though it would appear that most of Jesus' teaching would have been done in Aramaic, since it takes place among the Jewish population of the towns and villages, all of the New Testament writings were composed in Greek. To that extent, they show us by their very language how rapidly Christianity spread outside its Jewish Palestinian environment to the world of Greek-speaking Jews and of Gentiles (non-Jews).

You can also see that the New Testament has been involved with translation from one language to another and from one cultural context to another since the very beginning. You can also see that there will never be "one translation" that will be the definitive rendering of the Bible. Not only do we learn more about what particular words and phrases meant in biblical times, we also find the meanings and nuances of words and expressions in our own language shift so that what was an adequate rendering of a biblical passage at one time may not be suitable a generation later.

Sometimes a passage is so difficult or complex that any translation is really an interpretation of what the translator thinks the author meant to say in the passage. This task can be especially difficult if the writer is using sarcasm or irony. Here is an example. In 2 Cor 10:10 Paul is responding to accusations that some people have made against him. A fairly literal translation might be:

They say, "On the one hand, his letters are weighty and strong;
but his bodily presence is weak and his speech contemptuous."

However, Paul is very sarcastic. His enemies seem to be able to persuade the Corinthians that they should not listen to Paul because Paul does not put on as good a "religious show" as they do. Therefore, many modern translations try to capture that tone. Here are two of them:

> "His letters," they say, "are severe and forceful, but when he is here in person, he is unimpressive and his word makes no great impact." [*New American Bible*]

> Someone said, "He writes powerful and strongly worded letters, but when he is with you, you see only half a man and no preacher at all." [*Jerusalem Bible*]

Both of these modern translations are easier for people to understand when they first hear them read. The first is perhaps closer to the literal rendering of the sentence, but the second is more successful at capturing the strong irony of Paul's words.

In addition, you may have noticed that the second speaks as though one person, "someone," made the accusation, while the other versions speak of what a group of people are saying. If you were to look at a scholarly commentary on 2 Cor, you would find out that there is a problem in understanding the situation being spoken about in this section of the letter. It appears to be addressed to a group of outside preachers who have gotten into the church at Corinth and are causing serious problems. But the first part of 2 Cor speaks of a different situation. Paul had gone to Corinth on a visit. While he was there, someone in the Corinthian church had humiliated Paul. Paul had had to leave Corinth and had written the Corinthians a stern letter. But now he is patching things up with the Corinthians and telling them to forgive the man who had caused the offense (2 Cor 2:1–11). Some people think that these later chapters are from the harsh letter and that the man from the Corinthian community is the one responsible for the kind of accusations that Paul has to face. If you were reading the *Jerusalem Bible* translation, that interpretation would appear to be backed up by this passage. The Greek is sufficiently ambiguous to make either translation possible.

You can see from this example that there is no simple answer to the question of what is the "best" translation of the Bible. Each one has strong points and weak ones. One translation may be more successful in rendering particular sections of the Bible than another. But it is important to distinguish between a translation of the Bible which attempts to use all the words that the biblical author used in sentences which come in the same order and a "paraphrase" of the Bible. A paraphrase doesn't preserve the words or sentence structure of the original at all. Sometimes it is even much shorter because it leaves things out. Sometimes it retells the story with things added by the translators that are not there at all. There are three versions of the Bible currently on the market which fall into this category: *The Reader's Digest Bible, The Word,* and *The Book.* They might be all right for private reading but to use them for studying the Bible is like trying to use Monarch Notes to follow an analysis of a chapter in a novel.

The most important thing for the beginner is to pick a translation of the Bible that you can read comfortably. Some of the most popular translations are: *The Good News Bible; The New American Bible* (which is the basis for Catholic church readings in the USA); *The New English Bible; The Jerusalem Bible; The New International Version* (a fairly literal rendering popular with conservative Protestants). The most universally used translation for study purposes and in mainline Protestant churches is the *Revised Standard Version.* An ecumenical edition, which includes the apocryphal books that were part of the early church's Greek Old Testament but were not in the Hebrew Old Testament and so were rejected by the Protestant reformers, is often used by Catholics as well as Protestants. The latest version also contains a few additional works that are part of Scripture in the Greek Orthodox church. Most of these versions come in a number of editions. Some have extensive aids for Bible study such as introductory essays, notes, maps, and cross-references to other parts of the Bible. You can also buy short concordances for the main translations of the Bible. They list the major words that occur in the Bible and then the most important passages where those words are to be found. Of course, if you wanted a complete concordance that listed all the words and all the places they are found, you would have to go to a library because that's a large book. Some study Bibles even have a brief concordance with them. A concordance is handy when you are trying to find a passage or when you want to know what the Bible has to say about a particular topic.

Entering the New Testament World: Archeology and History

Though new translations of the Bible occasionally make news, the most publicized developments are connected with archeological discoveries. Sometimes people expect that archeology simply proves the truth of what is in the Bible by discovering the remains of cities, roads and other places mentioned in the biblical narrative. Actually, the relationship between archeology and the Bible is much more complex than that. Certainly, the growth of biblical studies in our century would have been impossible without the equally striking growth in archeological investigation and interpretation of sites in the Near East, Turkey, North Africa, Greece and Italy.

Archeological discoveries have included important written remains of the cultures surrounding the Bible. The rich religious and mythological symbolism of the sea peoples of Phoenicia, of the Sumerians, the Babylonians, the Assyrians, the Persians and the Egyptians, to name a few, has taught us a lot about the symbolic and mythic allusions attached to stories, events and persons in the Bible.

By New Testament times the symbolic interpretation of figures from the past was quite extensive. We often have to look outside the Bible to other Jewish writings from the period between 300 B.C. to 300 A.D. to gain some idea of the richness that informed the religious imagination. One of the major finds of the century occurred in caves near the Dead Sea. A whole library of writings that had been used by a Jewish sect, known as the Essenes, was discovered. The sect also had a community below the cliffs and the scrolls were probably copied by members of that community. It is sometimes referred to by the name of the site, Qumran. You will also find the scrolls referred to as the "Dead Sea Scrolls."

Even though the scrolls were first discovered ca. 1947, the work of unrolling them, piecing them together, editing them and translating them still goes on. We knew something about the Essenes from brief references in first century A.D. Jewish writers. And we even possessed a version of their community rule that had been found among the manuscripts of an old synagogue in Cairo. We know that in addition to Qumran there were groups of Essenes in cities and villages. But we would have had no idea that the sect had endured for over two centuries without the discovery of their writings and the "monastery" at Qumran, which was inhabited from the mid-second century B.C. until the Roman destruction of Jerusalem. In addition to providing our oldest manuscripts of the Hebrew Bible and some fragments of the Greek Old Testament, the Aramaic writings in this collection provide us with our most important evidence for the Aramaic that was spoken in Palestine at the time of Jesus.

The Essenes also composed commentaries on biblical texts, which have provided us with insights into how passages from the Jewish law, the Torah, were applied as well as how the Psalms and the prophets were interpreted in light of the experiences of the Essene group. The various rule books of the community show a pattern of complex organization that provide some parallels to patterns of organization in the New Testament.

Discoveries of whole libraries of legal and religious writings like these are the most exciting to those who are primarily interested in interpreting texts. But more often archeology presents us with much less in the way of written material. Excavating burial sites may produce inscriptions on tombstones. The number of Greek inscriptions used by Jews from the first century B.C. onward shows that Greek could be understood as well as Aramaic or Hebrew.

A lengthy inscription that reports a decree of the emperor against desecrating tombs was found in Nazareth. The style of the letters allows archaeologists to date it in the first half of the first century A.D. But, since Galilee was not directly ruled by the Romans until the death of king Herod Agrippa in 44 A.D., the emperor who issued it would have to be Tiberius or Claudius. The inscription is in Greek, although scholars think it was originally composed in Latin:

DECREE OF CAESAR

It is my pleasure that sepulchres and tombs, which have been erected as solemn memorials of ancestors or children or relatives, shall remain undisturbed in perpetuity. If it be shown that anyone has either destroyed them or otherwise thrown out the bodies which have been buried there or removed them with malicious intent to another place, thus committing a crime against those buried there, or removed the headstones or other stones, I command that against such person the same sentence be passed in respect of solemn memorials of humans as is laid down in respect of the gods. Much rather must one pay respect to those who are buried. Let no one disturb them on any account. Otherwise it is my will that capital sentence be passed upon such person for the crime of tomb-robbery. [from Eric M. Myers & James F. Strange, *Archaeology, The Rabbis and Early Christianity*, Nashville: Abingdon, 1981, p. 84]

A cemetery in Beth She'arim, a town in Western lower Galilee, contains tombs from the first to the sixth century A.D. Some of the inscriptions connected with burials from the first century A.D. mention resurrection. Others speak in Greek fashion of immortality or eternal life. Since the language of epitaph is brief and often standardized, it is difficult to know how much such inscriptions can tell us about what people actually believed about the fate of the person after death. But at least we learn that both language about resurrection of the body and that about immortality of the soul could be found in first century Palestine. The old division between Hebrew thought, which was supposed to be oriented toward the person as bodily, and Greek thought, which identified the true person with the soul, not the body, does not adequately describe the archeological remains of first century Palestine.

Even under the best conditions, we cannot always give precise dates for buildings, or determine the use of certain structures or objects. It is not uncommon for material from an earlier building to be used in construction of a later one. In other cases, we would like to know more about the occupants of a building than we do. The pious desire to see things exactly as they would have been in the Bible frequently leads to misrepresentations in tourist books. Well-known examples are found in Capernaum. The New Testament mentions a synagogue there in which Jesus taught (Mk 1:21; Lk 4:31). Ruins of a magnificent synagogue have been found at Capernaum, but they do not come from the first century. A late fourth century A.D. pilgrim to Capernaum, Egeria, mentions seeing a synagogue there. Excavations show that this building was erected on earlier buildings from the first part of the fourth century A.D. The synagogue at the time of Jesus was probably considerably smaller and less imposing.

Even the proper architectural reconstruction of the remaining synagogue has generated some dispute. It used to be presumed that the rows of columns on three sides, two running north-south and one running along the transverse side, supported a gallery. It was also often presumed that this gallery served to isolate the women from the men during synagogue services. Both those assumptions appear to be extremely doubtful. In synagogues of this type, there are no remains of stairs to provide access to such a gallery. Nor do we find in the written traditions any early rulings that would make such segregation mandatory. The excavators at Capernaum are convinced that the columns there supported a simple shed roof at a height of about five meters.

Another popular "Christian" site at Capernaum is a house that is sometimes claimed to be that of Peter's mother-in-law (Mk 1:29–30). The Christian excavators have tried to use every argument possible to link the remains of a first century house from Capernaum that was a Christian "house church" in the fourth century A.D. and later a basilica with the "house of Peter." But, of course, the evidence is never that simple. No one doubts the conversion of the structure into a Christian church in the fourth century A.D. and the rebuilding there of a basilica type church in the fifth century. The problem lies in interpreting the story of the occupation and use of the building in the previous centuries. The excavators claimed that plastering of the central room toward the end of the first century A.D. and the graffiti in the plaster, which are claimed to be Christian, though they are not well enough preserved to be sure, imply earlier conversion to public use. Therefore, they insist that building was continuously venerated as the "house of Peter" and was, in fact, "Peter's house."

From a more rigorous historical and scientific point of view, we cannot be that confident. We can say that the "house church" at Capernaum is one of our oldest examples of a public building used for Christian worship. We can also say that the type of first century house represented in excavations from this part of Capernaum gives us some idea of what Peter's house would have been like. It was part of a block of houses founded in the first century B.C. The blocks of one story houses were about forty meters by forty meters. Each house consisted of a number of rooms around a central courtyard, which contained the oven. Outside stairs led up to the flat roofs. Roofs were normally made of beams, branches, rushes and mud. They would be relatively cool in the summer and warm in winter. The only windows were small, and high up in the wall. They let light into the house but did not provide a view outside.

Biblical scholars comb the results of archeological excavations to see what they can learn about places, persons, events, symbols and language used in the Bible. Sometimes the connections that we are able to make between archeology and the Bible help us to understand things that were obscure in the Bible. Sometimes archeology forces us to put the biblical picture into a larger perspective. Sometimes the biblical text provides a key hint as to how to interpret the physical remains at a given site, or, perhaps, to look for things there that we might otherwise ignore. One of the most important developments in modern archeology and biblical studies has been emphasis on reconstructing the lives of the people. Archeology used to focus on the "big figures and monuments," the palaces, temples and city gates. Now we are asking about the evidence for houses, streets, diet, burials, ages and beliefs of the population as a whole.

The New Testament and Christian Life

Even those who are not Christians participate in the study of New Testament times through archeology and historical research. The New Testament reflects the origins and earliest development of a religious movement which was to shape the course of Western civilization and through it the history of the world. Everyone in the world comes into contact with Christianity in some way whether directly or indirectly through values in Western culture that have their roots in Christianity. Similarly, anyone who wishes to understand much of Western literature, art or music has to have some introduction to the Bible and to Christian beliefs.

When most people think of studying the New Testament, they don't think about the cultural role which it plays. They think about the role which the Bible plays in the lives of believing Christians. There is no

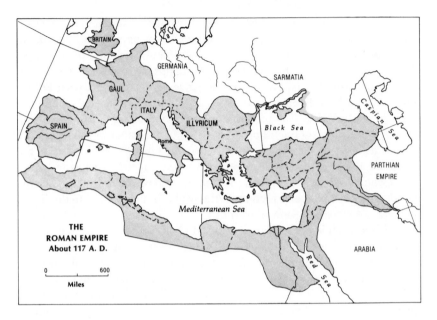

Christian group, Protestant or Catholic, which does not give the Bible, and especially the New Testament, a central role in its life. Because the Bible is shared by all Christians, it plays an important role today in bringing Christians together. A common interest in the Hebrew Bible and the history of Israel also brings Christians and Jews together. Many churches have Bible study groups for lay people that include Christians from different denominations.

We will see that there were a number of different groups of Christians in New Testament times. Some Christians of Jewish origin still continued to follow the customs of Judaism and to worship in the synagogue and temple. Other Christians of Gentile origin focused their whole religious experience around belief in Jesus. All that they took from Judaism was their scripture, the Greek translation of the Old Testament, a firm belief in one God over against the pagan gods and goddesses, and general ethical principles about justice, charity and sexual morality.

We will also find in the New Testament that there are different lines of Christian tradition that are linked with important apostles. James, the leader of the church in Jerusalem, becomes the focal point for Jewish Christianity. Peter, who apparently left Jerusalem for missionary activity in the Antioch region, becomes the sponsor for a Christianity which retains its ties with Judaism through the Old Testament symbolism. Antioch became an important center of Petrine tradition. Churches in rural Asia Minor had apparently been founded by missionaries associated with this tradition. And, after Peter's death in Rome, writings in that tradition are sent from Rome to those Asia Minor churches. Paul, the most famous missionary to the Gentiles, established churches in the cities of Asia Minor and Greece. Finally, the churches of the Johannine tradition developed a unique symbolic language and a clear perception of the divinity of Jesus. The New Testament was entirely written in Greek and reflects the churches of the Greek speaking part of the empire. Further to the East, in Eastern Syria and part of India, an equally strong Christian tradition grew up around the memory of the apostle Thomas.

If you remember the basic fact that the New Testament permits some differences in Christian traditions and practice, then you will understand that it is possible for a number of different Christian churches to all be faithful to the Bible. For some churches everything depends upon the Bible. The sermon is the focus of the service surrounded with readings from the Bible, responsive readings of the Psalms, prayers often formulated in biblical language and singing of hymns. Members of those churches may spend time in private Bible reading and often bring their Bibles to church with them. They may have memorized large portions of the Bible in summer camps when they were young. Whenever they run up against a problem, they will look for a solution or for words of comfort in the Bible. The particular interpretations of biblical passages given by members of churches like that tend to reflect the views of a particular minister or preacher. Sometimes Christians in these churches accuse other Christians of not following the Bible because they don't use the Bible in the same way.

The Catholic Church is a good example of a church that is often attacked as "not biblical" by other Christian groups. This charge has a long history. Part of it is true. For Catholics, the Bible is not the only way to approach God. Nor is the Bible the only source of church teaching and practice. Catholics insist that sacraments, especially the weekly (or daily) celebration of the Lord's Supper (Eucharist, Mass), bring a person into God's presence and are sources of God's grace for a person's life. The reading of the Bible and preaching form the first part of the service. They call believers to remember Christ and the Christian life that they have promised to lead in baptism and confirmation. But, to a Catholic, it would seem strange to stop with the prayers and service of the word. The Catholic wants to respond with a "yes" to God's word and the affirming presence of God's grace by participating in the meal which Christ left to his followers. As St. Paul told the Corinthians, the Supper commemorates the sacrificial death of Christ for us until Christ comes again (1 Cor 11:23–26).

The Bible also plays another role in the religious lives of those Catholics who belong to religious orders. From very early times the monks developed services of prayer based on reciting the Psalms. These prayers were established to mark the key turning points of the day and came to be known as the "Divine Office." Some religious groups are devoted to chanting the entire Office each day, which along with the daily celebration of the Eucharist can mean several hours spent in community prayer. Naturally, priests and members of religious orders who are engaged in working in schools, hospitals and the like cannot drop everything for such extensive prayers. Shorter versions of the Office have been developed for them to use. Sometimes Catholic lay people will also use these shorter versions as the basis for their private prayer.

In recent years, more and more Catholics are also beginning to read and study the Bible through courses, workshops and parish Bible study groups. They find that Bible study enriches their faith in a number of ways. The Bible readings that are part of the liturgy become more meaningful. Psalms and other passages from the Bible become the focal points for private prayer and reflection. Study of the Bible also puts some of our modern problems in better perspective. It teaches us that faith is never "finished" or simple. It has a story. It develops. The first Christians often had to struggle to figure things out just as we do. Because they were successful, they established a tradition of faith that has continued for two thousand years. We have to preserve that tradition and hand it on into the twenty-first century.

Summary

You can see that there is a lot to studying the Bible. There are also a number of different reasons that a person might have for wanting to do so. Those who are interested in the history of Western culture need to know "what is in the Bible." They need to know what the most important themes, symbols and images are so that they can recognize them in Western literature and art. They also need to know what the major "ideas" found in biblical writers are. Those "ideas" have played a role in shaping Western thought and values. And they continue to play an important role in our understanding of what is just and good in a society.

Others may come to study the Bible because they are interested in the history involved. Or they may be interested in comparative religions. They may want to know how such a powerful religious movement as Christianity started and developed. They may eventually want to compare Christianity's story with that of other religions which emerged as a kind of "protest" within an existing religious environment and which continue to guide the lives of people around the world such as Islam or Buddhism.

Still others come to study the Bible because they are Christians. For some Christians, Bible study is a way of getting back in touch with a faith they might have been taught as children but then had lost contact with. For other Christians, Bible study is a necessary part of their personal reading of the Bible. They realize that you can only go so far by just reading a translation of the Bible, or even memorizing one. Eventually, it is necessary to try to understand what the world of the Bible writers was like. What did the various words, images, symbols and ideas sound like to an audience in their time? What was the challenge being presented by faith? How did people respond to that challenge in their lives? Believing Christians will then try to apply the insights gained from the biblical stories of faith to their own lives today.

These are all important reasons for studying the Bible today. A person may share all of these goals or only some of them. This book is written from the perspective of a person who shares all of these goals. But as an introduction to reading the New Testament, the emphasis lies on becoming familiar with basic information about archeology, history, language, religion, and socio-cultural background of NT times. It is not about how to translate the ideas and images of the New Testament into Christian life or theology today. When you have finished your introduction to the New Testament, you may want to pursue further study in one of these directions.

STUDY QUESTIONS

Facts You Should Know

1. How many "books" are in the New Testament? What are the main types of writing found in the New Testament?
2. What do we mean when we speak of the Bible as "canon"? What do we mean when we speak of the Bible as a "classic"?
3. What languages were spoken in Palestine during Jesus' lifetime? What language was the New Testament written in?
4. How does archeology help us understand the Bible? Describe each of the following archeological discoveries: (a) Essene settlement at Qumran; (b) synagogue at Capernaum; (c) "Peter's house" at Capernaum.

Things To Think About

1. If someone asked you to tell a favorite story from the New Testament, what story would you tell? Do you know where to find it in the New Testament?

2. What approach to the Bible is the most interesting to you? Learning about the people and their times? Learning the Bible as a source for personal inspiration and guidance?

3. When was the last time you heard, read or studied any passage from the Bible? What do you remember about that passage?

Chapter 2

THE WORLD OF JESUS

Galilee, Samaria and Judea

We have all seen those humorous maps which claim to give the distorted view of the world held by particular persons or groups. We have also all watched the embarrassment of TV commentators when a crisis breaks out in some part of the world with which we are not familiar. Even lessons learned years ago in geography are not much good as names, boundaries and alliances shift with the turmoil of world events. If we are so unclear about the basic geography of the world we live in, it is hardly surprising to find even more confusion about the geography of the world in which Jesus lived.

Some of the political realities of that time (and of the area in our own time) were determined by the geographical location of the Jewish states. For all of its history, Palestine either has been dominated by a greater power, which left some autonomy to the local inhabitants, or when the great powers in the area were weak, it has managed to enjoy independence under a local dynasty and to expand its rule over the surrounding countryside. These periods of independence under David and Solomon in the tenth century B.C. and under the Hasmonean kings in from the mid-second century B.C. until Pompey's [Roman] conquest in 63 B.C. were often idealized. People looked back to them as the source of hope for a new independence in the future.

In 198 B.C. the Seleucid king of Syria, Antiochus III, gained control. His empire stretched from the Persian Gulf to the Aegean. He created larger administrative districts than had been the case under the Ptolemies, Samaria was the center of a district which included Galilee, Judea and Perea. But as the Maccabean revolt against Syrian rule in the 160's B.C. spread, Judea again became an independent district. Another district was

23

created along the coastal plain and one east of the Jordan. The Seleucid rulers also favored the establishment of independent Greek cities, since they found their most loyal supporters in the aristocracy of such cities. A number of cities east of the Jordan took the name "Antioch." Some Jews in Jerusalem also wanted to create a "Greek city," "Antioch," there. It was located on the western of the two hills that made up the ancient city and contained a marketplace and a fortress known as Acra. During the revolt, the city of Jerusalem was divided. The Jews were established on the temple mount, called "Mount Zion," and the Syrians and their Jewish sympathizers, called Hellenizers because they advocated Greek culture, were entrenched around the Acra.

Although the Seleucid generals were unable to relieve the fortress and although the rebels had established control over the other part of the city by 162 B.C., the struggle for complete independence from Syria would continue for several decades. In 152 B.C. the Syrians, beset by internal strife over succession, appointed Jonathan high priest and de facto ruler of Judea. He began to enlarge the territory over which he held control. But it was not until 141 B.C. that his brother Simeon, the last of the family of Maccabee brothers, was able to capture Acra and reunite Jerusalem. He also captured Joppa and made it a Jewish town and an outlet to the sea. His successor, John Hyrcanus, set about gaining a foothold on the "king's highway," which lay east of the Jordan, and then gaining the other international highway through Palestine, the Via Maris. After that he turned to conquer Samaria. The Samaritan temple on Mount Gerezim was destroyed. But the Samaritans continued to maintain a distinctive national and religious identity, venerating Moses and their version of the Torah, and tensions between Samaritans and Jews are clearly evident in the New Testament.

Fresh from clearing the Mediterranean of pirates, the Roman general Pompey took Jerusalem and its temple in 63 B.C. He returned the Greek cities to their former Gentile inhabitants. The Jews lost Joppa and the agricultural estates in the Jezreel valley. In addition, Pompey created a league of Ten Cities east of the Jordan, the "Decapolis." This league included Sythopolis on the west of the Jordan. Pompey seems to have intended that these cities would form a buffer zone between the Roman empire and the Arabian steppe. Augustus made them subject to Herod. Later they were part of the Roman province of Syria. These ten cities were thoroughly Greek in their outlook. We also have evidence for Jews continuing to live in Sythopolis, Gadara, Hippos, Trachonitis, and Gaulanitis. And in Roman times there was considerable traffic between Galilee and this area of the Transjordan. Mt 4:23–25 includes people from the Decapolis among those who listened to Jesus. Mk 5:1–20 and 7:31 even presume that Jesus went there to minister. The territories of Hippos, Gadara and Gaulanitis reached to the eastern shore of the lake.

Herod and His Kingdom

Herod the Great was named "king" of the region by the Romans in 40 B.C., though he required Roman help to assume the throne in 37 B.C. Herod was able to win favor with Augustus, who expanded his domain by giving Herod the coastal cities from Gaza to the Tower of Straton (except Ascalon), the city of Samaria and the cities of Gadara and Hippos. In order to show his gratitude Herod rebuilt and expanded the cities of Caesarea (formerly the Tower of Straton) and Samaria, renamed Sebaste, Greek for Augustus. In Caesarea, Herod built a great temple to Augustus. This temple is probably the one represented on coins by Herod's son Philip. Caesarea was also provided with a deep-water harbor, which provided the only secure anchorage between Joppa and Accho. Sebaste was provided with new city walls, a forum, a theatre and a temple of Augustus. Caesarea lay outside the boundaries of Galilee proper and probably did not have much influence on the lives of Galilean peasants. But Bethsaida, which Philip renamed Julias after Augustus' daughter Julia, lay on the shores of the lake and may have had frequent contacts with such Galilean settlements along the lakefront as Capernaum and Corozain.

The city of Tiberias was founded by Herod's son, Herod Antipas, in A.D. 13 and named after the emperor. It was on the lake in the most fertile part of Galilee and was noted for its hot springs as a "tourist attraction." However, the city was also built over an ancient cemetery, a site forbidden by Jewish law. (Even today, ultra-orthodox Jews instigated a lawsuit to stop building of a modern hotel over the old tomb area, claiming that that would hinder the resurrection of those buried there.) It appears that the Jewish inhabitants of this city belonged to the aristocratic circles associated with the Herodian court. Antipas is also said to have populated the city with the poor, who were given houses and plots of land.

Herod's kingdom comprised quite a mixed population, a Jewish element (Judea and Galilee), Idumeans (Herod was an Idumean), Samaritans (who already had a long history of friction with the Jews), and the non-Jewish population of the Greek towns. Herod's perpetual fear of an uprising led him to expand and strengthen the old fortresses of Alexandrium, Hyrcania, Machaerus and Masada and to build a new one at Herodium, the site of the royal tomb. Part of his rebuilding in Jerusalem included a fortified palace protected on the north by three towers. The lower part of one of these towers (archeologists are divided over which one it was) can still be seen today. Another fortress, Antonia, dominated the temple.

Herod initiated an expansive rebuilding of the temple, which continued into the middle of the first century A.D. The Jewish historian Josephus claims that when it was finished some 18,000 people were out of work. Herod Agrippa II is said to have undertaken repaving the streets of Jerusalem in order to provide them with employment.

When Herod died (4 B.C.), the kingdom was divided between his three sons. Archelaus, the eldest, received Judea, which had the bulk of the Jewish population, Idumea and Samaria (including the cities of Caesarea and Sebaste). He was given the title "ethnarch." The other two only received the title "tetrarch." Herod Antipas, the second son, ruled over two widely separated areas, Galilee and Perea. The third, Philip, received the lands east of the Jordan. Herod's sister, Salome, received the towns of Jamnia and Azotus and the domain of Phasaelis in the Jordan valley.

Archelaus proved a bad administrator and after a short, turbulent reign was deposed in 6 A.D. His region was administered by a "prefect" of equestrian rank responsible to the legate of Syria. When Philip died in A.D. 34 his land was provisionally taken over by the imperial administration. In A.D. 37 Herod Agrippa (Agrippa I), Herod's grandson, was given the tetrarchy of Philip together with the region of Chalcis and the title "king" by the emperor Caligula, with whom he had grown up in Rome. In A.D. 39, Caligula exiled Herod Antipas and gave Agrippa his territory. Then the emperor Claudius gave Agrippa I Judea and Samaria. Thus, he regained almost all of the territory of Herod the Great. Agrippa I only ruled this domain for three years (A.D. 41–44). His son Agrippa II received Chalcis from Claudius in A.D. 53, and two-thirds of Perea and half of lower Galilee (Tiberias and Tarichaeae) in A.D. 54 from Nero. After he died (c. A.D. 95) the Herodian dynasty ceased to rule any part of the Jewish people.

Jesus grew up in Nazareth, a small town (pop. ca. 1200), which had been occupied since the second century B.C. It lay a couple of miles off a main road through lower Galilee. Sepphoris was the next large town to the northwest and was the administrative headquarters of the region. Galilee's southern boundary separated it from the Herodian estates in the Jezreel valley. Three important localities mentioned in the New Testament lie along the Sea of Galilee—Tiberias, Tarichaeae, or, as it is called in Aramaic, "Migdal Nunaiyya" (home of Mary Magdalene), and Capernaum. Upper Galilee consisted of highlands. In this region, there are peaks of over 3,000 feet. Mount Meron, the highest, is 3,963 feet. It is an area of rugged peaks, valleys, basins and gorges. Traffic did pass through the area destined for the port of Tyre along a road which appears to have run from Damascus over Paneas and through the Dishon valley. It is a region of independent village life, which appears to have been strongly attached to ancestral custom. The principal city in this area was Gishala. Josephus complains that during the revolt against Rome, the peasants of Upper Galilee were more interested in farming than in defending the city (*War* 4:84).

Although it is possible to establish boundaries between various territories and administrative regions, it is more difficult to describe the ethnic make-up of a particular area or city. From Hasmonean times, we find a desire to establish Jewish areas especially in Judea proper. But in Jamnia and Azotus their status as imperial estates would suggest some admixture of Gentiles, since the higher administrative ranks would probably have been filled by non-Jews. Similarly, Gentiles would have been involved in administering the royal estates in the Jezreel valley. (An example of such a person would be the "royal official" of Jn 4:46.) Some Greeks may even have moved into Jerusalem under Herod. The two large Galilean cities, Tiberias and Sepphoris, are careful to avoid human images on their coins and appear to have been Jewish municipalities. Yet, Herod Antipas is also reported to have settled Gentiles in Tiberias when he founded the city. Even Capernaum, which sat on the border of two regions as is evident by the customs collector there, appears to have had some Gentiles. Herod had settled colonies of veterans at Gaba, and a number of mercenaries may have stayed on after their discharge to become prominent figures in local villages. The centurions mentioned in the gospels may have been former legionary officers, who were now in charge of drilling native auxillary troops (Mt 8:5–13; Lk 7:2–10). The Jewish population of Jerusalem was constantly increased by an influx of Jews from other countries.

Jerusalem: A Pilgrimage City

Jews from outside Palestine, called "the diaspora," regularly made pilgrimages to Jerusalem to celebrate the great feasts. Synagogues in the city appear to have been established to accommodate them. Excavations in Jerusalem have uncovered a large complex that had been donated by a person whose name clearly shows Roman origins:

> Theodotus, the son of Vettneus, priest and *archisynagogos* (ruler of the synagogue), son of the *archisynagogos*, grandson of the *archisynagogos*, built this synagogue for the reading of the Torah and the study of the commandments, and the hostel and the rooms and the water installations for needy travellers from foreign lands. The foundations of the synagogue were laid by his fathers and the elders and Simonides.

The combination of synagogue and lodging facilities would have made it easy for persons from a particular region to meet others who spoke the same dialect and to obtain help and advice. Tombstones in Jerusalem also attest to the influx of people from outside Jerusalem, perhaps to spend their last days and be buried there.

The Old Testament law commanded that adult males make the pilgrimage to Jerusalem three times a year (Ex 23:17; Deut 16:16). Persons from the diaspora could not fulfil that obligation literally. But diaspora communities sent representatives with the half-shekel tax for support of the temple that was required of all Jewish males. A Roman edict protected that offering as "sacred money" and mandated harsh penalities against any who might attempt to seize it.

Although only men are bound by the law, women and children clearly took part in pilgrimages and ceremonies. They are mentioned in inscriptions referring to Jews from the diaspora. In the diaspora itself, some wealthy women seem to have built synagogues and are honored with inscriptions conferring on them the same title as Theodotus, *archisynagogos*. Others who came for the great festivals were proselytes, Gentiles who had converted to Judaism.

The great pilgrimages and offerings strengthened the ties between Je-

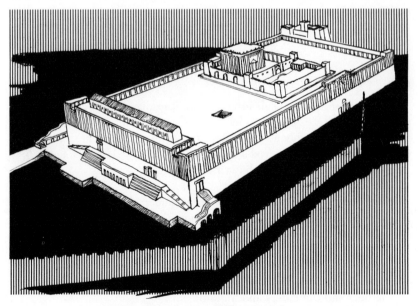

Reconstruction of the Temple.

rusalem and Jewish communities outside Palestine. Envoys and letters might then be sent from Jerusalem to the communities in the diaspora. The very early spread of Christianity from Jerusalem outward into the Roman world followed the patterns already established in Jerusalem's relationships to diaspora Judaism. The first converts at Pentecost are Jews visiting in Jerusalem for the Passover feast (Acts 2:5–11).

The Political and Social World

Our survey of the shifting boundaries, provinces, cities and rulers has already shown something of the "large scale" realities of political and social life in Jesus' time. The destiny of the country was in the hands of others far removed from most people. Excavations in Jerusalem's Upper City have revealed the luxurious villas and palaces of the high priests and other wealthy persons who might be the equals of members of Herod's court. But even the Herodian monarchs owed their position and what part of the land they ruled to personal ties and loyalty to Rome and even to personal relationships with members of the imperial family.

With the Herodian monarchy and the consolidation of Roman power in the region, Palestine was relatively peaceful and prosperous. The Jewish revolt of A.D. 66–70 was quickly extinguished in Galilee. Diaspora Jews made no move to join in an uprising, which they may have considered more a local struggle for power than the overthrow of a great oppressor. Roman edicts protected certain Jewish practices. The temple tax was protected as "sacred money" and exempted from prohibitions against the export of gold and silver. The sacred Torah scrolls were also protected. Any Gentile who stole the temple offering or Torah scrolls could be prosecuted for a sacrilegous act. The punishment was confiscation of one's property. Roman edicts also protected the Jewish sabbath by stipulating that Jews could not be issued a summons to appear in court on the sabbath, since failure to do so would cost them the case. Jews were exempt from obligations to perform certain "civic liturgies," that is, to pay for various public works projects—often enough with religious associations—and from compulsory service in the military. We find repeated complaints against local officials in the eastern part of the empire, which required Roman intervention to protect these rights.

Loyalty to a demanding and tenacious set of religious beliefs contributed to the cultural vitality of Judaism and provided a common bond between those who might otherwise have been sharply divided. Even considerable diversity between Jewish groups like the Pharisees and the Sadducees over religious practices and observance of the law did not shake the common core of devotion to the temple and to the religious practices of Judaism. We do find sectarian groups, most radically the Essenes, who attacked the Jerusalem priesthood and the common interpretations of the law. A non-Zadokite priesthood, a religious calendar and an interpretation of the law that was not acceptable to the Essenes led them to paint a particularly dark picture of their fellow Jews. The sect had been founded by a member of a high priestly family in the mid-second century B.C. The founder, known to us only by the "code name" used in the sect, "Teacher of Righteousness," had apparently opposed the Hellenization of the Hasmonean monarchy and their assumption of the high priesthood. The sect gave cryptic interpretations of prophecies by Habbakuk, which were said to reflect their origins. A certain "wicked priest" is said to have come and attacked the Teacher. Whatever the political events surrounding the sect's founding, its invisibility in the first century suggests that intense sectarian piety and isolation from fellow Jews were more characteristic of the Essenes than social or political critique.

This fact does not mean that Herod was always a model ruler. When John the Baptist spoke out against his marriage to his brother's (former) wife, he had John imprisoned and finally killed. Some of his attempts to ingratiate himself with the emperor Tiberius behind the back of the Syrian legate Vitellius only netted him an angry ally. When the Nabatean king, father of Herod's first wife, attacked, the Roman legate left Herod to suffer a stinging defeat. The Markan picture of village leaders, Herodian nobles and Roman military commanders gathered to celebrate Herod's birthday provides a likely image of the political unity in the region (Mk 6:21). The emperor Caligula exiled Herod Antipas in A.D. 37 in order to make his friend Herod Agrippa king. But in general the Galilee of Jesus' day appears to have been politically stable.

One must also raise cautions about over-dramatizing the economic divisions. No one doubts that the wealthy, especially the absentee landlords in Jerusalem, engaged in conspicuous consumption well beyond anything that the temple functionaries, petty traders, merchants, laborers and the like could ever imagine. But in the life of hundreds of Galilean villages the divisions are between rich and poor peasants. Although some of the best lands had come under royal and imperial control by the first century, there is no evidence for major disruption in village life or land ownership. Jesus' parables show us two types of land owner. There is the Herodian noble with slaves to act as stewards and peasants beset by their debts to such landowners. But there is also ample evidence for the continued viability of small holdings. In the parable of the prodigal son, the father, his sons and a few servants work the land (Lk 15:11–31). A father and two sons are involved in cultivating a family vineyard (Mt 21:28–31). Zebedee, his sons and hired servants are working the fishing boats (Mk 1:16–20). The main hazards are natural disasters that lead to a bad harvest rather than policies of deliberate oppression of the poor.

It is difficult to measure the burden of taxation in this period. Taxes were levied on the produce of the land, on men, property, sale of animals and all transport of goods across boundaries. In addition, Jewish males paid a half-shekel for support of the Jerusalem temple. Religious law also commanded that people pay "tithes," a portion of the fruits of a person's labor, to the priests and Levites. What was subject to tithing, the strictness with which it was observed and whether tithes were paid to priests living in the local area or were paid in Jerusalem were all questions of some dispute in Jesus' day. The "tax collectors" who are scorned by the people in the gospels are those, like Levi, who collected the customs tolls and other fees connected with transporting goods across borders. They were generally suspected of becoming wealthy by various forms of fraud in collecting such taxes (see the story of Zacchaeus in Lk 19:1–10).

Taxes on the produce of the soil were supplemented by a "head tax." This tax applied to all who were subject to the Romans directly. Persons had to be registered on the tax rolls of the town or city in which they lived. When the Roman governor took over Judea in A.D. 6, a census was taken for tax purposes. Lk 2:1–2 thinks that Jesus' birth in Judea occurred when his parents went to Bethlehem for the census. However, they would not have done so for that reason. Taxes were collected according to place of residence, which was clearly in Herod's Galilee, not in Judea. By linking the two events together, Luke is able to present Jesus' parents as loyal Jewish subjects in the larger Roman empire. In Jesus' time, the "head tax" appears to have been set at "one denarius" or approximately a day's wage.

The wealthy, Hellenized Jews of the Herodian court and the high priestly families in Jerusalem served as intermediaries between Roman power and the populace. Agrippa even complained to the emperor that Pilate was cruel, took bribes and executed people without trial. The causes behind the eventual revolt against Rome in A.D. 66–70 are difficult to establish. However, it does seem clear that under the later governors, the Jewish upper class, which tended to be moderate, lost its ability to mediate potential conflicts. Josephus insists that as the war went on, moderates lost all voice to hot-headed radicals. The radicals were worse tyrants and oppressors than the Romans had ever been, he claims. The people may have been sympathetic early on, but by the end they were simply victims of violence that could no longer be controlled. Finally, in August of 70, Roman legions stormed the temple and fortress of Jerusalem, looting and burning the city. The Roman capture of Jerusalem is commemorated on the triumphal arch set up in Rome by the victor, Titus. There you can see the great seven-branched candlestick from the temple being carried off in triumphal procession.

Before the Jewish revolt, there was a sizable Christian community in Jerusalem. We meet them in the letters of Paul and the Acts of the Apostles. Tradition holds that they fled the fighting by going across the Jordan to Pella. Some scholars think that many of them may have gone up to Galilee, which had surrendered early on in the war and settled in towns and villages there. The Jerusalem church had provided Christianity with a strong center of Jewish identity. Paul insisted that his Gentile converts show their gratitude by making an offering for the poor there (2 Cor 8–9; Rom 15:25–29). After A.D. 70, this center is lost. Christianity becomes independent of Judaism and emerges as a predominantly Gentile religion.

Religious Parties and Sects

The various religious parties within first century A.D. Judaism are grounded in both religious and political developments of the previous two centuries. Since the temple at Jerusalem formed the center of Jewish life, it is hardly surprising that the high priestly families in the city formed a wealthy, aristocratic elite. They are the owners of the large, richly decorated houses that archeologists have found in the Upper City. We have seen that some two centuries before, the high priesthood had become a political appointment. The high priest served at the pleasure of the rulers of Palestine. He might also be expected to exercise some influence with the ruling powers.

Of course, the elaborate services and sacrifices of the temple required many other priests, Levites and others to carry out the daily rounds of offering. The hereditary priestly families from the different regions had appointed times to come up to Jerusalem and serve in the temple. Priests were expected to observe special rules of purity. No one could be a priest who had any physical imperfection. There is a story that when Antigonus, a contender for the Jewish throne, was given the high priest Hyrcanus as a prisoner, "Antigonus mutilated his ears with his own teeth so that never again could he resume the high priesthood" (Josephus, *War* 1:270). In addition, appointment to the high priesthood was limited to a few families, who were often referred to as "high priests" or "sons of high priests."

The high priest did not minister in the temple every day. He would appear there on the sabbath, on special festivals and on the annual day of repentance, Yom Kippur, when he alone entered the most holy sanctuary of the temple. Here is the description that Josephus gives of the splendid garments that the high priest wore for that occasion:

> When ministering, he wore breeches which covered his thighs up to the loins, a linen undergarment, and over that a blue robe reaching to his feet, full and tasseled; to the tassels were attached alternately golden bells and pomegranates, the bells signifying thunder and the pomegranates lightning. The embroidered sash that bound the robe to the breast was adorned by five bands in different colors—gold, purple, scarlet, linen and blue, with which the curtains of the sanctuary were also woven. The same combination appeared in the high priest's *ephod* [possibly a cape to which the breastplate was attached], gold being predominant. Shaped like an ordinary breastplate, it was held by two golden brooches set with very large and beautiful sardonyxes [an un-known gem] engraved with the names of the twelve tribes. On the other side were twelve more stones in four groups of three— sardius, topaz and emerald; carbuncle, jasper and sapphire; ag-ate, amethyst and jacinth; onyx, beryl and chrysolite—and on each of these was the name of one of the heads of the tribes. On his head the high priest wore a tiara of fine linen wreathed with blue and circled by another crown of gold on which were em-bossed the four sacred letters [of the name Yahweh]. (Josephus, *War* V:231–35)

If you look at a diagram of the temple area, you will see that it was divided into a number of chambers and courtyards. Only the officiating priests entered the court immediately in front of the temple where the great altar and the places for slaughtering the sacrificial animals were lo-cated. Only Israelite males were permitted beyond the walls which sep-arated the temple area from the court of the women. Non-Jews were not even permitted as far as the court of the women. Israelite men who were not in a state of ritual purity were confined to the court of the women. Persons suffering from leprosy or related types of disease were barred from the holy city of Jerusalem altogether. (Notice that Jesus sends a leper he has healed to the priests to make an offering and to have it attested that he is no longer unclean—Mk 1:40–44.)

A group generally known as "the scribes" had emerged as interpreters of the law in the period after the exile. But it is the group known as the Pharisees, who had the widest influence on the interpretation of the law in the time of Jesus. They originated sometime in the second century B.C. out of the various groups known as "the pious." These groups had re-

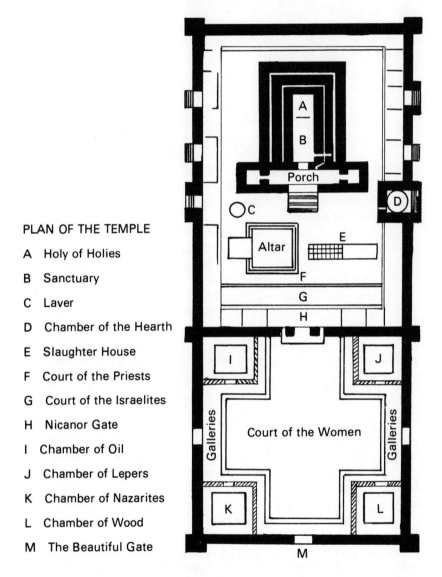

PLAN OF THE TEMPLE

A Holy of Holies

B Sanctuary

C Laver

D Chamber of the Hearth

E Slaughter House

F Court of the Priests

G Court of the Israelites

H Nicanor Gate

I Chamber of Oil

J Chamber of Lepers

K Chamber of Nazarites

L Chamber of Wood

M The Beautiful Gate

sponded to the threats of Hellenism by emphasizing the importance of carefully observing the law in daily life.

Both priests and lay people might belong to the party of the Pharisees. The aim of Pharisaic interpretation of the law was to make every sphere of life holy. The developing tradition of oral interpretation of the law enabled the Pharisees to advocate interpretations that could not be strictly maintained on the basis of the written text. Essene writings appear to be attacking Pharisaic interpretations of the law when they claim that many are being led astray by the "seekers of smooth things." This objection shows that the Pharisees were not always rigid conservatives in interpretation. Their goal was to find an application of the law that both respected its importance and could be lived out in the circumstances of ordinary life.

The name "Pharisee" comes from the Hebrew *p'rushim*, "separated ones." What this meant was that the Pharisees tried to separate themselves from all that was impure. They were careful to observe the rules for food preparation and meals, perhaps even taking on as laymen rules that had originally only applied to those who were priests. They were also careful to pay tithes on everything that might possibly be subject to the tithing. Although the Christian parable holds him up as a figure of scorn, the Pharisee in the parable of the Pharisee and the tax-collector (Lk 18:10–13) is a good example of the serious devotion to God felt by members of this sect. The Pharisees were the ones who were able to restructure Judaism after the destruction of the temple and its cult. The oral law was codified in a work known as the *Mishnah* around 200 A.D. Thus, the Pharisees, not the high priests, were the ancestors of rabbinic Judaism and, through the rabbinic traditions, of the various forms of Judaism that we know today.

In the first century B.C., the Pharisees had been engaged in political struggles for influence with another party known as the Sadducees. The Sadducees represented the wealthy aristocracy and the priestly families. They opposed the "oral law" of the Pharisees along with other innovations in Jewish belief such as belief in resurrection or an afterlife.

Religious Customs and Beliefs

A COVENANT PEOPLE LIVING BY GOD'S TORAH.   The law, which had been given by God, provided the basic framework for Jewish life. The different parties and sects might dispute one another over the interpretation and application of the law, but no one would think that a person who lived "outside" the law could expect to enjoy God's blessing. For those who lived in Palestine, the law was also the basis for all legal relationships between people. It was not just a set of religious rules. Jews living in minority communities in the diaspora were probably allowed to conduct their own internal affairs according to the law as well.

We may have a hard time understanding why the law is so important or why challenges to it from the early Christians excited so much controversy even among Christians. One must remember that "the law" is not an arbitrary set of rules. The law was understood to be God's revelation to

Plan of the Monastery of Qumran.

Moses on Sinai. There the nation had entered into a covenant, a solemn pact, with God to abide by the law and to honor no other gods. In return, the people of Israel would enjoy a special place as God's chosen people. God would protect, guide and bless them throughout their history.

When things did not go well for Israel, many people sought the cause in Israel's failure to remain faithful to the law. The Essene sect saw most of the history of Israel as infidelity. Here is a description of the prayers said when new members were accepted into their group. You will notice that joining the sect was said to be entering into a "covenant before God." This "new covenant" replaces the disobedience of the old covenant. (Christians would later insist that they had entered a new covenant with God through Jesus' death on their behalf.)

Everyone who joins the community must enter into a covenant before God to do everything He has commanded and not to turn away from Him through fear or through any trial to which one may be subjected by Belial [= Satan] . . . then the priests are to recount the bounteous acts of God and to recite His tender mercies toward Israel. The Levites are to recite all the sins and transgressions that the children of Israel have committed as a result of the dominion of Satan. Everyone who enters should make a confession saying: "We have acted wickedly; we have transgressed; we have sinned and done wickedly, we and our fathers before us by going against the Truth. God has been right to bring His judgment on us and on our fathers before us. But from ancient times, He has been merciful to us and always will be." Then the priests are to bless all those who cast their lot with God . . . and the Levites to curse all who have cast their lot with Belial.

The Essenes believe that God's mercies to Israel will be given to faithful members of the sect.

Most Jews would not have drawn the sharp division within Israel that is presupposed by the sectarian Essenes. They might agree that the people had sinned against God through disobedience but would expect God to raise up a new king and to bring the nation out of sinfulness to righteousness. Here is an example of such expectation from one of the "Psalms of Solomon." They are a collection of eighteen psalms apparently written in the middle of the first century B.C. PsSol 2:30–35 alludes to the death of Pompey in Egypt in 48 B.C. The Psalms of Solomon emphasize the covenant, the coming destruction of sinners and the eternal life which awaits those who are pious. PsSol 17:23–51 describes an "anointed" king like David who will come to lead the people:

> . . . we hope in God, our deliverer. For the might of our God is forever with mercy. And the kingdom of our God is over the nations in judgment forever. You, O Lord, chose David as king over Israel, and swore that his kingdom would never fail before you. But, because of our sins, sinners rose up against us . . . They did not glorify your name . . . They destroyed the throne of David in tumultuous arrogance . . . Look on their plight and raise up for them, their king, the son of David . . . and gird him with strength so that he can destroy the unrighteous rulers, and throw out of Jerusalem the nations that trample her to destruction . . . and he shall gather a holy people and lead them in righ-

teousness . . . and he shall force the pagan nations to serve under
his yoke; and he shall purify Jerusalem, making it holy as of old;
so that nations will come from the ends of the earth to see His
glory.

The selection from the Psalms of Solomon supposes that God can
bring about the blessings of the covenant by raising up a king from the
Davidic line who will cast out foreign rulers and create a holy and great
nation. In the early days of the Maccabean revolt, people had thought that
such a reform might come about. But by the time the Psalms of Solomon
were written, it was evident to all that the ruling kings could not be described in such terms.

GOD'S NEW ORDER TO DESTROY EVIL.   Another writing from
the very end of the first century B.C., the *Assumption of Moses*, proposes
a somewhat different version of this hope for a nation free from evil. Ass.
Mos. 6:2–6 lashes out at Herod the Great:

An insolent king will succeed them [the Hasmoneans], who will
not be of the race of the priests, a man bold and shameless, and
he will judge them as they shall deserve. And he will cut off their
chief men with the sword, and will destroy them in secret places,
so that no one may know where their bodies are. He will slay the
young and the old, and he will not spare anyone. And fear of him
will be bitter . . . for thirty-four years.

Ass. Mos. describes a bitter period of persecution suffered by the righteous. This persecution originally reflected the conditions under Antiochus IV. But the author sees it as the final wicked bloodshed that will
demand God's response:

His [= God's] Kingdom will appear throughout creation.
And then Satan will no longer exist, and sorrow will depart with
him.
And the hands of the angel appointed chief will be filled, and he
will avenge them against their enemies.
For the Heavenly One will arise from His royal throne, and He
will go forth from His holy dwelling, with indignation and wrath
on account of His children.
The earth will tremble and be shaken to its depths.
The high mountains will be leveled and the hills be shaken and
fall.

And the horns of the sun be broken and it will turn dark; the
moon will not give her light and be turned to blood . . .
For the Most High, the only Eternal God, will arise, and He will
appear to punish the Gentiles, and He will destroy all their idols.
Then you, O Israel, will be happy . . . and God will exalt you,
and bring you near to the stars. And you will look down from
above and see your enemies in hell. And you will recognize them
and rejoice. And you will give thanks and praise to your creator.

(Ass. Mos. 10)

This vision breaks the boundaries of mere earthly rulers. God arises
from the heavenly throne and creates the new order of things. Indeed,
God's action follows directly upon the death of a martyr, Taxo and his sons.
Taxo, a righteous person, chooses to suffer that death so that God will come
and deliver the people. This understanding of the martyr's death is very
important in the New Testament. It originates with the promise of Deut
32:43 that God will avenge the "blood of his children." The same promise
is invoked in the martyr story of the heroic mother and her sons in 2 Macc
7. Sinful Israelites deserve any fate that comes to them. But when the innocent righteous suffer persecution and death, God must become their
defender. In the New Testament, Christians were able to understand the
death of Jesus as the offering of an innocent, righteous person to free a
sinful humanity from the punishment due its sins against God (Rom 3:24–
26).

You may have noticed that human sinfulness is not the only reason
given for evil in many of these passages. Perhaps you were not surprised
to find references to Belial (or Satan) as the source of evil. But if you look
carefully in the Old Testament, you will see that there is little mention of
Satan. Evil is human doing pure and simple. Sometime in the period after
the exile, the Israelites picked up a new idea, the idea that there was a
demonic principle of evil that worked in the world to corrupt God's creation and to lead human beings astray. As a result, it would never be possible to have humanity obey God as it was meant to without destruction
of this evil power.

The Essenes give a dramatic expression to this view. They speak of
human beings as divided into two types. Some are guided by the "angel
of light," others by the Satanic "angel of darkness":

Now God created man to rule the world and appointed two spirits whose direction he would follow until the final Judgment: the
spirits of Truth and of Falsehood. All who practice righteousness
are under the domination of the Prince of Light and walk in light;

all who practice evil are under the Angel of Darkness and walk
in darkness. Through the Angel of Darkness, however, even
those who practice righteousness are made prone to error. All
their sins and transgressions are the result of his domination,
which is permitted by God's inscrutable design until the time He
has appointed. But the God of Israel and His Angel of Truth are
always there to help the sons of light. God created these spirits
of light and darkness and made them the instigators of every action and thought.

New Ideas and Symbols

These selections show us that a number of new ideas had come into
circulation in the two centuries prior to the time of Jesus. These new religious ideas and symbols were ways of understanding the significance of
what was happening in Israel's history. First, the direct links to the Davidic kingship and to the Zadokite priesthood had been broken. The existing kings and high priests were no longer in that line of descent. Had
God broken the promise to sustain the Davidic line forever? Some people
might have been political pragmatists and presumed that the Davidic kingship no longer mattered. Israel simply had to get along in the world she
had. But other people, observing the abuses of the present monarchy, answered that God was always faithful and merciful. God would soon raise
up a righteous and just king of David's line. Along similar lines, groups
with a strong attachment to the priesthood like the Essenes held that God
would also restore the true priesthood. A recently published Temple
Scroll from the Essene collection speaks of an entirely new temple and of
special rules of purity that would be observed in the holy city of Jerusalem.

Second, there is clear disagreement over the relationship between
human action and divine action in bringing about this new order. Some
writings speak as though the new leaders, king (and priest), would simply
emerge from the people as had been the case in the past. Others have
given up on that view. Only direct divine intervention, or divine intervention through a heavenly figure, can destroy the wicked from the earth
and break the power of Satan. Here is a long passage from a Jewish writing
describing the ideal high priest. The passage is presented as a revelation
given by the dying Levi to his sons:

Then the Lord will raise up a new priest. And all the words of
the Lord will be revealed to him, and he will judge the earth
righteously for many days. His star will arise in heaven like that

of a king, and light the light of knowledge as the sun does the
day. He will be magnified in the world, and shine forth on the
earth like the sun, and remove all darkness from under heaven.
There will be peace in all the earth, and the heavens will exult
in his day, and the earth will be glad. And the glorious angels of
the Lord's presence will be glad in him. The heavens will be
opened and sanctification will come upon him from the temple
of glory, with the Father's voice as from Abraham to Isaac. The
glory of the Most High will be uttered over him, and the spirit
of understanding and holiness will rest upon him. And no one
shall ever succeed him. In his priesthood the Gentiles will increase in knowledge [= religious devotion to God] and be enlightened through the graciousness of the Lord. In his priesthood
sin will come to an end, and the lawless will stop doing evil. He
will open the gates of paradise, remove the threatening sword
against Adam, and give the holy ones the tree of life to eat, and
the spirit of holiness will be upon them. He will bind Beliar, and
give his children power to tread on evil spirits. And the Lord will
rejoice in his children, and be pleased with his beloved ones forever. Then Abraham and Isaac and Jacob will exult, and I [=
Levi] will be glad, and all the holy ones will clothe themselves
with joy.

You can see that like the passage from Ass. Mos. this image of the coming
high priest goes beyond the boundaries of possibility for the world as it is.
Various signs indicate his coming. (Some of them should be familiar to you
from the Christmas stories in the gospels.) This high priest is not limited
by human knowledge since "all the words of the Lord will be revealed to
him." His appearance will bring about an era of peace when even the Gentiles will come to acknowledge God.

Sin will come to an end and a redeemed humanity will enjoy the fruits
of paradise. However, only those who are found righteous at the judgment
inaugurated by this high priest will participate in this glorious future. The
theme of a universal judgment at the end of history and the world as we
know it is another one of the "new ideas" which had developed in this period. The patterns of "salvation history" in the Old Testament had the nation as a whole suffer divine judgment through natural disasters or at the
hands of enemy nations. Balancing punishment and rewards with each individual was not an issue. The persecution and suffering of righteous persons in the post-exilic period sparked reflection on how God's "justice" was
present in individual lives as well as the corporate life of the nation. A judg-

ment scene such as that presupposed in this passage was one way of answering such questions.

A fourth "new idea" is embodied in the dualism associated with the emergence of Satan and myths of angelic (demonic) forces at work behind the evils of the world. Such dualism could never become absolute, since the Israelite believed in God's sovereign power as Creator of all things. Therefore, judgment is also a time in which God's rule over all of human history is made evident. Everything which had been contrary to God's purposes is destroyed. Some writings of this period introduce the idea of set periods of history. God knows the evils that are to come in each. God also controls their unfolding. Usually, most of the ages are said to have passed. The author assures the readers that they live close to the end of the times. Frequently, the overwhelming evils of the present are seen as symptoms of the final evil age in which people are living.

Global wars, famines, persecution of the righteous and an increase in evil are commonly presented as signs of the "end-time." One of the most influential "historical surveys" is that in the concluding section of the book of Daniel (Dan 7–12). It employs a traditional scheme of four world empires. This scheme is combined with mythic images of four beasts coming out of the sea. The myth of the god defeating the dragon monster of the watery chaos in order to establish order is a very ancient one in the near east. Yahweh slays the dragon in creating the world (Job 26:7–13), or with the exodus (Is 51:9–10). The terror and chaos of the mid-second century B.C. is evoked in these images.

"One Like a Son of Man"

Dan 7 switches to a scene of heavenly power, also derived from mythic symbols. "One like a son of man" ascends to the throne of the Ancient of Days. Israelite imagery describes Yahweh as the one who rides on clouds. But the image is taken from the Canaanite myths of Baal, the divine figure who conquers the evil sea monster. Baal is a younger god, subordinate to 'El, the father of gods and human beings. Daniel is using this imagery to assure the readers that the persecution of Antiochus is the culmination of demonic evils. It will come to an end with glorious divine victory. Instead of analyzing the situation of his time in human terms, Daniel sees it in the cosmic terms of archaic symbols.

The New Testament applies "Son of Man" to Jesus. The heavenly origins of the "Son of Man" figure are evident in the association with angels (Mt 13:41; 16:27; 24:31; 25:31; Mk 8:38; 13:27,41; Lk 9:26) and the exercise of judgment. Here is a description from a Jewish writing of the New Testament period that pictures the "Son of Man" enthroned in judgment. Notice that the righteous and elect have been raised up from the earth to a joyous fellowship with the Son of Man:

> And the Lord of Spirits seated him on his glorious throne and the spirit of righteousness was poured out upon him and the word of his mouth slays all the sinners . . . and they shall be downcast. Panic will seize them when they see the Son of Man sitting on his glorious throne. The kings, the mighty and all who possess the earth will glorify and praise the one who rules over all and who was hidden, for the Son of Man was hidden from the beginning; the Most High preserved him in his mighty presence and revealed him to the elect . . . And the righteous and the elect will have risen from the earth and cease to be downcast. And they will be clothed with glorious garments. (1 Enoch 62, 2–15)

You can see that later writers understood the heavenly context of Daniel's judgment scene. When "Son of Man" is used in connection with Jesus it should evoke images of a heavenly savior figure who represents the righteous community on the supernatural level. The revelation of the Son of Man at the judgment is the ultimate vindication of the righteous and their cause. "Son of Man" was not intended to make a point about Jesus' humanity in contrast to the expression "Son of God." In fact, "Son of God" was an expression with more human overtones than "Son of Man." It could be used for the king or for Israel as a whole or for a person who was particularly wise or righteous.

Writings like Daniel are often called "apocalyptic" from the Greek word for "reveal" because they claim to reveal the secrets of God's plan for the world, the judgment and secrets of the heavenly world. Apocalypses frequently repeat the same sequence of events in parallel visions using different symbols. Dan 8 and 10–12 form such a parallel. Dan 9 interprets the prophecies of Jeremiah 25:11–12 and 29:10 that seventy years after the Jews were taken into captivity by the Babylonians (587 B.C.) they would be restored to their land. The focus of the interpretation is on the last "week of years," the time in which Dan is being written. During that time there was an "anointed one" (Onias III, reported in 2 Macc 4:3) and the temple is profaned. However, these evil days are coming to an end. Dan 10–11 explains that there is a great conflict of heavenly powers behind the historical struggles of the sage Daniel during the Babylonian period and of the author's own time during the persecution of Antiochus IV. Dan 11:32 predicts that Antiochus will "seduce with flattery those who violate the covenant," that is, those Hellenizing Jews who supported the Syrian king's policies. But the people who "know God" will be led by "the wise" to stand firm.

Resurrection of the Righteous

Dan 12:1–3 introduces another new theme for Judaism in this period: the resurrection or exaltation with the heavenly hosts for the righteous. Here, that destiny is a special reward for the "wise." "Shining like stars" means that they become companions of the angels in heaven. This image of the resurrection of the righteous appears in 1 Enoch 39:5: "the dwelling places of the righteous are with the holy angels." Jesus uses it in Mk 12:25 to answer the Sadducees' objection that resurrection is a foolish idea. The Essene writings do not contain explicit reference to resurrection, but some scholars think that resurrection is presupposed in the Essene view that members of their sect are purified and given a place with the angelic host as in this hymn:

> You [= God] have taken a spirit distorted by sin, and purged it of the stain of transgression and given it a place in the host of the holy ones, and brought it into communion with the sons of heaven. You have made mere humans to share the lots of the spirits of knowledge; to praise your name in their chorus. (1 QH 3,19–21)

Many other images of exaltation in God's presence or resurrection to new life or new creation can be found in this period.

It is also the view of apocalyptic writers that the events in history are guided by powers that are beyond human control. Without heavenly revelation, one would never know that the events on the stage of human history are really part of God's salvation. Salvation must come with God's divine power. The apocalyptic writers do not think that human beings can create God's rule on earth by some political and religious revival. Evil has much too much power for that. Some apocalypses even speak of salvation as a form of heavenly life.

Because Christians refer to Jesus as *the* messiah (the word simply means "anointed"), they sometimes imagine that there was a special agent of divine intervention, "the messiah," whom all Jews were waiting for. It's not that simple. Both kings and priests were "anointed." Some people thought that God would deliver the people from their present evils by restoring a king from the descendants of David to rule over Israel. Others thought that the corrupt high priesthood would be replaced with a true one. Others believed that God would raise up two "anointed" figures, a king and a righteous high priest. Still other people thought that salvation would be brought through a heavenly figure—for example, the angel Michael might defeat the evil angels, or, perhaps, the mysterious, heavenly "Son of Man" would come in judgment and defeat the enemies of God's people. And many other apocalypses speak as the prophets do of God acting directly in human history.

The Religious Life of the People

Apocalyptic visions and their prophecies about the great empires of the world have contributed much religious symbolism to the New Testament. But much of Jesus' audience was from the general populace. They were not members of any special religious group devoted to the study of the law or to interpreting such visions. For them, religious life was part of the daily routine of the home and the local synagogue.

SYNAGOGUE.   The structure of the sabbath services in the synagogue appears to have been quite simple. Singing a Psalm was followed by reciting the "Shema" (Deut 6:4–9; 11:13–21; Num 15:37–41) and the Blessings. A reading from the law would be followed by a reading from one of the prophets. Then someone would give a sermon on the scriptures. A blessing by the president of the synagogue was followed by the priestly blessing from Num 6:24–36. Some scholars think there was a three year cycle for the readings from the law. The "president of the synagogue" was often a person who had donated the synagogue building. NT examples suggest that any adult male could be called upon to read and explain the law, though it may have been normal to pick out persons who were known for their knowledge of the law.

The religious center of Judaism remained the temple. The synagogues were places to meet, pray and study the law. They were not "sacred places" like the temple which was the place in which God dwelt. Jews living outside Judea would make pilgrimages to Jerusalem. Many could not make the three yearly journeys called for in the religious calendar. So Jews adopted the practice of praying at the times when sacrifices would have been offered to God in the temple (Dan 6:10–13). The first century Jewish historian Josephus retells the story of Moses to include the command to pray three times a day (*Antiquities* 4:212).

Our earliest example of a synagogue building comes from the beginning of the third century B.C. It is referred to by the Greek word for prayer (*prosuche*). Other examples have been found in every part of the

Roman world. After the Roman general Pompey conquered Judea he brought Jewish prisoners to Rome (63 B.C.). By the first century A.D. there was a large Jewish community in that city. It was the basis for the earliest churches there, which were established by 41 A.D. However, the extensive remains of synagogues in Galilee are all from the third century A.D. onward. The New Testament remains our only evidence that there were already synagogues there in Jesus' day. They were probably much simpler than these later synagogues, which had been built along the lines of a "temple," with a special ark for the Torah scrolls and more elaborate decoration.

GREAT FESTIVALS.   Pilgrimages to the temple in Jerusalem were linked with the agricultural seasons. Galilean villagers probably thought that God's faithfulness was tied to their harvest as well as to the events of salvation that were remembered at each feast.

Passover (Pesah) is probably the best known to Christians because Jesus' death and resurrection occurred during this feast. Passover commemorates the fact that God brought the Israelites out of slavery in Egypt. They are told to *remember* (Ex 6:7; Num 15:41) what God has done forever. We do not know exactly how the Passover meal was celebrated in Jesus' time. Groups large enough to consume a lamb would gather for the meal. Lambs were slaughtered in the temple the day before Passover. The basic rules for Passover observance are derived from Exodus: (1) remember annually (Ex 13:3); (2) eat unleavened bread (Ex 12:18); (3) cleanse all leaven out of one's house. Today, cleansing all the leaven from the house can involve an orthodox Jewish family in an extensive house cleaning—putting away all dishes used during the year; purifying ovens and refrigerators, cleaning silver and utensils so that no particles of leavened food are left on them.

Traditions which go back to Jesus' time claimed that the leaven represented the "evil inclination" which leads people away from God. A first century Jewish philosopher from Alexandria, Philo, explained that leaven "puffs up" bread. Therefore, it symbolized the arrogance of the pharaoh who would not let the people go. The negative associations of "leaven" should be remembered when reading Jesus' parable of the leaven in Mt 13:33.

It is also important to notice how important *remembering* is in the Passover context. Christians would speak of the Eucharist as "remembering" the death of Jesus (see 1 Cor 11:24–25). Remembering in this context is not just looking back into the past, it is a call to put ourselves back with those events and to recognize that they are also about us. The Mishnah tractate on Passover gives us an example of what is meant by commemoration:

Rabbi Gamaliel used to say: "Whoever has not said the verses concerning these three things at Passover has not fulfilled his obligation. They are Passover, unleavened bread and bitter herbs. "Passover" because God passed over the houses of our ancestors in Egypt; "unleavened bread" because our ancestors were redeemed from Egypt; "bitter herbs" because the Egyptians embittered the lives of our ancestors in Egypt. In every generation a person must regard himself as if he, himself, came forth from Egypt, for it is written, "And you shall tell your son on that day, It is because of what the Lord did for me when I came out of Egypt."

(*m. Pesahim* 10.5)

Pentecost (*shavuot*), was a more popular festival than Passover according to Josephus. Lev 23:9–22 prescribes that an offering be brought fifty days after the *omer* offering. The *omer* was a grain offering that marked the beginning of the spring grain harvest. This festival marks its end. Two loaves of leavened bread were presented in the temple. If you live in a farming area, you can see why the end of the spring wheat harvest would be an important feast for Galilean villagers. After the temple was destroyed by the Romans in A.D. 70, there was no place to make such offerings. The feast had also been associated with the giving of the law on Sinai. It could even be seen as the conclusion to the season that began with Passover. Today, there are no special rituals associated with Pentecost. Custom dictates that some Jews will decorate their homes and synagogues with green plants and eat dairy foods at Pentecost.

Tabernacles (*sukkot*) was the third agricultural festival. It celebrated the fall harvest (Ex 23:16). Lev 23:39–43 prescribes a seven day festival like Passover. The people are to dwell in huts during the festival and are to come to the temple waving branches of citron, palm, myrtle and willow, while singing praises to God. Zech 14:16–19 prophesied that when God judged the world all the nations that had oppressed Israel would annually go to Jerusalem at Tabernacles. Any nation that failed to do so would not receive rain for its crops. The gospel of John has Jesus deliver two discourses in the temple during the feast (7:14–39). They refer to Jesus as the source of living water, picking up the symbols of light and water from the temple celebration, and to Jesus going to teach the "Greeks," non-Jews.

Today, whenever they can, Jews build booths for Tabernacles. People will eat in them, especially on the first day of the feast, and perhaps hold discussions of the law there.

New Year. All cultures celebrate the New Year. Judaism marks it with solemn holy days, usually referred to as the "high holy days." They begin with the first day of the year, *Rosh Ha-Shanah*, and end ten days later with the Day of Atonement, *Yom Kippur*. This is a period of serious reflection on the ways in which one has failed to be faithful to God during the past year. The people are to devote *Yom Kippur* to fasting and repentance before God (Lev 23:23–32). In ancient times, the day was marked by special sacrifices. A "scapegoat" bearing the sins of the people was driven out into the desert and killed. The day of Atonement was the only day on which the high priest went into the most sacred part of the temple, the Holy of Holies.

In the New Testament, Heb uses the symbolism of the Day of Atonement for Christ. He is the High Priest who has entered the heavenly sanctuary by offering an atonement sacrifice that will never need to be repeated. Rabbinic traditions linked *Rosh Ha-Shanah* with creation. Synagogue worship focused on the theme of God as King over creation and as the one who continually renews creation. The three blessings recited in the synagogue reflect three fundamentals of Jewish belief: (1) God is King of the universe; (2) God intervenes in the world to punish the wicked and reward the good; (3) God has revealed himself in the law at Sinai and will do so again at the end of days.

Hanukkah. Unlike the festivals which go back to early times, the festival of Hanukkah originated in the second century B.C. under the Maccabees. It commemorates the rededication of the Jewish temple and is an eight day holiday modeled after Sukkot, which the people had been unable to celebrate while the temple was in pagan hands (2 Macc 10:6–7). Hanukkah is a minor feast in the Jewish calendar except in countries like the United States where it competes with the Christian celebration of Christmas. On each day of the feast, another candle in the eight branched candlestick, the menorah, is lit. During later centuries people forgot that the festival celebrated a military victory, and circulated a legend that although there had only been one flask of oil left in the temple, it kept the lamps burning for eight days. Sometimes the feast is also tied to the story of the mother and her seven sons who were martyrs for refusing to renounce Judaism (see 2 Macc 7). Or people may read the story of another heroic Jewish woman, Judith, who saved the people from a foreign enemy. Customs include playing games, singing special songs and gifts of money to the children.

Summary

Worship at the local synagogue, daily prayers, sabbath meals, the great pilgrimage feasts and other holidays of the Jewish calendar reminded people of their special relationship to God. They did not worship the gods and goddesses of their pagan neighbors. Although it sometimes seemed that God had left the people at the mercy of the great powers, the Jewish people continued to look forward to the day when God would send them salvation.

Of course, they had many visions of what salvation would be like. Some thought that a new king like David would make Israel a great nation. Others imagined that the basis for a new life would be the complete renewal of the temple and its priesthood. Still others thought that evil had such a grip on the nations and on human institutions that they would all have to be judged and condemned. Salvation would be a heavenly, angel-like existence for those who had remained faithful to God. Some people felt that they should show their devotion to God by joining a sect which had a stricter interpretation of the law than that followed by most people. They might become Pharisees or Essenes. Others responded to John the Baptist's call to repent because the time of judgment was at hand. The gospels show us that many of those who followed Jesus came not from such pious sects but from the ordinary people who had been farmers or fishermen or collectors of taxes and the like.

STUDY QUESTIONS

Facts You Should Know

1. How were Galilee, Samaria, Judea and the Decapolis governed in the first century A.D.?
2. What were the three pilgrimage festivals? What did each one celebrate?
3. What was the "temple tax"?
4. What were the special Jewish privileges which Roman edicts protected?
5. What were the distinguishing characteristics of the following groups within Judaism: (a) priests and Levites; (b) scribes; (c) Sadducees; (d) Pharisees; (e) Essenes?
6. What expectations for the future did groups of Jews associate with each of the following: (a) "anointed king," like David; (b) "anointed priest"; (c) new covenant; (d) God's rule or kingdom; (e) judgment of the world; (f) "Son of Man"; (g) resurrection and/or heavenly exaltation of the righteous?
7. What was a synagogue? How is it different from the temple?

Things To Do

1. Read Daniel 7–12. Pick out the mythic images of battle between heavenly powers and demonic beasts. How do they describe the political situation of God's faithful people in the world dominated by great empires? Pick out the prayers uttered by the visionary and the words of consolation spoken by the angel. What message do they give the pious?

2. Read the story of the mother and her seven sons in 2 Maccabees 7. Pick out the words which the mother and sons say against the tyrant. What picture do they give of life as a faithful Jew? What does the hope of resurrection mean for the martyrs in this story?

Things To Think About

1. The three Jewish pilgrimage festivals connect the agricultural cycle with events in God's salvation and creation of a people. How do the great Christian festivals link "nature" and events of salvation? What symbols and customs express this connection?

2. What modern symbols are used to give an "apocalyptic" picture of a world in which evil has the "upper hand" and which will soon come to an end in a great catastrophe or war? Do those images carry with them pictures of divine salvation and hope for a new order like the apocalyptic visions of Jesus' day? What do people put their hope in today?

Chapter 3

THE LIFE OF JESUS

Seeking Jesus of Nazareth

Almost as soon as anyone becomes famous in our culture, whether that person is a political leader, a rock star or a famous athlete, people will start writing books about that person. There will be TV and radio talk shows to further arouse our curiosity. We sometimes find it hard to imagine how the early Christians spread the message about Jesus for several decades before there were any written accounts of Jesus' ministry. Sometimes we imagine that the gospel writers engaged in the same sort of interviewing and research that people do today. So we need to constantly remind ourselves that the gospels are not like a modern biography. Each one tells the story of Jesus differently. Each has a special point of view which often provides us with clues about the particular church or group of Christians that the writer had in mind.

Now you may be wondering whether the gospels tell us anything at all about Jesus of Nazareth. Some people have even written books claiming that they do not. Such people argue that all we learn from the gospels is what each writer thought Jesus was like on the basis of stories that he had heard handed down in his church. They argue that what Christians believe about Jesus is really based on those gospel images of Jesus and that it is not necessary to ask what Jesus' life would look like if it were possible to study it in the way we can the life of some famous person in our own time.

We cannot simply stop with describing what the earliest Christians believed about Jesus without asking how they came to that belief. "Jesus" was not a figure of the distant, mythical past. He was a definite person known by some of the first generation of Christians, someone whose disciples and relatives were known to other members of the Christian movement. What was remembered and said about Jesus could not be

51

completely divorced from the person who had been known to such people. Of course, we know even from our own experience that the same persons and events are not remembered in the same way by all of the participants. We also know that sometimes our understanding of something a person said or did changes radically when we are able to set the person in a larger perspective, perhaps learning something else about the person or seeing how an individual's life turned out. Both of these basic experiences are met with in the gospels.

But scholars can also use their growing knowledge of the world of Jesus to show that the gospels preserve stories and sayings which fit into that world. They can use that information to help fill in the picture of what Jesus was like. They can ask how the people who first heard Jesus' words in Galilee would have understood them. Thus, we are constantly building up a more detailed picture of Jesus and his world. There may always be parts of the picture which are unclear to us because we do not have enough information about Jesus or first century Palestine to fill in the necessary details. But with patient study of literary materials, inscriptions, archeological remains and the traditions preserved about Jesus in the gospels, we can learn a great deal about Jesus of Nazareth.

How the Stories Are Preserved

Jesus' disciples did not use writing to help memorize what Jesus said and did. They traveled about with him, heard him teaching the crowds, asked him questions themselves, and saw him healing the sick. The stories of what Jesus had said and done were then repeated to others. In order to make them easy to remember many of the stories about Jesus follow a set pattern. The sayings of Jesus also fall into patterns which could be remembered. If you were familiar with the basic pattern, then you would only need to remember enough detail about a particular episode or saying to fill in the pattern. When they classify these patterns, scholars call them "forms."

MIRACLE STORIES.   One of the easiest types of story to recognize is the miracle story. People are always interested in miraculous events and cures. Here is a story about a Syrian (non-Jewish) healer from Palestine:

Everyone has heard of the Syrian from Palestine, an expert at such things. Whatever moonstruck—rolling their eyes and filling their mouths with foam—people come, they arise and he dispatches them away healthy, when they are free from the terror

[= a demon, thought to be possessing the person] and for a large fee. When he stands by them as they are lying there he asks from whence they came into the body. The sick man is silent, but the demon answers in Greek or some other barbarian tongue. The Syrian levels oaths at him, but if the demon is not persuaded, he threatens and expels the demon.

This type of healing is called an "exorcism" because it involved curing a person thought to be possessed by a demon. A number of such stories were told about Jesus. Here is one from Mk 1:23–26:

And immediately, there was in their synagogue a man with an unclean spirit; and he cried out, "What have you to do with us, Jesus of Nazareth? Have you come to destroy us? I know who you are, the Holy One of God." But Jesus rebuked him, saying, "Be silent, and come out of him!" And the unclean spirit, convulsing him and crying with a loud voice came out of him.

This story is told in a much more direct and dramatic way than the report about the Syrian exorcist. But you can see that it has the basic features of an exorcism: (1) demonstration of the symptoms of the illness, here of possession; (2) verbal conflict between the demon and the exorcist; (3) demon departs from the person with some form of violence. Miracle stories then conclude with some indication that the person has really been healed. In Mk 1:27, for example, the people begin to talk among themselves about the event:

And they were all amazed so that they questioned among themselves saying, "What is this? A new teaching! With authority he commands even the unclean spirits and they obey him."

In the story about the Syrian exorcist, the main point of the man's activity was to get money from the people he cured. Many people were suspicious of persons who claimed to have powers of healing. They thought that such people were working with the demons, or they thought that people like that were "getting rich" with fake cures. You can see that the second charge does not apply to Jesus. He was teaching in the synagogue according to Mark's version of the story when he was interrupted by the possessed man. He was not looking to make money. You also notice that as the miracle story was told among Christians, it had a double purpose. For those who didn't yet believe in Jesus, it might persuade them that he had to be "from God." For those who did believe, the demon's reaction to Jesus is really a very "religious" one. The demon knows Jesus' true identity. It also knows that Jesus' ministry is going to break up the power of demons. Jesus is not working with them but against them.

You can see that the earliest Christians retold stories about Jesus' miracles as part of their desire to convince people that Jesus was a person sent by God. They may have made collections of miracle stories about Jesus to use in missionary preaching. Some scholars have suggested that Mark used such a collection in composing the opening chapters of his gospel. You will notice that in Mark we even find two versions of the same miracles. Jesus feeds a large number of people (Mk 6:30–44 [5,000 people]; 8:1–10 [4,000 people]). Jesus also works two miracles in which he calms severe storms at sea for his disciples (Mk 4:35–41; Mk 6:45–50). You might think that Jesus simply did the same thing more than once. That is not impossible. But it creates a problem. If you look closely at each of the double stories you will notice that the disciples are just as bewildered the second time around as they were the first. They would not seem to have learned anything. That is why many scholars think that the double stories are really two different versions of a single incident. The gospel of John, which does not seem to have used the gospel of Mark, has its own versions of the feeding and storm stories (Jn 6:1–13; 6:16–21).

Scholars have suggested that the early Christians had a collection of Jesus' miracles with these two stories in it. Mark may have known two different versions of the collection and used them both for his gospel. John had a slightly different version of the same collection. Matthew and Luke each appear to have had Mark's gospel available when they wrote their gospels. But Luke leaves out the section of Mark that contains the duplications. Matthew, on the other hand, takes the second storm story in which Jesus rescues the disciples by walking on water and adds another episode. Peter asks Jesus to make it possible for him to walk on water. But as Peter begins to do so, his faith in Jesus wavers. Jesus must rescue him from sinking. This episode leads Jesus' disciples to worship him as "truly, Son of God," (Matt 14:28–33).

Matthew's addition tells you something important about how the gospel writers treated their material. They did not simply copy what they had in front of them. They were able to expand stories and add new ones so that the church of their time could see how the story of Jesus applied to them. In Matthew's case, Peter was the founder of the church. Throughout the gospel, Matthew shows Peter being prepared for this role of leader. Here, Peter has to learn an important lesson about faith. Some scholars have pointed out that Matthew's church was passing through a time of turmoil. Christians would have read this story of Jesus and Peter as addressed to them. Jesus would guard and protect the church as long as Christians kept up their faith in him.

PRONOUNCEMENT STORIES.   Other stories were told about Jesus in addition to miracle stories. A popular type of story was the "pronouncement story." Stories of this type were often told about famous teachers in antiquity. They begin by creating some form of "tension," perhaps a question by disciples, a paradox posed by opponents or even a problematic situation. The wisdom of the hero is demonstrated when he or she resolves the situation using an appropriate saying or pronouncement. Naturally, the saying that forms the resolution of the story might well be independent of its setting. Sometimes such sayings are proverbial and might have been used in any number of contexts. The pronouncement story often serves to show the superiority of its hero over others, since he or she is able to "master" the situation.

Here is one of many such stories about the Cynic philosopher Diogenes. The Cynic philosophers wandered from city to city in a coarse cloak with few possessions. They often chastised their hosts and audiences for concern with luxury, bodily pleasures and all the cares that make life difficult for people. The Cynic, who lives without such possessions and cares, is the one who is really "free." Here, Diogenes has suffered a fate feared by many in antiquity. He has been captured by pirates and is about to be sold into slavery:

> [Speaking to his fellow captives] . . . then he [= Diogenes] said this in sport and ridicule: "Stop pretending ignorance and crying over your imminent slavery, as if you were really free before you fell into the hands of pirates and were not slaves to even worse masters. Now perhaps you will get moderate masters who will cut out of you the luxury by which you were ruined, and who will instill in you perseverance and self-control, the most honored of good things." As he went through these things, the buyers stood and listened, amazed at his freedom from emotion. Some also asked him whether he was skilled at anything. And he said that he was skilled at ruling men. "So, if any of you needs a master, let him come forward and strike a bargain with the sellers." But they laughed at him and said, "What free man needs a master?" "All," he said, "who are base and who honor pleasure and despise toil, the greatest incitements to evil."

You can see that the Diogenes story is meant to demonstrate the superiority of the Cynic teaching. Like the pronouncement stories in the gospels, this one is part of a longer exposition of Diogenes' adventures.

Often pronouncement stories in the gospels preserve points of Jesus' teaching that had become critical for the later development of the community. Here is one in which the "hero" is a pagan woman, who asks Jesus to perform a miracle for her:

THE SYROPHOENICIAN WOMAN   *[3–1]*

Mark 7:24–30:
And from there he arose
and went away to the region
of Tyre and Sidon.
And he entered a house and
would not have anyone know
it; yet he could not be hid.
But immediately a woman
whose little daughter was
possessed by an unclean
spirit, heard of him, and
came and fell down at his
feet. Now the woman was a
Greek, a Syrophoenician by
birth. And she begged him
to cast the demon out of
her daughter.

Matthew 15:21–28:
And Jesus went away from there
and withdrew to the district
of Tyre and Sidon.

And behold a Canaanite woman

from that region came out
and cried,

"Have mercy on me, O Lord, Son
of David; my daughter is severely
possessed by a demon."
But he did not answer her a word.
And his disciples came and begged
him saying, "Send her away for she
is crying after us."
He answered, "I was sent only to
the lost sheep of the house of
Israel."

But she came and knelt before him,
saying, "Lord, help me!"

And he said to her,
"Let the children first be
fed, for it is not right
to take the bread of
children and give it to
the dogs."

And he answered,
"It is not fair to take the
children's bread and throw it to
the dogs."

But she answered him, "Yes, Lord; yet even the dogs under the table eat the children's crumbs."	She said, "Yes, Lord; yet even the dogs eat the crumbs that fall from their master's table."
And he said to her, "For this saying, you may go your way; the demon has left your daughter." And she went home and found the child lying in bed and the demon gone.	Then Jesus answered her, "O woman, great is your faith! Be it done as you desire." And her daughter was healed instantly.

Make a careful comparison of the two versions of this story. In Mark's version, the woman's "saying" wins her case. Matthew has Jesus comment on her faith. Look back at Mt 14:31. Jesus chides Peter for being a person of "little faith." By praising the woman's faith, Matthew makes her an example for all Christians. You will also notice that she has to overcome more obstacles in Matthew than in Mark. Jesus ignores her. The disciples want to get rid of her. And Jesus insists that his mission is only to the Jewish people, "the lost sheep of the house of Israel."

The expansion of the obstacles in Matthew shows us the role that this story came to play in early Christian communities. Jesus' mission had been to Israel. But the early Christian missionaries quickly found converts among non-Jews as well. When we study Paul's letters, we will see that they had to struggle with the question of whether Gentile converts would have to become Jews. Finally, most of the leaders of the church agreed that Gentiles could be part of the community without becoming Jews, "children of Israel." In that context, a story of Jesus' healing the daughter of a Gentile takes on new life. It shows that even a Gentile was capable of showing the kind of faith in Jesus that would lead to salvation. Matthew's gospel is written from the perspective of a strong Jewish Christian tradition. Many scholars think that at the time Matthew wrote his church was undergoing a transition from evangelizing Jews to preaching among the Gentiles. (See the strong affirmation of that mission in Mt 28:16–20). This story would support that mission.

SAYINGS AND PARABLES.   While some of Jesus' teaching is preserved in stories about him like the pronouncement stories, much of it is preserved in sayings and stories which are reported as direct instruction to the crowds or to disciples. Here too we find a number of different types of saying. We also find allusions to the Old Testament, to what appear to have been folklore themes and to common proverbs. We also find that Jesus' stories and sayings often come down to us in a number of different versions. Sometimes there are sayings of Jesus which are reported in other early writers that are not in the gospels. For example, Acts 20:35b; 1 Cor 9:14 (indirectly), and 1 Thess 4:15 all refer to words of the Lord which are not in the gospels. Lk 1:1–4 and Jn 20:30 both refer to the fact that the evangelists are conscious of selecting their material from a larger pool of available traditions about Jesus. These traditions may have circulated in both oral and written form.

Parables

One of the most popular forms of Jesus' teaching remains the parable. Jesus' parables range from very short, "one-liner" comparisons and analogies to miniature stories in which one or more characters take part. One of the best known short parables is that of the shepherd who goes in search of a lost sheep:

PARABLE OF THE LOST SHEEP   [3–2]

Matthew 18:12–14:
What do you think?
If a man has a hundred
sheep, and one of them has
gone astray,
does he not leave the
ninety-nine on the
mountains and go in search
of the one that went
astray?
And if he finds it,
truly I say to you,
he rejoices over it more
than over the ninety-nine
that never went astray.

Luke 15:3–7:
So he told them this parable,
What man of you,
having a hundred sheep,
if he has lost one of them,
does not leave the
ninety-nine in the
wilderness and go after
the one which is lost
until he finds it?
And when he has found it,

he lays it on his shoulders,
rejoicing.

And when he comes home, he
calls together his friends and
his neighbors, saying to them,
"Rejoice with me, for I have
found my sheep which was lost."

So it is not the will of my Father in heaven that one of these little ones should perish.	Just so, I tell you, there will be more joy in heaven over one sinner who repents than over ninety-nine righteous who have no need of repentance.

Gospel of Thomas 107:
Jesus said, "The Kingdom is like a shepherd who had a hundred sheep. One of them, the largest, went astray. He left the ninety-nine and looked for that one until he found it. When he had gone to such trouble, he said to the sheep, "I love you more than the ninety-nine.""

Once again we have two versions of the parable in the synoptic gospels. If you look up the context of the parable in each of the gospels you will see that Matthew has Jesus address the parable to disciples, especially to those who are going to be leaders of the community. They must care for all members of the community and not despise the "little ones." Luke has Jesus address the parable to hostile Pharisees who were critical of his associations with sinners. They thought that the messiah should be sent to the "righteous of Israel," those who were really looking for God's salvation.

You will also notice that Luke's version of the parable has an additional scene between the parable and the application of the parable to the audience. The shepherd collects his friends for a celebration. Again, if you were to look carefully at the parables in Luke 15, you would notice that the chapter has three parables about things which are "lost": a sheep, a coin and a son (the prodigal son). Each one ends with a celebration and rejoicing, doesn't it? The feast of celebration is critical to the action of the prodigal son. It looks as though Luke has used that theme to structure the whole chapter. Go to the beginning of the chapter. There, we find a meal as the context in which the criticism of Jesus has been raised. You might say that it is the reverse of the "celebration" of repentance and forgiveness being called for in the stories.

We can also use non-gospel tradition to provide us with an additional clue that the story of the lost sheep circulated in the oral tradition without the second part. A version of this parable has come down to us in a second century collection of sayings of Jesus, the Gospel of Thomas. This version lacks some of the urgency conveyed by the gospel versions. It also avoids the troubling problem of whether the shepherd was so concerned about the lost one that he actually left the other sheep exposed, since it doesn't refer to the mountains or the wilderness. And it seems to feel the need to explain the special relationship between the shepherd and the lost sheep by making it the best one in the flock. Such shifts easily can occur in a story as it is handed down in the tradition. But whatever the shifts, the Gospel of Thomas version confirms the view that the story originally had a simple structure of seeking the sheep, finding and reaction. The Lukan calling in neighbors and the application of the lesson to the audience are expansions.

Instructions for Disciples

In addition to the parables, many of Jesus' sayings take the form of "rules" or instructions about the life of discipleship. These were often gathered together by the tradition or by the individual evangelists into collections of related material. Naturally, instruction on prayer plays an important role in the life of the community. Matthew and Luke each contain a section of Jesus' teaching on prayer, which includes the Lord's Prayer. Matthew's, from the Sermon on the Mount, explains how Christian piety differs from that of Jews and pagans (Mt 6:1–18). Luke has the teaching on prayer result from the disciples' observation of Jesus at prayer and their desire to be taught about prayer (Lk 11:1–13). Compare the two versions of the Lord's Prayer. You can see that Matthew's has been "filled out" to provide the parallel phrasing that would make it appropriate for communal worship:

THE LORD'S PRAYER   *[3–3]*

Matthew 6:9–13:
Our Father
who art in heaven,
hallowed be thy name.
Thy kingdom come;
thy will be done,
on earth as it is in heaven.
Give us this day
our daily bread;
And forgive us our debts,
as we also have forgiven
our debtors;
And lead us not into
temptation,
but deliver us from evil.

Luke 11:2–4:
Father,
who art in heaven,
hallowed be thy name.
Thy kingdom come.

Give us each day
our daily bread;
And forgive us our sins,
for we ourselves forgive
everyone who is indebted to us.
And lead us not into
temptation.

Jewish Kaddish Prayer:
Magnified and sanctified be His great name in the world that He created according to his will. May He establish His Kingdom in your lifetime; in your days; and in the lifetime of the house of Israel, even speedily at a near time.

> **Mark 11:25:**
> And whenever you stand praying, forgive, if you have anything against any-one; so that your Father also, who is in heaven, may forgive you your tres-passes.

The first part of Jesus' prayer focuses on the coming of the kingdom of God. It reflects a Jewish prayer (the Kaddish prayer). The second half speaks directly of the needs of those who are to be Jesus' disciples. They must be preserved from "temptation," that is, from the "testing" of God's people that might lead them astray from God's will. The bread petition reflects Jesus' more general teaching against anxiety (cf. Mt 6:25–34; Lk 12:22–34; 16:10–13). Jesus links God's forgiveness with our treatment of others. This point is emphasized in Mt 6:14–15. Although the gospel of Mark does not contain the Lord's Prayer, it does contain another saying of Jesus which makes the same point (Mk 11:25). The addition that is made in Christian liturgies, "for thine is the kingdom and the power and the glory forever and ever," appears in an early Christian writing from the end of the first century, the *Didache*, as "for thine is the power and the glory forever." This document instructs Christians to recite the Lord's Prayer three times a day. Matthew includes prayer in a triad of pious practices: almsgiving, prayer and fasting. The Gospel of Thomas preserves a saying on true piety that takes this triad and adds to it the question of dietary food laws:

> And his disciples questioned him and said, "Do you want us to fast? How shall we pray? Shall we give alms? What diet shall we observe?" Jesus said, "Do not tell lies, and do not do what you hate, for all things are plain in the sight of Heaven. For nothing hidden will not become manifest and nothing covered will re-main without being uncovered." (Gos. Thom. 6)

Jesus' rejection of Jewish concerns about kosher food laws is preserved in the synoptic tradition in Mk 7:14–23 (cp. Mt 15:10–20).

Gos. Thom. 6 makes use of a form of saying that is sometimes referred to as a judgment saying. The passive verb represents God as the author of the action. Whatever is hidden now will be revealed in the judgment. Mk 4:21–23 combines that saying with a saying about a lamp, which occurs in many forms in both the canonical gospels and in the traditions outside the gospels:

> And he said to them, Is a lamp brought in to be put under a bushel, or under a bed, and not on a stand? For there is nothing

hid, except to be made manifest; nor is anything secret, except
to come to light. Let him who has ears to hear hear.

The saying about the lamp probably existed in proverbial form such as we
find in Mt 5:15a, Lk 8:16 or 11:33, to the effect that no one lights a lamp
and puts it under a vessel or a basket. The gospels use this proverb to warn
the disciples that they must not hide what they have received. The element of warning is intensified by incorporating the saying into a context
of judgment sayings.

In addition to proverbs and judgment sayings, there are sayings which
are described as "legal sayings." Although most of these sayings are not
"laws" in our sense of the word, they are intended to set forth the way in
which Jesus' disciples are to live their lives. The one which has been most
frequently embodied in the legal system of Christian countries has been
Jesus' saying against divorce (e.g. Mt 5:31–32; 19:3–9, in the context of a
debate with the Pharisees). Jesus rejected the rather liberal standards for
divorcing a wife in his time as contrary to the intention of God in creation,
though he knows that the law of Moses does allow for divorce so long as
the husband follows the proper legal procedures and gives his wife a divorce decree. Some Christian sects have even taken other sayings from the
Sermon on the Mount as strict rules of conduct. The prohibition against
swearing oaths in Mt 5:33–37 they take to mean that they cannot swear an
oath of allegiance or an oath in court. Of course, if people always told the
truth directly as Jesus commands, then the use of oaths to back up a person's word would not be necessary.

Jesus' legal sayings do not represent a system of law to replace the law
of Moses by which Jews lived their lives and governed themselves under
Roman supervision. Rather, they seem to be a challenge to the type of
person who thinks that the will of God is perfectly embodied in the law.
Such a person might presume that as long as "it's legal" in the Mosaic law,
it represents the will of God. But Jesus keeps insisting that the law cannot
come close to the real perfection of God or the change of heart demanded
of those who live for God alone.

SAYINGS COLLECTIONS.   Naturally, as the early Christians handed down the various sayings and parables of Jesus, they also made collections of them just as they did of the miracles of Jesus. The Gospel of
Thomas, which in its present form stems from a second century gnostic
sect, seems to be based on just such a collection of sayings. It's not even
a gospel in the way we think of a gospel because it does not narrate the
ministry of Jesus in Galilee, the concluding days in Jerusalem and the
death and resurrection as the gospels in the canon do. Gos. Thom. appears

to preserve a collection of sayings that circulated in the eastern part of the church in Syria, which was an area of strong Christian churches in the early centuries.

Long before Gos. Thom. was discovered, scholars had proposed that there was a collection of Jesus' sayings and parables that both Matthew and Luke had used to supplement the teaching material that they found in Mark. This source was called "Q" from the German word for source, "Quelle." They reached the conclusion that this source had to have been a written collection of sayings because of the close verbal overlap between the material common to the two writers. At the same time, differences in their versions and in the order of material in their respective gospels make it unlikely that Matthew copied the material out of Luke or vice versa.

You have already seen some examples of Q material in the parable of the lost sheep and in the Lord's Prayer. If you look back at those passages you can see what we mean by common source material. In general the Lukan form of the Q material is less elaborately reworked than that in Matthew, so we will give the passages commonly assigned to Q in their Lukan version. Jesus is pictured in the Q sayings as the Son of Man who comes to bring the end-time salvation. Satan will be defeated, judgment is coming and the faithful perseverance of the disciples of Jesus will win them salvation.

Many scholars think that this collection of sayings was shaped by the earliest Christian missionaries in Palestine and Syria. Their way of life was much like that of Jesus himself. They traveled from village to village announcing that the kingdom of God was at hand. Jesus, the Son of Man, who is coming in judgment, had demonstrated the defeat of Satan's kingdom in his exorcisms. His disciples are continuing Jesus' summons to Israel to repent.

You can also see that all of our reports about what Jesus said and did have been handed down within the context of a believing community. Neither the gospel writers nor their sources were engaged in "investigative reporting." The stories about Jesus, the collections of his miracles and his sayings are all intended to awaken and nourish faith in Jesus as the one sent by God to bring salvation.

Jesus as Teacher and Miracle-Worker

All of the traditions about Jesus emphasize two aspects of his ministry: teaching and healing. Mk 1:21–28 combines these two features of Jesus' ministry in an opening scene at the synagogue in Capernaum. While Jesus is teaching the people, a possessed man begins to cry out, "What have you

MATERIAL ASSIGNED TO Q   *[3–4]*

Narrative:
Centurion's Slave (Lk 7:2,6b–10)

Ethical Exhortation:
Serving Two Masters (16:13)
Light/Darkness Within (11:34–36)
Faith and Forgiveness (17:3b–4,6)

Eschatological Warning:
Judgment Preached (3:7–9)
Baptism with Spirit and Fire (3:16–17)
Judging and Eschatological Judgment (6:37–42)
Woes on the Cities (10:13–15)
Woes on Scribes and Pharisees (11:39–52)
Fire, Baptism, Sword and Division (12:49–53)
Signs of the Time (12:54–56)
Repent (12:57f)
Prepare for the Crisis (13:24–29)
Lament: Doom of Jerusalem (13:34–35)
Judgment: Careless and Preoccupied (17:24,26f,33–37)

Eschatological Conflict:
With the Devil (4:2–12)
Defeat the Prince of Demons (11:14–22)
Dispel Unclean Spirits (11:23–26)

Eschatological Promise:
Beatitudes (6:20b–23)
Love Enemies (6:27–36)
Lord's Prayer (11:2–4)
What God Will Give (11:9–13)
Seek the Kingdom (12:22–31)
Treasure in Heaven (12:33f)
Role in the Kingdom (22:28–30)

Eschatological Discipleship:
Gratitude for Knowledge Revealed by God (10:21–24)
Fitness for Kingdom (9:57–60)
Kingdom Near (10:2–12)
Fearless Confession (12:2–12)
Bearing the Cross (14:26f)

Eschatological Parables:
Watchfulness (12:39–40,42–46)
Leaven (13:20f)
Great Supper (14:16–23)
Lost Sheep (15:4–7)
Talents (19:11–27)
House Built on Sand/Rock (6:47–49)

Jesus Brings Eschatological Salvation:
Fulfills Scripture (7:18–23)
Brings the Kingdom (7:24–35)
Fulfills the Law and the Prophets (16:16–17)
To Receive Jesus Is To Receive God (10:16)
Sign of Jonah (11:29b–32)
Jesus' Table in the Kingdom (14:15; 22:28–30)
Messiah Coming to Jerusalem (13:34–35; 19:41–44)

to do with us, Jesus of Nazareth? Have you come to destroy us? I know who you are, the Holy One of God" (v. 24). We have seen that that is quite a theological insight for a demon. The crowd reacts in amazement at Jesus' teaching and his authority over the demons. Mark suggests that Jesus' reputation as a healer drew people to him from all over.

Of course, as we have seen, Jesus was not the only person in his time reputed to work miracles (see Mt 12:27). Sometimes, as in the case of the Syrian miracle worker that we quoted earlier, such persons were accused of being in the business to make money from those who were gullible. Neither Jesus, nor his disciples, are ever accused of profiting from the power to heal. Pagans often sought to be healed by going to a temple of the healing god Asclepius. In the reports attached to famous shrines, we sometimes find the motif of doubt and conversion to belief in the god. Here is an example of such a story:

A man who could move only one finger of his hand came to the god as a supplicant. When he saw the votive tablets in the sanctuary he did not believe the cures and made fun of the inscriptions. In his sleep [in the sanctuary] he had a vision. It seemed to him that as he was playing dice in the room under the temple and was about to throw, the god appeared, jumped on his hand and stretched out his fingers. When he had stepped off, he saw himself bend his hand and stretch out each finger on its own; when he had stretched them all out straight, the god asked him whether he still did not believe the votive tablets, and he said no. "Because you had no faith in them, though they were worthy of belief your name in the future shall be Apistos [= 'without faith']," said the god. When day came he emerged from the sanctuary cured.

This story illustrates the theme of faith, which plays an important role in Jesus' miracles. Jesus, too, is able to cure persons who are paralyzed as several stories about him suggest (Mk 2:1–12; 3:1–6). In the gospels, we frequently find faith in a different location in the story. Instead of Jesus using the miracle to convince someone who does not believe, Jesus only performs the miracle after he or the disciples (by trying to push the person aside) have challenged the person's faith (Mk 2:5; 5:34; 5:36; 7:27–29; 10:48–52).

The emphasis on faith in connection with the miracles of Jesus was one way in which the tradition could make it clear that Jesus was not some sort of "magician" or "money-seeking wonder worker." Even so Jesus had to reject two different types of "crowd reaction" to his abilities. One was the desire to set him up as some sort of mass leader and wonder-worker (Jn 6:15). The other was to credit Jesus' miracles to some clever manipulation of demonic or at least dubious powers (Mk 3:20–22; 5:17). Even in our own day, versions of these views are represented in attempts to discredit Christian belief in Jesus. Certainly, Jesus' miracles did bring him popular attention as Mark suggests. But the gospels also show a certain reserve in their narration of the miracles that is unlike other accounts of miracle-working.

Scholars suggest that this reserve may go back to Jesus himself. Because miracles are ambiguous, they have to be set within a larger context. Jesus, unlike other miracle-workers, sees his exorcisms as signs of liberation and hope. Casting out of demons shows that God's kingdom is present (Mt 12:28). Other sayings attributed to Jesus speak of a vision in which he sees Satan falling from heaven (Lk 10:18), his kingdom falling apart (Mk 3:24–26), and his house being robbed (Mk 3:27). Another way of connecting the miracles and Jesus' coming to fulfill the Old Testament promises of salvation is to connect them with the promises in Is 35:5–6 that the blind shall see, the deaf hear, the lame walk and the dumb speak. Mt 15:30–31 uses this Isaiah passage as a summary of Jesus' healing activity. All of these themes are represented in the miracles of Jesus (dumb, Mt 9:32–34); deaf and dumb, Mk 7:32–35; blind, Mk 8:22–26; 10:46–52; Mt 9:27–31; Jn 9:1–11; lame, Mk 2:1–12; Jn 5:1–9).

Of course, Jesus' miracles are not limited to those which can be linked to Old Testament prophecies. But by making the connection between the two, it was possible for Jesus and his disciples to insist that the time of salvation had come. The limitations and evils that held people in bondage were no longer insurmountable. People could experience the saving power of God in their lives. They are not "trapped" in a world dominated by evil. As the early Christians retold these stories about Jesus' miracles, they showed that the miracles pointed to Jesus as the one who embodies God's power just as we have seen the demon in the Markan story hail Jesus as the "Holy One of God."

Jesus as Teacher

Jesus' teaching also called upon the hearer to recognize that God was bringing forth a new time of salvation. Some people may have thought that Jesus was like one of the scribes, a person who was going to engage in interpreting the law. But Jesus breaks with their tradition of interpreting the law so that it could be lived in this age by proclaiming that salvation and healing and even human need take priority over such important obligations as observing the sabbath (Mk 2:23–28; 3:1–6). Some people apparently expected Jesus to be like the Pharisees or other pious laymen, who went beyond what was required of the law in their personal lives. Jesus is criticized for not observing ritual washings before meals (Mk 7:2) and for not teaching his disciples to fast (Mk 2:18). Neither practice is required by the law. Nor were Jews, in general, required to avoid contact with fellow Jews who were sinners, though Jesus was criticized for failing to do so (Mk 2:15–17; Lk 7:34). Mk 7:15 preserves a saying of Jesus which shifts the focus away from external purity rules to the inner dispositions of a person, "There is nothing outside a person, which by going in can defile, but the things which come out of a person are what defile." Such debates suggest that some considered Jesus to be a teacher who sought to expand the sphere of observance of the law and personal holiness. Yet, his teaching and conduct sometimes conflicted with what people expected from such teachers.

In other respects, Jesus may have appeared to be closer to the prophets. He often spoke directly of the will of God for the people. Some of his puzzling actions and sayings have also been compared to the prophets— for example, the saying in Mt 8:22 (Lk 9:60), "Let the dead bury their dead." Such disregard of filial piety would have been shocking to anyone, Jewish or pagan, in antiquity. If we look back at the Old Testament, however, we find two examples in which the prophet is commanded to break with burial rites. Jeremiah is told not to take part in mourning because an age is coming in which burial will be neglected (Jer 16:5–7). Ezekiel is told not to observe the usual rites when his wife dies (Ez 24:15–18), as a sign of how the people will behave when Yahweh brings judgment on them by destroying the temple and permitting the death of many of the young. Jesus' command to a would be disciple, then, can be understood as a prophetic sign that the kingdom is at hand. The usual conventions of piety and behavior are broken because God's salvation and judgment are coming into the experience of Jesus and his generation.

The idea that Jesus' presence and actions show people that they are facing an "exceptional time" is also evident in the responses given to the charges of breaking the sabbath, "so the Son of Man is Lord even of the sabbath" (Mk 2:28). It is used in the collection of sayings that defend Jesus and his followers for not fasting (Mk 2:19,21–22). Other "prophetic" elements in Jesus' teaching are more difficult to establish in their original form as they have been recast in the gospel traditions in light of later events. Jesus appears to have made predictions about the impending destruction of the temple in Jerusalem (Mk 13:2; 14:58). He may also have predicted his own suffering and death in a saying that linked his fate with the death of John the Baptist (Mk 9:12–13). But the elements in Jesus' ministry that would have most reminded people of the prophets would have been linked with the immediacy of the kingdom of God, the sense that people now stand at a time of God's salvation/judgment.

The radical character of some of Jesus' sayings can only be understood when we recognize that they do not stem from a world which "goes on as usual." They are not calculated to assure success in an on-going pattern of human relationships. Instead, Jesus speaks of a "new age" which reverses the values of the old one. This reversal is evident in the activities of healing and liberation for the sick, poor and oppressed, which are associated with the Old Testament (as in Lk 4:18–21). It is also evident in the sayings that speak of changing evaluations of persons and status, "becoming like a child" (Mk 10:15) or the "first" as servant of all (Mk 10:43). And it is evident in the call for a radically different way of relating to others as in the sayings about non-retaliation and love of enemies (e.g. Lk 6:27–36). We cannot simply take Jesus' sayings as though they describe the way in which we think people are likely to act. They are a summons to changing our hearts in light of the coming of the rule of God.

Jesus and His Followers

Everyone knows that Jesus was accompanied by a group of disciples. The gospels preserve stories about how some of those people came to follow Jesus (Mk 1:16–18 [Simon Peter and Andrew], 19–20 [James and John, sons of Zebedee] and Mt 4:18–20,21–22; Lk 5:1–11 combines the call of

Peter with that of James and John but omits Andrew; Mk 2:14//Mt 9:9//Lk
5:27–28 [Levi, in Mk/Lk, Matthew, in Mt]; Jn 1:35–50 has an independent
tradition about an unnamed person, Andrew, Simon Peter, Philip and Nathanael). Most people are also familiar with the fact that Jesus had a special
group of disciples known as the Twelve. Mk 3:16–19 lists their names as
Simon Peter, James and John the sons of Zebedee, Andrew, Philip, Bar-
tholomew, Matthew, Thomas, James son of Alphaeus, Thaddaeus, Simon
the Canaanite, and Judas Iscariot. But the gospels mention other persons
who followed Jesus around as well. Mk 4:10 speaks of "those who were
about him with the twelve." Lk 8:1–3 speaks of Jesus preaching accompanied by the twelve and some women whom he had healed and who contributed to the support of the group. Jn mentions two disciples of Jesus
whom he does not name, Nathanael and a disciple called the "Beloved Disciple," who was the source of the community's tradition (Jn 1:35–36,45;
13:23; 18:15; 19:26–27,35; 21:2,7,20,24). The circle of Jesus' followers
seems to have been larger than the special list of "twelve."

The importance of the number "twelve" can be found in the twelve
tribes of Israel. A saying in Mt 19:28//Lk 22:30 speaks of the position the
twelve will have in the new age as judges over the twelve tribes of Israel.
Lk, conscious of Judas' impending betrayal, omits the number "twelve"
from his version of the saying. Psalm 122:4–5 speaks of the tribes going up
to Jerusalem where thrones have been set up in judgment. The association
of "judging the tribes" and thrones suggests a vision of the new age in
which the "twelve" will be rulers over the renewed people of God. Acts
1:23–26 describes the followers of Jesus at Jerusalem choosing another
person who had been among them from the beginning, Matthias, to replace Judas. Once the number "twelve" had been restored it was not necessary to continue to appoint persons to the circle of the "twelve."

However, the twelve quickly become confused with another group in
early Christianity, "apostles." Luke uses the "apostles" for the twelve (e.g.
Lk 6:13; Acts 1:26). But the term "apostle" referred to persons who were
emissaries or missionaries sent to preach the gospel and has its background
in the Jewish idea of specially commissioned emissaries. You can see how
the two terms differ if you read 1 Cor 15:5–9. Paul, who is himself an "apostle," speaks of Jesus appearing to Peter and then to the "twelve" separately
from appearances to James, the brother of the Lord not the son of Zebedee, other apostles, other believers and finally to himself. The confusion
between the twelve and the larger group of apostles is rooted in the fact
that the gospels also describe the twelve as being sent out by Jesus to engage in a mission of preaching and healing (Mk 6:7–13; Mt 10:1–15; Lk 9:1–
6; Lk 10:1–16). Read one of those passages. You will notice that it gives a
number of rules which the disciples are to follow in their preaching. These

rules make them radically dependent upon the hospitality that they receive from others along the way, since they are not to take money or provisions. They are also very close to the way in which the gospels picture Jesus conducting his ministry. Many scholars think that the first missionary efforts in Palestine were carried out by followers of Jesus who adopted this style of life based on what they had seen and heard about Jesus.

There are a number of different situations in antiquity in which a person might leave family and occupation to become the "disciple" of a popular leader. The most familiar would be persons who went to become students of a teacher, a particular Pharisee or teacher of the law, or, for the non-Jewish person, a particular philosopher teacher. Some of the latter also led a wandering life-style, warning the crowds of humanity about the blindness of their ways. A person might also join a gang of robbers, preying on travelers, or might follow a leader of a band of persons aimed at overthrowing the Roman occupation. These persons are also described as "robbers" in first century writings. Barabbas and the two "thieves" with whom Jesus was crucified may have been rebels of this sort. Or one might belong to a group of disciples surrounding a prophetic figure. John the Baptist when he began to preach to the people that they should repent gathered a group of disciples distinct from the crowds who came to hear him and be baptized as a sign of their repentance.

The Baptist was executed by Herod Antipas as a result of his popularity among the people (Josephus, *Antiquities* 18:118–19), and the fears that his preaching might cause an uprising among the people. Similar fears may have motivated the Jewish officials responsible for turning Jesus over to Pilate as a potential rebel. But in neither case do the suspicions that are said to be responsible for their condemnation imply that the Baptist or Jesus was actually the leader of a "Zealot" gang devoted to the violent overthrow of a corrupt political regime. Both Jesus and John preached a message of God's impending judgment. Both called upon people to repent. Jesus insisted that the time of God's rule was already becoming present in his ministry. In addition to a lack of evidence for armed resistance by Jesus' followers (or the Baptist's), the general picture of Galilee in the time of Jesus suggests that much of the territory was peaceful. Even when the Jews did revolt against Rome in A.D. 66–70, the resistance in Galilee was quickly extinguished. Therefore, there is little to recommend the view that Jesus and his disciples saw themselves as rebels seeking to establish a new political order in which justice and obedience to the law would be realized.

Jesus' concerns for interpreting the will of God often lead his teaching to overlap with that of Pharisees and others devoted to interpreting the law. But he does not seem to have pursued the kind of detailed interpre-

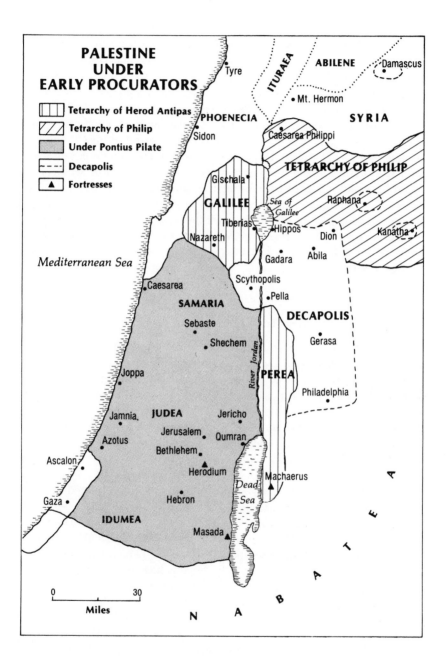

PALESTINE
UNDER
EARLY PROCURATORS

▯▯▯ Tetrarchy of Herod Antipas
▱ Tetrarchy of Philip
▨ Under Pontius Pilate
---- Decapolis
▲ Fortresses

Tyre

ITURAEA   ABILENE   Damascus

Mt. Hermon

PHOENECIA   SYRIA

Sidon   Caesarea Philippi

Gischala   TETRARCHY OF PHILIP

GALILEE   Sea of Galilee   Raphana

Tiberias   Hippos

Nazareth   Dion   Kanatha

Mediterranean Sea   Gadara   Abila

Caesarea   Scythopolis

SAMARIA   Pella   DECAPOLIS

Sebaste   Gerasa

Shechem

Joppa   PEREA

Philadelphia

Jamnia   JUDEA   Jericho

Azotus   Jerusalem   Qumran

Ascalon   Bethlehem

Herodium ▲   Machaerus ▲

Gaza   Hebron   Dead Sea

IDUMEA

Masada ▲

0   30
Miles

N   A   B   A   T   E   A

tation and exegesis of the letter of the law that we find elsewhere. There-fore, his followers may have seen in him a popular religious teacher but they are hardly disciples of a scribe or rabbi. In addition to teaching, Jesus' ministry is also characterized by prophetic sayings and actions and heal-ings. Charges that Jesus' activities were inspired by a demon (Mk 3:22–27; Mt 12:22–30; Lk 11:14–23) led to the view that Jesus was a magician and deceiver of the people. Josephus uses similar language about messianic prophets and Zealot leaders during the Jewish revolt against Rome (Jo-sephus, *War* 2:259; 6:288). It is evident that how a person described Jesus and his disciples in the first century usually carried with it a judgment about Jesus himself. If Jesus comes in the name of God, then his teaching, prophetic warnings and healings must all be signs of God's activity. If not, then Jesus can be identified with any of the negative images for a popular leader: deceiver, rebel, magician. We will never know what led Judas to betray Jesus, but we can see that Jesus was a problematic figure even for his own disciples.

The Trial and Death of Jesus

One of the most certain historical facts about Jesus is that he was con-demned to be crucified by the Roman prefect of Judea, Pontius Pilate. We know from the references to crucifixion in literary sources that it was con-sidered the appropriate punishment for slaves and the most hardened criminals. St. Paul comments that Jesus' death on the cross is under a curse pronounced by God's law in Deut 21:22–23 (Gal 3:13). His interpretation is borne out by the legal rulings of the Essene sect such as the following passage from the recently published Temple Scroll:

> If a man has informed against his people and has delivered his people up to a foreign nation and has done evil to his people, you shall hang him on a tree and he shall die. On the evidence of two witnesses and on the evidence of three witnesses, he shall be put to death . . . their bodies shall not pass the night on the tree, you shall bury them that very day, for what is hanged on the tree is accursed by God and humanity and you shall not defile the land I am giving you for an inheritance.

You can see just from the tone of this passage that many of those who saw Jesus on the cross or heard that he had been crucified would have pre-sumed that he was guilty of a terrible crime. The cross would be a real stumbling block to belief just as St Paul says it is in 1 Cor 1:18–25.

Archeologists have discovered the skeleton of a young Jewish man, Yehohanan, who had been crucified in the first century. He was buried in his family tomb, which shows his family to have been a prosperous one. One of its members was a potter. Another had been active in the building of Herod's temple. Since it seems unlikely that someone from that family would be a common robber (and certainly not a slave), we can only guess that he had engaged in some form of activity that the Romans found suspect. Whatever his crime, the family had been able to obtain possession of the body and to bury it in their own tomb.

Our only evidence about the accusations against Jesus comes from the gospel accounts which were written decades after the event. Even though the evangelists may have been able to draw on earlier accounts of Jesus' trial and death, we do not have anything resembling a contemporary court record. In addition, we are in the dark about critical legal issues. Some historians agree with the assertion in Jn 18:31 that a Jewish court could not have condemned Jesus to death so that even if they had thought Jesus guilty on the religious charge of deceiving the people, they would have to get the Roman governor to condemn Jesus on political grounds. Others insist that the Sanhedrin could still exercise the death penalty in any case where the offense was clearly a religious one.

While the gospels all agree that Jesus was handed over to Pilate by Jewish authorities, the nature of the Jewish proceedings against him is unclear. It was possible for a private party to bring someone before the governor on the charge that that person was an evildoer. Then it was up to the proconsul to decide how to deal with the case. No more than two or three persons were needed as accusers. Thus, you should not imagine that Jesus was handed over by the entire Jewish people or even the entire Sanhedrin. Mk 14:55–65 (and Mt 26:59–68) presumes a trial before the council in which various conflicting testimony was brought forward, and Jesus was finally condemned as a blasphemer. Lk implies that no verdict was reached (Lk 22:71; Acts 13:27–28). Jn presumes that the decision to have Jesus executed had been made before Jesus was arrested (11:45–53). Charges of blasphemy are leveled at Jesus throughout the gospel (Jn 5:18; 8:59; 10:31). Prior to being turned over to Pilate, Jesus is interrogated by the former high priest Annas (Jn 18:19–24). Lk 23:6–12 has a peculiar episode in which Pilate sends Jesus off to Herod. Although offenses were tried where they occurred regardless of the defendant's origins, some scholars think Pilate might have taken such an action since Herod had the extraordinary privilege of extraditing offenders who fled his jurisdiction for other parts of the empire.

It is possible that Jesus was never condemned by a Jewish court. With its members from differing parties and traditions of interpreting the law, it may have been very difficult to obtain a verdict in the Sanhedrin even if that body did have the authority to render a death sentence. Josephus (*War* 6:300–305) tells the story of a prophet, Ananias (ca. A.D. 62), who upset the authorities by predicting the destruction of the temple. He was turned over to Roman authorities who let him go as a "lunatic." It is also possible that the Sanhedrin session was never intended to be a trial but merely a hearing to determine grounds on which Jesus might be turned over to Pilate. Thus, while it is clear that some of the Jewish leaders had decided that Jesus' words and actions were potentially dangerous, it is far from clear that there was any consensus that Jesus had committed a capital offense. Sometimes Jesus is presented in a way that makes him an opponent of the whole religious tradition of his people, Israel. Were that the case one would expect a much clearer tradition about the religious charges against him.

Pilate was free to handle the case put before him in any way that he chose. The formulation of the charge "king of the Jews" reflects a Roman viewpoint: the condemned is a rebel leader trying to stir up the people. What we know of Pilate does not suggest a person overly concerned with the niceties of Jewish feelings or the guilt or innocence of those he condemned for seditious behavior (cf. Lk 13:1–2). Later in A.D. 35 Pilate sent soldiers to Samaria to prevent the Samaritans from following one of their prophets up Mount Gerezim. Some of the people were killed, and the aftermath led to Pilate's recall to Rome (Josephus, *Antiquities* 18:86–87). Since the high priest Caiaphas lost his office soon after Pilate was removed, historians presume that Pilate and Caiaphas had some sort of political understanding. Thus, a person sent to his jurisdiction as an evildoer from the high priest would hardly have caused Pilate much concern. The gospel writers seem to paint Pilate in a better light than other evidence suggests he deserves. They may have wished to avoid giving others the impression that Christians were, in fact, the subversive movement they were sometimes accused of being.

Of course, we have only looked at the trial and death of Jesus through the eyes of an historian trying to figure out the legal facts of the case. Even from that perspective, it appears to be an example of human evil, the thoughtless destruction of an innocent person. But the early Christians were able to look at Jesus' own acceptance of that death through the image of the suffering servant from Is 53:6–12. They saw that Jesus suffered for the sins of humanity to bring us back into a living relationship with God (e.g. Mk 10:45b; Rom 4:25; 2 Cor 5:21). They used the language of sacrifice, of the expiation for sin on the Day of Atonement to describe it (Heb 9:11–15; Rom 3:25–26). And they also saw in Jesus' death the supreme manifestation of God's love (Gal 2:20; Rom 5:8; Jn 3:16). For Christians, then, the death of Jesus also demonstrates a power of love that goes beyond the worst of human evil and sin.

Summary

We have seen that the New Testament does not provide us with the kind of information that would be found in a modern historical biography of a famous person. One of the most critical events in Jesus' story, his trial and death, poses a number of historical questions, which we cannot resolve. Jesus' deeds and teachings were remolded as they were handed on so that they addressed the problems faced by later groups of Christians. Sometimes it is easy to detect the concerns that have led to new emphases in this material as in the link between the story of the Syrophoenician woman and the mission to the Gentiles. Or we may see the fuller and more balanced expressions in Mt's version of the Lord's Prayer as representative of the use of that prayer in Christian worship. But in other cases it is much more difficult to decide how a particular tradition may have developed.

We have also seen that as Jesus healed and preached among the people, he gathered around him a diverse group of followers. A special group of "twelve" represented the renewal of Israel through Jesus' ministry. But there were other disciples, women and men, who followed Jesus as well. Then there were persons drawn to him in the hope of being healed or out of curiosity about his preaching. Some may have become disciples. Some may have thought of Jesus as just another healer, prophetic preacher of repentance or interpreter of the law. And at least some persons among the Jewish leaders in Jerusalem were so offended or concerned about the impact of Jesus' activities that they initiated the events which led to his execution by the Roman prefect in Judea, Pontius Pilate.

We have also seen that it is not easy to fit Jesus into any of the established categories for popular, religious or political leadership. Jesus was not an authority in one of the groups of the time like the Pharisees or Essenes. His family did not belong to the priestly tribes, so he could not be a priest. The infancy narratives in Luke 1–2 and Mt 1–2 claim a relationship to the "house of David." But that relationship is clearly indirect. Jesus' family was not recognized as "heirs to the throne of David." If some people thought of Jesus in political terms as "messiah" or "anointed" leader of the people, they might have thought that he would establish a new dynasty or might bring about the final judgment of God. For those in the crowds, Jesus' leadership did not stem from any established role but was based on popular appeal as healer or prophetic figure. You can also see that for many of these people Jesus' death would be the end of the story, since both political leaders and healers have to be alive to draw a following. Prophets and teachers may continue to influence others through disciples, who preserve their teaching. We will see that Jesus' disciples do far more than preserve his teaching. They claim that God has raised Jesus from death and that Jesus is the decisive turning point in salvation for all of humanity.

STUDY QUESTIONS

Facts You Should Know

1. Name the two basic types of stories about Jesus and give the characteristics of each type.
2. Name three different types of sayings by Jesus and give the characteristics of each type.
3. Why do we find different versions of the same parable, saying or incident in the gospel traditions?
4. What is the *Gospel of Thomas?* The "Q" source?
5. What other miracle-workers were active in the first century A.D.? How do the stories of Jesus' miracles compare with stories told about others?
6. Give two examples of "radical" or "shocking" elements in the teaching of Jesus. What do these examples tell Jesus' audience about the "time" in which they live?
7. What is the significance of the "twelve"? How is that group distinguished from "disciples of Jesus" and from "apostles"?
8. Why would the crucifixion of Jesus by the Romans have led some people to conclude that he could not have been God's spokesperson?
9. Describe three unresolved historical questions about the trial of Jesus.

Things To Do

1. Study the stories of the Syrophoenician Woman (3–1) and the Lost Sheep (3–2). Make a list of the common details and of everything that is special to each version. Pick out the special features which a particular author might be directing at the later situation of Christians. Can you find any similarities between Mt's versions of the two stories?

2. Read the stories of Jesus' trial(s) in Mk 14:53–15:20 and Lk 22:54–23:25. First make a list of the common elements in the two accounts. Then find the differences between them. What reasons can you think of for some of the differences?

3. Take a concordance and look under the word "faith" to find all of the times in which "faith" is used in connection with a miracle of Jesus in the synoptic gospels (Mt, Mk, Lk). Compare the use of "faith" by the gospel writers with the use of faith in the story of the healing by the god Asclepius.

Things To Think About

1. What significance do the miracles of Jesus have for today's Christian? Should Christians expect Jesus to heal them of disease? What do they need to remember when they pray to Jesus for healing?

2. What kind of popular leader(s) might Jesus be confused with today? What parts of his ministry or teaching might make him such a threat that he might suffer injury or death? What kind of "follower" of Jesus do you think you would have been?

Chapter 4

THE PREACHING OF JESUS

Proclaiming the Kingdom of God

The expression "kingdom (or "reign") of God" frequently introduces Jesus' message (e.g. Mk 1:15). It would evoke images of God ruling over the people. For some the true experience of God's rule could only come with the messianic age when evil had been destroyed, Israel was obedient to her God, and even the nations would be able to see the Lord's presence as ruler of Israel. In Jesus' preaching the "kingdom" is not just a reference to some distant event. Its presence makes itself felt in persons whose lives are changed. But the kingdom is not identical with what happens in this world either. There is still the future coming of the kingdom in which its promise of salvation is completed. Mk 14:25 has Jesus say to his disciples at the Last Supper, "I will no longer drink of the fruit of the vine with you until that day when I drink it new in the reign of God." Drinking "new wine" at a banquet with the Lord is a symbol of the banquet of rejoicing in the new age.

One of the most famous sayings of Jesus pointing to the presence of the reign of God is Lk 17:20–21:

> Once Jesus was asked by the Pharisees when the reign of God would come, and he answered, "It is not by observation that the reign of God comes; people will not even say, 'Look, here it is, or there!' For the reign of God is among you."

This saying captured the imagination of early Christians. Several versions of it found their way into the Gospel of Thomas:

> His disciple said to him, "On what day will the kingdom come?"
> [Jesus said,] "It does not come with the expectation of it. People

will not say, 'Look, here or Look, there!' Rather the Kingdom of
the Father is spread out on the earth and human beings do not
see it."

[Gos. Thom. 113]

Jesus said, "If those who draw you on say to you, 'Look, the Kingdom is in heaven,' then the birds of heaven will be there before
you. If they say to you, 'It is in the sea,' then the fish will be there
before you. But the kingdom is within you and outside you. . . ."

[Gos. Thom. 3]

Though Jesus had disciples pray for the coming of the kingdom in the
Lord's Prayer, there is a firm tradition that he rejected speculation about
the time and place of its arrival. Disciples should learn to discern the presence of the kingdom in their midst. Lk 11:20 preserves a saying in which
Jesus points to his exorcisms as one sign that the kingdom is present. There
is even a very puzzling saying in which Jesus says that some of those present "will not taste death until they see the kingdom of God" (Lk 9:27; Mk
9:1). Jesus' contemporaries might have assumed that he meant that the
final manifestation of the reign of God, judgment and new creation, was
right around the corner.

Another way that Jesus proclaims the "reign of God" is in the parables
which point toward what it means to experience the kingdom. Mk 4:11
speaks of the parables as revealing the "mystery of the kingdom." Those
who fail to grasp the parables are cut off from the kingdom. Some parables
like the parable of the seed growing secretly (Mk 4:26–29) and the parable
of the mustard seed (Mk 4:30–32) speak of the kingdom by comparing it to
a small, almost unnoticed seed. But when the seed is fully grown then
there is a harvest or a nesting place for the birds. In this way, Jesus shows
us that the kingdom is not something that God brings about with a dramatic, cosmic gesture as the myths of the end of the world have it. The
kingdom may begin in a way that is almost invisible.

Jesus also spoke about the kinds of persons who would "enter the
kingdom." Mk 12:28–34 contains a pronouncement story in which a scribe
asks Jesus what is the greatest commandment. Jesus summarizes the law
by speaking of the obligation to worship only God: to love God with our
whole heart, and to love our neighbor. The scribe approves and repeats
what Jesus had said. Then Jesus concludes by saying of the scribe, "You
are not far from the kingdom of God." So we can see one type of person
who is close to the kingdom. This person perceives what the essentials of
a religious life are in terms of the love of God and neighbor. This scribe is
not like some of the others in the gospel who try to trap Jesus or who take

offense at things which are not part of the essential love of God and neighbor. Another very famous saying of Jesus compared persons who would enter the kingdom of God to children (Mk 10:13–16). This saying was also widely repeated:

> Truly I say to you, whoever does not receive the kingdom of God like a child shall not enter it (Mk 10:15).

> Truly, I say to you, unless you turn and become like children you will never enter the kingdom of heaven (Mt 18:3).

> Truly, truly I say to you, unless a person is born anew, that person cannot see the kingdom of God (Jn 3:3).

> Jesus saw infants nursing. He said to his disciples, "These nursing infants are like those who enter the kingdom" (Gos. Thom. 22).

These sayings suggest that a change is required in persons who become part of the kingdom. The versions in John and the Gos. Thom. even think of beginning all over again like a new-born infant. Jn 3:5 links this new beginning with the ritual of baptism when the person is born of "water and the Spirit."

Parables as a Language of Faith

One of the ways in which Jesus showed what he meant by faith was through the parables. Some of the parables show us people doing surprising things. They suggest that the kingdom can radically change a person's life. For example, Mt 13:44–46 preserves two parables in which the characters take quick action. A day laborer digging in a field finds a treasure. He quickly buys the field for himself. A pearl merchant finds a really valuable pearl so he sells everything else in order to get it. We can understand both of these acts as things that human beings might do in extraordinary situations. Jesus is telling us that the kingdom creates that type of situation.

Other parables challenge us to evaluate the actions of particular characters in the stories. Their actions and success or failure indicate how persons should live in the presence of the kingdom. Sometimes the parable may have been given an introduction by the gospel writer that links it to the kingdom. A striking example of the link between the kingdom and unusual human behavior occurs in the parable of the vineyard workers in Mt 20:1–15. Matthew has added a proverbial expression, "The last shall be first and the first last," which was often used of the reversal to take place in the new age to the end of the parable (v. 16). The parable reflects a situation common in the agricultural economy of the time: when it was necessary to harvest the grapes a vineyard owner would have to hire day-laborers to do the work. Roman books on agriculture advise people to plant grapes that ripen at different times so that they would not have to hire too many people or work for too many days to pick them. Since the grape harvest was one of the busiest times, the story presumes a situation of serious unemployment. If day-laborers could go all day without work at this time of year, things must have been much worse at other times.

You can see from reading the story that the experience of the persons in the story depended upon which group one belonged to. The people who worked all day, even though they may have been happy to accept the work when they started, go away unhappy. We don't hear from the other workers, but we would certainly guess that those who had waited all day without work and then found themselves with a day's pay at the last minute were rejoicing. The owner, though free to do as he chooses, does have to face the complaints of the first group. He may claim that he is "good" but the first group no longer experience his behavior as good even though he has honored their original contract and has also followed the law which instructed people to pay the worker his wages on the same day (Lev 19:13; Deut 24:15). If this parable is about the coming of God's reign, then it turns out that the reign of God does not create universal peace and harmony. Some people are unable to share in its coming. This parable is a good example of how we may have to change our lives and our presuppositions about what is fair and just if we are to experience the reign of God.

Another parable in which a "good" or generous action on the part of the character whose acts have the possibility of deciding the destiny of others is the parable of the prodigal son in Lk 15:11–32. The younger son, like the figure of Joseph in the Old Testament, finds himself among pagans (Jews do not eat pork) at a time of famine. But instead of lifting the whole country to prosperity and becoming second only to the ruler as Joseph had done, the younger son is a starving pig-herder. So he decides it would be better to return home and beg his father for mercy than to remain where he is. The father surprises the younger son by throwing a party in his honor. The older son, who has remained at home helping his father, becomes angry. He says what many of us would feel in his situation. The younger son has done nothing to deserve such treatment. He has stayed home and worked hard and never been given anything like the welcome his brother is getting. Notice that the father does not reject the elder. He reminds him that everything the father has will be his. But the father does say that it is wrong of him to be angry and resentful. He insists that it is right to celebrate the return of the younger in this fashion.

The story reminds us that there is forgiveness and rejoicing for persons who seek to change their lives no matter what they may have done. The younger would have agreed with his older brother that he did not "deserve" a large banquet. He wasn't even asking his father to take him back as though he were a "son"—just to treat him like a hired hand. But the father does not want the younger back in disgrace. He wants him back as the "son" he should be. The banquet is a way to show that reality. Other parables of Jesus have this pattern. Luke puts two of them just before the parable of the prodigal son in his gospel, the lost sheep (Lk 15:3–7; cp. Mt 18:12–14), and the lost coin (Lk 15:8–10). Some scholars think that Lk 15:1–2 provides an important clue as to why Jesus emphasized parables of this sort. Luke says that Jesus was severely criticized by the Pharisees for associating with sinners. They thought that a good or righteous person would gather those who are also good and righteous. In that way, a group of righteous persons would be built up that might turn others to God. Jesus claimed that his message about the coming of the rule of God was not just for the righteous. He came to seek for those who were "lost" and who might never have thought that they would have any hope of salvation. Instead, Jesus teaches that God is something like a shepherd finding a lost sheep, a woman finding a lost coin, or the father in the story of the "prodigal" (= lost) son. God is overjoyed when what has been lost returns.

Wisdom in the Sayings of Jesus

Another very common form of teaching in Jesus' time was the collection of "wise sayings" or proverbs. Sayings of this sort do not have any particular situation in mind. They are cast as general pieces of wise advice for a person. A wisdom saying can apply to a number of different situations. Proverbs do not claim to be new insights. Since proverbial wisdom is often aimed at the young, they may concern advice about how to be successful in friendship, family, work etc. Wisdom traditions often draw a sharp contrast between "the wise" and the "foolish." Most people, it appears, fall into the latter category.

Proverbs and Ecclesiasticus (or Ben Sirach) contain wisdom sayings of this sort. Here is an example from Ben Sirach about lending money:

Lend to your neighbor in the time of his need; and in turn, repay your neighbor promptly. Confirm your word and keep faith with him, and on every occasion you will find what you need. Many persons regard a loan as a windfall, and cause trouble to those who help them. A man will kiss another's hands until he gets a loan, and will lower his voice in speaking of his neighbor's money; but at the time for repayment he will delay, and will pay in words of unconcern, and will find fault with the time. If the lender exerts pressure, he will hardly get back half, and will regard that as a windfall. If he does not, the borrower has robbed him of his money and he has needlessly made him his enemy; he will repay him with curses and reproaches, and instead of glory will repay him with dishonor. Because of such wickedness therefore many have refused to lend; they have been afraid of being defrauded needlessly. (Sir 29:2–7)

You can see that the sage expects his audience to lend to those in need. But he also recognizes the rather dismal record of human relationships when such loans are at stake. Such experiences might cause people to refuse to make loans altogether. Those who borrow are to keep their word and repay the loan as they said they would do.

We also find Jesus speaking about lending to others and about keeping one's word. Here are some of the sayings attributed to him:

Again you have heard it said to your ancestors, "You shall not swear falsely, but shall perform to the Lord what you have sworn." But I say to you, "Do not swear at all, either by heaven, for it is the throne of God, or by the earth, for it is his footstool, or by Jerusalem, for it is the city of the great King. And do not swear by your head, for you cannot make one hair white or black. Let what you say be simply 'Yes' or 'No'; anything more than this comes from evil." (Mt 5:33–37)

Give to him who begs from you, and do not refuse him who would borrow from you. (Mt 5:42)

You can see that Jesus agrees that people should give and keep their word honestly. He even goes so far as to reject the "oaths" that they swear to prove their honesty. He also agrees that they should be generous in lending to those who wish to borrow. But you may notice something different in Jesus' tone. He does not engage in pessimistic reflection on the fact that most persons will abuse that privilege. This does not mean that Jesus was blind to the kind of human failings treated in Ben Sirach. We have already seen parables in which he uses such examples very vividly. But Jesus' teaching springs from the presence of God's reign. It is not simply good advice about how to maintain one's integrity in a world of fools and less than honest people.

Sirach also tells his audience that the pursuit of God's commandments is more important than the pursuit of wealth:

> Lay up your treasure according to the commandments of the Most High, and it will profit you more than gold. Store up alms-giving in your treasury and it will rescue you from all affliction. (Sir 29:11–12)

Jesus reminds his followers that service to God cannot be combined with service to money:

> Do not lay up for yourselves treasures on earth where moth and rust consume and where thieves break in and steal, but lay up for yourselves treasure in heaven, where neither moth nor rust consumes and where thieves do not break in and steal. For where your treasure is, there your heart will be also. (Mt 6:19–21)

> No one can serve two masters; for either he will hate the one and love the other, or he will be devoted to the one and despise the other. You cannot serve God and mammon. (Mt 6:19–21)

Jesus was clearly able to use the traditions that circulated in the wisdom sayings of his people to shape his own instruction.

Summons to Discipleship

You can see that Jesus' preaching of the reign of God as present and his use of the wisdom sayings both presume that his disciples will begin to live in a new way. Sometimes people think that Jesus' words are just a vision of how things "ought to be" or will be when there is a new age in which God's rule is not "hidden" like the seeds in Jesus' various seed parables (see Mk 4:3–8, 26–29, 31–32), but is established among people. However, Jesus is represented as speaking directly to his audience about their life and behavior, not about some future ideal order of things. On the other hand, you will notice that the explicit sayings and deeds of Jesus do not play a major role in the ethical teaching of the other writings of the New Testament. Clearly, the first Christians did not think of Jesus as a person who had set up an elite "sect" within Judaism that had a special interpretation of the law to follow as the Teacher of Righteousness had done for the Essenes. So we would also be making a big mistake if we thought of Jesus' preaching as a "new law" or even a special form of interpreting the law such as we find it among the Pharisees or the Essenes.

The Lord's Prayer

Although Jesus does not propose a set of legal requirements for Christian behavior, his preaching does give us a sense of the ways in which Christians will act. The Lord's Prayer combines the future expectation of the rule of God and our present life as Christians. Look at Mt's version of the prayer (Chart 3–3). Each section has a conclusion to balance out the petition to which it is attached. These petitions also make the eschatological side of the reign of God evident. The first petition that the name of God be "sanctified" or made holy can be related to the prophecy of Ez 36:22–28. Yahweh is about to "vindicate the holiness" of his name which had been "profaned among the nations" because of the sinfulness of the

Synagogue at Capernaum.

people. You can see that this image does not simply refer to praising God as holy. It means that the people of God show that God is holy in their lives. The addition that Mt makes to this section of the prayer emphasizes that point. God's rule, already a reality in heaven, still has to become a reality on earth. But God, not merely some form of human moral or legal renewal, brings about the coming of the kingdom in the "heaven-like" obedience to God's will on earth.

The second half of the prayer addresses petitions to God from the community of believing disciples. These petitions express their own desire to live in a way that does manifest the holiness of God. The conclusion which Mt gives to the third petition makes the eschatological character of "temptation" evident. Just as the Essenes spoke of the danger of the "evil inclination" and the "Angel of Darkness" leading righteous persons away from following the law, so Mt understands "temptation" to mean falling into the power of "the evil one." (The tendency to translate the Greek as though it were an abstract noun "evil" conveys the impression that this phrase is simply a variant of the previous petition.) The Christian community acknowledges the power of evil to lead people away from devotion to the will of God and must rely on God's aid to keep it from that evil.

The petition for bread, which Luke's version has generalized from "today" to "every day," contains an unusual word to describe the bread— *epiousion*. English speakers are used to "daily" as a guess about the meaning of that word. Some church fathers thought that the bread being referred to was the bread of the Eucharist. However, if you read through Mt 6, you will notice that much of the rest of the chapter concerns anxiety about material things and the basic necessities of life (vv. 19–21,24,25–34). It would seem that Mt understands the petition to be related to these anxieties. The symbolism attached to the bread might then be that of the "manna" which God had given the Israelites to keep them from starving in the wilderness. Prv 30:8 has the wise person ask God to provide only the food that the person needs. Therefore, the best guess about the meaning of the word *epiousion* is to follow the church fathers who thought that it meant the bread "of our need" or "for our sustenance." This understanding means that Jesus' disciples are to have a particular relationship to material things. They are not to hoard or rely on them, but are to rely on what God provides.

The petition about forgiveness appears to have been altered by Luke from "debts" to "sins," from "debtors" to "persons who have done wrong to us," and from "have forgiven" to "forgive." These shifts are understandable within a Gentile context that did not know the religious significance of forgiveness of debts in the OT tradition. The most dramatic examples of this tradition are associated with the legislation about the "jubilee year" which is a time of "release" for the poor. Special times, the "sabbath" and jubilee years, required Israel to recall her own bondage and liberation by God. Slaves were to be freed and the land allowed to lie fallow (e.g. Ex 21:2–6; 23:10–11; Deut 15:1–18; Lev 25). Jesus' parable of the "seed growing secretly" (Mk 4:26–29) draws upon the image of the land producing food "of itself," what persons were allowed to harvest during the sabbatical year, to describe how fruitful the kingdom is. Within this context, to speak of Christians as "having forgiven debtors" makes life in light of the kingdom a continual enactment of the redemption and liberation of the jubilee year.

God's Forgiveness

Other passages in the teaching of Jesus also emphasize the radical nature of the forgiveness that is part of Jesus' understanding of God. Mt 18:21–35 links the parable of the unforgiving servant to Peter's request for a ruling on how often we have to forgive others for a wrong they have done us. Both Jesus' answer to the question and the parable make it clear that there are no limits on forgiveness. Mt 7:1–5 contains a sharp warning against judging others, while Mt 6:14–15 adds a reminder that the forgiveness we receive from God requires that we forgive others their wrongs. Various formulations of the "love command" expand beyond the love of neighbor to love of enemies as in Mt 5:43–48. You will notice that Mt uses that passage to cap off a collection of sayings against retaliation for specific wrongs, including "debt," that is, Christians are to lend without demanding repayment. Thus, one of the most important parts of Jesus' ethical teaching is the "love command." Jesus expects his disciples to make the experiences of redemption and forgiveness a reality of their lives. He tells them stories in which the characters do extraordinary things in order to demonstrate what forgiveness, generosity and mercy mean. In the parable of the unforgiving servant, the king was willing to wipe out a debt that was much bigger than the annual revenue of Herod's whole kingdom (Mt 18:24–27). Unfortunately, the servant didn't learn anything from that experience. He went out and threatened a fellow servant over a small debt (vv. 28–34).

Jesus did more than talk about mercy and forgiveness. He also scandalized some people by welcoming sinners and eating with them himself. Luke 7:36–50 contains a dramatic story in which Jesus is a guest of one of the local Pharisees. A woman known to be a sinner suddenly comes in weeping and anoints Jesus' feet. When the Pharisee is puzzled because

Jesus permits a sinner near him, Jesus replies with another tale about debtors. He asks who will love the lender more, the one who is freed of a large debt or of a small one? When Simon agrees that the person forgiven a large debt will love the lender more, Jesus applies the case to the sinful woman. Her love has already been shown in what she has done for Jesus. Therefore, her many sins are forgiven. Other passages in the gospels show that people who wished to attack Jesus spoke of him as a friend of tax collectors and sinners (Mt 11:16–19). Levi, a tax collector, became a disciple of Jesus (Mt 9:9–13; Mk 2:13–17; Lk 5:27–32).

We sometimes forget how amazing Jesus' behavior toward sinners is because we think of a "sinner" as someone like us, a person who is trying to live a good life but who falls short and has to ask God's forgiveness. In Judaism, a person like that is not a "sinner." That person can use the rituals of atonement to receive forgiveness for the failings in his or her efforts to follow God. A "sinner," on the other hand, is a person who deliberately turns against God. That person is leading a life which he or she knows is contrary to the law. The "wicked" scorn righteousness, justice and piety to pursue their own desires. Tax collectors were considered to be engaged in an occupation which excluded them from the "people of God" because they were working for the Romans in collecting taxes and other fees. Tax collectors also had a reputation for defrauding people by demanding more taxes and pocketing the difference and for using violence against people in collecting fees. So you can see that it was the kind of occupation in which a person could hardly claim to be "just" and "merciful." When the prodigal son squandered his father's money in sexual immorality and then wound up working as a pig-herder for a pagan (pigs were considered "unclean" by Jews, who do not eat pork), he was acting like one of the "wicked."

Most people thought that when God brought salvation to the people, only the righteous, those who were trying to follow God's will, would be saved. The "wicked" would be condemned for their evil ways. Jesus, on the other hand, insists that God's reign reaches out to the wicked. He told a parable about a shepherd and a lost sheep (Lk 15:1–7; Mt 18:10–14) to demonstrate the attitude of God toward the wicked. The "righteous" are all right. Jesus has come to seek out those who are lost. People like that do not even think that they have a chance of being accepted by God. Matthew's version of this parable makes it clear that Jesus' disciples are expected to continue that concern for those who are "lost." Matthew realizes that there is a danger of Christianity becoming a group just for the pious, the good people. So he surrounds Jesus' parable with a warning that the angels of the "little ones" stand before God. Church leaders must seek out the wandering and lost. They must never take an attitude of self-righteousness and "despise" such persons.

Summary

When Jesus preached about the "reign of God," he was not only speaking about God's power in the future. He was also calling his disciples to experience what God's power could do to change their lives now. We are expected to live in a way that depends upon the power of God and not upon our human prejudices, divisions, cares and anxieties. Otherwise, we will not experience the joy of salvation when the reign of God is completely manifest.

The central feature of the new life of disciples can be found in Jesus' vision of the mercy, love and forgiveness of God. This love also has to govern the relationships which Christians have with one another. They cannot judge or condemn others. They must be looking for ways in which they can show what love, mercy and forgiveness mean in their lives by extending them to others. And they must also be willing to seek out persons who are not part of their own group of pious or righteous people. They must be willing to help the poor and suffering. They must go even further and seek for the "lost sheep," people who are so marginal to society and to religion that they would not even think of approaching God or a church.

STUDY QUESTIONS

Facts You Should Know

1. Give examples from the teaching of Jesus that point to the kingdom as "present" in the experience of disciples and as "future expectation."
2. What do the sayings about "becoming like a child" tell disciples about entering the kingdom?
3. Describe the objections raised to the behavior of the central character in the parables of the workers in the vineyard and the prodigal son.
4. How do Jesus' sayings about lending and wealth differ from similar sayings in the wisdom traditions of Israel?
5. What does each petition of the Lord's Prayer tell us about the kingdom and discipleship?
6. Why was Jesus' behavior toward "sinners" a scandal to his contemporaries?

Things To Do

1. Read Lk 15. How do each of the parables in the chapter answer the objections against Jesus raised in vv. 1–2? Compare Lk's version of the

parable of the lost sheep with the other versions (Chart 3–2). What elements in Lk's version fit in with themes in the rest of the chapter?

2. Use a concordance to find the passages in Mt which warn disciples that they must show forgiveness to others if they are to expect it from God. Read the parable of the unforgiving servant. How does the parable illustrate this teaching?

3. Read Mk 4. Find all the allusions to "secrecy" and "hiddenness" in the chapter. How is this theme related to the seed images used in the parable?

Things To Think About

1. Make yourself a list of the characteristics of discipleship in the Lord's Prayer. How would you make them part of your life?

2. How do you think the conflicts that are left hanging at the end of the parables of the vineyard workers and the prodigal son might have been resolved?

3. What situations today call for forgiveness and reconciliation? How might Jesus' parables be applied to those situations? Could you write such a parable for today?

Chapter 5

THE RESURRECTION OF JESUS

Images of Death and Life in Judaism

Christians celebrate Jesus' return from death to life at Easter. Jesus' disciples announced that he had been raised up by God to a position of glory and honor. We have seen that images of "resurrection" and the exaltation of the righteous were among the "new" symbols that came to be used by some Jews in the two centuries before the time of Jesus. But for most of the Old Testament death remains the end of human relationships, whether with other humans or with God. Only God lives forever (Ps 90:1–6).

The New Testament mentions the fact that the Pharisees believed in a resurrection of the dead, while the Sadducees argued that such an idea was absurd. Not only was it missing from the scriptures, it led to bizarre consequences if one assumed that when God "raised the dead," God returned them to a bodily type of existence (Mk 12:18–27; Acts 23:6–9). Jesus is shown to be on the side of the Pharisees in this dispute. The Sadducees are too materialistic in asking "whose wife" a woman will be in the resurrection. They should think of resurrection as being a spiritual existence like that of the angels. St. Paul makes a similar point against an overly materialistic interpretation of resurrection in 1 Cor 15:35–55.

Martyrs and Suffering Righteous Ones

When we first begin to hear about resurrection among Jews some two hundred years before Jesus, we also find that it is an answer to a serious religious crisis. Those people who were most faithful to God's commandments were being persecuted and martyred. Dan 12:1–3 promises that those who have suffered will be delivered and those who have done evil punished, even if God has to bring them out of the grave to do so. It also has a special promise for those who have led the people in righteousness during these evil times. They will shine like stars.

The story of the mother and her seven sons who were martyred by the evil king that is found in 2 Macc 7 also contains promises of resurrection. The second brother tells his torturers, "You accursed wretch, you dismiss us from this present life, but the King of the universe will raise us up to an everlasting renewal of life because we have died for his laws" (7:9). The fourth brother proclaims that while there is hope of being raised for those who die because they are faithful to God, there is no "resurrection to life" for the wicked (7:14). 2 Macc does not expect Antiochus and his associates to be raised for judgment. They will experience God's judgment when God drives them out of the land (7:37). The author demonstrates this punishment in a legend about the horrible death of the tyrant in anguish, his body rotting with worms. With his last breath he attempts to gain God's favor by renouncing his own divine pretensions, claiming he would build a sanctuary for God and even become a Jew. Naturally, such promises were too late to spare Antiochus his agonizing death (9:5–28).

Another promise of eternal life for the righteous who have suffered at the hands of the wicked occurs in Wis 2–5. Its author is familiar with Greek philosophical thought and so speaks of the "souls of the righteous" resting at peace with God (Wis 3:1–3). Wis 2 contains a dialogue among the evil people, who argue that there is nothing to stop them from oppressing the poor and doing anything else they can get away with. Since this life is all there is, they may as well enjoy it. However, the existence of righteous people angers them, so they claim that they will "test" the righteous person's claim to being a "child of God" by killing him. The wicked only get their answer when they die. Then they discover that they are condemned to vanish into oblivion, but that the righteous person lives in the presence of God, among the angels forever (Wis 5:1–16).

Resurrection, Vindication and Judgment

You can see that the idea of resurrection is connected with a central point in the whole biblical tradition: human beings are to live their lives according to the order which God has established. If they do so, then they are blessed by God. If they rebel and try to create their own order apart from God, then they will be condemned. Israel was to create a society in which God's justice and mercy were expressed. Exile and captivity were seen by the prophets as God's punishment. One of the martyred brothers in 2 Macc prays that God will accept their deaths as an atonement for the sins of the nation and lift the curse against the land (2 Macc 7:32–33). The author of 2 Macc wants the reader to understand that without the faithful sufferings of the martyrs, the military victories of the Jews against Antiochus IV would never have happened. God did accept those sufferings as an atonement for the sins of the people.

This example reminds us that the resurrection of the martyrs, which is predicted in 2 Macc, was more than a personal reward for the individual. It was a statement that their deaths had not been "in vain." Though Antiochus IV killed them, the martyrs were proved right in the end. God's justice triumphed. Thus, resurrection is frequently associated with scenes of divine judgment. In this world, we often do not see that goodness and faithfulness to God are victorious. Sometimes the idea of resurrection included a cosmic scene in which all people would be gathered in front of God's throne and would be judged either by God or by a heavenly figure referred to as the "Son of Man." This figure appears in Dan 7:13–14. He ascends to God's throne and is given an everlasting rule over all the nations of the earth.

Here is a passage from a Jewish apocalyptic writing, 1 Enoch. It describes God, the Lord of Spirits, judging the nations through the Son of Man. The powerful rulers of the earth, who have persecuted the righteous, "the holy and elect ones," are being judged:

> On the day of judgment, all the kings, the governors, the high officials and the landlords shall see and recognize him—how he sits on his throne of glory, and righteousness is judged before him, and no nonsensical talk shall be uttered in his presence. Then pain shall come upon them as on a woman in travail with birth pangs— . . . and pain shall seize them when they see the Son of Man sitting on the throne of his glory. . . . For the Son of Man was concealed from the beginning, and the Most High One preserved him in the presence of his power; then he revealed him to the holy and the elect ones. On that day, all the kings and governors, and high officials, and those who rule the earth shall fall down before him on their faces and worship and raise their hopes in that Son of Man; they shall beg and plead for mercy at his feet. . . . He will deliver them to the angels for punishments in order that vengeance shall be executed upon them—oppressors of his children and his elect ones. . . . The righteous and elect ones shall be saved on that day; the Lord of the Spirits will abide over them; they shall eat and rest and rise with that Son of Man forever. They shall wear the garments of glory. These garments of yours shall become the garments of life from the Lord

of Spirits. Neither shall your garments wear out, nor your glory come to an end before the Lord of Spirits. (1 Enoch 62)

In this passage, the righteous receive "eternal garments" and life in the presence of God forever as the reward for their righteousness and suffering. You can also see that while the wicked are condemned and punished, the primary focus of resurrection language is positive. It refers to the vindication of the righteous. They will live forever with God and experience the salvation for which they had been hoping.

The Resurrection of Jesus

In the Jewish traditions of martyrdom, suffering and righteousness, we see people expressing their faith that God's power to save and God's concern with justice extends beyond this life. We have seen that those who condemned Jesus to death passed a negative judgment on his relationship to God. Jesus' own disciples were confused and afraid when Jesus was arrested and executed. They may have hoped that God would raise and vindicate Jesus at the judgment along with the other righteous people who had suffered persecution.

However, the story of Jesus' resurrection is not just a reaffirmation of this Jewish hope. The disciples did not simply remember that Jesus had believed in resurrection, get their courage back and pick up the preaching where Jesus had left off. Instead, their experiences of the risen Jesus persuaded them that God had already raised Jesus up from the dead. God had already enthroned Jesus in heaven like the Son of Man described in Dan and 1 Enoch. Jesus is alive with God and will be the one to judge the world.

Our earliest evidence for Christian belief in Jesus' resurrection comes from the letters of St. Paul. Paul had been persecuting the early Christian movement when God revealed Jesus to him. This vision of the risen Lord changed Paul from being a bitter opponent of Christianity to being one of its most important missionaries (Gal 1:15–16). In 1 Cor 15:3–5 Paul repeats an early creed, which he said all Christians were taught:

For I delivered to you as of first importance what I also received, that Christ died for our sins in accordance with the scriptures, that he was buried, that he was raised on the third day in accordance with the scriptures, and that he appeared to Cephas [Peter], then to the Twelve.

He goes on to mention others who had seen the risen Lord, concluding with his own experience (vv. 6–8). Unlike the gospel writers who belong to the next generation of Christians, Paul is speaking about people who belonged to Jesus' generation. Peter, the Twelve and James had all known Jesus intimately. Neither they nor Paul have left us any first-hand descriptions of what their visions of the Lord were like. But they make it clear that they are not claiming simply that Jesus had an immortal soul which is now resting peacefully in heaven. They are claiming that God has taken the Jesus of Nazareth, whom they knew, and done something which had not happened to any other person. God has raised Jesus from the dead and exalted him to the heavenly throne.

No one actually saw Jesus being raised. The gospels contain stories about an Easter morning visit to Jesus' tomb. When it is found to be empty the women are confused and frightened. Jn 20:1–2, 11–15 describes Mary Magdalene as thinking that someone had either stolen or moved Jesus' body. In the earliest version of the tomb story (Mk 16:1–8a), an angel announces the news that Jesus has been raised. Originally, Mark's gospel ended with the women fleeing from the tomb. Later additional material was put at the end of Mark (Mk 16:9–20) to give an account of an appearance of the risen Lord like those found at the end of the other gospels.

As you can tell from the Jewish images of resurrection and judgment, resurrection was described as coming out of the tomb or the earth. The righteous would either become like angels or have new "eternal, glorious garments" to put on. No one thought that resurrection would simply mean the physical body coming back to life. But the most obvious explanation for a body missing from a tomb was that the tomb had been robbed or the body moved. At first, Jesus' disciples could hardly imagine that Jesus had actually been raised. That took the revelations by the angel and by Jesus before they could believe it. Only after they were convinced that Jesus lives exalted in heaven could the disciples link Jesus' resurrection with the fact that his body was missing from the tomb.

Summary

The earliest creed quoted by St. Paul focuses on two points, Jesus' death and Jesus' resurrection. Jesus' death is proclaimed as the source of forgiveness for all people. It is not limited to atoning for the sins of the nation of Israel at a specific time like the death of the Maccabean martyrs. Jesus' resurrection also goes beyond what people expected on the basis of the martyr traditions or the stories of the suffering righteous in Wisdom. Jesus' resurrection is a present reality. Jesus is proclaimed as alive with

God. Death has not cut Jesus off from his disciples. Instead, he remains present with them though in a new way.

Without the Easter message, Jesus might be remembered as a righteous person who healed people and taught about the kingdom of God. He might have been the founder of a small Jewish sect as John the Baptist or the Teacher of Righteousness had been. But the message of Jesus' resurrection claims much more than that. It claims that Jesus has been exalted and vindicated in a way that no other person ever has been. Jesus lives in a special relationship with God. Naturally, it is not possible to prove that what Christians believe about Jesus' resurrection is true by some sort of historical investigation. We can talk about Jesus' teaching in that way, and we can compare Jesus' teaching with that of other famous teachers. We can even talk about Jesus' death from an historical point of view. We can compare it with the deaths of other martyrs and servants of God in his own time and even in our time.

When we come to resurrection, however, we are speaking about the center of Christian faith. People today often find it difficult to imagine how resurrection could be true in our scientific and technological world of astronauts and space shuttles and cosmological distances and times. People in Jesus' day found it difficult to believe for other reasons. As we have seen, many Jews did not believe in resurrection at all because it was a new innovation. It wasn't part of their oldest tradition. Even Pharisees who did believe in resurrection would find it difficult to believe that God had raised up someone of their own generation, especially since God had not yet judged the world. And those who were at all familiar with Jesus' death would find it particularly difficult to believe that God had raised Jesus, since they would think that such a death implied God's curse, not salvation. 1 Cor 15 shows that Paul's Gentile converts in Corinth also had difficulty believing in resurrection. Paul has to insist that it is at the heart of the Christian faith. He also insists that what God has done in raising Jesus is the beginning of a resurrection that will encompass all Christians. Therefore, Paul tells them that if they do not believe in resurrection, their whole Christian faith is in vain.

STUDY QUESTIONS

Facts You Should Know

1. Give three arguments that a Jewish person who heard Jesus' disciples preaching that God had raised Jesus of Nazareth, a person crucified by

Pontius Pilate, from the dead might give against the Christian claims.

2. Based on the images and resurrection of the righteous that were circulating among Jews in Jesus' time, what would the claim that a person had been raised say about that person's relationship to God?

3. What was the first reaction to the announcement that Jesus' tomb was empty?

Things To Do

1. Read the stories of the finding of Jesus' tomb empty in Mk 16:1–8a, Mt 27:26–28:15 and Lk 24:1–11. First list the common features. Then list the differences between the versions. How do the variants in Mt and Lk seek to answer objections that outsiders may have made against Christian preaching of the resurrection?

2. Read the stories of encounters between the risen Jesus and disciples in Mt 28:16–20 and Lk 24:13–49. List all the examples of doubt and uncertainty in these stories. What do these examples tell the reader about the process by which the followers of Jesus came to believe in resurrection?

Things To Think About

1. What do you think of when you recite the words about resurrection in the creed? Which of the stories about Jesus' resurrection comes closest to expressing your feelings about resurrection?

2. Imagine yourself in Jerusalem hearing Jesus' followers talking about Jesus' resurrection. How would you react? Would you raise objections? If so, which ones?

Chapter 6

THE BEGINNINGS OF CHRISTOLOGY

Asking "Who Is This Jesus?"

Even Jesus' own disciples found it difficult to answer the question of "who" Jesus is. We are told stories of doubts and disbelief among Jesus' relatives and fellow townspeople (e.g. Mk 3:21,31–35; 6:1–6; Jn 7:2–8). Enemies looked at Jesus' miracles and presumed that he was a magician in league with Satan (Mk 3:22–27). They suggested that his association with tax collectors and sinners, people who were known to have turned against the commandments of God, made his claim to speak for God dubious (e.g. Mt 11:19; Lk 15:1–2). Comments about his origins often appear to have been used against him (e.g. Mk 6:3; Jn 6:42). In the end one of Jesus' own disciples, Judas Iscariot, turned against him.

In our own time, historians have suggested a number of approaches to answering the question of "who" Jesus is. Some emphasize the importance of his miracle working and exorcisms in drawing a crowd. Others look to the movements of resistance that sprung up at the death of Herod the Great around 4 B.C. and again before the outbreak of the Jewish revolt in the 60's A.D. They suggest that Jesus appealed to the independent peasantry of Galilee with his message of the rule of God and the reversal of all social orders and distinctions. Jesus would be reviving the old idea of an anointed leader or "king" of Israel, a person chosen directly by God, not a Hellenistic monarch like Herod. A variant of this view emphasizes the impoverishment and the outcast status of many of Jesus' followers. Jesus is the leader of a movement among the outcasts who had little hope of improving their lot or participating in the existing social order. He proclaimed that these persons are the beloved children of God and will soon experience God's salvation. Still other scholars picture Jesus in the mold of the ancient prophets. Jesus' prophetic word unmasks the injustice and

98

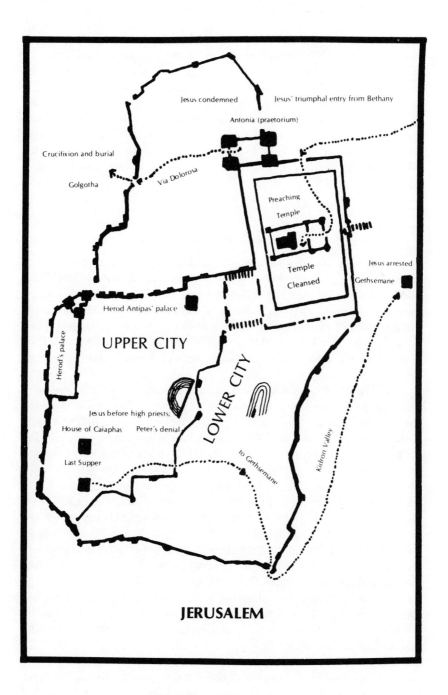

JERUSALEM

departure from God's will of the present, warns of the judgment against those who do not heed it, and promises salvation to the faithful.

All of these views can claim some support in the evidence from the New Testament and what we know of Palestine in Jesus' time. Their relative merits will be debated by Christian and non-Christian scholars alike. However, Jesus' disciples and believers who have come after them ask the question "Who is Jesus?" in another way. They are convinced that in Jesus God's saving power has come to humanity in a unique way. The question "Who is this Jesus?" is tied to the question of Jesus' role as an agent of salvation.

Resurrection, Jesus and God

Belief in Jesus' resurrection points out some answers to the question of who Jesus is. Not only does resurrection imply vindication of Jesus' mission by God, it also places a special stamp on Jesus' life. Jesus is more than the righteous martyr for God, since God has exalted Jesus to the heavenly throne. Exaltation to God's throne suggests that Jesus has a special place in God's rule over the world. One might say that Jesus' mission did not end with death. It took on a new dimension with Jesus' exaltation to heavenly rule.

We have also seen that the motifs of vindication and judgment were closely linked to resurrection symbols in Judaism. Not surprisingly the risen/exalted Jesus is understood by Christians as the one who will come in the future to exercise God's judgment. Paul alludes to an early creed in 1 Thess 1:9–10. His converts have turned from their false gods to the true God, and they wait for Jesus, God's Son, to come in judgment.

In such images of Jesus' heavenly exaltation we see the young Christian community looking to Jesus for its salvation. You can see another example of how the exalted Jesus becomes the focus of Christian hope if you compare Mark 13:11 and Luke 21:15. When Luke recasts the Marcan promise of divine help for Christians who must testify in judicial proceedings about their belief, he speaks of Jesus rather than the Holy Spirit as the agent of divine assistance. This shift does not reflect any neglect of the Spirit's role on Luke's part, since the Spirit plays a critical role in guiding the young community in Acts. But it does show that the exalted Jesus was felt to exercise divine functions in guiding and protecting the community (also see Mt 28:20).

Although the New Testament does not directly affirm that Jesus is God, we see that the exaltation of the risen Jesus led Christians to give him divine functions. This development may have been eased by the fact that some Jewish groups pictured angelic beings as the ones who would exercise such functions in regard to humanity. The mysterious "one like a Son of Man," i.e. "an angelic figure in human likeness," ascends to the divine throne in Dan 7:14–15. Dan 12:1 speaks of Michael, the angelic prince of the people, coming at the time of judgment to deliver the righteous. The exalted Jesus could be seen to play the role of such heavenly figures. Heb 1:4–14 contains an argument based on a number of Old Testament quotations which shows that Jesus, the exalted Son, is higher than any angel. Thus an "angel Christology" cannot quite capture the special relationship that exists between Jesus and God.

Jesus as Messiah, Son of God, Son of Man, Lord

Another way of capturing the significance of "who Jesus is" was to use titles which pointed to various aspects of Jesus' role in salvation. There are a number of these expressions in the New Testament, but the most frequent are "messiah," "Son of God," "Son of Man," and "Lord." When New Testament writers use these expressions, they already have in mind the fact that Jesus has been exalted to the right hand of God. You may have noticed that Heb 1:4 says that the superiority of the exalted Jesus to the angels is grounded in the superiority of his name to theirs. The "name" which the author has in mind is "Son." God has not called any of the angels "Son" (Heb 1:5). Rom 1:3–4 is based on an old confessional formula in which the earthly Jesus is described as a descendant (= son) of David, while the risen Jesus is designated "Son of God." The expression "Lord" is also used to speak of Christian belief in Jesus (vv. 4,7).

We will not be concerned with how each of the four expressions was used by different writers. For our purposes it is enough to have some idea of what the various expressions meant within the context of first century Judaism and what it tells us when Jesus' followers used these titles to explain who Jesus is. It is important to remember that the earliest Christians did not have the gospel narratives to shape their understanding of Jesus. They depended upon the various miracle stories, controversies, parables and sayings that could easily be remembered and passed on by word of mouth. They also summed up what they believed to be true about Jesus in short formulas such as we find in Paul's letters (e.g. Rom 1:3–4; 1 Thess 1:9–10; 1 Cor 15:3–5).

MESSIAH.   The word "messiah" is derived from the Hebrew *masiah*, "anointed one." It is translated into Greek as *christos* and so becomes the basis of the "Christ," which we often think of as part of Jesus' name. Anointing of a king or a prophet indicated that that person had been chosen by God to protect or rule the people. Some Jewish writings in Jesus' time look for anointed figures, a king, a priest or prophet, to come as a leader of the people in the last days. Such expectations might be attached to the Davidic kingship, since the anointing of David by the prophet Samuel had shown that God had selected him to rule over the people in place of Saul (2 Sam 6:21). David is also described as "anointed" of God in 2 Sam 23:1–17 and in the Psalms (18:51; 89:39,52; 123:10,17). In Jesus' time the kings were not descended from David. The prophet Jeremiah had predicted the end of the pre-exilic Davidic line and the coming of a new ideal king, David (Jer 33:15; Ez 37:23–24). He does not speak of that king as "anointed," but we do find such expectations for an anointed king in Dan 9:25 and Psalms of Solomon 17:23,36. Essene writings speak of several anointed figures coming as God's agents in the last days. Luke 3:15 describes the people as wondering whether or not John the Baptist was such an "anointed" person.

You can see from these examples that the expression "messiah" does not convey much information about a person. It merely indicates those who were felt to have a special role from God. The expectation of "anointed" figures in the last days did not specify whether such persons would be political leaders like the Davidic king, prophetic leaders like the Baptist, or anointed priests like the expectations for a renewed high priesthood that we have seen existed in this period.

Because "messiah" could be applied to different types of leader, many scholars think that people might have easily referred to Jesus as "anointed" during his lifetime. He did preach that the rule of God was being realized in his own ministry. And if he had a role in bringing people to the rule of God, then one can easily see that Jesus would become the focus of such expectations. In addition, the crucifixion of Jesus as "king" suggests that such speculation may have been the basis for the charge against him, that he was a political danger to the state because he claimed to be the "anointed king" in the Davidic line. Mark 8:30–31 portrays Jesus himself as critical of the "messianic" claims attached to him because they do not embody the element of suffering that is central to his mission. Indeed, none of the "anointed" figures that were expected to serve as God's agent were expected to die even a martyr's death. The coming of the "anointed" was to bring an end to the evil and corrupt rulers that caused righteous persons to suffer and even to be martyred for their loyalty to God. The "anointed" was to gather the righteous of Israel and to bring about the "new covenant" with God, the people as God had intended it to be.

You can see that crucifying Jesus as one who claimed to be "anointed king" was a way in which his enemies could deny any claims that Jesus was God's agent for the last days. Without the resurrection, that strategy would have succeeded. Jesus' followers might have been able to continue following some of his teachings; they might have continued their fellowship with one another and outsiders; they might have spoken of Jesus as a righteous martyr, and they might even have hoped for a future manifestation of God's rule. But they could never have claimed that the crucified Jesus was God's "anointed one," sent to lead the people in the last days. With Jesus' resurrection, they not only spoke of Jesus whose life ended in crucifixion as "messiah," but they also expected that Jesus would play a role in the salvation of the "last days" when he appeared as judge (cf. Acts 3:20–21). Luke 24:26,46 show that Christians still felt compelled to explain how the "messiah" came to suffer. These verses suggest that they had to reread the scriptures to show that, contrary to what people had thought, suffering had been part of the destiny of the messiah in God's plan.

SON OF MAN.   The expression "Son of Man" is one of the most puzzling expressions in the gospels. We have seen that in Dan 7:14–15 a mythic story of "one like a Son of Man" pictures the heavenly defender of righteous Israel ascending to God's throne. In a section of 1 Enoch that may postdate the earliest use of "Son of Man" for Jesus, we see God seating the "Son of Man" on the throne at the time of judgment. Sinners are condemned and the righteous are exalted into heavenly glory. Some of the images of Jesus as "Son of Man" in the gospels clearly allude to the scenario of heavenly judgment (e.g. Mk 8:38; Mt 19:28; 25:31–32). To speak of Jesus as "Son of Man" in such a context is to attribute to him the role of God's heavenly agent in judgment.

Unlike the expression "anointed," "Son of Man" does not appear to have been common in either Judaism or early Christianity. Dan 7 does not speak of the angelic figure as *the* Son of Man but as *one like a* "son of man." In other words, the visionary claims to have seen a heavenly being which had human form ascending to God's throne. The passages in 1 Enoch are metaphoric expansions on the Dan image. They do not suppose that the reader already expects a "Son of Man" to be the agent of divine judgment. The mysterious figure of judgment is referred to in a number of other ways in this section of 1 Enoch, such as "righteous and elect one" (1 Enoch 49:2–4) and "Lord's anointed" (48:10). 1 Enoch 71:14 identifies this figure with Enoch himself. However this section of 1 Enoch was apparently composed in the second half of the first century, too late to be evidence that "Son of Man" was being used among Jews generally as a designation for the expected messianic leader of the people. Some scholars even think that the concluding identification of the Son of Man with Enoch was a direct response to Christian claims about Jesus.

We also find that the expression "Son of Man" is almost entirely limited to the gospels, where it is placed on the lips of Jesus. The only exceptions are in passages that draw upon the imagery of Dan to describe the exalted Jesus (Acts 7:56; Rev 1:13; 14:14). In some of the sayings of Jesus, there seems to be a distinction between Jesus and the "Son of Man" as a heavenly judge who will vindicate Jesus' own mission (e.g. Mk 8:38; 13:26; 14:62). Mt 16:28 identifies the "kingdom of God" (from Mk 9:1) as the kingdom of the Son of Man, who comes "with his angels in the glory of his Father" (16:27). This description apparently presumes that the reader will make the necessary identification of Jesus with the coming Son of Man.

Although it is possible to trace the images of a heavenly "Son of Man" back to the interpretation of Dan 7, we have not discovered any evidence that the expression referred to an individual, whether heavenly or human, in a way that would make it an intelligible identification for people to have used to describe Jesus. Scholars have turned to the Aramaic which Jesus spoke to see what else the expression might have meant. In the Aramaic of the first century bar 'enas can be used either as a generic, "a human being, a mortal," or as an indefinite expression, "someone." Some of the sayings of Jesus appear to have used this generic expression (e.g. Mk 2:10). We also find the expression used in passion predictions, where it may have been put on the lips of Jesus by the evangelist (Lk 9:22; contrast Mt 16:21, "he"). Luke 17:24–25 contrasts the heavenly drama of the coming of the "Son of Man" in judgment with the suffering which he must endure.

As you can see from the imagery surrounding the expression "Son of Man," the combination of "Son of Man" with suffering (Mk 8:31; Lk 9:22) is every bit as strange as speaking of a "suffering messiah." Some scholars have tried to link use of the expression "Son of Man" in connection with vindication for the suffering righteous of Dan 7:19 to Jesus' own interpretation of the suffering servant theme found in passages such as Is 42:1; 43:10; 49:6; 52:13; 53:11. They suggest that Jesus used the Daniel metaphor. The combination of these motifs is evident in the sayings about the suffering Son of Man, but it is difficult to show that that interpretation was already part of Jesus' teaching. It may have been part of the process of reinterpreting the scriptures to explain the "messianic suffering" of Jesus after the resurrection. Other scholars, admitting that we do not have enough evidence to fill in the links that would account for Christian use of this expression, suggest that we view the interpretations of Jesus as "Son of Man" as developments that were attached to Jesus' use of the generic expression *bar 'enas* in his sayings.

SON OF GOD. Mindful of the monotheistic context of Judaism, we are not surprised to find that the expression "Son of God" is not necessarily a direct affirmation of Jesus' divinity. Within Judaism the expression "son(s) of God" might mean angels (e.g. Gen 6:2; Job 1:6; Ps 29:1; Dan 3:25). It might mean Israel as "God's son" (Ex 4:22; Deut 14:1; Hos 11:1; Wis 18:13). It might be a title of adoption for the king (Ps 2:7; 2 Sam 7:14). Or it can even be used for the righteous individual (Sir 4:10; Wis 2:18).

However, we do not find the expression in Palestinian Judaism for a "messianic" king, that is, for a person whom God will send to lead the people in the last days. The expression does appear in some Qumran texts for a Davidic king (e.g. 4QFlor 1–2 i 10), but the text does not speak of that king as "anointed" and could refer to any Jewish king. But we do know from the formulas that Paul quotes in 1 Thess 1:10 and Rom 1:3–4 that the expression "Son of God" had been used to express belief in Jesus' exaltation with God from a very early period. The imagery of Ps 2:7 played a role in the conviction that God had designated Jesus "Son" as we can see from Heb 1:5. The gospel narratives picture God naming Jesus "Son" at the baptism (e.g. Mk 1:11) and the transfiguration (e.g. Mk 9:7).

The expression "Son of God" played an important role in early Christianity. It could describe Jesus' special obedience to God's will by using "Son of God" in the sense of the righteous one who suffers. It could express Jesus' exaltation in heaven by using "Son of God" in the sense of the king "adopted" by God to rule over the people. It could express the special character of Jesus' relationship with God, by using "Son of God" to express the idea of being chosen as it had been used for the special relationship between God and Israel. And because "son(s) of God" could also refer to the chosen people, the expression was used for Christians too. Jesus is "God's own Son" but through baptism every Christian is adopted as a "son of God" (e.g. Rom 8:14–17).

LORD. One of the most common titles for Jesus in the New Testament is "Lord." Where "son of God" could express the new relationship of the Christian to God, "Lord" could be used to express the relationship between the Christian and the exalted Jesus. Christians are all "servants" of the one Lord. The ethical consequences of this expression were very important in the Christian communities. Not only was the Christian obedient to the "Lord," the Christian was also told that being servants of the one Lord meant that no one could claim to be superior to others. Paul describes Christians as those who call on the name of "our Lord Jesus Christ" in every place (1 Cor 1:2). Although men and women are different, "in the Lord" they are dependent upon each other (1 Cor 11:11–12). People in the church have to use different talents in serving the Lord (1 Cor 12:4–11). Christian masters are told to be just in their treatment of slaves, since they know that they have a "Lord" and master in heaven (Eph 6:9).

Of course, the expression "the Lord" does not always refer to human beings who have power over others. If it did, it would hardly have come to be such an important title for Jesus. In the Old Testament, "the Lord" is used to refer to God. The New Testament continues to use "the Lord" to mean God as well as to refer to Jesus. There are some passages in which we cannot tell which is meant. A very early hymn which Paul quotes in Phil 2:6–11 speaks of the exalted Christ receiving the name "Lord." Since all the powers of heaven and earth are subject to Christ as Lord, it clearly means that Christ has divine authority. We can trace the use of "Lord" as a title back to the earliest Aramaic-speaking Christians. One of their prayers or confessions of faith was *marana tha,* meaning "Our Lord, come!" Paul preserves this prayer in 1 Cor 16:22.

Gentile Christians were also familiar with the use of the Greek word for "Lord," *kyrios,* as a title used to address a god or goddess. Paul reflects this practice when he refers to the "so-called gods and lords" in 1 Cor 8:5. He contrasts this view with the confession that there is one God, the Father and source of all things, and one Lord, Jesus Christ (v. 6). In both a Jewish and Gentile environment, then, calling Jesus "Lord" indicated divine status. You can see that the passage in 1 Cor 8:6 preserves the monotheistic character of Judaism by making clear that the Jesus whom Christians confess as "Lord" is an agent of God, not a separate divinity like the many "gods and lords" that the Corinthians had worshiped before they became Christians. The language of "Father" and "Son" was also used to preserve the distinction between Jesus and God. It would take several more centuries for Christians to find a way of expressing the divinity of Jesus in a way that preserved belief in one God. Greek philosophical terms would be used for the task, but the New Testament language of Father, Son and Spirit maintains the links between the earliest Christian beliefs and the doctrines of the incarnation and the Trinity in these later formulations.

Jesus in Worship: Acclamation and Hymn

We are familiar with the titles for Jesus from the gospels and the letters of Paul. But before the gospels or the letters were written, Christians were using these titles to express their faith. Paul's letters make it very clear that Christian worship was the place where such expressions were used. Remember the expression *marana' tha*, "Our Lord, come!" You can see that that is an exclamation or a prayer for the coming of the Lord. Paul mentions it in 1 Cor 16:22. When we look at Paul's description of the Lord's Supper, or Eucharist, in 1 Cor 11, we find Paul telling the Corinthians that the Supper is a memorial of Christ's death until he comes (1 Cor 11:26). Therefore, many scholars think that the prayer for the return of the Lord was also part of that service along with the "holy kiss" between members of the church that is mentioned in 1 Cor 16:20.

1 Cor 12:3, which is also trying to explain how worship of Christ is different from the idol worship that the Corinthians had known, refers to saying "Christ is Lord" in the Spirit. An acclamation that Christ is Lord may have occurred in other contexts of worship. The Spirit also inspires the newly baptized Christians to call on God as "Abba," Father. When they do so they are expressing their new status as adopted children of God (e.g. Rom 8:15–16; Gal 4:6). Of course, they are also recognizing that Jesus, the Son of God, made that new reality possible. Many of the short formulas which Paul uses in his letters (e.g. 1 Cor 8:6; Rom 1:3–4; 1 Thess 1:9–10) were probably also familiar to his readers from their use in worship.

Early Christian Hymns

We also find in the New Testament longer passages, which we designate as "hymns," though we do not know whether they were sung or recited. Their language and form set them apart from the surrounding material even though the New Testament authors are using these hymns to illustrate points about Jesus. They have not copied them simply to provide information about hymns that should be used. In these hymns we see early Christians finding new ways of expressing the uniqueness of Jesus.

Our earliest example of such a hymn, Phil 2:6–11, stresses Jesus' willingness to abandon divine status in order to be obedient to God. If you remember the story of Adam in Gen, you can see that this hymn makes Christ the opposite of Adam. He doesn't try to "be like God," which Adam and Eve thought they could do by eating of the tree of "knowledge of good and evil." He is not disobedient at all. Instead, Christ is even willing to give up "being like God" and suffer the humiliating death on the cross:

[Christ Jesus], who, though he was in the form of God,
did not think being equal to God something to be grasped
but emptied himself,

taking the form of a slave,
born in human likeness.
And being found in human likeness,
he humbled himself,
becoming obedient to death,
[even death on a cross].
Therefore God has highly exalted him,
and given him the name above every other name,
that at the name of Jesus every knee should bend,
[in heaven and on earth and under the earth],
and every tongue confess that Jesus Christ is Lord,
to the glory of God, the Father.

Unlike Adam and Adam's descendants, Jesus is the one "without sin" (2 Cor 5:21). There is no reason for him to suffer the death he does, which is the penalty for human sin. But, the hymn asserts, because Jesus showed such obedience, Jesus is entitled to exaltation. He can be worshiped as "Lord."

The short formula in 1 Cor 8:6 hinted that the Lord Jesus was somehow identified with the power through which God brought all things into being. Other New Testament hymns use this idea that Jesus embodies God's wisdom or word, the power by which God created all things, to fill out the hint that Jesus had surrendered "being like God" in order to save humanity through his obedient death. The pattern of these hymns often shifts from the humiliation/exaltation of Jesus, to speaking of Jesus as an "image," "radiance" or "likeness" of God (words used to describe God's creative wisdom or word in some Jewish philosophers of the first century). Heb 1:2b–4 has all the elements of this type of hymn: (a) the Son is God's creative wisdom, which is of divine nature and which upholds the world; (b) the Son died for the sins of humanity; (c) the Son is exalted at the right hand of God above all the angels, with a "greater name" than any other powers in the universe.

The hymns in Col 1:15–20 and in John 1:1,3–4,(5?),9(?),10–12,14a,c,16 omit the exaltation. They focus on the identification of Christ with God's eternal wisdom and on the redemption which Christ has brought to humanity. Redemption involves descent into the world in John's hymn. However, that coming is already prepared by the fact that God's word/wisdom is active in the world as its light and life. Redemption is pictured as revelation, accepting the "light" visible in the incarnate Son. Col 1:15–20 focuses almost entirely on the heavenly reality of Christ. Verses 15–17 describe the "first-born" of God as agent of creation. Verses 18–20 speak of the reconciliation of all things to God in Christ's body, the church. Only the final verse mentions Christ's death on the cross as the means by which reconciliation takes place.

While the various titles used of Jesus have been shaped by the conviction that Jesus is exalted at God's right hand, the acclamations and hymns make it even clearer that the early Christians found Jesus to be more than just a holy person or righteous teacher or great healer or martyr. Jesus is not just "with God" as a reward for his righteous suffering like the martyrs or the suffering righteous person of Wis 2. Instead, Jesus embodies God's own power in creating and maintaining the world, in ruling over the world as "Lord" and as Savior or Judge of humanity. The community's experiences of the Spirit drawing persons into a new relationship with God which was expressed in their calling upon God as "Abba" or hailing Jesus as Lord played an important role in shaping these beliefs.

Jesus and God

Though the risen Jesus is imagined as an exalted, heavenly figure and worshiped as a manifestation of God, the early Christians would have insisted that Jesus is not "God" in the sense in which the Father is God. They know that Jesus is also a human being who really experienced suffering and death. Neither God in the Jewish tradition nor the gods of the pagan cults could be said to "die." Archaic myths sometimes spoke of a god or goddess being held captive by death and later liberated, often only for a time. Such myths explained the apparent death of nature in winter and its return to life in the spring. But these myths were not part of the early understanding of Jesus' death and resurrection/exaltation. (Later Christians sometimes appealed to the ancient myths to prove that God had also prepared the pagans to receive the truth of Christianity.) Some of the hymns and formulas antedate the letters of Paul. They must have been used among persons who were also contemporaries of Jesus. Paul himself had met Peter, James and probably others who had known Jesus during his lifetime. He knows that the Jesus whom Christians worship as "Lord" is a real human person just as surely as he knows that God is the invisible, eternal Creator of everything that exists (cf. Rom 1:20).

If you read through the New Testament carefully, you will notice that Jesus is rarely spoken of as "God." The most direct example, John 20:28, occurs as an acclamation or gesture of worship. The fourth gospel is acutely aware of charges made against Christians for blasphemy because they made Jesus, a human being, God (e.g. Jn 5:18). The author uses the imagery of Father/Son to explain that Jesus is not a rival god but the faithful emissary of the Father. What Jesus does is what God does. Jesus' powers to judge and give life have been given him by the Father (Jn 5:19–30). The

Philippians hymn makes a similar point by emphasizing the contrast between Jesus' obedience and Adam's disobedience. Jesus did not consider
"being divine" something to be "grabbed," "held on to" or "exploited for
his own advantage," (the Greek word *harpagmos* in verse 6 can carry all
of these connotations).

Christology as a special topic in Christian theology emerges when
Christians began to work out explanations for who Jesus is and what Jesus'
relationship to God is in a systematic fashion. The New Testament authors
do not engage in such explanations. They present us with their emerging
convictions about Jesus in a number of different images and literary forms.
Often, as we have seen, these images have their roots in different Jewish
traditions. Some are based on beliefs about God's agents of salvation, both
human and angelic. Others, like the identification of Jesus with God's
word/wisdom active in creation, come from more philosophical reflection
on how God can be said to be active in the world when God is so far above
that world and so different from anything in it. Many of these Jewish traditions had to be given a new meaning when applied to Jesus. It was not
easy to see how the "messiah" could be identified with a crucified person.
Nor was it easy to see how a human being who had recently lived and died
could be said to be God's creative wisdom. Often the various images occur
in different places in the New Testament traditions. They are not put together in a single account of who Jesus is.

Stories and the Identity of Jesus

Several weeks ago, one of my students was interviewing me for the
school paper. She said that the editors of the paper had told her that they
wanted "stories," idiosyncracies, etc. as part of the articles on different
faculty members. I referred her to some former students. The editors of
the paper recognized something important about how we identify people.
We don't always look for titles, lists of accomplishments, social position,
family etc. Often we are most interested in people when someone else tells
us a story about them.

You already know that much of our material about Jesus was preserved in stories and sayings that people repeated to one another. Miracle
stories identify Jesus as a sort of "divine man." He is able to exercise exceptional powers over demons, over the forces of nature, and to heal.
Many of the stories carried an additional message about Jesus' healing. A
person was said to be healed because of his or her faith in Jesus. Or a miracle is presented as a sign of forgiveness of sins. Jesus' treatment of the

demons shows their power over human life, but Jesus is greater than they are.

Jesus' sayings and parables not only show us Jesus as a teacher, they also ask us to compare Jesus with other teachers. The sayings which are part of a debate contrast Jesus' answers with the false views or even the inability to answer of his opponents. Sometimes Jesus' teaching invites comparison with similar themes in the Old Testament. Jesus may affirm what is in the Old Testament. He may present it in an intensified form. Or he may consider it insufficient or subordinate to some other expression of the will of God. The evangelists frequently remind their readers that Jesus' teaching was different than that of others. Mark 1:27 mentions Jesus' teaching in the context of an exorcism. The reader is to see the same power in Jesus' words as in his deeds. Mt 7:28–29 concludes the Sermon on the Mount with the observation that Jesus' teaching caused amazement because it had an authority different from that of the scribes. Luke 4:22 has the people praise Jesus' teaching and wonder at the "gracious words which came from his mouth." Since the Scripture quote about which Jesus had spoken begins with the prophet saying the Spirit of God rests upon him (v. 18), Luke's reader is to understand that Jesus has spoken in the power of the Spirit.

These brief examples show how stories carry important messages about who Jesus is, which are not easily represented in titles, creeds or hymns. We have concentrated on the shorter stories which people repeated to one another. However, each of the evangelists has also told the story about Jesus from a unique perspective. Study of how each gospel is structured and which themes about Jesus it develops helps us to present the picture of Jesus that is given in each of the gospels. Just as you may find that two people disagree about the way in which a particular character is presented in a book or a movie, so scholars have different views of what the "Christology" of each of the gospel writers is.

Often a gospel presents us with a number of puzzles that we have to fit together. Mark, for example, begins with an emphasis on Jesus' powerful miracles, but also has Jesus tell both demons and humans that they are to be silent. The second half of Mark emphasizes the necessity for the Son of Man to suffer. The disciples in Mark become almost as hostile to this teaching as Jesus' enemies in the gospel are to other parts of his teaching. At the end of the gospel, the women run away from the tomb frightened and don't tell anyone. No one doubts that an important part of Mark's Christology is that Jesus is the "suffering Son of Man." But how are the powerful miracles to be fitted in? Some scholars have argued that Mark wanted to oppose the image of Jesus that would come from emphasis on the miracles, that of a "divine man," because it did not make room for the necessity of suffering. Others see the miracles as reassurance to a suffering community. Even though Jesus had to suffer and even though Christians have to follow Jesus in suffering, Jesus does have the power to save us.

We have a hint that that is how Matthew understood the story of Jesus calming the sea. Mt 14:22–27 is based on the story in Mk 6:45–52. But Mark's story ends with the disciples not understanding anything about Jesus. The miracle did not increase their faith. Matthew substitutes a story about Peter walking on water for the Marcan ending (Mt 14:28–32). When Peter's faith in Jesus wavers, he begins to sink. Jesus rescues Peter and reprimands him for his "little faith." Then when Jesus enters the boat the disciples worship him as "Son of God." Matthew's version of the story is clearly aimed at teaching Christians that they must have faith in Jesus to save them from whatever trials they suffer. They should not be persons of "little faith," since the Jesus they worship is really "Son of God."

You can see that Matthew has used one of the titles for Jesus in a gesture of worship. This gesture also links the miracle story to the confession that Jesus is "Son of God." Matthew has shifted the ending of the story that he found in Mark in order to make it clear that these beliefs in Jesus should also have a message for the church of his day. They will be saved if they continue to trust in Jesus.

Summary

We have explored a number of ways in which the early Christians began to express their belief that Jesus has a special relationship with God which no other human being can have. In theological terms the word "Christology" is used to refer to explanation of who Jesus is in relationship to God. The New Testament does not use the abstract categories of the theologians. It uses the titles and images of its Jewish background. It also tells stories about Jesus which identify who he is. Jesus is not confused with God the Father. But Jesus is "next to God." Not even the angels are as close to God.

The New Testament insists that Jesus shares the powers of God in a special way. But the whole point of Jesus' divine power is to make salvation possible. Jesus can forgive sin, can give life and can act as judge. Therefore, those who believe in Jesus are to be confident that they will be saved. In many different ways, the New Testament tells its readers that Jesus is much more than a good, loving and wise human being. Jesus is God coming to save humanity.

STUDY QUESTIONS

Facts You Should Know

1. How does the New Testament distinguish the sense in which Jesus is spoken of as divine from the "one God" of its monotheistic creed?
2. Be able to explain the meaning of the four titles "messiah," "Son of Man," "Son of God" and "Lord" within the context of first century Judaism.
3. How is belief in Jesus' resurrection as exaltation tied to the use of the titles "Son of Man" and "Lord"?
4. Give examples of how the title "Lord" was used in early Christian worship.
5. How did early Christian hymns associate Jesus with divine powers?

Things To Do

1. Look up the short formulas that express Christian belief in some of Paul's letters (e.g. Rom 1:3–4; 1 Thess 1:9–10; 1 Cor 15:3–5). List the beliefs about Jesus and God which are found in those formulas.

2. Look up the "hymns" about Jesus in Phil 2:6–11; Heb 1:1–4; Col 1:15–20 and Jn 1:1,3–5,9–12,14ac,16. How does each hymn express the "before" of Jesus' existence, the turning point of obedient death and the final exaltation of Jesus?

3. Use a concordance to find examples of the three uses of "Son of Man" in Mark: (a) heavenly figure, coming judge; (b) suffering Son of Man; (c) "son of man" as an indefinite expression for any human being.

Things To Think About

1. Try writing your own "Christological hymn." What are the crucial elements in the "before," obedience and exaltation of Jesus for you?

2. If you had to make up short prayers or formulas for Christian worship what titles or phrases would you use to express the reality of who Jesus is? (Do not limit yourself to those found in the New Testament.)

Chapter 7

THE WORLD OF PAUL

Christianity in an Urban Environment

Jesus and his disciples came from the rural world of villages and farmers. But the most dramatic spread of Christianity occurred in the cities. Paul himself had been brought up in one such city, Tarsus. It was a prosperous commercial city on the southeastern coast of Asia Minor. It was also the Roman capital of its region, Cilicia. Major roads led out of the city to Asia Minor and to Syria in the East. When Paul was growing up, Tarsus was at the height of its prosperity. Its university rivaled those of Athens in Greece and Alexandria in Egypt. Growing up in the Jewish community of this city, Paul would have spoken Greek rather than a semitic language. His education probably also included some of the popular wisdom of Greek philosophy and the techniques of Greek rhetoric. We find evidence of such knowledge in Paul's letters.

THESSALONICA.   Some of the cities in which Paul established churches were important Roman centers. One of his earliest letters is to Thessalonica, a city in Macedonia. It had only been founded in 316 B.C. by one of Alexander the Great's generals. Like Tarsus, it became the Roman capital of the province. Cicero spent part of his exile there in 58 B.C. and the city had supported Octavian (Augustus) and Anthony in their war against Brutus, which had ended with the battle of Philippi in 42 B.C. It was also a very prosperous city, since it lay on a major Roman road, the Via Egnatia. Archeologists have found a number of remains that attest to the religious life of the ancient city. Not only was there a Jewish community, there was also a synagogue of Samaritans. In addition to favorite Greek gods, Zeus, Dionysus and Demeter, people also worshiped the Egyptian gods Serapis and Isis, and some gods of Phrygian origin, the Ca-

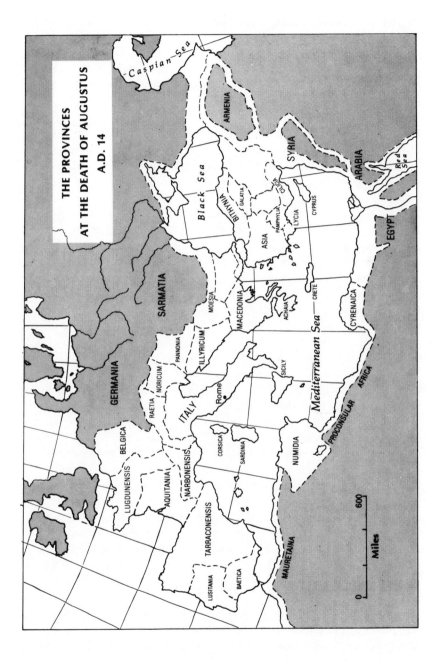

THE PROVINCES
AT THE DEATH OF AUGUSTUS
A.D. 14

Caspian Sea

ARMENIA

SYRIA

ARABIA

Red Sea

EGYPT

SARMATIA

Black Sea

BITHYNIA

GALATIA

CILICIA

PAMPHYLIA

LYCIA

ASIA

CYPRUS

GERMANIA

MOESIA

MACEDONIA

ACHAIA

CRETE

Mediterranean Sea

CYRENAICA

RAETIA

NORICUM

PANNONIA

ILLYRICUM

ITALY

Rome

SICILY

AFRICA

PROCONSULAR

NUMIDIA

BELGICA

LUGDUNENSIS

AQUITANIA

NARBONENSIS

CORSICA

SARDINIA

TARRACONENSIS

LUSITANIA

BAETICA

MAURETANIA

0   600

Miles

biri, who were very popular with sailors as well as with farmers. They were confused with the twins Castor and Pollux and a huge carving of them guarded the western gate of the city. The city also maintained civic cults in honor of its Roman benefactors. Divine honors were paid to the goddess Roma, to emperors like Julius Caesar and Augustus and to other benefactors.

PHILIPPI.　　Philippi lies in northeastern Greece and is another major stopping place on the Via Egnatia. It did not come into prominence until the Roman conquest in A.D. 168. After defeating Brutus on the plains west of the city in 42 B.C., Anthony settled many of the veterans of his army here and established it as a Roman colony. Augustus sent more colonists after he defeated Anthony and Cleopatra in 31 B.C. These Roman settlers along with a few of the original inhabitants were the "citizens" of the city. The city was governed by "Italian law," rather than local codes. However, the religious life of the city is much more diversified than its Roman origins might suggest. In addition to a Jewish synagogue, there were sanctuaries to the Thracian goddess Bendis, to Phrygian Cybele, and to gods from Egypt. Excavations in the ancient forum area have uncovered temples as well as rock reliefs of various divinities.

CORINTH.　　Corinth was the "newest" city among those in Greece. The older city had been completely destroyed by the Romans in 147 B.C. Corinth was refounded by Julius Caesar in 44 B.C. Like the other cities, it was the capital of its province. The city was populated by Italian freedmen, though by Paul's time in the mid-first century A.D. many Greek speaking settlers had also come to the city. Excavations of the city have uncovered an inscription which appears to refer to the "synagogue of the Hebrews," the numerous pagan temples with the dining rooms in which banquets to honor the gods were celebrated (cf. 1 Cor 8:10), the meat markets where meat from sacrifices was sold (1 Cor 10:25), the platform in the forum where Paul's trial before the governor Gallio may have taken place (Acts 18:12,17), the rows of small shops like the leatherworking shop of Aquila and Prisca in which Paul worked (Acts 18:1–3; 1 Cor 9:3–6,12) and the type of houses in which the community must have gathered for its meetings (1 Cor 11:17–22,33–34; 16:19).

ANTIOCH.　　A number of other cities are also mentioned in the Pauline mission. For a time, Paul had been a missionary sent by the church at Antioch on the Orontes river in the Roman province of Syria (now in Turkey). Christianity had come to the Jewish community of that city when the Hellenists associated with St. Stephen were driven from Jerusalem ca.

A.D. 40 (Acts 11:19–20). There Jesus' followers were first called "Christians" (Acts 11:26). That church began to accept Gentiles into its fellowship without requiring that they become Jews first. This decision caused such controversy that a meeting in Jerusalem was convened to settle the question (Acts 15:1–19; Gal 2:1–10). It was agreed that Gentile Christians did not have to adopt the customs of Judaism, nor did they have to submit to circumcision. Later in the first century, Antioch would be linked with preserving Petrine traditions. Many scholars think Matthew's gospel was written in Antioch. We hear more of Antioch in the beginning of the second century. Its bishop Ignatius (died ca. A.D. 117) wrote a series of letters to churches in Asia Minor as he journied to his martyrdom in Rome.

ROME. Rome, the ancient capital of the great empire, had all the features of the other cities magnified. It was a flourishing melting pot of commerce and trade. Slaves and merchants from the East brought their gods and goddesses with them to the capital. Rome also had a large Jewish community. Sometime around A.D. 40 unknown Christian missionaries had brought the message about Christ to that city. Riots over the "name of Chrestus" [= Christ] led the emperor Claudius to expel some Jews from the city. Paul's friends Prisca and Aquila had been forced out of the city at that time (Acts 18:1–3). Of course, other Jews and Christians remained in the city and eventually those expelled from Rome may also have returned. Paul and Peter were both among the Christians martyred at Rome (ca. A.D. 62) when the great fire under the emperor Nero was blamed on Christians.

Competing Religions and Philosophies

One of the things you may have noticed about these cities is their diversity. People came to them from quite different parts of the empire and along with them came numerous gods, goddesses and competing philosophies—not to mention the magicians and astrologers who were in evidence everywhere. In addition to such private cults and philosophies, cities also had their public festivals honoring important local gods or the "good fortune" of Rome or even the imperial family. Such festivals would be celebrated with elaborate festivals, processions, slaughtering of animals in the appropriate temples and often feasting. The Jews were known for refusing to engage in such religious practices. Since these festivals were civic celebrations, the Jews often had the reputation of being "haters of humanity" when they would not participate. However, other people admired the strict monotheism and the ethical code of Judaism. Some would even attend Jewish synagogues, though they would not necessarily convert to Judaism. To do so, a person would have to break with family, friends and social customs. Many of the first Gentile converts to Christianity probably came from this group of people.

ASTROLOGY AND MAGIC.   Naturally as people found their old world being uprooted when they moved from their native country to cities in which they did not enjoy the status of being citizens, they also became worried about what governed the world and people's lives. Both astrology and magic were widely practiced among all classes. Fate was sometimes pictured as a stern goddess. Astrology would tell you your destiny. And, if you were lucky, the magician might help you get control over some part of your life. Magic spells might be used to obtain victory at the track or to obtain the love of another. Here is a pagan love spell in which names of the Jewish God are included:

> I abjure you, demonic spirit, who rests here, by the sacred names Aoth, Abaoth; by the god of Abraam and the Iao of Jahu . . . hearken to the glorious and fearful and great name, and hasten to Urbanus son of Urbana and bring him Domitiana, daughter of Candida, so that he, loving, frantic, sleepless with love and desire for her, may beg her to return to his house and become his wife. . . . Make it so that he, loving, shall obey her like a slave and desire no other wife or maiden but have Domitiana alone, daughter of Candida, as his wife for the whole of their life, at once, at once, quick, quick!

ISIS CULT.   Magic was not the only way to deal with the problems of fate. The Egyptian goddess Isis was worshiped in the Hellenistic world as a powerful ruler over fate. Frescos from the Roman houses at Pompeii show ceremonies in her honor with the sacred jug of Nile water, priests with their shaved heads dressed in white and Egyptian plants. A temple to Isis built in Rome (ca. A.D. 38) is represented on coins. A large granite carving of Isis' husband Osiris had been imported from Egypt for the temple. A large complex in honor of Isis was found near the harbor warehouses at Corinth. She was thought to aid sailors.

The elaborate list of praises of Isis that could be found in carvings as well as in some writers showed that she was the origin of all human culture. Here is part of such an inscription from Asia Minor:

> I am Isis, mistress of every land.
> I gave and established laws for humans which no one can change.

Priestess of Isis.

I am the one who finds fruit for humans.
I am the one who rises in the Dog Star.
I am the one called goddess by women.
I divided earth from the heavens.
I showed the paths of the stars.
I set up the course of the sun and moon.
I devised business in the sea.
I made justice strong.
I brought women and men together.
I established that women should bear children after nine months.
I ordained that parents should be loved by their children.
I and my brother Osiris put an end to cannibalism.
I revealed mysteries to humans.
I taught them to honor images of the gods.
I consecrated the temples of the gods.
I broke down governments of tyrants.
I put an end to murders.
I caused men to love women.

I made justice stronger than gold and silver.
I established marriage contracts.
I assigned languages to Greeks and barbarians.
I ordained that nothing should be more feared than an oath.
I deliver the person who plots evil against others into the hands of
    those he plots against.
I established penalties for the unjust.
Justice prevails with me.
I am the Queen of rivers, winds and sea.
No one is honored without me.
I am Queen of War.
I am Queen of the thunderbolt.
I stir up the sea, and I calm it.
I am in the rays of the sun.
I free captives.
I created walled cities.
I am called the Lawgiver.
I overcome fate.
Fate listens to me.
Hail, O Egypt, that nourished me.

You can see that Isis is the mistress of everything humans need for
civilization. She is in charge of the stars and the weather, of trading and
founding cities. She establishes languages, laws and religions. She sees to
justice and she can also free her worshipers from captivity and fate.

In addition to public processions, temples, inscriptions, wall paintings and myths about Isis, there were also secret rituals. These rituals,
which are associated with a number of different gods and goddesses, are
what we mean when we speak of ancient "mystery religions." Areas in the
sanctuaries that were partly underground may have been the places in
which the person initiated into the "mysteries" saw visions of the sacred
myth or of items linked with the god or goddess. Strict prohibitions against
describing what went on in these cults were so well honored in antiquity
that we know little about them.

An account of Isis initiation does survive in a second century novel,
The Golden Ass. Its author, Apuleius, appears to be drawing upon his own
experience in the Isis temples of Corinth and Rome. The novel concerns
the adventures of a young man whose fascination with magic (in the service
of love) leads to his being turned into an ass. Finally, the goddess appears
to him and tells him that she can save him from the fate he is suffering.
When he goes to a public procession of the goddess, Lucius is restored to

human shape. The priest tells him that he should be grateful to his powerful protector:

> O Lucius, after enduring so many labors and escaping so many storms of Fate, you have finally reached the safe port of rest and mercy! Neither your noble birth, nor your high rank, nor your great learning did anything for you because you turned to slavish pleasures; by youthful stupidity, you won the grim reward of your unfortunate curiosity. And yet though Fate's blindness tortured you, she has brought you to this religious blessedness. Let Fate go elsewhere and rage in her wild fury. Let her find someone else to torment. For Fate has no power over those who have devoted themselves to serving the majesty of our goddess. . . . Now you are safe and protected by a "Fate" who is not blind but who can see and who by her light enlightens other gods. Therefore rejoice, put on a happy expression matching your white robe and follow the procession of this savior goddess with happy steps.

When it was time for him to be initiated into the mysteries, Lucius had to abstain from meat and wine for ten days. Then he had to purify himself with a ritual washing. The ceremony took place at night in the innermost part of the temple. Though he does not describe the ceremony, he claims to have descended to the gates of hell and returned reborn. The new initiate was then shown to other worshipers almost like a god himself:

> Hear then and believe, for I tell you the truth. I drew near the confines of death . . . I was carried again through the elements and returned to earth. At the dead of night I saw the sun shining brightly. I approached the gods above and the gods below, and worshiped them face to face. . . . As soon as it was morning and the solemn rites had been completed, I came forth in the twelve gowns worn by the initiate. . . . For in the middle of the holy shrine, before the statue of the goddess, I was directed to stand on a wooden platform, arrayed in a linen robe so richly embroidered that I was something to see. The precious cape which hung from my shoulders down to the ground was adorned wherever you looked with the figures of animals in various colors. . . . The cape the initiates call Olympian. In my right hand, I carried a flaming torch, and my head was decorated with a crown made of white palm leaves, spread out to stand up like rays. After I had

been adorned like the sun and set up like an image of a god, the curtains were suddenly drawn and people crowded around to gaze at me.

Lucius goes on to describe his daily devotions to the goddess in her temple and further initiations. He claims to have spoken to her husband Osiris, god of the underworld, in a dream. He also credits Osiris with helping him to a flourishing legal practice in Rome.

The story of Lucius and Isis gives you some idea of the emotional heights of ancient paganism. Though Jewish and Christian writers often speak of the pagans as worshiping the statues of the gods and goddesses, some people, at least, claimed to have a special relationship with particular gods and goddesses. You can also see something of the practical side of religion. The mystery cults were not primarily concerned with the afterlife, though someone who had been to the underworld had little to fear there. They were concerned with finding the right powers to help a person be successful in all the troubles and confusions of this life. Lucius is now under the personal care of a powerful divine being. You can also see why belief that Jesus had been exalted to be Lord over all the powers of the cosmos might appeal to people who were looking for salvation from the powers of fate. Paul reminds the Galatians that before they became Christians, they were subject to the powers of the universe and to beings who were not gods (Gal 4:8–9). But Christianity also had two things the pagan cults did not. It had an ethical code which sought to establish justice, love and peace among believers. And it created a new community which embodied these values and in which one would be welcomed wherever one went.

PHILOSOPHICAL SCHOOLS.   Philosophers also promised that people who followed their teachings could find a way to happiness. They promised a rational account of the place of humans in the cosmos. They insisted that reason could get control over the passions and false ideas that led humans astray and made them unhappy. Philosophers traveled from city to city. Young men from aristocratic families might go to famous schools like those at Athens or Tarsus to study philosophy. Philosophic literature was not confined to the great thinkers you may read about in college courses. It included anecdotes about the lives of famous philosophers, letters and handbooks that summarized philosophic teaching. We find New Testament authors drawing upon elements of such popular philosophic teaching. The image of the divine as something that pervades the universe and is not captured in religious cults is exploited in Acts 17:23–28, for example. The idea that humans should make moral and intellectual progress from being "children" driven by ignorance and passions to the perfection and maturity that comes with wisdom and virtue is exploited effectively in Paul's warning to the Corinthians that they pride themselves on a wisdom that they do not have. They are still in need of "baby food" (1 Cor 3:1–3).

Since Christianity taught people that they were to live their lives in a certain way, it naturally came into dialogue with the ethical teachings of philosophers. Each philosophy described what was wrong with humans, and how they could become happy. Philosophical systems also described the structure of the world which supported their picture of human life. Here is a quick sketch of three leading schools of philosophy in the New Testament world:

(a) *Epicureanism.* You might have read in a science book that the Epicureans held that the whole world was made up of different shaped atoms and empty space. They thought that if we humans would just really remember that fact, we could overcome our three main fears. First, we should never be afraid of death. All we are is a composite of different types of atoms (including those for the mind or soul). When we die, these atoms all come untangled and go off to become parts of something else. There is nothing left to experience death or to live afterward. Second, we should not fear the gods. Epicureans believed that gods did exist. People had seen them and people all over the world believed in them. Like everything else, gods had to be made up of atoms too, even if theirs don't come apart the way ours do. Epicurus argued that the main attribute of the gods is "blessedness." But if the gods are blessed, they are not going to worry themselves about what human beings, destined to be dissolved into atoms anyway, might do. Third, we should not worry about misfortune or fate. We cannot do anything about that. But we should attempt to arrange everything that we can in our life so that it will give as little pain and as much pleasure as possible. This meant withdrawing from politics or public affairs where one was likely to have enemies and troubles to a private, tranquil life. Epicureans often fostered small circles of "friends" devoted to these ideals. Women are sometimes mentioned as members of such circles.

(b) *Platonism.* The philosophic teachings that were developed by followers of Plato challenged the materialism of other philosophic schools. The material world is a mere shadow or image of the divine realities which are associated with the Good and are often described as "ideas" in the mind of the divine. Human beings can come into contact with the divine through the mind when they turn away from the world of sense impressions to the world of reason, often represented as embodied in mathematical forms. Since the "mind" is not material but belongs to the divine, it cannot "die" as the body does. Instead, some Platonists held out the image of the soul of the philosopher fleeing its bodily prison for its true home among the stars. Souls which had remained captive of the material world and its senses were often thought to be reincarnated in human or animal bodies. But this reincarnation was not correlated with a strict system of punishment and reward for the deeds of a past life as in some doctrines of karma. It is merely a necessity for a soul which has not been freed from its attachment to this world through philosophic contemplation.

(c) *Stoicism.* The first two philosophies were named after their founders. Stoicism was named after the place, the painted Stoa in Athens, where its founder Zeno used to teach. Like Epicureanism, Stoicism was a materialistic account of the world. But the Stoics claimed that everything came into existence through the condensations out of an original fire, or divine spirit. This spirit is also rational. The comprehensive order of the universe is due to the fact that the divine penetrates everything which has come to be in it. Periodically, the Stoics thought, the cosmos would return to its original fiery state and the process would start over again. Stoic philosophy was often accused of being the most fatalistic of all, since everything in the universe was connected and happened according to the laws that governed the "tensions" in the divine spirit. (One author has described the spirit as a "good and wise gas.") Sometimes the Stoics also spoke of the spirit as the divine word pervading all things.

The main attraction of Stoic ethics was its ideal of "passionlessness." Passions, after all, are merely movements or types of "tension" in one's soul. The wise person will gain control over the passions and be able to face both good and bad fortune with peaceful detachment. There is no point, the Stoic philosophers argued, in being worried about what we cannot change, the external things that happen to us in life. But we can be concerned about what really is under our control, that is, our reactions to external things. They cause most of our misery anyway. We are like dogs tied to a cart. If we resist the motion of the cart by lying down when it starts to move, we will be injured. But if we get up and run along with the cart, then we will arrive at the same place as the dog who is dragged but without pain and injury.

Here is a passage on this time from the famous Stoic philosopher, Epictetus (b. ca. A.D. 50). Epictetus had spent part of his life as a slave:

> Keep this thought ready for use at dawn, by day and night. There is but one way to calm, and that is to give up all claim to things that lie outside the sphere of moral purpose; to regard nothing as your own; to surrender everything to the deity, to Fortune; to yield everything to those whom Zeus had made supervisors; and

to devote yourself to one thing only, that which is your own. . . .
That is why I cannot yet say that someone is industrious until I
know for what reason . . . for I would not have you praise or
blame a person for things that may be either good or bad, but
only for judgments, because they are a person's own possessions,
which make one's actions either base or noble. . . . If you have
gotten rid of or reduced a malignant disposition . . . if you are
not moved by the things that once moved you, at least not to the
same degree, then you can celebrate day after day. . . . How
much greater cause for thanksgiving is this than a consulship or
governorship.

The language and ideas of Stoicism were very popular. They would come
to play an important part in the formation of Christian ascetic traditions.
Since Stoics held that all people were citizens of the cosmos, which is a
living organism, some scholars think that Stoic ideas influenced Paul's descriptions of the church as body of Christ.

Social Status of Pauline Christians

What we see of the early communities in Paul's letters suggests that
Christians came from diverse backgrounds. Yet they did claim to distinguish themselves from others by their way of life. When Paul speaks of
himself as laboring not to be a burden to his converts whom he treats like
a father or even a nurse gently caring for children (1 Thess 2:7–11), he
reminds the reader of the philosopher's claim to be sent as a healer for a
sick humanity. When he tells the Thessalonians to live in love for one another, to mind their own affairs, to live by the work of their hands and not
be dependent upon anyone (1 Thess 4:9–12), he would remind them of the
Epicurean ideal of quiet withdrawal. Paul's harsh words against those who
have confused Christianity with "wisdom" and "rhetorical preaching" at
Corinth (1 Cor 1:4) show that there were those Christians who identified
Christianity with the ideals expounded by philosophy. And they seem to
have thought that Christianity endowed them with a certain status and superiority to others. Indeed, they had even started to fight among themselves. Paul castigates them for forgetting the true paradox of the cross.
God's wisdom is not the same as human wisdom. They have also forgotten
the example of patient suffering and humility set for them by apostles like
Paul and Apollos.

We are better able to understand some of the divisions that broke out
in churches like Corinth when we consider the kinds of persons who made

up the first churches. We have already seen that in some cases difficulties arose between Christians of Jewish and of Gentile background. Clearly persons who were moved by the presentation of Christianity in relationship to the ideals of popular philosophy also had some education. Such persons are craftsmen, traders, merchants and the like. Paul frequently gets information about his churches from others who are traveling. He learned about some of the problems at Corinth from "Chloe's people," presumably the household slaves of this woman who were traveling on other business. He writes a letter of recommendation for Phoebe, the patron or deaconess of the church in one of Corinth's ports at the end of Romans (Rom 16:1–2). Some Christians had to be wealthy enough to possess houses in which the church could meet. Based on the average size of the dining room and atrium area of houses excavated at Corinth, we know that a church could not have been more than thirty or forty people.

In large cities like Corinth or Rome, we presume that the Christians were actually divided up into a number of "house churches." When Paul reprimands the Corinthians for their divisions at the Lord's supper, he speaks of some members of the church eating and drinking lavishly, while the poor go hungry and are dishonored. Probably the person who owned the house provided a special banquet at the "Lord's Supper" in the dining room and left the rest of the community in the atrium area with only the ritual meal of bread and wine. Such behavior imitates the kind of sharp social divisions that we find in ancient society. Persons would often give banquets in which their special friends were given choice food and wine while lesser associates might have poor wine and skimpy food at some distance from the host.

One of the most intriguing discoveries at ancient Corinth was paving stone marked with the name Erastus. The paving was donated in return for holding the civic office of aedile, one of the highest in the city. Paul mentions a man by the name of Erastus in Rom 16:23 as someone who held an office of "oikonomos" in the city. The title suggests a person in charge of civic funds. If the same man is the donor of the pavement, then he went on to the office of aedile, one of the highest in the city. Some scholars have noticed that the inscription does not have enough room for an indication of Erastus' father's name. Therefore, they have concluded that Erastus was probably a wealthy freedman. Christianity may have appealed to persons like Erastus, since it insisted that in Christ there was no distinction between slave and free (cp. 1 Cor 12:13). In ancient society as a whole, a former slave like Erastus could never be accepted into the aristocracy. Status was not simply based on wealth or success. It depended upon one's family origins as well. In a "new city" like Corinth, there may have been more opportunity for such persons than there would have been in a city

with old, established families. Nonetheless, Erastus' name itself would be
a sufficient indication of his origins.

Women as Converts

Another group of persons attracted to Christianity, judging by the
number of women Paul mentions by name as associates or patrons of the
Christian movement, were women whose economic and social position
was improved in the ancient city. Stoic philosophers had claimed that
women and men must practice virtue in the same way. Women should be
educated in philosophy so that they will be better managers of their households. Female slaves were often freed to marry their patrons. Women
were also active in trade and manufacture. Some lent money to finance
such ventures. Like comparable men, though not as frequently, wealthy
women might donate buildings to their community. At Pompeii a woman
who had made her money in brick-making donated a building to a work-
man's association and was rewarded with the title *sacerdos publica* ("public priest," though this does not mean that she exercised any particular
cultic functions). Another woman built the temple to the "genius of Augustus." Women appear in lawsuits as independent litigants. A few women
are named on coins and in inscriptions as benefactors of cities and even
officials.

Though not as frequently, women also joined the clubs and other cultic groups that are often linked to a particular craft. They are also patrons
and founders of groups whose membership is primarily male. A patron
might provide her home for meetings, build a separate building, or pay
the expenses for sacrifices, festivals and the like. Scholars think that between five and ten percent of the private associations had women as patrons and protectors. Women also played roles in private and civic cults.
Some religious cults were exclusively for women, but others had a mixed
membership. The philosopher Plutarch thought that a husband ought to
teach his wife philosophy so that she would not be prone to joining foreign
cults. He commented:

> It is becoming for a wife to worship and to know only the gods
> that her husband believes in, and to shut the door tight upon all
> queer rituals and outlandish superstitions. For with no god do
> stealthy and secret rites performed by a woman find any favor.

The wives and mother of king Izates of Adiabene played an important role
in his conversion to Judaism. Other women among the Roman aristocracy
were sometimes accused of Jewish sympathies. The cult of the goddess Isis

was particularly popular with women. Isis was among other things the goddess who protected marriage and chastity. There is no evidence that
women were particularly responsible for religious innovation. But they did
play a more substantial role in the newer religious cults of the ancient cities
than in the more established, traditional ones. Their position in Christian
churches seems to follow this pattern. Like that of freedmen, it was en-
hanced by the group's insistence that "in Christ" ethnic, social and gender
differences are of no importance.

The Church and the Forms of Association

The early churches had several models around which they might
shape their association. For Jesus' disciples and their Jewish converts, the
synagogue, home and even the temple in Jerusalem continued to form the
center of religious devotion. Early synagogues in the Hellenistic cities appear to have been private homes that were converted for community use.
However, the early Christian communities do not seem to have adopted
the terminology for synagogue officials that we find in a Jewish context.
Some scholars think that the sharp warning against disciples claiming titles
like "rabbi" in Mt 23:5–8 was directed against such a possibility. However,
certain elements of early Christian worship such as reading and interpretation of scripture, prayers, Psalms and ethical exhortation were doubtless
taken from the Jewish synagogue. The Jewish communities also provided
"courts" to settle disputes between their members. In 1 Cor 6:1–8, Paul
chastises the Corinthians for their lawsuits. He acknowledges that the
"love command" should make a Christian willing to suffer wrong rather
than to drag another into court (v. 7). But he clearly does not think that
the community as a whole will live by that principle. Therefore, he encourages them to find someone wise enough to settle disputes between
Christians rather than take such cases to outside courts (vv. 4–5).

We have already noted that there were a number of voluntary associations in the Greco-Roman cities. These served to link persons in a similar trade, such as burial associations, and to promote the worship of a
particular god or goddess. Jewish synagogues were often legally organized
as such voluntary associations. We do not know anything about burial practices among Christians at this early stage. 1 Cor 15:29 contains an enig-
matic reference to "baptism for the dead" and the Thessalonians were
concerned about the fate of Christians who died before the second coming
of the Lord (1 Thess 4:13–5:11). Therefore, it certainly seems probable that
Christian churches did function as "burial associations" for their members.
We have also seen that the voluntary associations often depended upon

wealthy patrons to provide for sacrifices, feasts and a place of worship. Patrons of this sort played an important role in the Pauline churches as well. But there are some striking differences. The voluntary associations, though they may cross some social and gender boundaries, are much more limited in scope than the early Christian communities, which sought to convert anyone who would believe in Christ. Voluntary associations did not recruit members by propagating their cult deity as the sole source of salvation. Often they might be limited to persons with ethnic origins in the country from which the deity being worshiped had come. Nor do we find among early Christians the elaborate offices and titles that are characteristic of the officials of cult associations.

Still other possibilities for organization were provided by the philosophical schools, particularly the groups of "friends" who followed the teachings of Epicurus. We have seen that emphasis on the moral conduct of one's life was an important part of popular philosophical teaching at this time. A badly burned collection of Epicurean writings was found among the remains at Herculaneum. These groups stressed friendship among members of the group and may have followed the practice of their founder in exchanging letters between groups which expounded the philosophic teaching of the school. In the second century, pagans would lump Christians and Epicureans together as "atheists," since both groups challenged the accepted beliefs about the gods. But, again, the participation of such diverse persons as the prosperous freedmen and women along with slaves, of Gentiles and Jews, in a single community is quite different from the philosophical school.

The fourth institution which contributed to shaping the early Christian community was the "household." We have seen that Christians met in the houses of wealthy patrons. They also adopted the language of family relationships: all are children of God, brothers and sisters of one another and of Christ. Sometimes the negative patterns of hierarchy, wealth and deference that were typical of ancient society were also experienced in the household churches as we see from the problems at the Lord's Supper in 1 Cor 11:17–34. The ancient "household" was considerably more complex than what we think of as a "family." Roman law held that all persons, male and female, were ultimately under the authority of the oldest male head of their family. (Women remained part of their paternal family while their children belonged to the father's family.) In addition, slaves and others dependent upon a wealthy person would be considered part of the latter's household. Even a peasant farmer or a craftsman in the city might have a number of persons living in his or her household who were not "family" in the sense in which we use the term.

Ethical writers emphasized the necessity for a hierarchy of good order and obedience within the household. Sections of such advice, called "household codes," found their way into early Christian preaching. They emphasized the fact that not only should wives, children and slaves show appropriate respect and obedience to husbands, parents and masters, but the superior parties also had an obligation to treat those under their care with love and concern. Husbands had to love their wives. Parents had to take care not to overburden their children. Masters had to treat their slaves justly. They should not exercise the absolute domination and cruelty which the law permitted (e.g. Col 3:18–4:1; Eph 5:21–6:9; 1 Pet 2:13–3:7). When the Pauline churches came to establish a list of qualities for "bishops," they insisted that such a person had to be able to manage his own household well (e.g. 1 Tim 3:4–5). Proper behavior also insisted that wives, who were usually much younger than their husbands, should defer to the latter and should not speak in public. These rules too found their way into the Pauline churches (e.g. 1 Cor 14:33b–35; 1 Tim 2:11–12).

Today many of these rules seem peculiar, since our households are much different. We forget that even fathers were subject to obedience and deference to the oldest male in their families, that women were much younger than their husbands and usually not as well-educated, and that children were not considered to be real persons at all. St. Paul speaks of the child as being a "slave," indeed assigned a slave to look after it, until coming of age (Gal 4:1–2). While a wealthy convert to Christianity might bring his or her whole household into the community, that was not true for many converts, especially women and slaves. Their conversion to Christianity might arouse suspicion. 1 Peter suggests that suspicions often led to ridicule and punishment of Christians. The church was something like a new "household community." But its members also had to continue to live in the households to which they belonged, which were not usually Christian. The Christian churches sought to show others that their "household" contained what was best in human life. It did not try to destroy the non-Christian "households" in which its members lived.

None of the four models—synagogue, cult association, philosophical school or household—quite captures the shape of the early Christian communities. Perhaps one of the most important things which is left out is captured by the special sense of belonging to a "church" which is not just the group that meets in a particular household; nor is it just the group of households that represent the Christians of a specific city; nor is it just all the Christians in churches that belonged to Paul's mission. From the beginning, the church also had a universal model. It was the "new Israel." That meant that everyone in the world who worshiped Christ belonged to "the church" (e.g. 1 Cor 1:2) just as all Jews anywhere in the world belonged to "Israel." The Greek word for church, *ekklesia*, stood for the assembly of citizens. But the expression for the church, "church of God" (cf. 1 Cor 10:32), has its roots in a biblical phrase, "assembly of the Lord," which referred to all the tribes of Israel gathered together. One of the ways in which the sense of a universal church was maintained was through the constant traveling by Christians. They were able to find hospitality among Christians in the cities through which they passed and were also able to share news of other churches. Apostles and missionaries were not the only ones involved in this process. Often ordinary Christians involved in trade sought hospitality with other believers. They may have been following a practice already established in the Jewish community.

The Workshop and Paul's Missionary Practice

Sometimes we think of Paul's mission as comprised of stirring sermons given in synagogues, the public places or private homes of people in the cities. Certainly he did use all of these places. However, there is one other element of Paul's missionary activity that we forget—he worked at the trade of "tent-making." This trade probably involved all kinds of leather-working. Some people think that Paul's father might have been granted Roman citizenship because he had been involved in making tents and other leather items for the Romans. Others have pointed out that Paul could have carried the tools of his trade with him. He could have scratched out a living on his long journeys by repairing leather goods for other travelers.

Paul sets himself up as an example for the Thessalonians. He works to support himself and not be a burden to anyone (1 Thess 2:9; 4:11–12). Paul links this work with his preaching and with his "fatherly care" for his converts. But others sometimes looked at it differently. Some philosophers praised a life in which one was dependent on no one. A person who could adopt the poverty and hardships of the tradesperson proved that he was not preaching in order to gain wealth and popularity. But there was another way of looking at the situation. Most people felt that the only truly respectable life was led by those not compelled to labor for a living. The philosopher should live from his teaching if he was not wealthy enough to live off the produce of estates. The great Stoic philosopher Epictetus even went from being a slave to being a person of wealth and importance. You can already imagine what persons who held this view must have thought of Paul. Paul's letters to Corinth show that a number of people criticized Paul for continuing to live such a "slavish" life (e.g. 1 Cor 9; 2 Cor 10–13). They knew that other apostles like Peter not only received support for themselves but also for their wives (and presumably their families). They knew that Jesus had told his disciples to get their support from preaching the gospel (1 Cor 9:4–5,14). Paul admits all that. But he insists that he is freely giving up the right to support so as to make the gospel available "for free."

If you have ever been in the Middle East or lived in an area of this country with craftsmen and small shops, you know that "doing business" is not the same as it is in most of our cities. You may sit and chat, even have a coffee or make general suggestions. The shopkeeper or tradesman may know your family. Often those relationships will go back several generations. If new people arrive, you might introduce them personally to the owners of the shops you use. Since he traveled, Paul would not be able to build up such long-standing relationships. He would have to work in someone else's shop. But he would have had plenty of time to talk with the people who came into the shop. Such conversation would not be confined to arranging and paying for the job as it is in an impersonal society. By using the workshop as part of his mission, Paul made it possible for persons to hear him who would not have met him in the homes of wealthier Christians at Corinth. He said that as much as possible he wanted all people to hear about Christ so he was willing to "make myself a slave to all, that I might win the more" (1 Cor 9:19).

Summary

The diversity of these cities seems a long way from the small, stable Galilean villages, where most behavior was set in tradition and where travel was usually limited to the five or so miles that were required to go to market. People sought others from their own country or trade to form smaller communities within the cities. They brought gods and goddesses from their homelands into the Greco-Roman cities. At the same time, each city had its own religious cults and festivals. And many of the Pauline cities, which owed either their origins or their prosperity to Rome, might have temples in honor of Rome, her gods and her emperor.

The Jewish community had learned to live in such cities by separating itself from others. Jewish religion, protected by Roman edict, prohibited participation in any civic religious activities. Jews could not be summoned to court on the sabbath. They had their own food laws which also limited contacts with outsiders. Marriage to a non-Jew was severely discouraged. The earliest Christian missionaries were part of that Jewish environment. But St. Paul insists that God called him to preach to the Gentiles (Gal 1:16). He was not the only Christian missionary to recognize that the gospel had to be preached beyond the boundaries of the Jewish community.

The task of preaching Christ in the cities of the ancient world was as great as any that has ever faced Christians. Apostles like Paul had to find a way to relate the gospel message to those who had not grown up with the Jewish faith and its scripture. They had to relate Christ to the religious and philosophical movements that were competing for people's attention in the ancient city. And they had to come up with some form of community structure that could embrace all persons. Christ could not be limited to a particular group, class or gender. People had to learn to call each other "brother" and "sister" across every possible boundary that might divide them. People had to care for others, even for churches they had never seen. As you read the letters of Paul, you will see that the first churches were not perfect. People did not understand what Paul had taught them. They quarrelled with each other. Sometimes they even did things which were clearly wrong. We shouldn't be surprised at those things. What family or organization of human beings doesn't have such problems? We should be amazed that Christianity managed at all. The gospel message had to touch the depths of the human spirit for it to have shaped a new form of human belonging in the Roman world. Only the tiny minority of Christians ever would have predicted that those who followed the Lord would outlast the greatness of Rome.

STUDY QUESTIONS

Facts You Should Know

1. Give a brief description of each of the following cities: (a) Thessalonica; (b) Philippi; (c) Corinth; (d) Antioch; (e) Rome.
2. Describe the Isis cult in the Roman world. How was the universal rule of the goddess expressed in the cult?
3. Describe the following philosophic views: (a) Epicureanism; (b) Platonism; (c) Stoicism.
4. Describe the diverse social origins of persons in the Pauline churches. Include two examples of conflict in the Christian communities that resulted from tension between ideas of social status in the larger society and the new realities of life "in Christ."
5. Give the characteristics of each of the following forms of association and indicate how that type of association contributed to the structuring of early Christian communities: (a) synagogues; (b) trade associations; (c) philosophical schools; (d) the Greco-Roman household.

Things To Do

1.   Locate on the map all of the cities mentioned in the chapter and the provinces to which they belonged.

2.   Read 1 Cor and find all of the phrases which refer to "social status" among the Corinthians. Include those which show a preoccupation with appearing to be among the "educated." Then make a list of the "status" language that Paul uses for himself. What does Paul think about the Corinthian views of social status?

3.   Look up maps for the ancient cities of Rome, Corinth and Antioch (e.g. in the *Harper's Bible Dictionary*) and identify areas and buildings common to ancient cities.

Things To Think About

1.   How diverse are the backgrounds of people in your church? What does diversity contribute to the life of the community?

2.   If you had to make a list of social institutions in modern society that are "like churches" or that have influenced the way churches are run and the way Christians understand themselves as a community, what would they be?

Chapter 8

THE LIFE OF PAUL

Sources for Paul's Life

Naturally, Paul's own letters are our main source for information about his life. Paul was not one of the original disciples and had not known Jesus. He tells us that he had been a zealous Pharisee. He had also been persecuting the Christians when God suddenly revealed the risen Lord to him (Gal 1:11–28). Paul says that his first response to God's call was to preach in Roman Arabia and then in the region of Damascus. After three years, he went to Jerusalem where he spent two weeks with Peter and James. Then he returned to Syria and his home region of Cilicia. Fourteen years later Paul is part of the delegation from the Antioch church at a meeting in Jerusalem, which accepted the principle of Paul's Gentile mission that Gentiles could become Christians without converting to Judaism (2:1–10). Shortly after that meeting, Paul left the Antioch church and began his own mission in Asia Minor and Greece. Paul's letters are written to the churches of this mission. When he writes to a church he did not found, Rome, Paul is winding up that phase of his life. At some risk to himself, he is going to deliver a collection for the poor at Jerusalem. He then hopes to journey to Rome and after a visit with the churches there go on to a new mission in Spain (Rom 15:22–32).

We also learn from Paul's letters that he often had to change or interrupt his travel plans. Paul suffered from illness, which he says God used to teach him that God's power could work through what is weak (2 Cor 12:7–10). Paul preached in Galatia when he was stranded there by illness (Gal 4:13). He also speaks of his illness as one of the trials that his new converts had to overcome in believing (Gal 4:14). Paul also mentions other forms of suffering, the hardships of his work, being driven out of cities, the hardships of journeys (including shipwreck), being beaten and even imprisoned (e.g. 1 Thess 2:2; 1 Cor 4:9–13; 15:32; 2 Cor 11:23–27). When he was in jail, Paul often did not know if he would live or die or when his case might be resolved (e.g. Phil 1:19–26; Phlm 22–23).

However, none of Paul's letters is dated. The various journeys he mentions in passing and the very rough hints at time intervals in Gal provide our only clues for relating the letters to one another. Acts, written several decades after Paul's death, fills out the story of the apostle by expanding upon other material that had been preserved in the community. Although Acts is written by a "Luke" who appears in the list of Paul's associates in Phlm 23 and Col 4:14, Luke is not one of Paul's regular associates. Many of the problems referred to in Paul's letters never appear in Acts. Acts 15 reports a very different agreement about the Gentiles than Paul does in Gal 2. Paul says the only requirement was that a collection would be taken up for the poor of Jerusalem. Paul was on his way to deliver it when he wrote Romans. Acts says nothing about the collection. Acts claims that Gentiles who become Christians should avoid food that has been strangled, food that has been used in a sacrifice to idols and sexual immorality (Acts 15:28–29). Paul tells the Corinthians that as long as they bought meat in the market or someone served it in a private home and as long as another person's conscience won't be offended, it is permissible to eat meat offered to an idol (1 Cor 8). Some scholars think that Luke may have found a copy of the decree by James and presumed that it came from the Jerusalem council. They suggest that it might have been formulated after the break between Paul and Peter reported in Gal 2:11–14. You can see from this example that it is not always easy to fit the information in Acts together with what Paul says in his letters.

Pauline Chronology

Scholars attempt to patch together references to events that we can date approximately in Paul's letters and Acts, the chronological hints in Gal, Paul's movements as reflected in his letters, Paul's journeys in Acts where they can be correlated with the letters and signs of development within the letters to arrive at a chronology for Paul's life and letters. Naturally, this process is open to numerous difficulties. You yourself can see that it is not easy to tell when the periods of three and fourteen years mentioned in Gal are to begin. Paul says that his missionary work in Damascus occurred under the ethnarch king Aretas (2 Cor 11:31–32). Consideration of the political relationships between Aretas and Rome suggests that this period must have been between the late summer of A.D. 37 and the death of Aretas in A.D. 39. Fourteen years from this period until the Council at

Jerusalem would place the latter in A.D. 51. Other reconstructions of Pauline chronology date the Council in A.D. 49.

Acts 18:12–17 report that Paul was brought before the proconsul Gallio in Corinth. Fragments of an inscription at Delphi contain a letter from the emperor Claudius in which Gallio is mentioned. A proconsul's term of office ran from July 1 and normally lasted for a year. The letter opens by saying that the emperor had been acclaimed for the twenty-sixth time and that the proconsul Gallio had reported a serious problem of depopulation in Delphi. Therefore, the instructions are likely to be addressed to Gallio's successor. He is instructed to recruit "well-born" persons from elsewhere to settle at Delphi and to give them the privileges of citizens. We know that Gallio did not serve an entire term as proconsul, since both his brother Seneca and the Roman writer Pliny report that he became ill and left the province by sea. Therefore, he must have left before the dangers of winter travel (referred to in Acts 27:9; 28:11). It would seem that Gallio was only in Corinth between June and October of the year he served as proconsul.

It is somewhat more difficult to determine when the twenty-sixth and twenty-seventh acclamations of Claudius took place. If the twenty-sixth acclamation took place after the first significant victory in the spring campaign of A.D. 52, then Claudius must have written the letter in the spring or early summer. How long did it take Claudius to receive Gallio's report and to act on it? Again, we are unsure. But it would seem likely that Gallio's term of office was in 51/52, which would narrow the encounter with Paul down to July–October of A.D. 51. Other scholars think that Gallio's term of office was in the year A.D. 50/51. This example gives you an idea of the complex task of establishing dates for events in the ancient world. When we come to the end of Paul's life we face another problem of Roman dating. Paul's arrest and imprisonment at Jerusalem takes place under the procurator of Judea, Felix. Paul's departure for trial in Rome occurs after Felix had been replaced by Festus (Acts 25:1–26:32). Felix was an imperial freedman, known for his cruelty. One of his wives was the Jewish princess Drusilla, daughter of king Agrippa I. The date of his recall by Nero is uncertain. The most common date is around A.D. 60. However, some argue for an earlier date, since his brother Pallas still had enough influence to protect him from the charges he faced in Rome. If one accepts a date around A.D. 60 for the change, then Paul was probably imprisoned sometime in A.D. 57. He would have arrived in Crete in the fall of A.D. 60 (Acts 27:9).

With the later date for the Felix/Festus change, Paul's trial, whose outcome Acts does not report, would probably have ended in the verdict that led to his death ca. A.D. 62. The seven letters, which scholars are certain were written by Paul himself, Rom, 1 and 2 Cor, Gal, Phil, Phlm, and 1 Thess, belong to the period prior to Paul's departure for Jerusalem. Rom, the last of these, was written from Corinth in A.D. 55/58. 1 & 2 Cor follow upon at least one earlier letter after Paul's expulsion from Corinth. But since 2 Cor appears to be a composite of several letters, the exact relationship of its sections is a matter of controversy. These letters stem from the period between A.D. 51 and Paul's return sometime in A.D. 55/56. Phil and Phlm are both written from an imprisonment. People used to think that that must have been Paul's final imprisonment at Rome. They failed to take into account Paul's own statement that he had been in prison as a result of his preaching (2 Cor 11:23) and the evident closeness to churches in Macedonia and Asia Minor. The Philippians have sent Paul aid and are well-informed about his circumstances. Philemon is the head of a house church that meets in Colossae (Col 4:9,17). Paul expects to visit there upon his release from prison (Phlm 22). 1 Cor 15:32 speaks in a metaphorical way of Paul "fighting with the beasts at Ephesus." This allusion would become the basis of stories of Paul's encounter with a lion he had baptized in the arena. Some scholars think it may be a gloss by a scribe who knew that legend. Others think that Ephesus was the place in which the imprisonment of Phil and Phlm occurred. The reference to the "praetorium" in Phil 1:13 and "Caesar's household" (4:22) point to the presence of imperial freedmen and soldiers in this city, the fourth largest in the empire.

You will notice that in Phil 1:12–26 Paul is uncertain how his case will be decided. Phlm 22, on the other hand, hints that Paul is about to be released. If 1 Cor 15:32 does refer to this imprisonment, then Phil and Phlm must have been written before the Corinthian letters. When we come to 1 Thess and Gal, we do not even have these slender clues to help us. Gal must have been written after the Jerusalem Council and Paul's departure from Antioch. But was the church at Galatia founded after that separation or does it stem from an earlier period in Paul's mission? When compared with Rom, Paul's argument about the law seems much less nuanced. Paul defends his teaching about salvation through Christ without the law against opponents who have attacked it. But he does not show the concern to avoid misunderstandings that we find in Rom. Gal 2:10 alludes to the collection for the poor as something known to the audience. Unlike the Corinthian letters and Rom, Paul does not refer to provisions for gathering the collection. Rom 15:26 speaks of the churches in Macedonia and Achaia as contributors to the collection Paul is taking to Jerusalem. Galatia is not mentioned. Nor does Gal itself make plans for any future visits by Paul. Some scholars think that Gal may have been written late in Paul's ministry. Others, more influenced by the contrasts with Rom, believe that it is a relatively early letter. The "Judaizing" (demanding that Gentile converts adopt Jewish customs of circumcision, kosher food rules and holidays) is also an issue in Phil 3:2–21. Some even suggest that Galatia is not mentioned in Rom because Paul's appeal was not successful.

1 Thess does situate itself in the apostle's travels. Paul had come to Thessalonica from Philippi. Unable to journey north from Athens (due to illness, 2:18), he had remained alone at Athens and sent Timothy to check on the young church (3:2). 1 Thess is written in response to Timothy's glowing report. However, Paul does not refer to Athens in that context. Most scholars think that he was writing from Corinth during his first visit

---

CHRONOLOGY OF PAUL'S LIFE *[8–1]*

ca. A.D. 10	Born (father a Roman citizen; leather worker)
	Raised in Tarsus (family may have had ties to Judea, e.g. Paul's insistence that he is a "Hebrew" [2 Cor 11:22] and from the "tribe of Benjamin" [Phil 3:5])
	Became a zealous member of the Pharisees
ca. A.D. 31/33	Is actively persecuting members of a new Jewish sect centered in Jerusalem that claimed Jesus as messiah (Gal 1:13; 1 Cor 15:9)
ca. A.D. 33/35	Called by God to preach to the Gentiles
ca. A.D. 35/38	Missionary activity in Arabia and Damascus (expelled under Aretas)
ca. A.D. 37/38	Two week visit to Jerusalem; meets Peter and James but not the larger church (Gal 1:22)
after A.D. 37/38	Missionary activity in Cilicia; Syria; from the Antioch church; [also Greece?]
ca. A.D. 47/50	1 Thessalonians (?)
ca. A.D. 50/51	Gallio episode at Corinth
ca. A.D. 49/51	Jerusalem Council
ca. A.D. 52/57	Missionary activity in Asia Minor and Greece Gal; Phil; Phlm; 1 and 2 Cor
ca. A.D. 56/57	Writes Rome from Corinth
ca. A.D. 57/58	Arrives in Jerusalem with collection; arrested; two year imprisonment at Caesarea
ca. A.D. 59/60	Sea journey to Rome
ca. A.D. 62	Executed after imprisonment at Rome

there. But some scholars think that the mission in Philippi and Thessalonica referred to in these letters occurred in the mid-40's A.D. They suggest that the Gallio episode belonged to a later visit to Corinth. This letter does not contain any of the concerns over the relationship between Paul's mission to the Gentiles and Judaism that appear in the later letters. Nor is Paul under an obligation to take up the collection in the Macedonian churches that figures in Gal 2:10. Therefore, these scholars argue, 1 Thess represents a phase of Paul's mission prior to the Council in Jerusalem. In any event, 1 Thess appears to be the first surviving letter from Paul to a church that he had founded. Our available evidence is so fragmentary or apparently contradictory that we must make a number of likely guesses in order to reach any results at all. Chart 8-1 gives you a rough outline of Paul's life.

Reading a Pauline Letter

Students often find Paul's letters the most difficult part of studying the New Testament. Unlike the gospels, letters are not in story form. Yet every letter belongs to a bigger story, the story of Paul and the church to which he writes. We can often tell that Paul is writing at a time of crisis. What a given church did in response to Paul's letter is also part of the story. We can often tell what Paul is hoping they will do from the way in which he writes. But we have already seen that sometimes we cannot be sure things actually happened that way. The Galatians, for example, may have resisted Paul's advice, though they did preserve the letter he sent them.

Paul is also difficult for us to understand because we are not trained to write letters or to make complex arguments in the way in which Paul was. The Greek language permitted very complex patterning of clauses within a single sentence. Here is a list of some of the rhetorical tricks of style that you should watch out for in reading Paul.

Paul also draws upon material which his readers would accept as "traditional." They should recognize in Paul's words something which is generally accepted by people, not something new which the apostle has said for the first time. It is often possible to recognize traditional material by its vocabulary (one finds words Paul does not use elsewhere), by a special introductory formula such as "we all know . . . " or "I handed on to you . . . " or by its form as a hymn, a list of virtues or vices, a set piece of ethical exhortation, a creedal formula, an acclamation like *marana tha*, an apocalyptic warning or judgment saying. You will also notice that Paul does not quote Jesus very often. Yet he must have taught his churches sayings and stories about Jesus. We find direct references to things the Lord taught in

---

RHETORICAL FEATURES IN PAUL'S LETTERS *[8–2]*

1. Use of parallel words and phrases or antitheses such as "life/
   death"; "flesh/spirit."
2. Chiasm: words and phrases developed in ab—b′a′ patterns.
   Putting an element in the middle of a chiasmus so that the
   pattern becomes ab—c—b′a′ emphasizes "c".
3. Use of paradoxes and expanding on metaphorical images.
4. Grouping of items for dramatic effect (pleonasm as in Gal
   4:10, "You observe days, and months, and seasons, and
   years").
5. Diatribe style: Address a question, usually an objection to the
   line of argument that "someone" would raise (e.g. Rom 6:1,
   "What shall we say, then? Shall we remain in sin so that
   grace may abound?").
6. Use of a negative expression to convey a positive meaning
   (e.g. 1 Cor 1:25).
7. Formulaic summaries.
8. "Preaching" style, elaborate and solemn references to God,
   e.g. Rom 14:12, "So let each of us give account of himself to
   God . . . "
9. Autobiographical style: Paul makes use of autobiographical
   references in several different ways: (a) simple autobiography
   (e.g. Phil 1:12ff; 2 Cor 7:5); (b) apostolic autobiography,
   Paul's life as an example to be imitated (e.g. 1 Thess 2:1–12; 2
   Cor 1:8–10); (c) apologetic: Paul is defending himself or his
   mission against charges made by others (e.g. 1 Cor 9; Gal
   1:11–2:14; 2 Cor 12:1ff); (d) "pseudo-autobiography," as a way
   of generalizing (e.g. Rom 7:7ff).

---

1 Cor 7:10f (Mk 10:11 par.); 1 Cor 9:14 (cp. Lk 10:7); 1 Cor 11:23f (a version
of the words at the Last Supper); 1 Thess 4:16f (cp. traditions behind Mk
13). Allusions to other sayings of Jesus have been suggested for: 1 Cor
14:37; Rom 12:14; 1 Cor 4:12 (Lk 6:28); 1 Tim 5:15, Rom 12:17 (Mt 5:39);
Rom 13:7 (Mt 22:15–22); Rom 14:13 (Mt 7:1); Rom 14:14 (Mk 7:18f); 1
Thess 5:2 (Lk 12:39f); 1 Thess 5:13 (Mk 9:50); 1 Cor 13:2 (Mt 17:20). Whenever you come across Paul using traditional material like this, you need to
figure out what the purpose of the appeal to tradition is.

Writing the Letter

We are also strangers to the formal divisions of an ancient letter. Many of the letters which survive from antiquity fall into three groups: (a) relatively short, private letters whose purpose was to transact business between the parties, request a favor, recommend the bearer to the recipient, or convey some piece of news; (b) official, public letters such as that of Claudius concerning Delphi in which Gallio is mentioned, which was written to the proconsul but was engraved on stone as a formal notice to the populace; (c) philosophical letters such as Epicurean and Stoic philosophers wrote, sometimes to friends and then later collected and published, whose purpose was to explain the teachings of the sect.

Here is an example of a business letter. Notice that the whole family expects to work at making women's garments. They are planning to join the groups of free workers in the small shops, who were textile manufacturers in Philadelphia:

> Greetings to Zenon from Apollophanes and Demetrius, brothers, makers of all sorts of woolen clothes for women. If you would like to and if you happen to have need, we are ready to supply what you want. We have heard of the glory of the city as well as of the goodness and justice with which you administer it. That is why we have decided to come to you, to Philadelphia, with our mother and wife so that we might be workers. Summon us if you would like us to work. We make, as you wish, cloaks, tunics, girdles, dresses, belts, ribbons, split tunics, trimming, everything to size. And we can teach our trade, if you wish. Tell Nicias to provide lodging for us. So that we won't seem strangers to you, we can provide references from people known to you, some from here whom you can trust, others from Moithymis. Farewell.

This letter gives you an idea of the kind of shop in which St. Paul worked.

One of the problems faced by people living in the Roman provinces was having labor, animals and crops seized for use by the military (see Mt 5:41). Here is an official letter/decree from the emperor Domitian to the procurator in Syria forbidding such a practice:

> From the orders of the Emperor Domitian Caesar Augustus, son of Vespasian Augustus, to the procurator Claudius Athenodoros: Among the special problems demanding great concern I am aware that the attention of my divine father Vespasian Caesar was directed to the cities; privileges, intent upon which he com-

**The overpass of Robinson's Arch
leading to the Royal Portico.**

manded that the provinces be oppressed neither by forced rent-
als of beasts of burden nor by importunate demands for lodgings.
But purposely or not . . . that order has not been enforced. . . .
Therefore I order you, too, to see to it that no one requisitions a
beast of burden unless he has a permit from me; for it is most
unjust that the influence or rank of any person should occasion
requisitions which no one but me is permitted to authorize. Let
nothing, then, be done which will nullify my order and thwart
my purpose . . . to come to the aid of exhausted provinces, which
with difficulty provide for their daily necessities; let no one in
defiance of my wish, oppress them and let no one requisition a
guide unless he has a permit from me; for if the farmers are
snatched away, the lands will remain uncultivated. [The rest is
lost.]

You may have noticed that ancient letters are very formal. Scribes and
secretaries were used to write letters. Here is a letter to a husband and

wife, who have just lost a child. Even the phrases of comfort are typical formalities:

> Mnesthianus to Apollonianus and Spartiate, be brave! The gods are witness that when I learned about my lord, your son, I was grieved and I lamented as I would my own child. He was a person to be cherished. I was starting to come to you, when Pinoution stopped me, saying that you, my lord Apollonianus, had sent him word that I should not come because you would be away in the Arsinoite nome [= a region in Egypt]. Well, bear it nobly, for this rests with the gods. . . . [The sender goes on to discuss business details.] I too have had a loss, a houseborn slave worth two talents. I pray that you remain well, my lord, together with my lord [= Apollonianus' father], in the benevolence of all the gods.

You can see from this letter that travel plans, especially when the sender does not come as might be expected, are often at issue in private letters. You can also see that many people in antiquity had little else to say in the face of death beyond "keep your chin up" or "it's the gods' will." No wonder Paul's Thessalonian converts were concerned about the death of fellow Christians (cf. 1 Thess 4:13–18).

Teaching in Letter-Form

One group of ancient philosophers, called Cynics (after the Greek word for "dog"), taught that people should give up all the false values, pleasures and weaknesses created by society. They wandered about giving advice, possessing as little as possible, and challenging the false values of the rest of humanity. Here are selections from letters of the philosopher Crates to his wife Hipparchia, also a Cynic philosopher:

> It is not because we are indifferent to everything that others have called our philosophy Cynic, but because we robustly endure those things which are unbearable to them because they are effeminate or subject to false opinion. It is for this reason that they have called us Cynics. Stand fast, therefore, and live the Cynic life with us, for you are not by nature inferior to us, for female dogs are not by nature inferior to male dogs, in order that you may be freed even from nature, since all people are slaves either by law [the Greek word "law" also carries the meaning of "customary behavior"] or through wickedness.

Crates objects to his wife following the accepted practices of weaving clothes for him rather than studying philosophy. He reprimands her:

> Some people have come from you bringing a new tunic, which they say you made so that I could have it for the winter. Because you care for me, I approved of you, but because you are still un-schooled and not practicing the philosophy I have taught you, I censure you. Therefore, give up doing this immediately, if you really care, and do not pride yourself in this kind of activity, but try to do those things for which you wanted to marry me. And leave the wool-spinning, which is of little benefit, to the other women, who have aspired to none of the things you do.

Crates wants his wife to be sure that their new son is brought up to be a little Cynic philosopher. These are his instructions:

> I hear that you have given birth—and quite easily, for you said nothing to me. Thanks be to god and to you. You believe, it seems, that toiling is the reason you did not have to labor [at giving birth]. For you would not have given birth so easily, if you had not continued to toil as athletes do while you were pregnant. Most women, however, when they are pregnant become enfee-bled; and when they give birth, those who survive childbirth bring forth sickly babies. Take care of this little puppy of ours. And you will take care of him, if you go into childrearing with your usual concern. Therefore, let his bath water be cold, his clothes a cloak [= a philosopher's cloak], his food be milk, yet not to excess. Rock him in a tortoise shell cradle, for they say that this protects against childhood diseases. When he is able to speak and walk, do not dress him with a sword as Aethra did Theseus, but with a staff, cloak and wallet [= Cynic philosopher's attire], which can guard men better than swords, and send him to Athens. As for the rest, I shall take care to rear a stork for our old age instead of a dog.

The Cynic answer to the problem of death was to practice separation from all the concerns with the body that bind us to life. Here is a selection from a long letter of Diogenes to Monimus on that topic:

> . . . practice how to die, that is, how to separate the soul from the body, while you are still alive. . . . The practice is very easy.

Examine carefully what death means to you. (Don't we do the same thing when we ask what is according to nature and what is according to custom?) For in death alone is the soul separated from the body, while in other experiences it is not at all. When a person sees, hears, smells or tastes, the soul is joined to it. It so happens that if we do not practice for death a difficult end awaits us. For the soul bemoans its bad luck as if it were leaving behind some darling boys, and it is released with much pain. . . . But whenever it meets the souls of philosophers [after death] they flee from it, since they know that it has erred in life by yielding direction of the whole person to the worst part of its nature. . . . If you have practiced how to die, this exercise will accompany you whenever you have to migrate from here. First, life itself will be sweet, for you will live free, a master and not someone who is enslaved, and in a short time you will strip away all that belongs to the body. Now this leads to harmony, when one keeps silent, exercises dominion and considers what the gods have provided for those who are moderate and restrain themselves from life like wild animals. For the rest of humanity, robberies and mutual slaughter are committed, not for great and noble reasons, but for trivial and common ones, and not against men only but against animals as well. For when it is a question of possessing more, eating, drinking and indulging in one's lusts, they are all worthless and no different from animals.

For some people, the life of the wandering Christian missionaries, dependent upon support from others, or, in Paul's case, upon working as a craftsman, seemed to be like that of the Cynics.

Paul's letters do not exactly resemble any of these types of letter. Most of his letters include concerns typical of the private letter. Paul must make arrangements for lodging, explain changes in his travel plans, and recommend his associates to the community. Another dimension of Paul's letters is the public side. Unlike imperial proclamations, they are not posted for everyone to see. But they are read to the churches. Therefore, we find liturgical language used in them. Where a private letter might have followed the opening "x to y, greetings" with the wish for the health of the recipient (this comes at the end of the condolence letter in our examples), Paul's letters usually contain a rather elaborate thanksgiving for the faith of the recipients. These thanksgivings often provide clues as to the topic in the main body of the letter. Paul's opening, a simple "greeting" in the private Greek letter or "grace and peace" in a Jewish letter, is also expanded with references to Paul's status as apostle, to those with him, to Jesus Christ and to God. The conclusion of the Pauline letter may have further benedictions and greetings. Thus, you can see a new form of Christian letter emerging in the Pauline collection. It is a very personal exchange between Paul and the Christians of a particular church. But it has also forged a new form of "public" speech out of the common language of worship and exhortation in that community.

Naturally, Paul's letters are also related to the philosophic letter. Each letter contains extensive sections of *paraenesis* (the word for ethical exhortation). Sometimes as in the case of the question about death in 1 Thess 4:13–18 the instruction Paul gives is in response to a specific question that he has been asked. Crates' letters to his wife are also triggered by specific incidents. In other cases, as in the general exhortation to a life of holiness in 1 Thess 4:1–12, Paul is reminding the churches of what they should know about Christian life generally. Diogenes' letter on practicing for death is an example of that type of exhortation in a philosophic letter. Sometimes we are not sure whether Paul's instruction has been triggered by a specific problem or question in the church or falls into this general category. But Christians have preserved Paul's letters because his words are not just limited to the peculiar problems of individual, first century churches. They speak about the roots of Christian faith and life.

Philemon: Letters and Apostolic Authority

We will begin our study of Paul's letters with the shortest and most specific, Philemon. Even here we find many of the characteristics of Paul's longer letters, although this is a personal letter from Paul to Philemon. It is sent from Paul and his associate Timothy to Philemon, Apphia, Archippus and the church which gathers in Philemon's house (vv. 1–2). It concludes with further greetings from Ephaphras, also in prison with Paul, and other fellow workers (v. 23). Thus, the letter is not just a private affair, but a public letter directed toward the whole church.

The occasion for the letter seems clear enough. Paul, who had converted Philemon and probably the others mentioned in the opening of the letter, is returning a runaway slave, Onesimus, to his master. Perhaps the slave had even known of Paul in his master's house. Legally, Philemon could punish his slave very severely. Paul's offer to repay in v. 19 suggests that Onesimus may have also stolen from his master when he ran away. The situation was not an unusual one. Nor is it peculiar to have a friend

OUTLINE OF PAUL'S LETTER TO PHILEMON   *[8–3]*

Greeting (vv. 1–3)

Thanksgiving for the love and faith Philemon has shown (vv. 4–7)

Body of the letter: Plea for Onesimus who is being returned as a
  beloved brother in Christ (vv. 8–16)

Body closing: Settling "accounts" between Philemon and Paul, which
  will settle Onesimus' account as well (vv. 17–22)

Final greetings (vv. 23–25)

intercede with the master for a runaway slave. Here is an example from a
plea by the Roman author Pliny on behalf of a young freedman (Epist.
9.21):

> The freedman of yours with whom you said you were angry has
> been with me, flung himself at my feet and clung to me as if I
> were you. He begged my help with many tears. . . . I believe he
> has reformed, because he realizes he did wrong. You are angry,
> I know, and your anger was deserved, but mercy wins the most
> praise when there was just cause for anger. You loved the man
> once, and I hope you will love him again, but it is sufficient for
> the time being if you let yourself be appeased. You can always
> be angry again if he deserves it, and will have more excuse if you
> were once placated. Make some concession to his youth, his
> tears, and your own kind heart, and do not torment him or your-
> self any longer—anger can only be a torment to your gentle self.

When you read Phlm, you will notice a different tone. Paul is not arguing the case simply in terms of "worldly" standards of behavior between
masters and slaves or ex-slaves. He is not pleading the case on the grounds
of mercy. Instead, the argument begins with a new set of relationships,
those between Christians. We are not told what Onesimus thinks about
having run away. Instead, we are told that Onesimus is now a beloved
brother in Christ. As such, he can even be said to represent the apostle
himself. Paul expects that Philemon will treat Onesimus as he would treat
him. In fact, Paul makes the future relationship of "fellowship" between
himself and Philemon depend upon the way in which Onesimus is re-

THE LIFE OF PAUL

ceived. Since Paul ends the letter with the request that Philemon prepare a guest room for Paul when the latter comes from prison, we presume that Paul expects the situation with Onesimus to have been settled as he directs.

We cannot tell concretely which of several actions Philemon might have taken. Clearly, to receive Onesimus back as a fellow Christian means that Philemon must cancel all "debts and punishments" that he might have claimed against Onesimus the runaway. Clearly, Paul does not expect that he has to make the "if he does it again" type of argument that we find in Pliny's letter. But since Paul also says that he would have liked to keep Onesimus with him, that Onesimus is his "heart," and that he would like Philemon to "refresh his heart," some scholars think that Paul is hinting that Philemon should free Onesimus and allow him to work with Paul.

You may also have noticed that unlike Pliny, Paul claims the authority to "command" Philemon to do what is right but says he would rather exhort him to act out of love (v. 8). By opening the body of the letter in this way, Paul turns from command to persuasion. If Philemon is persuaded to treat Onesimus as a fellow Christian rather than a runaway slave, then Philemon will once again demonstrate the faithfulness and love for which he is well known (vv. 5–7).

If you trace the themes faith and love in these verses, you will find an example of Paul's use of chiasm. Verse 5 introduces the pair: love (A) − faith (B). Then verse 6 picks up Philemon's acts of faith (B'), and verse 7 concludes with his love (A'). By having love at the beginning and end of the thanksgiving in this way, Paul puts special emphasis on "love" as the virtue he wishes to stress.

Phlm shows us something of how Paul exercised his authority. We are never in any doubt that as the one responsible for converting Philemon and at least some of the others mentioned in the letter to Christianity, Paul has the authority to tell them how the gospel is to be lived in concrete circumstances. Since Phlm is directed to the church which gathers at Philemon's house, the whole community is called to recognize that authority. However, Paul does not exercise that authority through command but by persuasion. Philemon has to see that the very foundation of Christian fellowship is at stake in how he responds to Onesimus. Maybe you think that the words are all a fancy cover-up for a command. But look at the letter again. Philemon is left with a certain freedom in how he receives Onesimus. Though he is clearly not to extract all the penalities that the law would have allowed, he may still put the debt down to Paul's credit; he may simply forgive Onesimus, who will then remain the Christian slave of a Christian master, or he may send Onesimus back to Paul to aid him. Furthermore, the letter makes any such response a positive sign of something good about Philemon, that he is a person who loves and cares for the community.

Phlm presents us with a picture of equality in an early Christian church which does not do away with all the elements of authority or even hierarchy. Paul refers to his converts, like Onesimus, as his "children." He has begotten them and remains responsible for them. But they are also able to be sharers in Paul's mission. They can be examples of love and goodness for others. As such, they are able to respond to persuasion rather than commands. The whole community must come to see that it is right to treat Onesimus in a new way, as a fellow Christian. They must all shift away from the worldly categories that make him a runaway slave. On the other hand, Christianity did not yet come to the position that it challenged slavery as such. We see Paul tell the slaves at Corinth that their "worldly" status as slaves does not matter in the Lord. Christians must all recognize that their real master is God. Therefore, the slave can make use of whatever situation he or she is placed in (1 Cor 7:20–24). But we can also see that the foundation for equality and rejection of slavery exists in Paul's insistence that Christians treat the slave and free person as equal brothers and sisters in the Lord. Thus, even this short letter contains an important message about how Christians are to relate to one another.

Missionary to the Gentiles:
1 and 2 Thessalonians

Paul spoke of his mission as a calling to preach the gospel among the Gentiles. We have seen that Thessalonica was a thriving Roman colony. Many different religious cults flourished in the city. Paul tells us that he came there after suffering persecution for his preaching in Philippi (2:3). When he was unable to visit the church again, Paul had sent his associate Timothy who has now returned with a glowing report about the Thessalonian Christians (2:17–3:6). Paul writes 1 Thess to encourage them to continue in their faith and to answer questions that have been caused by the death of some of the members of the church (4:13–18). You can see from the outline that much of the letter is taken up with thanksgiving for the Thessalonians. This thanksgiving is based upon the way in which they received Paul when he worked among them as well as upon the way in which they have continued to set an example for other Christians through their faithfulness.

2 Thess is more difficult to locate. The letter speaks of the possibility that the Thessalonians might have become confused by false claims of inspiration, false sayings or even letters claiming to be from Paul that tell

them that the day of the Lord (= judgment) has come. The way in which the theme is introduced, "concerning the coming of our Lord Jesus Christ and our assembling to meet him" (2:1), implies that the readers are familiar with the teaching of 1 Thess 4:17 that the Lord will come, along with those Christians who have died, and the rest of the Christians will be gathered together to meet him. It would appear that 2 Thess is written sometime after 1 Thess and that some Christian prophets were claiming that the day of the Lord had arrived or was at hand. 2 Thess makes the point that there are a number of mysterious events and figures who have to come before the judgment. It insists that God is restraining these figures from coming (2:3–10). 2 Thess 3:6–13 refers back to the ethical advice of 1 Thess 4:11–12. Christians are to gain respect from others by working at a trade and minding their own affairs. 2 Thess 3:6–13 warns against Christians who are not following this advice but are living in idleness and poking into other people's affairs.

Although the final verse of the letter stresses that it comes from the apostle (unlike the letters mentioned in 2 Thess 2:2), scholars have often noticed that 2 Thess is not quite like Paul's usual style. You can see for yourself that in comparison with 1 Thess this letter is much more impersonal. None of the details of the apostle's relationships with the Thessalonians or his past and future travel plans are mentioned. You may also notice that where 1 Thess 1:3 bases the thanksgiving on the triad, "faith, hope and love," 2 Thess 1:3 only speaks of faith and love. Where 1 Thess speaks of the rejoicing in the salvation of the Christians when Christ comes in judgment (e.g. 1:10; 4:17–18) 2 Thess is more concerned with the punishment that will come upon non-believers (2 Thess 1:6–9; 2:8–12). Therefore many interpreters wonder whether or not Paul himself wrote 2 Thess. We have seen that 2 Thess does remind the Thessalonians of Paul's teaching about the coming of Christ and the way in which Christians should live. But since the letter has no references to Paul's activities, many think that it might have been written by Silvanus or Timothy after Paul had been imprisoned in Rome. They would have heard that confusion was being created in the Thessalonian church and sent this letter to answer the confusion in Paul's name.

You can see from the outlines of the two letters to the Thessalonians that they deal with the basics of Christian life as they are set out in 1 Thess 1:9b–10. Christianity means converting from "idols to serve a living and true God." Most of us do not have the experience of having worshiped some other gods, but we still understand that Christians "convert" when they change their values or way of life from the "idols" of the modern world to serve God. Salvation is described in these verses as a future event. It means being spared the judgment which is to come upon all evil persons.

1 THESSALONIANS

Greeting (1:1–2)

Thanksgiving for the faith, hope and love of the Thessalonians (1:3–10)

The example set by Paul's ministry (2:1–12)

Condemnation of those unbelievers who persecuted Christians and
   hinder the spread of the gospel (2:13–16) [Because of its bitter
   remarks about the Jews, some scholars think this passage was added
   to the letter after Paul's death and the destruction of Jerusalem]

Paul's desire to visit Thessalonica again has been thwarted (2:17–20)

Timothy's visit and glowing report about the Thessalonians (3:1–13)

Exhortation: Live a life of holiness (4:1–12)

Exhortation: Resurrection of dead Christians at the parousia so that all
   will be with the Lord (4:13–18)

Exhortation: Be watchful, since we do not know when the Lord will
   return (5:1–11)

Exhortation: Relationships within the church (5:12–24)

Final greeting (5:25–28)

2 THESSALONIANS

Greeting (1:1–2)

Thanksgiving for the faith and love which saves Christians at the
   parousia (1:3–12)

What must happen before the parousia (2:1–12)

God has chosen Christians for salvation (2:13–17)

Prayer for the apostle and the steadfastness of Christians (3:1–5)

Exhortation: Christians are to follow Paul's example by working, living quietly and doing good to others (3:6–13)

Exhortation: How Christians should treat someone who will not follow Paul's words (3:14–15)

Final greeting: (3:16–18)

Christians expect that this divine judgment will occur at the "parousia," a Greek word that was used for the visit of an important figure like the emperor (or like a papal visit today). Christians took over the word "parousia" to mean the second coming of Christ when Christ would have the power of God and would judge the world. Paul and his associates must explain to Christians what kind of life they are supposed to lead now and what is meant by belief in the second coming. Both of these points continue to divide and confuse Christians today.

One of the most important characteristics of Christian life is the love that Christians show for each other and even for those outside their group (e.g. 1 Thess 4:9–10). This theme appears over and over again in Paul's letters. Another theme which appears often is that of sexual morality (1 Thess 4:3–8). Even though pagan philosophers warn against being slaves to passion and various laws punished adultery, the pagan world was known for its permissive attitude toward sexual behavior. Even the paintings on the walls of the houses at Pompeii showed scenes of sexual passion; comedy was full of sexual humor, and the gods of many of the myths were hardly examples of restraint. Grounded in their Jewish heritage, Christians insisted that the only appropriate place for sexual activity was in marriage. Paul has to tell the Christians at Corinth that they cannot go and buy sex from the prostitutes in the seaport (1 Cor 6:12–20). Christians also opposed the homosexual use of young boys as a perversion of God's natural order (e.g. Rom 1:26–27).

Perhaps you were also surprised to see Paul insisting upon the need for Christians to work and to live quietly, minding their own affairs. Remember that Paul's society despised the person who had to work for a living at some trade. The "gentleman" was able to live off the proceeds of his farms and could spend the whole day in public affairs, study, discussions and athletic activities at the gymnasium, in the company of friends or whatever. But those who were not wealthy enough to be completely independent might live such a "leisured life" if they could find a rich patron or benefactor to support them. Paul keeps insisting that the Christian should not be dependent upon others. He is thinking of that kind of relationship. 2 Thess suggests that the situation may have been made even worse by those Christians who decided that the events leading to the end of the world were already underway (2 Thess 2:2). They may even have been taking advantage of the charity of other Christians to support their idleness.

You can see that Christians generally expected the parousia (= coming of Christ at the end of the world) within their own lifetime. Even up to the present day there are Christian groups which preach the view rejected in 2 Thess 2:2 that the end of the world is underway. The final events in which evil would show its powers before the Lord came to defeat it (2 Thess 2:3–12) are happening. Paul and his true disciples reject that position. 2 Thess says that the evils of the present time are not the final evil times because they are being "held back" (2 Thess 2:6–7). 1 Thess 5:1–11 draws upon apocalyptic teaching that goes back to Jesus. We can never know when the "end" is coming by signs and the like. But since Christians are to live in holiness and not in evil and darkness, they don't have to worry about the exact timing of the end. Whenever the Lord comes, Christians will rejoice because for them it is a time of salvation.

The questions which troubled the Thessalonians about the dead Christians seem to have been raised by a worry that those who had died would miss out if they were not alive when the Lord came. Paul again appeals to earlier traditions. He argues that Jesus will not just come with the angels of God. He will come with the risen Christians so that the whole community will be restored. Paul insists that Christians should not treat death like the pagans, who had no hope for anything afterward. They should be confident that all Christians will be reunited in the Lord. You can see that in these short letters Paul has already sketched out the plan of a Christian life from the time of conversion to the glorious future that awaits Christians with the Lord.

Paul's Missionary Associates: Philippians

1 Thess 2:2 reports that before coming to Thessalonica Paul had been persecuted for preaching the gospel at Philippi. Nevertheless Paul was able to establish a strong church there. His close personal ties with that church are evident in the letter. We learn from Phil 4:15–16 that the Philippians supported Paul's missionary work in Thessalonica by sending him gifts. These verses speak of the Philippians as the only church which "entered into partnership in giving and receiving" with Paul. In Roman law persons could enter into "partnerships" on the basis of verbal agreement

between the parties. No written documents were required. A partnership was an association of persons formed for some common goal. Usually these objectives were commercial. All parties had to agree about the goal of their partnership and all parties would share the rewards or profits. It looks as though Paul and the Philippians have such a relationship. They share in Paul's missionary efforts both through gifts such as these and through the efforts of other members of the Philippian church who are Paul's "fellow-workers" in spreading the gospel. In Phil 4:2–3 Paul asks an unnamed Christian to help reconcile two women from that group, Syntyche and Euodia. Paul does not mention the source of their falling out, but he does tell us that they are part of a group which has worked side by side with him for the gospel.

Obviously the "profit" from such a partnership cannot be material reward as it would be in business. What the Philippians share with Paul are the "rewards" of his suffering (Phil 4:14; 1:7) and the "riches" which God bestows on those who sacrifice to serve the gospel (4:19; cp. 2 Cor 9:6–13).

Studying "partnership" language also helps us understand some of the tensions which we find in Phil. A partnership only lasted as long as the original parties were agreed about their common purpose and as long as all the original parties were alive. When those conditions ceased to exist, the partnership was dissolved. Paul alludes to both possibilities. There is the possibility that some people will preach the gospel out of rivalry or motives that are not part of the original intent (1:15–18). There is also the real possibility that Paul will not be released but will die in prison (Phil 1:19–26).

In order to ensure the spirit of the preaching which is required, Paul speaks of the "unity of spirit" which Christians should share (1:27–30). A business partnership depends upon unity about a single project. Paul shows that Christian unity goes beyond that to the example of humility and concern for others that was given by Christ. He uses the early hymn praising Christ's humiliation and exaltation (Phil 2:6–11) to make this point. Whatever happens to Paul, the Philippians must hold on to the truth of their faith. Paul even speaks of himself as though he were an athlete running to win a medal (a wreath was used for victors in Paul's time). He will only know that his "race" is successful if the churches that he has founded remain faithful to the gospel (2:15–16; also 3:12–16).

If you read through Phil carefully, you will notice that the tone of the letter is suddenly broken in chapter 3. Instead of continuing with the plans to send Timothy to Philippi and the account of Epaphroditus' serious illness (2:19–30), Paul begins to condemn some persons he calls "the dogs" (an expression of scorn and contempt in Greek), "evil workers" and "those who mutilate the flesh." Clearly such persons are rival preachers. Paul's opposition to them is much stronger than the warning about divisions within his own missionary association.

Those whom Paul condemns in Phil 3 hold views similar to those Paul opposes in Gal. They appear to have been Christian missionaries, perhaps associated with the church in Jerusalem, who taught that in order for Gentiles to become Christians the Gentiles had to follow at least some Jewish customs. Men had to be circumcised, which is why Paul attacks them for "mutilating the flesh." Christians also had to follow some of the Jewish food restrictions, which is why Paul says they have made their god their belly (3:19). And from what Paul says elsewhere, we presume that they also kept some of the Jewish religious feasts. Scholars use the term "Judaizers" to describe those who demand that non-Jewish converts to Christianity also take up Jewish practices. Even today there are small groups of Christians who hold this view. In addition to believing in Jesus, they also follow Jewish food rules and keep the sabbath and other feasts as Jews do.

Paul is violently opposed to this view. He uses one of his favorite antitheses, spirit vs. flesh to contrast the two positions. The Judaizer, he claims, puts confidence in what is fleshly or material. Christians, on the other hand, know that the salvation they have received from God is spiritual. Paul introduces another important theme in 3:7–11, "righteousness through faith" rather than the law. He will develop this theme in Gal and Rom. Paul's basic point is that the Jewish law is not the source of "righteousness," that is, of people being acceptable to God. The only way to become acceptable to God is through faith in Jesus Christ. And that faith is based on Christ having suffered for us. It is not a faith which needs to be finished off by taking up the Jewish law. Paul reminds his readers that he had been an extremely pious Jew. Indeed, he says, as far as any "righteousness" that could come from following the law he was blameless (3:6). But he has set all that aside now that he believes in Christ and expects to receive true heavenly salvation from him (3:20–21).

If you look at the end of Philippians you will notice that the reference to the Philippians' gift mentions Epaphroditus again (4:18) but gives no hint of the serious illness which had prevented him from returning to Philippi once he had delivered the gift. Neither chapter 3 nor chapter 4 speaks of the danger to Paul's life that we find in chapter 1. Scholars have suggested that these peculiarities would be easier to understand if we assume that Phil was made up of three shorter letters that Paul wrote to the church: (a) a brief note thanking the Philippians for the aid they had sent him; (b) a warning against Judaizing preachers; (c) a letter brought by Timothy when Paul thought he might be in danger of death and wanted to assure the unity of purpose in his missionary partnership.

OUTLINE OF PHILIPPIANS [8–5]

Sections from other letters that have been used in Phil:

Note thanking the Philippians for their gift, which Epaphroditus had just brought (4:10–20)

Letter warning the Philippians against the preaching of "Judaizing" missionaries (3:1–4:1)

Letter delivered by Timothy as Paul's case is about to be decided:

Greeting (1:1–2)

Thanksgiving for the "partnership in the gospel" with the Philippians (1:3–11)

Paul's situation: Whatever happens, it will advance the gospel (1:12–26)

Philippians' situation: Continue to be "of one mind" in following Christ (1:27–2:18)

Timothy and Epaphroditus are to come to Philippi (2:19–30)

[Against the Judaizers]

Exhortation: Euodia and Syntyche are to be reconciled (4:2–3)

Exhortation: Rejoice and be at peace (4:4–9)

[Thank-you for the gift]

Final greetings (4:21–23)

Summary

These short letters from Paul's mission in Asia Minor and northern Greece have shown us what it meant for people to become Christians. We have seen that becoming a Christian required a break with one's past. The gods and goddesses worshiped by the Gentiles in both private clubs and civic cults had to be abandoned for the God of Jesus. A person might also have to change his or her behavior. Sexuality could not be an "indifferent" pursuit of pleasure. It had to be controlled so that it reflected holiness and not lust. The old power and hierarchy could not be left unchallenged when it might destroy the relationships between fellow Christians. Even though Philemon had a legal right to punish his runaway slave, Paul makes it clear that as a fellow Christian with that same slave, he must not use that right.

We can also see that the early Christian communities were places of intense personal relationships between people. Paul was very much concerned with the welfare of the churches he founded. But he was often prevented from returning to visit them, so he relied upon his close associates like Timothy and upon his letters. And we can see that the churches kept those letters. They were read to the whole community. When there was confusion about Paul's teaching, an associate wrote 2 Thess to clarify the apostle's teaching. Both letters were then preserved. The Philippians appear to have put three of Paul's letters together into the longer version we have. Even Paul's thank-you note to them was preserved. Paul's letter to Philemon about Onesimus might have seemed to be just a private matter. Its importance might have ended when Paul visited after his release from prison. But the Christians in that church clearly thought that the message of even that small letter was important and so they preserved it.

All of these letters mention the suffering that was faced by the first Christians. Paul was forced out of Philippi and then Thessalonica and would later be forced out of Corinth because of the opposition to his preaching. He writes Phlm and Phil from prison, probably in Ephesus. For a time, he even thought that he might be killed rather than released. Paul admits in Phil 3:6 that he had even persecuted the Christian movement. We learn in 1 Thess that major figures like Paul were not the only ones who might suffer. Other Christians in both Judea and Thessalonica found themselves under attack. But in all of this suffering, especially in Phil with his life in danger, Paul's attitude is one of rejoicing. He constantly reminds his converts of the great salvation which they have from God. As long as they remain faithful to the gospel, no one can take that from them.

STUDY QUESTIONS

Facts You Should Know

1. Name the sources scholars use in constructing a chronology for Paul's life and indicate the difficulties they face in doing so.

2. What are the three main types of letter found in the ancient world? Explain how Paul's letters are both similar to and different from each type.
3. Describe the reasons Paul has for writing each of the following letters: (a) Philemon; (b) 1 Thessalonians; (c) Philippians.
4. What was the reason for writing 2 Thessalonians? Why do some scholars think that 2 Thess might have been written by one of Paul's associates?
5. What elements in Paul's exhortation and personal example in Phlm, 1 Thess and Phil might lead outsiders to think that the missionary was like a Cynic philosopher or was advocating a kind of Epicurean fellowship among Christians?
6. What was the special relationship between Paul and the church at Philippi? How was this relationship threatened by Paul's imprisonment?

Things To Do

1. Read Paul's appeal for the runaway slave in Philemon. Compare it with the letter from Pliny about a similar situation. What do the two letters have in common? Where are they different? What difference does the fact that Onesimus is now a Christian make in Paul's argument?

2. Read Paul's words of consolation in 1 Thess 4:13–18. Compare them with the approach to death reflected in the letters by Mnesthianus and Diogenes. How does the Christian approach differ from that of an average person (Mnesthianus) and that of a philosopher (Diogenes)?

3. Find as many examples of the rhetorical features of Pauline letter-writing (Chart 8-1) in 1 Thess as you can.

Things To Think About

1. What do you imagine Philemon's response to Paul's letter was? Do you feel that Paul was really forcing Philemon to give up his own authority over the runaway slave?

2. In reading these short letters, what elements in early Christian community life seem to you to be most appealing? What message do they have for people today?

Chapter 9

CHRISTIANS: JEW AND GENTILE

Jewish/Gentile Christianity: Its Variations

The letters of Paul are our earliest evidence for the missionary expansion of Christianity. There we find Paul calling non-Jews to believe in God and in Jesus, God's Son. They are promised that Jesus saves those who believe in him from divine judgment (1 Thess 1:9–10). Behind this mission lies a major shift from the preaching of Jesus and his disciples among the Jews of Galilee and Judea to converting people who lived completely outside the boundaries of Judaism. Acts 10–11 tells a story of Peter converting a Gentile, Cornelius. Acts 8:4 suggests that followers of Stephen began to preach to the Samaritans and to the Gentiles after Stephen's martyrdom. Mt 28:16–20 links the beginning of the mission to the Gentiles and a revelation by the risen Lord. Paul always speaks of God calling him to be a missionary to the Gentiles (e.g. Gal 1:16; 2:8; Rom 11:13). Eph 3:1–11 combines the tradition that Paul received a revelation to preach to the Gentiles (v. 3) with the tradition that this commission was given to apostles and prophets as a group (v. 5).

Mt 10:5–6,23 preserves sayings which limit the mission to Israel. They show that some Christians continued to think of their mission as one in which Jews were to be converted to believing that Jesus is the messiah promised by God. The conflict raised by the Hellenists in Acts and Paul's own actions in persecuting Christians (Phil 3:6; Gal 1:13–15; 1 Cor 15:9) point to a movement which is under the jurisdiction of local Jewish authorities. Paul links his actions with his "zeal" for the traditions of his ancestors. The speech which Luke attributes to Stephen in Acts 7:1–53 employs salvation history as a criticism of Israel's disobedience and idolatry. That pattern is continued in Jewish rejection of Jesus. Christian preaching which rejected the "traditions of Israel" may have been the cat-

160

Balustrade and Inscription barring Gentiles from the Temple.

alyst in the early conflicts between some of Jesus' followers and Jewish authorities.

We cannot write a history of how the mission to the Gentiles originated on the basis of the evidence in the New Testament. However, it appears that there were a number of possibilities for such a mission. When we turn to Paul's letter to the Galatians we learn of a heated dispute among various groups over the conditions under which a Gentile convert might be included in the Christian community (Gal 2:1–14). Although Paul reports that he, Barnabas and other Christians from the Jewish/Gentile church in Antioch and the leaders of the Jerusalem church, Peter, James and John, had all agreed that Gentiles did not have to become members of Israel by accepting circumcision, he also refers to others who continued to reject such agreements. Paul writes Gal in response to a fresh crisis. Some people have begun to persuade that community that Paul's "gospel" had been incomplete (perhaps designed to gain easy success, Gal 1:6–10; 5:7–12; 6:12–13). Christians should be circumcised and should follow at least some of the religious practices of Judaism (Gal 4:10, observance of the Jewish religious calendar?).

We have an example of a gradual conversion to Judaism in the report preserved by Josephus about king Izates of Adiabene. A Jewish merchant had converted the king's wives to "worship God in the manner of the Jewish people." Through them the king was also won over. The king's mother Helena was also brought over to the Jewish laws by another Jew. The conversion of the royal house was completed when a third Jew arrived preaching a stricter interpretation of the law. He also persuaded the king to be circumcised (*Antiquities* 20:17–54).

Fr. Raymond Brown suggests that we see four different types of Jewish/Gentile Christianity in the New Testament (R. Brown and J. Meier, *Antioch and Rome* [Paulist, 1983] 1–9). Given the diversity of early Christian preaching, there may have been other variations on these types involved in the disputes which surface in the New Testament.

(1) *Gentiles who became Jews.* Like king Izates, some converts to Christianity may have become Jewish proselytes. They would have received circumcision and taken on the full observance of the Jewish law which Paul says is required of anyone who seeks to "come under the law" (Gal 5:3). Paul refers to persons who were preaching this view among Gentile converts as "false brothers" and "spies" in Gal 2:4. They may also be the "dogs" against which he warned his Philippian converts (Phil 3:2–21). Acts speaks of persons "of the circumcision" (11:2) and "Pharisees" (15:5) holding such views.

(2) *Gentiles living within Israel.* This approach, probably that held by James and Peter (Gal 2:9; Acts 15), does not require that Gentiles convert to Judaism. But it did assume that they would follow some Jewish observances. The decree said to have been issued by James and the Jerusalem community (Acts 15:28–29) suggests that these requirements would have been those stipulated in the law (Lev 17–18) for non-Jews living within Israel. They are to reject all meat sacrificed to idols, keep from *porneia* (sexual immorality), that is, sexual relations within forbidden degrees of kinship, and avoid eating blood and meat which comes from an animal with the blood inside, that is, non-kosher meat. (City officials in Sardis were required to provide "suitable food" for the Jewish community in the public market; cf. Josephus, *Antiquities* 14:259–61.) Such rules would make it possible for Gentile converts to live together with their Jewish-Christian counterparts in one community. Some scholars think that the episode in which some Jewish Christians from Jerusalem refused to associate with Gentile Christians (= share the Lord's Supper) mentioned in Gal 2:11–14 was the occasion for the ruling in Acts 15:29.

(3) *Gentiles not under the law.* This is the view of Paul and other Christians with whom he worked. Salvation comes to all persons through Christ. It does not come through the law, which is broadly understood as the body of religious practices that governed the lives of Jews. Since even

Jews must believe in Christ to be saved, there is no reason to require that Gentiles come under the law in any sense (e.g. Gal 3:10–13). Nor does Paul think that the fact that Gentiles are not "under the law" creates a barrier between Jew and Gentile Christians when both are part of a single community (a view shared by Peter until objections were raised by "people from James"—Gal 2:11–14). Notice what this view does not say. It does not say that Jews who have come to believe in Jesus abandon their heritage. Paul insists upon his own place as a "Hebrew" (Phil 3:5; 2 Cor 11:22; Rom 11:1). But he also sees God making the Gentiles heirs to the promises to Abraham without requiring that they follow the law (Rom 10:1–4; 11:17–24). Acts 21:20–21 pictures Paul's opponents charging that he led Jews to abandon their traditions. Rom 9:4–5 suggests that Paul felt that it was possible for Jewish-Christians to find salvation through faith in Christ and maintain their Jewish heritage.

(4) *Jesus has replaced Judaism.* The radical critique of the Jewish temple and cult which is represented in the preaching of the Hellenists in Acts 6:8–14 appears in a number of forms in the New Testament. In John, Jesus symbolically replaces the Jewish temple, worship of God there, and the major Jewish feasts. The way to God lies only through Jesus, not Moses (e.g. John 1:14–18). Hebrews insists that Jesus' sacrifice as eternal, heavenly high priest has replaced all the imperfect images in the earthly cult of the Jewish temple and priesthood (e.g. Heb 7:1–10:18). Mark 2:22 insists that the "new wine" cannot be put into old wineskins. For these Christians, Scripture testifies to Jesus and provides instructive examples for Christians, but the coming of Jesus as messiah has led to a sharp break with the past.

Righteousness, Faith and the Law

Many Christians today would probably identify the fourth option as their view of the relationship between Christianity and Judaism. Small groups of "Christian Jews" do advocate some form of the first alternative. But the disappearance of mixed communities of Jewish and non-Jewish Christians quickly deprived the middle two options of their social grounding. The accommodations of the Petrine position were simply forgotten. Paul's arguments about "righteousness through faith in Jesus and not through the law" were transformed into timeless theological principle. The question became one of how God is gracious to humans who always stand condemned as "sinners," not simply one of how persons who were "sinners" because they lived outside the law and its holiness could be said to be righteous.

Scholars continue to argue over what led Paul to make such a radical disjunction between faith in Christ and "the law." Paul's view is not shared by others like Peter and James. Yet Paul also appears to be less radical than the "Hellenists." According to Phil 3:6, Paul was blameless in his observance of the law. We cannot conclude that he found in Christ freedom from an obligation that he was unable to meet as a Jew.

The same verse links Paul's "zeal" for the law with his persecution of the church. Some scholars find the key to our problem in this part of Paul's experience. The one failing which Paul repeatedly admits is persecuting the church, though his sufferings on behalf of the gospel certainly make up for that failure in his view (1 Cor 15:9–10; Phil 3:10). These scholars have suggested that Paul's description of how the "good law" can be "used" by sin to entrap humans in a "sin they do not even want to do," in bondage and death (Rom 7:13–25), is a generalization based on Paul's experience. When Paul was acting out of his own zeal for the law, he actually opposed God. Zeal for the law led him to consider the "crucified Christ," the source of righteousness for all humanity, accursed as he says in Gal 3:13–14. Thus, Paul speaks of his own conversion as nothing less than a complete reversal of everything he had valued in the past (Phil 3:7–8). Paul could not have freed himself from the impasse set by the law; only God acting in Christ could do that (e.g. Phil 3:9–14; Rom 8:1–3).

Paul's reflection on the experience of "bondage to sin and death," even by those who know the "good law," may also have been shaped by the story of Adam's disobedience. Rom 5:12–21 presents a complex type/ antitype relationship between Adam and Christ. Sin and death came to dominate humanity through Adam even before the law was given. But giving the law to Moses did not "lessen" or "erase" sin. It might be said to have "increased" it, since the law is the norm against which sin is measured. But if Adam's sin brought all that on humanity, Christ has brought much more, the "free gift" of righteousness which culminates in eternal life. Rom 7:7–13 appears to be a generalized repetition of this story of how "sin" exploits the "commandment," which is good in itself, to bring about death.

Freedom for the Gentiles: Galatians

The location of the churches to which Galatians is written remains a puzzle. Paul does not connect any cities with this mission. Had he been referring to the Roman province of Galatia, one would have expected reference to cities in that province. Acts speaks of a Pauline mission in four of those cities, Pisidian Antioch, Iconium, Lystra and Derbe, but never

OUTLINE OF GALATIANS   [9-1]

Greeting (1:1–5)

Curse against those who preach another gospel (1:6–10)

Proof of Paul's gospel based on past events (1:11–2:14)
  (a) Paul's call as apostle to the Gentiles (1:11–24)
  (b) Jerusalem agreement about the Gentile mission (2:1–10)
  (c) Antioch episode (2:11–14)

Thesis: Salvation only comes through faith in Christ (2:15–21)

Proofs from Galatians' experience, scripture and Christian tradition (3:1–4:31)
  (a) Galatians received the Spirit apart from the law (3:1–5)
  (b) Promise to Abraham is different from the law whose curse Christ removed (3:6–14)
  (c) The promise is fulfilled in Christ; the law is a later addition (3:15–20)
  (d) The law acts as "custodian" until all could become heirs of Abraham through Christ (3:21–29)
  (e) Gentiles were "under elemental spirits" until their adoption as heirs in Christ (4:1–7)
  (f) Galatians' experience of conversion and relationship with Paul (4:8–20)
  (g) Abraham's two sons (4:21–31)

Conclusion: Maintain your freedom in Christ (5:1–12)

Ethical applications: Freedom in the community (5:13–6:15)
  (a) Freedom is walking in the Spirit/Love (5:13–26)
  (b) Maxims for relations between Christians (6:1–10)
  (c) Final warning against Judaizers (6:11–15,17)

Final Blessing and Greetings (6:16,18)

speaks of those cities as "Galatia." Therefore, some scholars think that Paul must be referring to the ethnic area, the "Galatian country" of Acts 16:6. This area is located in the central highlands of Anatolia where tribes of Celts had settled in Hellenistic times. Paul's *O Galatai* in Gal 3:1 means "O Celts" or "O Gauls." Roman roads connected the three small cities in this area with such cities as Sardis, Nicomedia and Paul's home city of Tarsus. Paul mentions the fact that his mission in Galatia was the result of "weakness of the flesh" (4:13). He may have fallen ill while journeying through the region.

Paul does not have any immediate plans to return to the region (4:20). Nor does he indicate the source of his information about the crisis which has broken out in the Galatian churches. He indicates that persons are preaching a "different gospel" from the one he had preached to these Gentile converts (1:7–9). They are insisting that the Galatians be circumcised (5:2–12; 6:12) and observe certain Jewish holidays (4:10) and perhaps other provisions of the law, though Gal 5:3 and 6:13 suggest that they did not expect the Galatians to become Jews in the full sense. Paul insists that for the Galatians to seek to be "under the law" would be as bad as returning to the "slavery" to the various spirits of the universe they had worshiped as pagans (4:8–9). He is so disturbed by the problems in Galatia that Paul even omits the thanksgiving with which he usually begins his letters. Instead, he opens with a curse against anyone who would pervert the gospel message (1:6–10).

You can see from the outline of Galatians that much of the argument against the "Judaizing" position refers to past events which Paul claims vindicate the truth of his message. Salvation comes through faith in Jesus. Attempting to "add the law" to that faith is really a rejection of that salvation and a return to slavery (Gal 2:15–21; 3:1–5; 5:1)

During the course of his argument, Paul sets up a number of antitheses. These paired opposites lead the reader to negative associations with the proposed obedience to the law. Here are some of the most prominent:

faith in Jesus Christ	works of the law
live to God	died to the law
death of Christ	righteousness through the law
Spirit	flesh
blessing Abraham (promise)	curse of the law
freedom	slavery (to law; to "elemental spirits")
faith working through love	freedom used as occasion for desires of the flesh

You can see from our discussion of types of Jewish Christianity that Paul's treatment of the law would be controversial. Paul's opponents might even have used the example of Abraham's two sons to argue that the Galatians must adopt circumcision and some Jewish practices in order to be among the "free offspring" of Abraham, the descendants of Isaac.

Paul rejects that interpretation of the story. Isaac is the child of promise just as Christians who are born "according to the Spirit" are (Gal 4:28–29). He finds in the Genesis story an analogy with the present situation in which the "law-free" Christians are persecuted by those of the circumcision (Gal 4:29; cp. 5:11; 6:12).

Paul also invokes the early traditions of baptism in making his claim that "in Christ" differences between Jew and Gentile are abolished. Gal 3:27–28 apparently reflects a formula of the baptismal ritual. Other echoes of the formula are found in 1 Cor 12:13 and Col 3:11. It proclaims that baptism brings into being a "new human" in whom the fundamental divisions between humans—Jew/Gentile; slave/free; male/female—are eradicated. Many Jewish interpretations of Gen 1:26–27 thought of Adam as originally created "male/female." This androgynous Adam possessed the image of God as a "garment of light." After the fall, humans were divided into male and female, had become mortal, and the garment of light was replaced by the "garment of skin." Col 3:10 speaks of the renewal of the image of the creator. Paul holds that our transformation into the image of the heavenly Christ occurs at the resurrection (1 Cor 15:42–49). But the baptismal rite symbolizes the truth of this new reality. Gal 4:5–6 also refers to another aspect of the baptismal ceremony. The Christian cries in the Spirit, "Abba, Father!" The Spirit by which the new Christians proclaim their adoption as children of God is the Spirit of God's Son. Therefore, Paul insists that the Galatians know from their own experience that they are heirs to the promises of salvation. They do not need to add any additional religious rites to assure their salvation.

You will notice that the section of the letter devoted to ethical encouragement picks up themes from the body of the letter. Paul insists that the Christian, who is not under the law, will live a life which fulfills the positive elements of the law because it is based on love (Gal 5:14). Some scholars think that part of the appeal of the Judaizers' preaching lay in the ethical area. Gal 6:1 indicates that Christians had to be taught how to deal with those who have sinned. Paul expects Christians to handle this difficulty by mutual exhortation. He can even speak of such actions as fulfilling the "law of Christ." Christians who seek to walk by the Spirit do not need to supplement their freedom in Christ with some more formal allegiance to the law. Paul speaks of constantly seeking to "do good" (6:9). The actions prompted by the Spirit are not ones that can come under the law (5:22–23). Yet they are the ones that the Christian who has "been crucified with Christ" will seek out because Christians no longer live lives that are dominated by what Paul calls the "passions of the flesh" (5:24). You will notice that the examples which he gives of such passions are not limited to what we might think of as bodily desires. They also include a variety of "social sins" like jealousy, anger, enmity, strife, selfishness, divisiveness, envy and the like (5:19–21,26). Paul's vice list is "open-ended." The vices listed are only examples of the types of activity which come under this category.

Righteousness and Salvation History: Romans

Scholars are still uncertain about the relationship between the arguments in Rom and the actual situation of the church in Rome. Paul had not founded the church there. Nor had he ever visited it. He hopes to come to Rome after delivering the collection he has taken up among his Gentile churches for the poor in Jerusalem (Rom 1:10–13; 15:23–33). Paul then hopes to take his missionary work to Spain. He considers his work in the cities of Asia Minor and Greece to be completed. The greetings in chapter 16 include some twenty-five people. Prisca and Aquila (Rom 16:3) had been associated with Paul at Corinth (Acts 18:2–3) and then were living at Ephesus (1 Cor 16:19; Acts 18:11,18–19,24–26). Paul greets Epaenetus, the first convert in Asia (Rom 16:5), and writes a letter of recommendation for Phoebe, who is the patroness of the church in the eastern port of Corinth (Rom 16:1–2). Therefore, some scholars think that chapter 16 belongs to a copy of Rom that was sent to Christians at Ephesus as a farewell. (Acts 20:17–18 has Paul summon the leaders of the Ephesian community for a farewell.) According to this view, Romans is primarily a summary of Paul's experience in Asia Minor and Greece. Its concern with the problem of righteousness through faith and the relationship between the Christian movement and Judaism in God's plan is dictated by Paul's impending visit to Jerusalem.

Other scholars think that Prisca and Aquila, who had left Rome when Claudius expelled Jews for rioting at the name of "Chrestus," had returned to that city. The others whom Paul refers to as associates and heads of household churches (16:5,11,14,15) have also migrated to that city. A number of these people are Jewish converts to Christianity. Those who had been forced out of the city a number of years earlier may have found a Christian community quite different from the earlier churches based in Rome's extensive Jewish community. Paul's words to the Gentiles in Rom 11:13–32 warning against assuming a superiority to "unbelieving Israel" suggest a Christian community which is now largely Gentile. But Paul insists that God is the one who has given faith to those who have heard the gospel message. God is also behind the "hardening of Israel" and may yet "undo" that hardening. The Gentiles have benefited from the "disobedience" of Israel. But Israel remains the people of God's promise.

The situation of the Roman church has led Paul to reflect on the place of Israel in salvation history. You may also notice that he is much more positive about Israel in Rom 9–11 than he was in the allegory of Abraham's two sons in Gal 4:21–31. There he simply treated the present day Jerusalem and her "children" as slave descendants of Abraham. Only Christians are the children of promise, descendants of Isaac. Here, Paul is no less committed to the view that salvation comes to both Jew and Gentile through faith, but he leaves the story of Israel's salvation open to further saving acts of God. Paul's argument about the promise to Abraham in Rom 4 is also different. First, he argues that scripture bases Abraham's righteousness on his faith. Abraham had that faith before he was circumcised. Paul even allows that circumcision served as a sign of Abraham's faith (4:11). In this way, Abraham is father of both circumcised and uncircumcised believers (4:12). The example of God's promise to Abraham's descendants drops the idea of two sons, slave and free. Paul only tells the story of Sarah and Abraham's trust in the promise God made (4:16–24).

Paul still wrestles with the problem of the law in Romans. He opens the letter with an extensive argument indicating that all people, Jew and Gentile, are under sin and can only be saved through faith (Rom 1:16–3:31). Rom 3:24–26 uses a pre-Pauline formula to suggest how the death of Jesus "saves" a sinful humanity. You will notice that God is the primary actor in the drama. Scholars have suggested that this formula refers to ideas which had developed in connection with the death of the Maccabean martyrs. God responded to their faithfulness by forgiving the sins of the people and freeing the land from its oppressive rulers. This formula presents the death of Jesus as an "expiation" for all the sins of humanity, which God had not punished as they deserved. Paul insists that such a gift of righteousness to a sinful humanity does not destroy the law. It demonstrates God's righteousness and so upholds the law (3:26–31). Rom 5:6–11 returns to the theme of Christ's death for a sinful humanity. Here it is presented as an act which reconciles those who are "enemies" to God. It is also the basis of their future salvation.

You may notice from the outline of Romans that there is a structural parallel between the argument in chapters 5–8 and that in Gal 5. Paul follows his arguments that Christ has freed Christians from the law with reflection on what it means for the Christian to have "died with Christ" and to "live in the Spirit." Paul also makes use of references to shared convictions about baptism (Rom 6:3–5) and to the gift of the Spirit of God through which the "adopted children" call God "Abba" (Rom 8:14–17) as he had done in Gal 3:26–4:6.

OUTLINE OF ROMANS　　　　　　　*[9–2]*

Greeting (1:1–7)

Thanksgiving: Paul's desire to preach in Rome (1:8–15)

Thesis: God's salvation comes through faith for both Jew and Gentile (1:16–17)

Salvation through faith in Christ as God's response to the sinfulness of humanity (1:18–3:31)

Abraham as the ancestor of all believers (4:1–25)

As Adam's sin brought death to all, so Christ's sacrifice brings reconciliation with God and life for all (5:1–21)

The free gift of righteousness in Christ creates freedom, not increased sin (6:1–23)
  (a) Baptism is sharing in Christ's death so that we will share life with God (6:1–11)
  (b) "Dying" in baptism means dying to the passions which made us slaves to sin (6:12–23)

The law could not bring righteousness and life (7:1–25)
  (a) Human example: The law only binds those who are alive, not the Christian who has died with Christ and now lives by the Spirit (7:1–6)
  (b) Sin was able to pervert the law to awaken passions that led to death [Adam story implied] (7:1–12)
  (c) The law itself is good but the "fleshly" nature of humans makes it possible for sin to enslave us even when we want what is good [Paul reflecting on his story] (7:13–25)

Christ has freed us from bondage by making life in the Spirit possible (8:1–38)
  (a) Freedom is life in Christ/the Spirit and is opposed to the slavery of sin which works through the flesh (8:1–11)
  (b) Baptism is our adoption as children of God/Abba in the Spirit (8:12–17)
  (c) The Spirit helps us live in this world of creation waiting for its final redemption when we will have the image of Christ (8:18–30)
  (d) Nothing can separate us from the love of God in Christ (8:31–39)

Though Israel is rejecting Christ now, God may still bring the people of the promises and covenants to salvation (9:1–11:36)

Ethical instructions on mutual love, service and tolerance in the Christian community (12:1–15:13)

Paul's mission and plans to come to Rome (15:14–33)

Recommendation for Phoebe and greetings to fellow workers (16:1–16)

Final warning and greetings from Paul's associates (16:17–23)

[Doxology missing from many early manuscripts (16:25–27)]

You will also notice from the outline that Romans contains an extensive section of ethical exhortation (12:1–15:13). Many of the themes of this instruction, such as the necessity for Christians to love one another, the command to love and not retaliate against enemies, and the picture of the church as a body in which people exercise different ministries for the good of all (12:1–21) have parallels in earlier letters. But there are two new points, which some scholars think are linked to particular problems faced by the church at Rome.

The first new instruction occurs in Rom 13:1–7. Christians are instructed that they are to be subject to the governing authorities. Paul echoes a common theme in writers of the time when he insists that political authority has a divine origin. Its purpose is to see to it that good is rewarded and evil is punished. Since the Christian only seeks to do good, he or she has nothing to fear from governing authorities and should be obedient and respectful of the role God has given them. In this context Paul explicitly instructs the Christians that they are to pay taxes and revenues to the appropriate persons (vv. 6–7). This concrete detail is missing from the other New Testament example of this teaching (1 Pet 2:13–17). Some interpreters think that Paul may be concerned lest Christians become involved in the rebelliousness against customs duties that the emperor Nero had imposed in the city. Remember that the previous emperor Claudius had already expelled "Jews" from Rome for rioting at the name of Christ. Some of those expelled are greeted in Rom 16. Furthermore many of the Christians in the city may have been artisans, merchants and traders—exactly the persons most affected by the disputed levies. Paul makes obedience to the ruling authorities a matter of conscience (v. 5).

The second new element emerges in chapter 14. Paul speaks of Christians who differ over a number of religious customs: some obey dietary restrictions, others do not; some consider particular days holy, others do not (14:1–23). Though Paul himself does not think that the Jewish rules about clean and unclean foods need apply to Christians (v. 14), he argues that Christians should tolerate their mutual differences in love. The only thing that counts is whether or not someone is serving the Lord (vv. 6–9). Since the conclusion of the whole section speaks of Jesus welcoming both Jews and Gentiles (15:7–12), the differences to which Paul refers may have been those separating different "house churches" in the city of Rome. Some of these assemblies would have been made up of the original converts from within the Jewish community. Others are Gentile converts or fellow Jews who had worked with Paul in the mission to the Gentiles in Asia Minor and Greece. The first group may have continued to follow Jewish customs about kosher food and observance of the sabbath and other holidays. The second group would have considered itself free from such obligations. Paul is not trying to force all of the household churches in Rome into the same mold. Instead, he argues that as part of their service to the Lord, they should live together in harmony (15:5–6).

Summary

The specific problems of Jewish/Gentile Christianity which Paul faced in Galatians and Romans vanished as Christianity came to be a religion that was completely independent of its Jewish birthplace. Christians learned to read the Jewish scriptures as their own by looking as Paul did for ways in which those scriptures pointed to Christ. They also found there general examples of how to live which were not tied to the specific practices of Judaism. Certainly the "freedom in Christ" which Paul worked so hard to defend became a permanent possession of the Christian churches.

In the process Paul also came to understand the way in which sin could capture all people, even those who might consider themselves "righteous." He was able to see that our only salvation comes to us from God's love in Christ. We are not able to create salvation by our own efforts. At the same time Paul knew that God's love is not an excuse for a freedom which says that anything goes. He insisted that the baptized Christian really has received a gift of the Spirit and can live by the Spirit. We have seen that Paul knows that Christians will not always live up to their ideals. He tells the Galatians that they will have to correct each other and bear with each other's failings. He tells the Christians in Rome that they are not to judge and condemn one another.

Along with Paul's insights about sin and righteousness, Romans has important lessons to teach Christians for their daily relationships. Christians are not radical revolutionaries. They support the authorities and laws which are necessary to have order and goodness in society. Christians should also avoid thinking that the Jews and others who may reject Christ are automatically God's enemies. God may yet find a way to bring about the change of heart necessary for them to be heirs to the promises in Christ. Finally Paul's emphasis on the need for the different Christian house churches in Rome to accept each other should teach us how to relate to Christians who are of different churches. Their particular rules, customs and beliefs may be different from ours, but what is really important is that all Christian groups are seeking to serve the Lord.

STUDY QUESTIONS

Facts You Should Know

1. Describe the four different approaches to the conversion of Gentiles reflected in the New Testament.
2. What is the occasion for the writing of Galatians? How does the story of the conversion of king Izates help us understand the attraction of "Judaizing" among the Gentile converts of Galatia?
3. What is the relationship between Paul's teaching on "righteousness through faith in Christ" and the conflicts over the conditions under which Gentiles are to be included in the Christian communities?
4. What lessons does Paul expect the Galatians to draw from their experience of baptism and conversion?
5. Describe the situation in Paul's life at the time he writes Romans. What are his plans and expectations? How did those plans turn out?
6. Describe the situation in the Roman church as we see it reflected in Rom.

Things To Do

1. Read through Gal, making a list of as many different antitheses as you can find. What are some of the other words that appear in the negative column along with "law"? How might a Jew or Jewish Christian who faithfully observes the law as God's revelation respond to this set of associations?
2. Read Rom 1–8 and Gal 2:11–5:12. How is the treatment of Abraham different in the two letters? How does Paul argue for the universality

of sin and the necessity of righteousness through faith in Rom? How does he argue the case for righteousness through faith in Gal?

3. List all the allusions to baptism in Gal and Rom. How does Paul picture the lives of persons being changed by becoming part of Christ?

Things To Think About

1. What are the implications of Paul's picture of the place of Israel in salvation history in Rom 9–11 for relationships between Christians and Jews today?

2. What do Christians today have to learn from Paul's insistence upon mutual tolerance in Rom 14–15 and on the unity of all in Christ in Gal 3:16–18?

Chapter 10

DIVISIONS IN CORINTH

The Urban Environment of Corinth

Paul's Corinth was a city of "self-made men," descendants of the initial colonists who had turned Corinth into a thriving city in two generations. The city controlled two harbors, Cenchreae leading to Asia and Lechaeum to Italy, as well as the major land route from the Peloponnese. Merchants, envoys, pilgrims and other travelers passed through the city. Travelers used to eastern cities in which the population overflowed the city walls were impressed by the open-spaces within the city walls of Corinth, which even included wooded hills at the base of the city's acropolis.

We will hear of the city's temples and shops in Paul's letters to the Corinthians. Some of the Corinthian Christians apparently continued to attend banquets thrown by their friends in the dining rooms of such temples (1 Cor 10:18–21). Others worried about whether they could eat meat which had come from sacrifices at the temples and was being sold in the meat markets (*marcellum*—Paul uses the Latin word in Greek dress at 1 Cor 10:25). Paul himself labored at his trade of leather working in the shops of the city (1 Cor 9:3–19). Small shops were scattered throughout the city; others were clustered into blocks devoted to a particular trade. Excavations of the north market area show the shops to have been about 4 meters high and 4 meters deep and varying in width from 2.8 to 4 meters. Some had a door or window communicating with the next shop. The door was their only source of light. These shops would have been drafty and difficult to heat. Perhaps Paul's "big writing" (Gal 6:11) was caused by the effects of working long hours in cold, drafty conditions.

We will see that Paul constantly had to remind the Corinthian Christians that they should not seek to exalt themselves over others. Boasting about one's achievements and even expecting the apostles to demonstrate

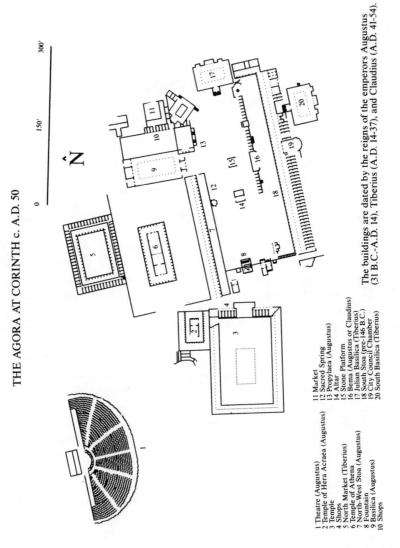

THE AGORA AT CORINTH c. A.D. 50

0   150'   300'

1 Theatre (Augustus)
2 Temple of Hera Acraea (Augustus)
3 Temple
4 Shops
5 North Market (Tiberius)
6 Temple of Athena
7 North-West Stoa (Augustus)
8 Fountain
9 Basilica (Augustus)
10 Shops

11 Market
12 Sacred Spring
13 Propylaea (Augustus)
14 Altar
15 Stone Platform
16 Bema (Augustus or Claudius)
17 Julian Basilica (Tiberius)
18 South Stoa (pre-146 B.C.)
19 City Council Chamber
20 South Basilica (Tiberius)

The buildings are dated by the reigns of the emperors Augustus (31 B.C.-A.D. 14), Tiberius (A.D. 14-37), and Claudius (A.D. 41-54).

their authority in "signs" such as persuasive speech, revelations and speaking in tongues turn out to be pervasive "sins" among the Corinthians. We can understand this tendency as one which is consistent with the city itself. Its leading families could include descendants of slaves and other colonists who would not have obtained such distinctions in an older city with an established aristocracy. We are not surprised, then, to find some people carrying this same attitude over into the church. An inscription says that the limestone pavement east of the city's theater was given by " . . . Erastus in return for his aedileship, at his own expense." This pavement dates before the mid-first century. Scholars think that the same Erastus is the one mentioned in Rom 16:23, where he is designated "treasurer of the city." That may have been an office held prior to becoming aedile. The aediles—two were elected each year—served under the two city magistrates. Their responsibilities included managing the public markets of the city.

Paul's readers might have had an image of the 14,000-seat theater flash through their minds when he spoke of the apostle as a "spectacle" (*theatron*) to the world (1 Cor 4:9). When Paul used athletic imagery to describe himself as an athlete in "training" (1 Cor 9:24–27), they could have imagined the great Isthmian games celebrated in honor of Poseidon. The games were held in the spring of A.D. 51. Paul himself might have been called upon to repair tents that housed those who traveled to the games. The officials in charge of these games had their offices in the upper agora of the city.

Finally, archeology also tells us something about the tensions that arose when Corinthian Christians gathered for the Lord's Supper (1 Cor 11:17–34). When the Corinthians met to celebrate the Lord's Supper, which took place during a meal, some people were eating well and even becoming drunk. Others, the poor members of the community, were being left out and going hungry. We know that in the society of the time a wealthy person might give a banquet in which his special friends were served good food and wine but lesser associates of the host or his friends would be served small portions of poor food and wine. Someone like Gaius (Rom 16:23) was wealthy enough to invite the whole church to meet at his house. Archeologists have excavated such houses. A meeting like this would have had to take place in the dining room which opened off the courtyard.

Only forty or fifty people could assemble at one time. The friends of the host would be able to recline in the dining area, but the others would be crowded sitting in the courtyard (1 Cor 14:30 indicates that they sat during such gatherings). It even appears that the host might have invited his friends to come before the other members of the church could arrive

(1 Cor 11:33). It is clear that the poorer members of the church were being treated like "second class" citizens. Paul cannot do anything about the space in which the church has to meet. But he can insist that the Lord's Supper is not like a private dinner party. All Christians are equal in the Lord. The Corinthians must see to it that their behavior treats all members of the church in this way. Otherwise, Paul says, the Corinthians are really mistreating the "body of Christ."

Paul and the Corinthian Community

Paul came up to Corinth from Athens, where he does not appear to have had much success (1 Thess 3:1). He spent about eighteen months working and preaching in Corinth before the controversy stirred up by his activities forced him to leave the city. It seems likely that by the time Paul wrote 1 Cor, there were groups of Christians meeting in different house churches in both the city itself and in its seaports. Since Rom 16:23 makes special mention of the fact that the "whole church" can meet in Gaius' house, the usual house church groups may have only comprised about twenty people.

1 Corinthians shows that Paul maintained contact with the church in Corinth. He had previously written them a letter which no longer survives (1 Cor 5:9). He has also heard about divisions between Christians at Corinth from members of "Chloe's household," presumably her slaves or freedmen traveling on business (1 Cor 1:11). The Corinthians themselves have written to Paul asking him to resolve some questions (1 Cor 7:1). And Paul has dispatched Timothy, who will arrive after the letter Paul is writing (1 Cor 16:10). But the Corinthians have also learned about Christianity from the preaching of another missionary, Apollos (1 Cor 3:5–4:7). Acts 18:24–28 identifies him as a Jew from Alexandria who had been converted at Ephesus by Priscilla and Aquila. He had become known for his powerful preaching. Some of the Corinthians have formed "parties" around the names of famous apostles—Paul, Apollos and Peter (Cephas, 1 Cor 1:11–13). We do not have any direct evidence that Peter had preached in Corinth as Paul and Apollos had, so scholars think that the "Peter party" may have formed because of reports of that famous apostle brought by others. Paul also speaks sarcastically of some who claim that they belong to a "Christ" group.

Just as he did not approve of divisions at the Lord's Supper, so Paul does not approve of these divisions either, even though one group claims to be his supporters. He insists that it is not possible to divide up Christ. Furthermore, only Christ is responsible for our salvation. The various apostles are just servants who will eventually be judged on the basis of the quality of their labor in preaching the gospel.

Episodes of division and misunderstanding continued throughout Paul's association with the Corinthians. Some people may have thought that Paul was responsible for the fact that Apollos had not returned to preach there. Paul claims that he had urged Apollos to go, but Apollos had decided it was not the right time (16:12). Some people at Corinth objected to Paul's working at a trade. In antiquity, the life of such a person was considered disgraceful, especially one like leather-working that meant being confined in a small shop and working "like a slave" for an uncertain livelihood. We know that Paul was not able to support himself entirely. The church at Philippi sent him assistance when he was preaching in Thessalonica and again when he was in prison. The Corinthians also know that other apostles were supported entirely by the donations of those to whom they preached. The rich Christians in Corinth may have even felt insulted that Paul continued to work at a slavish trade rather than accept money from them. Paul devotes 1 Cor 9 to this topic. He admits that most of the other apostles like Peter receive support for themselves and their families. He also says that both the Old Testament and Jesus teach that it is right for someone who is preaching God's word to be supported by it. But Paul does not think that "right" means that he has no choice in the matter. Paul says that he could never help preaching the gospel. God's call makes it impossible for him to do otherwise. But he can show that he is also preaching out of his "own free will" by giving up his "right" to demand support from the church and working at his trade instead. That way he can preach the gospel "for free." Even though laboring adds to the hardships that Paul suffers (cf. 1 Cor 4:12), Paul's willingness to take on this suffering means that he can "boast" about the freedom with which he preaches (1 Cor 9:15–18).

You can see that Paul's relationship with the Corinthians is very complicated. Since he is the founder of the community, he is responsible for it just as a "father" is responsible for the behavior and well-being of his children (1 Cor 4:14–21). He has authority over the community, which he exercises through his letters and his associates. Paul also has friends and supporters at Corinth. But Paul is not in control of everything that happens in the different house churches. Nor is he the only source of missionary preaching, since other Christians traveling though Corinth bring news of what other apostles like Peter do, and other missionaries, like Apollos, even came to preach in the community.

When we turn from 1 Cor to 2 Cor, we find an even more complicated situation. Some of the concrete problems about the Lord's Supper and spiritual gifts like tongues and prophecy and the questions about marriage may have been solved by 1 Cor. At least they are no longer mentioned. Nor are the "parties" attached to Paul, Apollos and Peter. But new problems have arisen and some old suspicions remain. Accusations surround Paul's support. These may have been fueled by charges that the collection for the poor at Jerusalem (1 Cor 16:1–4) was really going to the apostle (2 Cor 11:7–11; 12:14–18). The collection had not yet been completed. 2 Cor 8–9 makes an extended appeal to the Corinthians and those in the churches in the province of Achaia to imitate the generosity of the Christians in Macedonia. During a visit that Paul had paid to Corinth some incident had "pained" the apostle and evoked an anguished and tearful letter from him (2 Cor 2:1–4). But Paul had also cancelled another visit he planned to make to Corinth, which seems to have led to accusations about his integrity (1:15–24). 2 Cor 2:5–11 and 7:8–16 indicate that reconciliation between Paul and the Corinthians had taken place. Paul's letter and a subsequent visit by Titus have caused a change of heart. In addition, one member of the community, apparently responsible for the affront to the apostle, had been disciplined. Paul now wants the Corinthians to forgive the man and receive him back in affection.

But this situation of reconciliation does not fit with the bitter sarcasm of 2 Cor 10–13. There Paul rejects charges against himself and his mission that have been made by outsiders whom he refers to as "false apostles," "super-apostles" who boast in their spiritual achievements (10:12; 11:4–6,12–15; 12:11–12). Paul says that he is about to come to Corinth for the third time. If the Corinthians do not change their attitude, they will find Paul a stern father (12:14; 13:1–2,10–11). Many scholars think that 2 Cor 10–13 was actually taken from the "letter of tears." The cancelled visit would be the one referred to in these verses. But other scholars think that these chapters cannot be from the letter referred to as the "letter of tears," since they reflect an impassioned defense of the apostle against the claims of outside "apostles" who are trying to discredit the divine authorization of Paul's ministry. They do not refer to the painful visit. According to this view, the reconciliation of the earlier chapters has again broken apart. Paul must face yet another challenge to his apostleship.

Many scholars think that 2 Cor 1–9 was not from a single letter either. It is easy to see that chapters 8 and 9 refer to the collection for the poor at Jerusalem. 2 Cor 8:16–24 tells the community that Titus and those Paul is sending with him are authorized to complete the collection. The trustworthiness of these men guarantees that the money is being used for honorable purposes (2 Cor 8:20). You will notice that none of the defensiveness of chapters 10–13 occurs in this section. Since Paul refers to the example of the Macedonians twice (8:1–6, 9:1–5) and in the second instance speaks of "Achaia," the province of which Corinth was the capital, in slightly different terms than he speaks of the addressees in 8:6, the two chapters might even be from separate appeals. If so, the first is addressed to churches in Corinth, the second to the province as a whole. You may also notice some "breaks" in chapters 1–7. Paul took up the theme of reconciliation in 2:1–13 only to break off into a lengthy description of true apostolic ministry in 2:14–7:1. With 7:2–16 the tone of rejoicing and reconciliation as well as the narrative of events leading to reconciliation returns. But we also notice that 6:11–13 takes the form of an appeal to the Corinthians, which is picked up at 7:2. We lose sight of that appeal because

---

CORINTHIAN CORRESPONDENCE   *[10–1]*

Letters between Paul and the Christians at Corinth

(1) **"Previous Letter" (cf. 1 Cor 5:9):** May have contained exhortation to "holiness" like that of the fragment in 2 Cor 6:14–7:1

(2) **1 Corinthians**

(3) **"Letter of Tears" (cf. 2 Cor 2:3–4; 7:5,12):** May have contained 2 Cor 10–13

(4) **On Paul's Apostleship (2 Cor 2:14–6:13, 7:2–4?):** May have been an exposition of true apostleship against the claims of false apostles such as those mentioned in 2 Cor 10–13, since Paul opposes those who bring (and demand) "letters of recommendation" (cf. 2 Cor 3:1–3)

(5) **Letter of Reconciliation (2 Cor 1:1–2:13; 7:5–16):** Many scholars think that this letter also included the piece on apostleship and an appeal to complete the collection

(6) **Letter(s) of Appeal for the Collection (2 Cor 8–9):** The addressees are asked to complete the collection, which had been begun a year ago (9:1; cf. 1 Cor 16:1–2)

(7) **Against the "Super-Apostles" (2 Cor 10–13):** If these chapters are not from the "letter of tears," then they suggest accusations against Paul by traveling apostles [Paul's collection appeals could have refueled the debate about his finances and way of life—2 Cor 11:7–11; 12:13–18]

Paul writes Romans from Corinth before his departure for Jerusalem with the collection for the poor (Rom 15:25–28; 16:1–2,23)

of a section of dualistic exhortation that tells Christians to have nothing to do with unbelievers. These exhortations seem very unusual for a Paul who had told the Corinthians in 1 Cor 5:9–13 that he did not mean for them to avoid sinful non-Christians or they would have to "go out of the world." Is 2 Cor 6:14–7:1 something from that earliest letter of Paul which had led to the misunderstanding? Or is it from another type of Christianity altogether? It could easily be a piece of Jewish Christian preaching which sought to encourage Christians to isolate themselves from the pagan world and its evils just as God had told the Jewish people to do.

If all of the "pieces" which now make up 2 Cor came from different letters, we have quite an anthology of Paul's dealings with the community. In these days of xerox machines and "desktop publishing" with personal computers, we find it difficult to understand why churches would have created "anthologies" like 2 Cor and Phil from the letters which Paul had sent them. But we should also remember that all letters and books had to be hand-copied. People usually employed others to do the actual writing of their letters (cf. Rom 16:22). The loss of the "previous letter" and perhaps also of the "letter of tears" shows us that not all of Paul's letters survived. Putting sections of letters together may have helped save others from being lost. However, it is difficult for us today to know whether all the disjointed sections of such letters are from separate documents or simply represent breaks in Paul's composition.

Church as Body of Christ: 1 Corinthians

1 Cor deals with a variety of problems in the community. Ordinarily the thanksgiving section of Paul's letters mentions virtues like faith, hope and love. When we read 1 Cor 1:4–9, we find a different situation. Paul speaks of the Corinthian concern with "speech," "knowledge" and "spiritual gifts." The thanksgiving assigns these gifts their proper place. They are gifts of God for the purpose of sustaining and building the community so that it will be "guiltless" before God's judgment. 1 Cor 1:9 reminds the Corinthians that God called them into fellowship in Jesus Christ.

Many of the problems which Paul corrects can be traced back to an individualistic use of "knowledge," "speech" and "spiritual gifts." The Corinthians valued individuals who could demonstrate their spiritual powers in gifts like speaking in tongues and even persuasive preaching. Some Corinthians claimed that their "knowledge" of the mysteries of salvation in Christ meant that they were free of the restraints of this world. Paul accuses the Corinthians of "boasting" about a man who had married his stepmother. They should be sad and expel such a sinful person from the community (5:1–6). Others think that whatever they do with their bodies doesn't matter. Paul rejects their claim that it is "all right" for a Christian whose body belongs to Christ to have sex with a prostitute (6:12–20). Some Corinthians thought that since Paul himself was unmarried and thought that was a good way to serve the Lord, it was better for Christians not to have sex at all. They may even have been breaking up marriages and engagements to take on this new life. Paul insists that God gave humans marriage as the proper way to express their sexuality. It is not wrong for Christians to marry. But God also gives some people the special gift of remaining single in order to devote themselves completely to the gospel. However, those who are married or feel a strong desire to be married cannot claim to have been given that gift. So they ought to be married.

Paul also reminds the Corinthians that Jesus had spoken against divorce. He does think that Jesus' words do not cover every case. Christians should not seek a divorce to live an ascetic life. Nor should they seek a divorce out of fear that living with a non-Christian spouse would make them "unholy." If anything, the Christian will make both the spouse and the children holy. But if a Christian is divorced by a non-Christian spouse, then Paul thinks that Jesus would certainly have said that the Christian is free to marry again (7:1–40).

As Paul works through the different issues that come up in 1 Corinthians, he keeps returning to the idea that Christians should always see

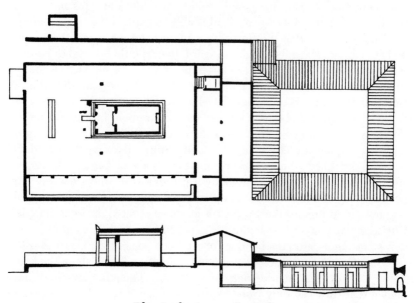

The Asclepion at Corinth.

themselves as part of a larger whole. We are not just isolated individuals who are free to do whatever we want. We have to think about how our actions affect other people. We have to be particularly concerned about actions which might cause them harm. Some actions which would be acceptable in one situation are not "allowed" by this principle in another. Remember the meat markets. Well some Christians felt that they should not eat any meat that had been used in a sacrifice to a pagan idol. Others argued that Christians know that the gods and goddesses are nothing. Slaughtering an animal in a rite devoted to one of them cannot make the meat different. Paul agrees that the meat itself is just meat. But he also recognizes that for some people who had been converted from such pagan rites it might be difficult to separate eating sacrificial meat from the feelings of worship they had once held for the pagan gods. These people could be drawn back into paganism. So Paul tells the "enlightened" Christians who have "knowledge" of the true God that their knowledge isn't worth anything without love for the others. They can buy any meat they want and eat it. But in a situation where another person's faith might be destroyed if they eat such meat their knowledge has to give way to love and they have to refrain (8:1–13; 10:23–11:1).

Paul develops an important symbol for the church in 1 Corinthians: the church is the "body of Christ." Some ancient philosophers described political communities as a "body" of which the citizens were members. The metaphor showed that people could have different roles and still act together in a harmonious way. Paul is able to expand the image because Christians believe that the Spirit links them together as members of the body of Christ. The gifts which the Spirit gives should be used to build up the whole community. They are not opportunities for individuals to exalt themselves over others. Paul emphasizes this point by reminding the Corinthians that the gift they should seek above all others is love (13:1).

The imagery of "body of Christ" links a number of themes together. The reason Christians do not abuse their sexuality is that they recognize that their bodies are also places for God's Spirit. Because the bread and wine of the Lord's Supper represent the "body of Christ," Christians should recognize that the same body is present in all who are at the Supper. They should not treat some members as "second class." They should also not try to mix up the Lord with feasts celebrated in pagan temples. Christians may accept invitations to a pagan friend's home (10:27), but a Christian cannot attend a banquet offered in a pagan temple (10:14–22).

In 1 Cor 15 Paul deals with another kind of confusion about the body. Some Corinthians are denying resurrection. Though they must have known that they can only worship Jesus as Lord if Jesus has been resurrected (15:3–8), the Corinthians apparently saw no connection between

OUTLINE OF 1 CORINTHIANS   *[10–2]*

Greeting (1:1–3)

Thanksgiving: Spiritual gifts to keep the community blameless (1:4–9)

Against divisions in the church (1:10–31)

True wisdom found in the cross (2:1–16)

Imitate the apostles: God's fellow-workers (3:1–4:21)

Against immorality tolerated by the Corinthians (5:1–6:20)
  (a) Man married to stepmother to be expelled (5:1–13)
  (b) Christians should not have lawsuits against each other (6:1–11)
  (c) Do not unite the body, the temple of the Spirit, with a prostitute (6:12–20)

Questions raised by the Corinthians (7:1–11:1)
  (a) Some are called to marriage and others to remain single for the sake of the kingdom (7:1–40)
  (b) Christians will not seek divorce (7:10–16)
  (c) Christians follow God's will in any way of life (7:17–24)
  (d) On meat offered to idols (8:1–13)
  (e) Paul's example: Give up rights for the sake of others (9:1–27)
  (f) Do not participate in cults at pagan temples (10:1–22)
  (g) Use your freedom for the good of others (10:23–11:1)

Questions related to worship (11:2–14:40)
  (a) Suitable dress for male and female prophets in the assembly (11:2–16)
  (b) Show unity with all at the Lord's Supper (11:17–34)
  (c) God gives different spiritual gifts to create unity in the body of Christ (12:1–31)
  (d) Love is the highest gift Christians can pursue (13:1–13)
  (e) Rules for prophecy and speaking in tongues (14:1–40)

Christians believe they will be raised like Jesus (15:1–58)

Gather the collection for Jerusalem (16:1–4)

Paul's future travel plans (16:5–12)

Respect those who serve among you (16:13–18)

Final greetings from Paul and his associates (16:19–24)

what happened to Jesus and what would happen to Christians. Paul insists that the whole point of all the apostles' preaching was that Christians would be raised as Jesus had been (15:12–28). He reminds those who think that it would be impossible to raise up the physical body that resurrection will not mean jumping back into the bodies we have now. It will mean being changed so that we have a new, spiritual body which carries the image of the heavenly Christ (15:35–58).

Division and Reconciliation: 2 Corinthians

We have already discussed the various sections of 2 Corinthians. We have seen that Paul faced serious challenges to his position as an apostle. As a result of these challenges 2 Cor contains two lengthy sections on the true nature of apostleship. 2 Cor 10–13 is a passionate self-defense in the heat of the struggle. 2 Cor 2:14–7:4 presents Paul as the apostle of a "new covenant" which God writes in the Spirit on the hearts of those who believe. A letter of reconciliation in which Paul instructs the Corinthians to forgive the man who had offended Paul provides the framework in which an early editor set these two pieces along with the appeal that Paul wrote for the collection at Jerusalem.

Scholars look for hints about the views of Paul's opponents in 2 Cor. It is difficult to draw a clear picture of their charges, since we are not always certain when Paul is representing actual accusations and when he is mocking the opposition. We know from 2 Cor 1:17–19 that Paul's cancelled travel plans had led to the charge that he was insincere, vacillating and perhaps even deceitful. Paul insists that neither he nor his associates have ever acted out of such motives. God is the source of both Paul's apostolic authority and the Corinthians' faith. They should know that such accusations are false. Though Paul cancelled his visit, his harsh "letter of tears" had brought the Corinthians around so that Paul is able to speak of a joyous reconciliation that will even include forgiveness for the person who had offended the apostle during his second visit (2:1–11).

Outside apostles carried with them letters of recommendation. They may have even suggested that Paul's apostleship was deficient because he did not have such letters. Paul argues that the Corinthians themselves should be a sufficient letter of recommendation. Their faith is a "letter" which all people should be able to read. Paul does not need to have written documents (3:1–3). [You may remember that Paul praised the Thessalonians for the way in which their faith had become known to others (1 Thess 1:7–9).] Along with a concern for letters of recommendation, Paul accuses

OUTLINE OF 2 CORINTHIANS [10–3]

Greetings (1:1–2)

Blessing God for comforting the apostle in his sufferings (1:3–11)

Reconciliation between Paul and the Corinthians (1:12–2:13; 7:5–16)

Paul's ministry: Ambassador for a new covenant (2:14–6:13; 7:2–4)
  (a) The apostle relies on God who writes with the Spirit in the hearts of believers (2:14–3:3)
  (b) The new covenant in the Spirit is not like the Mosaic covenant: it reveals God's glory (3:4–18)
  (c) The truth is only hidden from those who do not hear the call to believe (4:1–6)
  (d) The weakness of the suffering apostle demonstrates the glory of God which we will share in the resurrection (4:7–5:10)
  (e) Everything the apostle does is to call people to be reconciled with God in Christ (5:11–21)
  (f) The apostle is even willing to suffer to bring people to Christ (6:1–13; 7:2–4)

[Fragment on holiness as separation from the world (6:14–7:1), possibly non-Pauline]

Appeals for the Jerusalem collection (chapters 8–9)

Against the "super-apostles" (chapters 10–13)
  (a) Paul rejects their standard of boasting in human accomplishments (10:1–18)
  (b) Do not be led astray by their flattery (11:1–6)
  (c) Against suspicions raised by Paul's working and the collection (11:7–15)
  (d) True sign of an apostle is God's power manifested in suffering and weakness (11:16–12:13)
  (e) Paul's love for the Corinthians (12:14–21)
  (f) Paul's plans for a third visit to Corinth (13:1–10)

Final greetings (13:11–14)

these "super-apostles" of a false competitiveness, comparing themselves to one another in signs of their spiritual power, and also making comparisons unfavorable to Paul (10:12; 11:5–6, 18–20). They may have claimed that Paul did not have the spiritual revelations that they did. Paul answers by speaking of a "heavenly revelation" in an ironic manner. It doesn't matter what visions he has seen or what angelic languages he has heard. The true sign of Paul's apostleship is his consistent suffering and weakness for the sake of the gospel. This suffering is a "sign" that God would not even take away (12:1–10). Some even attacked Paul's letters. They claimed that the letters were a way of "lording it over" the Corinthians from a distance. But when Paul was actually present, he showed himself to be weak and not strong (10:8–10).

Paul does not deny that he seeks to correct the Corinthians and thus to exercise authority over their faith. Paul claims that God has given him the Corinthian community as part of the "assigned territory" for his mission (10:13–16). Unlike the outsiders, Paul sticks to his "territory" and does not try to "boast" of work which someone else has done. Paul also uses parental images to describe the special relationship between himself and the churches God has given him. He is like a father who is responsible for seeing that his daughter is a "pure virgin" for her husband (11:2). He is like a parent working hard to save up money for his children (12:14–15). His heart goes out to these "children," and he hopes that they will find a place for him in their hearts in return (6:11–13).

All of these images of the apostle as a loving parent who is willing to work and suffer for his "children" are grounded in an understanding of what it means to be an "apostle of reconciliation." Paul describes the new covenant in Christ as one in which the glory of God is made manifest. Every believer, who sees that glory, will also be changed into the "glory of Christ, who is the image of God" (3:7–4:4). But the apostle who is the minister of this new covenant should never think that the light and knowledge which he brings to others somehow "rubs off" on its messenger. Quite the opposite, the apostle shares in the "death of Jesus" through weakness and suffering (4:7–18). Like all Christians, Paul is confident that he will share in a glorious future, but that future is in heaven with Christ (5:1–10). He reminds the Corinthians that we cannot judge Christ "from a human point of view" or we would not see that in Christ's death God reconciles the world to himself (5:16–21). Anyone who looked at Paul from a "human point of view" without understanding the gospel would only see the weakness, suffering, poverty, punishment and "bad reputation" of the apostle. One would never suspect that the apostle is God's "co-worker" (6:1–10).

Summary

The Corinthian letters provide us with our most extensive look at Paul's ministry in a single community. We often wish we knew more about the Christians to whom these letters were addressed as we catch glimpses of their struggles and divisions. The Corinthians appear to reflect the city from which they come, a "new city" without many of the established ways of old cities; a thriving, mobile seaport; a city of diverse people who are often "on the move." Some of the problems which surface in Corinth seem quite "dated." Most of us are not likely to be invited to celebrate a banquet in honor of a pagan god or even to require rules for how men and women prophets should dress or for the conduct of speaking in tongues. We no longer assemble for worship in the house of a wealthy patron or celebrate the Lord's Supper in the context of a banquet. We are not likely to encounter Christian preachers who advocate breaking up a marriage so that the man can follow the "noble" practice of "not touching a woman" (1 Cor 7:1).

Even in these cases we see Paul looking for ways in which love and unity can be made the primary experiences of the community. We do still have lawsuits with one another, though we are not likely to call upon the churches to find people to mediate disputes between Christians and so keep them out of the civil courts (6:1–8). We are certainly as confused as the Corinthians were about the body, sexuality and marriage. Most of us have experienced divorce in our families or among our friends. Most of us know the pressure generated by the idea that the body can be used for anything, so that "date rape," incest and sexual abuse of young children are increasing problems in our society. To all these, not to mention our various forms of drug and alcohol abuse, the same advice Paul gave the Corinthians applies: the body is "for the Lord" and is to be treated like the "temple of the Spirit" which it is.

Paul has also given us a number of images for the church. The most significant is that of the "body of Christ." We have to remember that symbol when we are torn apart by conflicts and even competing "spiritual gifts." Paul gives concrete examples from his own life and suffering as an apostle of what it means to put love and the building up of others first. But the most important example stands behind Paul's own apostleship, the example of Christ. Paul never lets us forget that the cross is a "paradox," not an example of human wisdom or power. As a result the life of those who are Christ's servants must also image the glory hidden in weakness that we find in Christ.

STUDY QUESTIONS

Facts You Should Know

1. Describe the controversy over eating "meat sacrificed to idols" and participating in meals in the pagan temples in 1 Cor. What were the different views held by the Corinthians? How did Paul seek to resolve the conflict?

2. Describe the tensions which arose over the celebration of the Lord's Supper. How did those divisions reflect the social customs of the time? What is Paul's answer in his instruction to the Corinthians?

3. How does Paul use the metaphors of "body as temple of the Holy Spirit" and the community as "body of Christ" to deal with the following problems in Corinth: (a) sexual morality; (b) relationships between Christians at the Lord's Supper; (c) differences in "gifts" within the community; (d) the destiny of Christians after death?

4. What accusations were raised against Paul's apostleship in 1 Cor and 2 Cor? How does Paul use the imagery of the crucified Christ to respond to such charges?

5. Describe the various divisions in 2 Cor which some scholars think came from separate letters.

Things To Do

1. Find as many references to "body" in 1 Cor as you can. List those which refer to the physical body, those which speak of the community as a "body," and those which speak of "body" in connection with Christ.

2. Find as many references to the "weakness of the apostle" in 1 and 2 Cor as you can. How is "weakness" understood to be a "sign" of true apostolic ministry in Paul?

3. Find as many exhortations to "love" as the principle of relationships between Christians in 1 and 2 Cor as you can. What problems does Paul invoke the principle of love to resolve?

Things To Think About

1. Are we more like Paul or the Corinthians in our evaluations of persons, status, power and success?

2. Is our attitude toward the "body" shaped by any Christian symbols or expectations (e.g. the "body" as seed of the "body" we are to have in the resurrection)? Or do we tend to agree with those Paul opposes at Corinth that the body is an indifferent "tool" for humans to use as they will?

Chapter 11

UNIVERSALIZING PAUL'S MESSAGE

Pauline Christianity in Colossians and Ephesians

Colossae was famed for wool-working and cloth-dying, especially for a dark red wool known as *colossinum*. Ephesus, one hundred and ten miles to the west, was a major port city in Asia Minor. According to Acts 18:19–21, Paul sailed here from Corinth with Prisca and Aquila. Paul returned to Ephesus on subsequent missionary journeys. He was there when he wrote 1 Cor (1 Cor 16:8) and was probably imprisoned there when he wrote Phil and Phlm. Many scholars think that Paul's "fellow prisoner," Epaphras (Phlm 23), served as Paul's representative to Colossae and the neighboring cities of Laodicea (see Col 2:1; 4:13–16) and Hieropolis. You will notice that the thanksgiving in Col attributes the recipients' faith to Epaphras (Col 1:7–8).

According to Col 1:24 and 4:3–4,10, the apostle is once more in prison. If you compare Col with the letters from Paul's earlier imprisonment, Phlm and Phil, you will notice that this situation is different. In those letters, Paul expected to be released and resume his work among those to whom he writes. Col never speaks of either release, though Paul's imprisonment might still be an "open door" for the word (Col 4:3), or of any future visits by the apostle. Col 2:1–2 refers to those who have never seen the apostle. The letter takes great pains to emphasize the growth in faith which its recipients can experience through the ministry of persons who are Paul's associates (Col 1:7–8; 4:7–17) and by sharing letters with other churches in the region (4:16). Archippus, another person known to us from Phlm 2, is apparently being charged to undertake some form of permanent ministry in the area (Col 4:17). You have probably already figured out one reason for this new tone: Paul must be imprisoned in Rome.

191

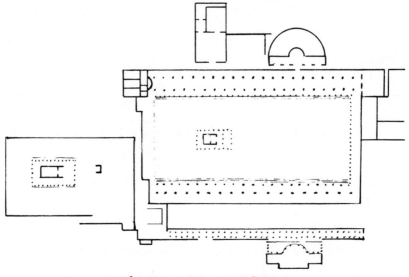

The Upper Square, Ephesus.

A severe earthquake was reported in the region of Colossae in A.D. 60 or 61. Colossae was already declining in contrast to Laodicea and Hieropolis before the earthquake. Afterward it seems to have become an insignificant town. Since Col shows no awareness of these events, many scholars think that it was written before A.D. 60/61.

Although Col follows the general outline of a Pauline letter (see page 193), many of the expressions and images do not quite sound like the Paul we are familiar with from the letters written during his missionary work in Asia Minor and Greece. Look for some of these differences in your reading. There is only one reference to the Spirit (Col 1:8). Instead of speaking about the perfection which Christians will have when Christ comes at the judgment (see Phil 3:20–21), Col speaks of Christians participating in a life oriented toward the Christ who is now in heaven (Col 1:5,12–14; 3:1–4). Notice that in Col 3:1 the author speaks of Christians as having been raised with Christ already and in 3:4 of Christians appearing with Christ in glory. Paul's earlier letters speak of some Christians coming with the Lord (1 Thess 4:16–17) and those who are alive being transformed (1 Cor 15:51–52). Look for the word "church" in Col. In Paul's earlier letters he spoke of "church" to refer to Christians gathered together in local communities just as he does when he refers to the "church" which meets in Nympha's

OUTLINE OF COLOSSIANS   *[11–1]*

Greeting (1:1–2)

Thanksgiving: Faith, hope and love of the community (1:3–8)

Prayer for the well-being of the community (1:9–14)

The exalted Christ as source of our heavenly salvation (1:15–2:23)
  (a) Hymn to Christ as image of God and Savior (1:15–20)
  (b) Apostle's ministry reveals God's salvation (1:21–2:7)
  (c) Against those who preach a false salvation based on "angelic worship" (2:8–23)

Living the Christian life (3:1–4:6)
  (a) Holiness manifests the "new creation" which Christians have become in baptism (3:1–17)
  (b) "Household code": Behavior of wives and husbands, children and fathers, slaves and masters (3:18–4:1)
  (c) Continue in prayer and wise conduct toward outsiders (4:2–6)

Concluding greetings (4:7–18)
  (a) Tychicus and Onesimus will report on what has happened to Paul (4:7–9)
  (b) Greetings from associates of Paul (4:10–14)
  (c) Greetings to those at Laodicea and instructions for an exchange of letters between churches (4:15–18)

house in Col 4:15. But here "church" takes on a new, universal sense. It is pictured as a cosmic "body" with the heavenly Christ as its head (Col 1:18).

Perhaps you have also noticed that Christ's death is only mentioned in the hymnic passage of Col 1:20 and very indirectly in Col 2:14. The elliptical way of speaking in that passage is very different from Paul's own emphasis on his preaching as "portraying Christ crucified" (Gal 3:1). It is also very peculiar for a Paul who gloried in his sufferings as ways of participating in the death of Christ (see 1 Cor 4:6–13; 2 Cor 11:21–29; Gal 6:14–17; Phil 3:10). Instead of looking to Christ crucified for the meaning of apostolic suffering, Col 1:24–29 makes the sufferings of the apostle an addition to those of Christ for the sake of the cosmic body of Christ, the church.

These verses also picture Paul as a triumphant revealer of the "mysteries" that God had kept hidden for ages. Elsewhere Paul either speaks of "mysteries" as the paradox of Christ's crucifixion (1 Cor 2:6–13) or as the "endtime" events of salvation (1 Cor 15:51–52; Rom 11:25–27).

Although Col 1:27, 2:11–15 and 3:11 speak of the salvation of the Gentiles "in Christ," a central theme of Paul's mission, the other pole, "the Jews" or "Israel," has disappeared. So have the links which Paul forged between his insights about "righteousness through faith" and the Old Testament. While it is not entirely impossible that Paul's theological imagery and his way of speaking about Christ, the church and his own mission had changed during his imprisonment, many scholars doubt that so many little details would be different. Instead they suggest that Col was composed by one of the associates mentioned in the letter, perhaps Timothy or Epaphras. Since they had worked with Paul for such a long time, they knew his general way of writing. The danger of false teachers (Col 2:4,8) and the impending death of the apostle made it imperative that the churches which had been left behind in Asia Minor be instructed and encouraged by apostolic letters. If Paul was still alive when Col was sent, he may have been able to add the final greeting (Col 4:18).

Ephesians: A Circular Letter?

When we turn to Ephesians the questions of authorship become even more complex. Col ended by instructing churches in the region to exchange letters. That was a way of saying that the apostle's letters were not just for one church and its problems. They were for the instruction of all churches. Eph may have originally been written as a circular letter. Our oldest manuscripts do not have any particular church named in the opening greetings. Nor does the conclusion refer to any particular people. The only one mentioned is Tychicus, and those verses (Eph 6:21–22) appear to have been copied from the conclusion to Col (Col 4:7–8). Now compare the opening of Eph (1:1–2) with Col (1:1–2). They are almost identical except that Eph does not mention Paul's associate Timothy, and its author is more "Pauline" in expression by adding the reference to "our Lord Jesus Christ" at the end of verse 2.

You can see from these simple examples something that a more complicated comparison of the two letters will also show. The person who wrote Eph was very familiar with Paul's language but that person also reworked parts of Col for this letter. Chart 11-2 gives the main parallels between the two letters:

PARALLELS BETWEEN EPHESIANS AND COLOSSIANS

[11-2]

Ephesians	Colossians
1:1–2	1:1–2
1:15–17	1:3–4,9–10
2:5–6	2:12–13
3:1–13	1:24–2:5
4:17–32	3:5–14
5:19–20	3:16–17
5:22–6:9	3:18–4:1
6:18–20	4:2–4
6:21–22	4:7–8

In some cases, Eph has taken the framework of a Col passage and expanded it considerably. We can see that Eph emphasizes the theme of the church as the body of Christ. For example, Col 1:19 and 2:9–10 describe Christ as the one in whom the "fullness" (*pleroma*) of God dwells. Eph understands that "fullness" to be embodied in the church as the body of Christ (1:23; 3:19–21; 4:10–13). Compare the two examples of the "household code" (Col 3:18–4:1 and Eph 5:22–6:9). You will notice that Col thinks that the code might address situations in which only one member of a pair is Christian. Eph, on the other hand, has given a Christian cast to the whole section. Marriage is compared to Christ and the church. Children are reminded of the ten commandments. Slaves are to view their masters as "the Lord," and masters are to remember that they too have a "Lord."

In reading through Eph, you may also notice that the image of Paul as the heroic martyr is emphasized even more strongly than it was in Col. The Gentile audience of this letter (1:11–14; 2:1–3,11–22; 3:1; 4:17–19; 5:8) is reminded that Paul's suffering is on their behalf (3:1,13). The author wants them to be inspired by the example of Paul's suffering (4:1). Following Paul's own example, Col refers to the apostle's prayer for the churches (Col 1:9; 2:1). Eph gives actual examples of Paul's prayer in addition to the normal thanksgiving with which Paul began his letters. Look at Chart 11-3. You will see that the first half of the letter, which is usually the theological part of one of Paul's letters, is mostly composed of prayer formulas.

You may have noticed that the content of Eph is very general. It is not possible to say that there is a particular problem which the author must resolve in the body of the letter. Instead, the author presents us with a

OUTLINE OF EPHESIANS   *[11–3]*

Greeting (1:1–2)

Thanksgiving for redemption and knowledge of heavenly mysteries in
Christ (1:3–14)

Through the apostle God has made the Gentiles alive in Christ (1:15–
3:21)
  (a) Prayer for the faith, love and hope of those whom God has made
       part of the body of the heavenly Christ (1:15–23)
  (b) Contrast between their old "death" in sin and life in Christ (2:1–
       10)
  (c) Reconciliation of the Gentiles to God in the one body of Christ
       (2:11–22)
  (d) Paul's suffering and ministry to bring the Gentiles into the body
       of Christ (3:1–13)
  (e) Prayer for faith and love among Paul's converts (3:14–21)

Christian life in the world (4:1–6:20)
  (a) Unity in the body of Christ which is built up by different
       ministries (4:1–16)
  (b) Old life in "darkness" contrasted with new life as "children of
       light" (4:17–5:21)
  (c) Household code: Marriage in Christ; children and parents; slaves
       and masters (5:22–6:9)

cosmic vision of the church as the source of salvation. Since Eph appears
to have used Col and since most of the particular names and references
that we find in Col are missing in Eph, scholars do not think that Eph was
written by the same person as Col. The emphasis upon Paul's heroic imprisonment on behalf of the Gentiles suggests that Paul may have already
been martyred. Eph is a way of providing a general summary of his teaching for the churches in Asia Minor.

Christ as Lord of the Cosmos: Colossians

Both Col and Eph have shifted from the earlier letters in which the
glory of Christ is pictured as coming at the end of the world to picturing
the heavenly glory of Christ as the reality of Christian salvation. Both use

the apocalyptic contrast of light and darkness to speak of the transformation which Christians have experienced in baptism. They have been taken from the world of darkness, a life lived in opposition to God, and been made part of the heavenly world of light (e.g. Col 1:12–13).

Col 1:15–20 appears to be taken from an early Christian hymn. The first section describes Christ as the "image" of God through whom the universe was created. The second section speaks of the risen Lord as the fullness of God and head of the "body," the church:

> who [= the Son, from v. 12] is the image of God,
> the first-born of all creation;
> in him all things were created,
> in the heavens and on the earth,
> visible things and invisible ones;
> whether thrones or dominions;
> whether principalities or powers—
> all things were created through him and in him;
> he is before all things,
> and all things hold together in him;
> he is the head of the body, *the church;*
>
> who is [the] beginning, first born from the dead
> so that he might be pre-eminent in all things;
> in him the whole fullness was pleased to dwell,
> and through him all things were reconciled to him [= God]
> making peace *through the blood of his cross* [through him]
> whether things on earth or those in the heavens.

You can see that the images of this hymn make an important point. The special role which Christ has in salvation is not something that was added to his earthly life when he was exalted into heaven. Rather, it is part of the role which Christ as the "image" of God played in creation. The fullness of God's creative power in Christ is the same fullness that brings salvation in Christ.

At first, you might think that Col has quoted this hymn simply to back up the exhortation in 1:21–23. Christ's death has made us part of this reconciliation, but we must continue to show that we belong to the "body" in lives of holiness. However, when we come to Col 2:8–23 we find out that this picture of Christ is being challenged by another form of religious teaching which the author refers to as "philosophy and empty deceit." The accusation of being "human tradition" might occur in debates between different philosophical schools. It implies that the opposition has simply "made up" their teaching and not derived it from any authentic sources. The contrast between "according to the elements of the universe" and "according to Christ" (v. 8) is more difficult to interpret. By the next century, "elements of the universe" could refer to demonic beings or astrological powers—usually opposed to the ascent of the human spirit into the heavenly regions. If so, the contrast would be between the sources or inspiration of the teaching. But the expression more commonly referred to the fundamental physical "elements" out of which the universe was made. If that is what the author means, then the contrast is between mere human speculations about the make-up of the universe, which usually associated the dark, heavy elements of earth and water with the realm of change and death, and the light elements, air and fire with the immortal stars, and the Christian picture of Christ as the one in whom all is created. The "fullness of deity" mentioned in verse 9 would refer to the "fullness" mentioned in 1:19.

Col 2:9–15 emphasizes the role of Christ in salvation of the Gentiles, who had been caught in sin and alienation from God. You will notice that several themes from Paul's earlier conflicts over the salvation of the Gentiles appear in a slightly different form here. In Christ, the uncircumcised are "circumcised," though not in a physical sense. Paul uses this distinction in Rom 2:29; cf. also Phil 3:3. The image of baptism as dying and rising with Christ (v. 12) recalls Rom 6:4. Paul had described the conflict between the crucified Christ and the law as Christ becoming "sin" (2 Cor 5:21) or "cursed" (Gal 3:13). Verse 14 pictures Christ setting aside the claims of the law against humanity by nailing its "bond" to the cross. While scholars are not clear about the practice being alluded to, it seems clear that the author wants the readers to connect this verse with verse 16. Christians should not accept new obligations or judgments being passed by others. We found a similar train of thought in Gal 4:8–11. Paul had told his Galatian converts that if they took on observances of the Jewish calendar, they might as well be going back to paganism.

Paul had made the argument against Judaizing practices by appealing to Christian freedom (e.g. Gal 5:1). Col uses the imagery of the cosmic role of Christ to make its point by pointing to the victory of Christ over all the powers in the universe (vv. 10,15).

It is difficult to reconstruct the religious practices which Col is opposing. Clearly regulations involving food, possibly some other cultic objects and subjection of the body through ascetic practices such as fasting and sexual asceticism are involved. So too is a religious calendar. The puzzling references to "elements of the cosmos" and "self-abasement and worship of angels" suggest that the ascetic and cultic practices involved were linked with some form of "heavenly ascent" or vision. Perhaps the "elements" were pictured as binding the soul to the earthly realm. Only through the practices of asceticism and worship of angelic guardians could the soul ascend to the divine realm.

Col assures its readers that Christ embraces the whole cosmos. Through baptism they have become one with the heavenly, risen Christ. They should not think of salvation as some dangerous trip which the soul still has to make through the "elements" which separate earth from the divine. Instead, Col 3:1–4 tells them, they should seek the "things above." The nature of that quest is spelled out in the ethical life by which Christians "put to death" the desires and passions which cut us off from God and "put on" the virtues of those who belong to the body of Christ (3:5–17). Col also speaks of the cultic practices of Christians, which are the basis of their salvation. Baptism has united all people in Christ (3:10–11). Christians continue to worship God through mutual teaching, encouragement, psalms, hymns and other "spiritual songs." They are not involved in worshiping angels or even claiming to share that offered by angels in heaven. Christians are giving thanks to God through Christ (3:16–17).

All United in Christ: Ephesians

You can see from Chart 11-3 that Eph emphasizes the contrast between life in Christ and that "in the world." Eph also stresses the unity which binds the whole church together as the body of Christ. Where Col presents us with the image of the cosmic Christ as the source of salvation, Eph shifts toward the embodiment of salvation in the "body of Christ," the church. Col speaks of "fullness" belonging to Christ and communicated to Christians (Col 1:19; 2:9,10). Eph 1:23 identifies the "fullness" with the church as Christ's body. The different ministries in the church seek to bring Christians to the maturity which is required for the "fullness" of Christ and the "building up" of Christ's body (Eph 4:11–16).

You may have noticed that the image of Christ's cosmic victory over the powers (Col 2:5) has been expanded in Eph 4:8–10. Eph cites Ps 68:19. Christ has filled the universe by descending to the earthly regions and ascending to the highest heavens. The "captives" of the psalm are presumably the "powers and authorities" mentioned in Col. Eph 4:11 picks up the second theme in the psalm text to explain, "He gave gifts to men." Those gifts are the spiritual gifts which enable the church to grow in love. Eph 3:10 pictures the church/body-of-Christ as the cosmic manifestation of God's wisdom. Once again we see what was originally a cosmological description of Christ: he is the "wisdom of God" (as divine image in Col 1:15; as the one in whom "treasures of wisdom are hidden" in Col 2:3), being transferred to the church.

Even though the symbolic language of Eph may be difficult for you to follow, you can see that Eph presents a very important insight about the nature of the church. "Body of Christ" is not just a nice image for a particular collection of people, which can be used to get those people to think of themselves as a group that is dependent on one another. "Body of Christ" says that the church really does have some of the same attributes which are given to Christ, her head. She is the manifestation of God's wisdom. She is holy. She is "different" from the world. You can see how deeply this idea is worked into Eph when you compare what Eph 5:22–33 says about the relationship between Christian husbands and wives with Col 3:18–19. Col merely adopts the conventional "ordering" of the household in its time. The teaching to husbands includes a common exhortation not to be harsh with their wives and a reminder to love them. Eph has taken over this rather simple pattern of ethical teaching and "explained it" by describing the relationship as like that between Christ and the church. This development describes the wife's relationship to her husband as like that of the church and Christ.

The major line of development concerns the role of the husband. It becomes the source of a reflection on love and self-sacrifice. This reflection is important on a number of levels. Some people think that because the New Testament tells wives to "be subject" to their husbands, women have to "put up with it" when their husbands abuse them or their children. You can see from this description of love that abusive behavior of any sort does not belong in a Christian marriage. On another level, you can also see from this passage that the holiness of the church is not something that she has on her own. The holiness of the church comes from the sacrifice and love of Christ for the church. Finally, we live in a time when people always seem to be criticizing the church. For some the church is too conservative; for others, she is too liberal. For some she is not involved enough in social causes; for others, she seems to have lost herself in them. Eph challenges us to forget all the squabbling and to imagine the church as the object of Christ's love. You know that when you love someone you treat his or her "faults" differently than when you don't. We may still criticize people we love. But we also are willing to accept their struggles and peculiarities and even weaknesses.

Just as holiness comes to the church as a gift, so salvation comes to Christians as God's "grace." Eph 2:1–10 reminds the readers that without God's grace they would have remained lost in sinfulness. Throughout the letter, Christians face a world of darkness and sin. The "new creation," which Christians become in baptism, is not some static form of divine salvation. It is reflected in the "good works" which are part of the new life of Christians (2:10). You will also notice that Eph speaks of Christians being strengthened by the Spirit and growing to maturity in love and knowledge (3:16–19; 4:11–16). Promoting such growth and unity is the primary function of the various "gifts" which God has given people in the church (4:11–13). Thus Eph reminds us that Christian life is not merely static or defensive, holding onto salvation like a possession. Rather Christian life requires constant growth. Christians cannot be naive about the task that faces them. Eph reminds us that "putting away" the old life of sin which shows itself in speaking deceitfully to others and in anger as well as in more obvious crimes like theft means working against a tough enemy, the "devil" (4:25–32; 6:10–18).

Summary

We have seen that Col and Eph reflect the situation of Pauline Christianity after the apostle himself has been removed from the scene by imprisonment and death. Eph is particularly conscious of how much the Gentile churches that Paul founded owe to his efforts and suffering on their behalf. Eph 3:3–4 also mentions the important role of Paul's letters in conveying his teaching to many Christians who had not known him personally.

Christians could read and exchange these letters. Remember that they had no official Christian scriptures to go with the Old Testament at this time. Even the collection of Pauline writings which we have been studying was not in circulation. We have seen that these letters preserve Paul's teaching by developing Pauline images in new ways. They emphasize the cosmic significance of Christ and the universality of the church as the body of Christ. They speak of others who must carry on the work of "building up" the body of Christ which the apostle has left behind. They remind Christians of the holiness that comes from being in Christ.

STUDY QUESTIONS

Facts You Should Know

1. How is Paul's imprisonment in Col and Eph different from the imprisonment in Phil and Phlm?
2. How does Col picture the cosmic role of Christ? List some of the ele-

ments of the religious movement that Col opposes. How does the "cosmic Christ" make those religious practices unnecessary for Christians?

3. According to Col and Eph, how do Christians show that they already live in unity with the "head" of the "body," Christ, who is exalted in heaven?

4. Explain how Eph has taken over and expanded the following metaphors found in Col: (a) the cosmic victory of Christ over the "powers of the universe"; (b) Christ as "head" of the church; (c) the relationship between husband and wife in Christian marriage.

5. According to Eph, what is the basis for the Christian claim that the church is holy?

Things To Do

1. The thanksgiving in Col praises the addressees for "faith in Christ Jesus," "love for all the saints [= Christians]," and "hope laid up for you in heaven" (Col 1:4–5). Read through the rest of the letter and find as many examples as you can of each of these virtues.

2. Compare the "household code" of Eph 5:22–6:9 with that in Col 3:18–4:1. How has Eph "Christianized" the moral teaching of the household code in each of the three cases?

Things To Think About

1. Do Christians today really believe that Christ is victorious over the "powers" that hold the cosmos in bondage to evil and sin? How do they demonstrate that they have such a faith?

2. Eph emphasizes the need for Christians to grow into Christ by putting aside the vices of their past, which the "rulers of this world" still encourage, and taking up the armor of Christ. What "vices" would go into a modern day catalogue of things which the Christian must struggle to put aside?

Chapter 12

MARK: JESUS, SUFFERING MESSIAH

The Composition of Mark

Paul's letters presumed that the readers knew some sayings of Jesus, that Jesus was a Jewish teacher who had followers including a special group referred to as "the twelve," and that Jesus had been crucified by the Roman prefect at the time of the Jewish Passover and had been raised from the dead. Paul also speaks of the origins of the Lord's Supper in the final meal which Jesus shared with his disciples. Clearly stories about Jesus played a role in the earliest Christian preaching and worship. But Paul never suggests that the "story of Jesus" as such was written down somewhere for his readers to consult. The kind of information about Jesus to which he refers could easily be transmitted orally and remembered by the hearers. Paul uses the word "gospel" to mean the message of salvation which he preaches (e.g. Gal 1:11; Rom 1:1; 2 Cor 4:3). The noun *euangelion* has its roots in the verbal form, "to bring or announce news," which is used in Is 40:9, 41:27, 52:7 and 61:1 for the announcement of the "good news" that God is going to bring captive Israel out of exile. A Roman inscription describes the birthday of the emperor Augustus as "good news" for the whole world.

Mark begins with the words, "The beginning of the gospel of Jesus Christ, Son of God," (1:1). "Gospel" does not mean "book" here either. Mark 1:14–15 uses "gospel" for Jesus' preaching that the reign of God is at hand. That usage reminds us of the OT use of "gospel" for the announcement that God is coming to free the people. (Luke 4:18–19 has Jesus begin his ministry with the words of Is 61:1–2.) The sayings about suffering for "Jesus' sake and for the sake of the gospel" (Mark 8:35; 10:29) link Jesus and the preaching about him (also 13:10; 14:9). Mark's opening, then, would not have led its readers to expect a reporter's biography about Jesus. They would expect preaching about Jesus as Son of God.

Look at Mark 14:9. It suggests something more is meant by "gospel" than just repeating stories and sayings. By promising that a particular woman's action will be remembered wherever the gospel is preached, it makes us think of the story of Jesus as something larger into which the sayings and stories about Jesus fit. Scholars think that some of the individual stories may have been gathered into collections. The parables which form the basis for Jesus' teaching in Mark 4:1–34 might be taken from such a collection. The doubling of several miracle stories (calming the storm: Mk 4:35–41; 6:45–52; feeding the multitude: 6:34–44; 8:1–9; healing the blind: 8:22–26; 10:46–52) suggests that there may have even been different collections that contained different versions of the same story. The story of Jesus' passion which we find in Mark 14–15 is probably based on an earlier written account of these events. While scholars can agree that Mark has probably used written sources as well as oral traditions about Jesus, it is much more difficult to move from the text of Mark as we have it back to the wording of a "pre-Markan" source.

As far as we know, Mark was the first person to bring the diverse stories about Jesus together in a single narrative. Mark writes in Greek for an audience that does not understand the Aramaic words which occur in some of the stories (5:41; 7:34; 15:34). They are also unfamiliar with Jewish customs (7:3–4). Mark 7:31 suggests that the author of the gospel was not familiar with Palestinian geography. (Try tracing the proposed route on a map!) Mark 13:2 suggests that the fall of Jerusalem to the Roman army has either occurred or will soon. The warnings against false messiahs and the command to flee (Mk 13:5–7,14–16,21–22) could be directed against expectations about the return of Jesus that had been awakened by those events. Mark has edited together these prophetic sayings with what appears to be an address to the situation of the readers in 13:9–13. They must expect to suffer for Jesus' sake at the hands of all the political authorities in the world: synagogue officials, Roman governors and even kings. This suffering is linked with the preaching of the gospel throughout the world. Mark 14:9 also referred to the gospel being preached "in the whole cosmos."

Church tradition later linked the author of the gospel with the Mark who is said to have been with Peter during his imprisonment in Rome (1 Pet 5:13). We also find a Mark associated with Paul's imprisonment there (2 Tim 4:11; Col 4:10). That tradition assumed that the references to suffering were to Nero's persecution. Another old tradition held that a "Mark" had founded the church in Alexandria. Citations from a gospel claiming to be a "secret version" of Mark preserved in Alexandria appear in a letter that is said to be by the third century teacher Clement of Alexandria. Some modern scholars think that the concern with the destruction of the Jerusalem temple and the theme of Jesus' kingship which appear in the final chapters of the gospel points to origins in the region of Syro-Palestine. As followers of Jesus who did not join the Jews in revolt, Christians would have suffered at the hands of both parties. To Jewish nationalists, they are traitors. To Roman officials and the Gentile inhabitants of the region, they are "Jewish sympathizers." Perhaps the promise that the disciples would see the risen Lord in Galilee (Mk 14:28; 16:7) was even addressed to the community's own flight from the hostilities.

Whatever the circumstances in which Mk was written, the gospel's composition leaves little doubt that the truth of Jesus is only found on the cross. The center of the plot comes with Peter's confession that Jesus is messiah, the passion prediction and the rebuke of Peter (Mark 8:27–33). Christians are told that they too must be prepared to suffer (8:34–38).

As you read through Mark you will notice that the story is broken up into small units that often begin and end abruptly. You will find other passages in which Mark has apparently provided a generalized summary to fill in between two episodes (see 1:21–22 which fills in between the call of the disciples and the first exorcism which attracts attention to Jesus). One of Mark's favorite methods of composition is to fit two stories together by putting one in the middle of the other. In Mk 2:1–12 and 3:1–6, miracles of healing have sayings about Jesus' authority to forgive and the appropriateness of healing on the sabbath inserted in the middle. The story of the withered fig tree forms the outside framework for Jesus' cleansing of the temple in Mk 11:12–25. The healing of Jarius' daughter is interrupted by the healing of a woman who had been hemorrhaging for twelve years (Mk 5:21–43). Both of these stories emphasize the faith of the persons who ask Jesus for healing. The mission of the twelve disciples frames the story of John the Baptist's death (Mk 6:6–30).

The biggest puzzles in Mark center on what is called the "messianic secret." Even though Jesus is Son of God and a powerful teacher and healer, he sometimes commands people to remain silent. This theme leads to a story of a leper in 1:40–45 immediately disobeying Jesus by telling everyone. The disciples are also commanded to keep silent about the transfiguration (Mk 9:9). Even Jesus' teaching seems to be somewhat of a riddle, which even his disciples have a hard time understanding (Mk 4:10–13). The key to this puzzle lies in the middle of the gospel. Peter recognizes that Jesus is God's messiah and is immediately told not to tell anyone (8:27–30). The reason for the silence must be connected with what follows. Jesus tries to explain to his disciples that his role as messiah is one of suffering and death (8:31–33). The "messianic secret" points to the paradox

OUTLINE OF MARK   *[12–1]*

Jesus comes preaching the kingdom (1:1–3:6)
  (a) Introduction to Jesus' ministry: John the Baptist (1:1–15)
  (b) Calling of the disciples and Jesus' powerful deeds (1:16–45)
  (c) Controversies with religious authorities (2:1–3:6)

Teaching and healing around the Sea of Galilee (3:7–6:6a)
  (a) Reactions to Jesus: Who are the true relatives? (3:7–35)
  (b) Disciples hear the parables (4:1–34)
  (c) Miracles of Jesus (4:35–5:43)
  (d) Rejection at Nazareth (6:1–6a)

Second cycle of teaching and powerful deeds (6:6b–8:21)
  (a) Sending out of the disciples / death of the Baptist (6:6b–30)
  (b) Feeding, walking on water, healing (6:31–56)
  (c) Controversies over keeping the traditions (7:1–23)
  (d) Healings, feeding (7:24–8:10)
  (e) Demand for a sign; the "leaven" of the Pharisees (8:11–21)

Discipleship: following the Son of Man who is destined to suffer (8:22–10:52)
  (a) Healing the blind (8:22–26)
  (b) Jesus is "messiah"; first passion prediction; discipleship means suffering (8:27–9:1)
  (c) Transfiguration; disciples fail to heal; second passion prediction (9:2–37)
  (d) Dispute over greatness / beware of temptation (9:38–50)
  (e) True discipleship: marriage, children, wealth (10:1–31)
  (f) Third passion prediction / dispute over greatness (10:32–45)
  (g) Healing the blind (10:46–52)

Jesus comes to Jerusalem as messianic king (11:1–13:37)
  (a) Entry to Jerusalem / cursing of the fig tree / cleansing the temple (11:1–25)
  (b) Controversies with religious authorities / parable of the wicked tenants (11:26–12:44)
  (c) How disciples are to react to the coming destruction of Jerusalem / no one knows the hour of the parousia (13:1–37)

Jesus' passion and death (14:1–16:8a)
  (a) Woman's anointing / Judas' betrayal (14:1–11)
  (b) Last Supper (14:12–31)
  (c) Gethsemane: Jesus' prayer / arrest (14:32–52)
  (d) Trials of Jesus (14:53–15:20)
  (e) Crucifixion / 'Truly this was the Son of God' (15:21–41)
  (f) Burial of Jesus / empty tomb: 'He has been raised' (15:42–16:8a)

of who Jesus is: the powerful Son of God who is destined to die on the cross.

Jesus as Powerful Savior

Take a look at the outline of the gospel. You will notice that the first half of the gospel can be described as a combination of Jesus' powerful deeds, that is, miracles which show powers of healing and control over nature, and his teaching. Jesus' teaching takes two forms. The parables about the kingdom of God in Mk 4 are directed toward sympathetic followers of Jesus. Perhaps you noticed that the seed parables of Jesus which are collected here all emphasize the "great harvest" that comes out of hidden, insignificant or difficult beginnings. The saying about the lamp in Mk 4:21–22 reminds the disciples that they are not to hide the light they have received.

The second form of teaching occurs in controversies between Jesus and religious teachers like the Pharisees. Mk 1:22 leads the reader to expect Jesus to teach with *exousia*, "power" or "authority," not like the scribes. The same word *exousia* reappears in the crowd response of Mk 1:27 after an exorcism. There it is used for the power by which Jesus cast out the demons. The same verse speaks of Jesus giving a "new" teaching, though Mark has yet to present any of Jesus' teaching. Jesus' teaching and exorcisms are linked again in the summary of his mission in 1:39. Mark has prepared the reader to expect a form of teaching in the controversy stories which is like the healings and exorcisms described in 1:23–27,30–31,40–44. Jesus will speak with authority. He will "command" and vanquish his opponents.

The debate over *exousia*, "authority," appears in the healing which opens the first cycle of controversy stories (Mk 2:1–3:6). Jesus exercises the authority to forgive sins. His opponents charge that he has blasphemed by taking on a power which belongs only to God (Mk 2:5–10). In this episode the physical healing of the paralytic takes second place to the issue of whether or not Jesus has the authority to speak God's word of forgiveness to the sinner. The reaction of Jesus' opponents and of the crowd shows us what is "new" in Jesus' teaching. This theme is repeated throughout the section. We see Jesus summoning a tax collector as disciple and are told that the scribes of the Pharisee party objected to the tax collectors and sinners who had become followers of Jesus (2:13–17). Jesus answers their objections by insisting that the sick are the ones in need of healing, not the healthy people.

The controversies which follow also have Jesus challenge some of the practices by which righteous people showed devotion to God: fasting and refraining from any kind of work on the sabbath. Jesus never denies that these practices have their place. But they cannot be used to obstruct the "new presence of salvation" which has appeared with Jesus' ministry. It is not right to fast when salvation is present. Jesus' ministry is "new wine" which cannot be forced into old skins (2:18–22). Jesus insists that even the law itself teaches that human need has priority over the obligation to rest on the sabbath (2:23–28; 3:1–5). Though Jesus defeats the arguments of his opponents, his teaching has created enemies. Mk 3:6 pictures the Pharisees and Herodians leaving to plot a way of destroying Jesus.

You can see from this example that the story in the first part of Mark moves on two levels. On the human level, Jesus' powerful miracles and teaching attract crowds of followers but they also lead to strong opposition from both religious (scribes, Pharisees) and political (Herodians) authorities. On the cosmic level, Jesus' ministry is pictured as a conflict with Satan. His healings and exorcisms are breaking up the hold which Satan has on human beings. Destruction of the power of evil is one of the signs of the coming of God's messiah (see Mk 3:22–27). Some of the demons even complain that Jesus is "destroying them" (Mk 1:24; 5:7). Jesus is also portrayed as having the power to control nature. He can provide food for the crowd from a small amount of bread and fish (6:30–42; 8:1–10) and rescue his terrified disciples from a storm at sea (6:45–52; 4:35–41).

You might think that anyone who has such divine powers would be able to silence all opposition: human and demonic. That is where we run into the paradox. No matter what Jesus does, misunderstanding and hostility seem to grow. People in Jesus' own region do not believe (6:1–6). We are told of the death suffered by John the Baptist, and of Herod's fears that Jesus might be another John the Baptist (6:14–29). And we even see that Jesus' own disciples have trouble understanding and believing in him (4:13,40; 6:52; 7:18; 8:21). The first half of Mark, then, presents us with a picture of Jesus as a powerful divine savior who is consistently misunderstood and rejected.

Jesus, Suffering Son of Man

The first part of the gospel builds up to the revelation of Jesus as the messiah who must suffer in Mk 8:27–33. Now you can also see why that revelation is so important. Jesus' mission does not depend upon using divine power to get the crowds to follow him and to destroy his various enemies. Jesus' mission is one of suffering and death. The rejection that he faced in Galilee is only a prelude to the final events of his life: his crucifixion by the religious and political authorities in Jerusalem.

Perhaps you noticed that in the outline of Mark there are only three healings in the second half of the gospel. The exorcism of the boy after the transfiguration repeats the lesson that faith is crucial to receiving salvation from Jesus. It shows that Jesus' disciples do not yet have such faith (9:14–29). Two others are healings of blind persons. Then there is one nature miracle, the cursing of the fig tree which is associated with Jesus' condemnation of corruption in the Jerusalem temple and his prediction that the temple will be destroyed (11:12–21; 13:1–2). You know that Mark often likes to create a "frame" for important parts of his gospel. Healing the blind men provides the frame for the revelation of Jesus as God's suffering messiah. There are three predictions of the passion in this section. Each one is more detailed. Each time the disciples become more and more frightened and perplexed (8:31–33; 9:30–32; 10:32–34). By framing this section with the healings, Mark points up the "blindness" of the disciples which will have to be healed.

Since Jesus' destiny is rejection and death, the final revelations about Jesus occur during the events of his passion. Jesus comes to Jerusalem "in the name of the Lord" (11:9), the royal messiah who is to restore the Davidic kingdom. His prophetic condemnation of corruption in the temple evokes the same official plotting to destroy him that his teaching had in Galilee (11:18; 3:6). A final sequence of controversy stories is introduced by a challenge to Jesus' *exousia*, "authority" (11:27–33). Jesus' response does not answer the question directly. Instead it exposes the falseness of the "chief priests, scribes and elders" who posed the challenge. They cannot answer because they did not recognize divine authority behind the Baptist's preaching. Nor would they dare reject the Baptist because they are afraid of the populace who revere John. Jesus' parable of the wicked tenants serves as a thinly veiled condemnation of the religious and political leaders of the people (12:1–11). It evokes further hostility (12:12).

Each additional controversy story brings forth a challenge from some group which claimed either political or religious leadership. Jesus' responses often do not speak to the question posed directly. Instead they show that these people are without any understanding of what it is that really belongs to God. They do not recognize the God "of the living" whom they claim to worship. Jesus even condemns the scribes as vicious exploiters of the poor and contrasts them and the other pious, wealthy people with a poor widow's offering (12:35–44). There is one other exception to this universal condemnation: the scribe in 12:28–34. You may have noticed that he is not sent to challenge or trap Jesus like the others. Mark pictures him as hearing the debates and asking Jesus about the "greatest commandment." They agree that worship of God and love of God and neighbor are the greatest commandments in the law. Jesus praises the scribe for his insight. At the same time, the wisdom of this one scribe makes the perversity of Jesus' opponents all the worse. It is not impossible to recognize that Jesus speaks as God's messiah if a person truly understands what God has revealed in the law.

The events of the passion show that Jesus dies as the messianic king of Israel. The woman who anoints Jesus in Mk 14:3–9 pours her costly ointment over his head as though anointing a new king. The charge that Jesus is "king of the Jews" runs through the trial before Pilate (15:1–32). Jesus is even mocked by the two men who are crucified with him for this claim. The onlookers insist that Jesus could not be "king" since he has no power to save himself or others. These accusations reflect the final irony of the gospel. As he dies, the Roman centurion will be the only one to see the truth: "Truly, this man was the Son of God" (15:39). God does "rescue" Jesus, not by giving him great earthly power, but by freeing him from death. Though his opponents may have appeared to have been victorious when they crucified Jesus, they were not successful. Jesus did not remain dead in the tomb (Mk 16:1–8).

Discipleship in Mark

We have already seen that discipleship is one of the central issues in Mark. The gospel was written for Christians who were suffering persecution. They may have wondered why the powerful Jesus, now exalted with God in heaven, did not step in to rescue them. They seem to have been in danger of following false messiahs who made promises about Jesus' return from heaven as Son of Man. Mk 13:32–37 warns about speculation like that. It insists that not even the Son knew when God would bring the judgment. If Jesus did not know, then no human being can claim to know either. The proper response for disciples is to always be ready for the coming of the Lord.

But discipleship will not be easy. Mk 13:9–13 prophesies suffering for those who preach the gospel. At the same time, they are to be confident that God is with them in suffering and that they will be saved. The same message about discipleship is delivered in the section framed by the healings of the blind. Disciples have to expect to suffer the same fate as their master (8:34–38). They are warned against thinking in terms of human greatness and power, when the example set by Jesus as the suffering Son of Man is one of humility, service and suffering (9:33–37; 10:35–45). The story of the rich man whom Jesus loved but who could not bring himself to give up that wealth to become Jesus' disciple points out that disciples may even have to make material sacrifices to follow Jesus (10:17–31).

Even at the very end of the story, the women who have heard the angel announce the good news that Jesus has been raised run away from the tomb in fear (16:7–8). But for all the fears, hesitation, misunderstanding, opposition and even flight that we see in Jesus' disciples, we also know as Mark's readers did that they finally did follow Jesus. We are only reminded of this knowledge twice. Though reprimanding the sons of Zebedee for seeking positions of honor in the kingdom, Jesus does prophesy that they will suffer martyrdom (10:39–40). The prediction of Peter's denial elicits a vehement protest of willingness to "die with Jesus" (14:29–31). Mark's readers cannot have failed to think of Peter's martyrdom in Rome just a few years before the gospel was written. Though Peter may have failed to follow Jesus to the death in Jerusalem, he has done so at the end of his life.

When we take the readers' familiarity with the subsequent story into account, we can see that the way in which Mark portrays the fears, weakness and lack of understanding by Jesus' first disciples is part of the encouragement he offers Christians. Their weaknesses just as much as the hostility of Jesus' enemies were part of the divine plan for suffering and service. The divine forgiveness and love which is extended to all in Jesus' death was not less because of human failure. At the same time, the readers are also encouraged to follow Jesus faithfully, since they know that he is the source of divine salvation.

Summary

Mark's gospel paints a powerful picture of Jesus as the suffering Son of Man. We see the divine authority of Jesus in both miraculous deeds and in teaching. We see a full range of human reactions to Jesus, from the extravagant love of the woman who anoints him before his passion to the fears of his disciples and the mocking hostility of religious and political authorities. Since Jesus has power to break up Satan's empire and to control natural phenomena, we cannot agree with the crowd that he failed to save himself from the cross because he was unable to do so. Instead, we are forced to accept the death of Jesus as part of God's plan for the salvation of humanity.

That insight about the cross is so central to Mark that it shapes the whole gospel. It also shapes Mark's vision of discipleship. For Mark the concrete issues of Christian life are very few. They are summarized in love of God and neighbor and the willingness to follow Jesus' example of self-sacrificing service. No persons are excluded from God's love and forgiveness. No one can claim that being a disciple of the suffering Son of Man gives him or her a position of superiority over others. No one should be so naive as to think that the life of discipleship will be without failures and setbacks. But whatever the difficulties and confusion, whatever the cost in personal or material terms, Mark insists that Jesus is there "ahead of his disciples," always reaching out to save them.

STUDY QUESTIONS

Facts You Should Know

1. What did the word "gospel" (*euangelion*) originally mean? How did it come to be associated with a narrative account of Jesus' life?
2. What hints does Mark give us about the situation of the Christians for whom the gospel was written?
3. How does the composition of Mk emphasize the paradox of the suffering Son of God?
4. How does Mark emphasize the "authority" (*exousia*) of Jesus? Why is this emphasis important for the gospel's portrayal of the suffering of Jesus and his disciples?

Things To Do

1. Using a concordance, find the passages in which "Son of God" is used for Jesus in Mk. Who knows Jesus' identity in each case? How does the final example illustrate Mk's theme of the "crucified savior"?

2. Trace the reactions of the disciples of Jesus to his deeds and words through the gospel. Where do misunderstanding and fear cause the disciples to fail Jesus?

Things To Think About

1. What is the cost of discipleship for Christians today? Are we just as repelled by the message of suffering and lowliness as the disciples in Mk?

2. What happens to faith that is based upon Jesus "the powerful miracle worker" in Mk's gospel? How do people today base their faith on demonstrations of divine power by religious figures? What would Mark say about such faith?

Chapter 13

MATTHEW: JESUS, TEACHER OF ISRAEL

The Composition of Matthew

Though Matthew preserves much of the material he found in Mark, comparison of the two writings shows that Mt also reshapes Markan traditions. He may do so to include material that he has derived from other sources. He may improve the ordering of Markan material or correct details. Or Mt may wish to bring out the message which he finds in a particular episode. You can see Mt at work in this way if you compare the opening presentation of John the Baptist and Jesus in the two gospels. Mk 1:2–15 contains four narrative episodes:

(a) Presentation of John the Baptist as the messenger in the wilderness (vv. 2–8)
(b) Jesus' baptism by John (vv. 9–11)
(c) Jesus' testing in the wilderness (vv. 12–13)
(d) Jesus comes preaching the kingdom (vv. 14–15)

Each episode has its counterpart in Mt. As we compare Mt's treatment of each one we can see Mt at work.

Mt 3:1–12 has reworked the appearance of the Baptist. The first change you might notice is one that your English teacher might tell you to make in a story. Mt moves the reference to John the Baptist from after the quotation to the opening of the story. He has provided a smoother introduction to the episode. Next compare the two quotations. You may need help from the footnotes in your Bible to figure this one out. Mt omits the part about the messenger in Mk 1:2. This is an example of a correction. The prophet being fulfilled is Isaiah. But Mk has used the words of another prophet Malachi 3:1 before he gets to the words of Is 40:3. You can see that the reference to a messenger preparing a way would make it natural to link the two together. But Mt, who is very interested in prophetic passages which point forward to Jesus, corrects the citation so that only the words of Isaiah are used. Now look at the content of John's preaching. Mt has several sayings about judgment (vv. 7–10,12) which are not in Mk. In addition he has picked up the reference to fire from the judgment sayings and added it to the prediction of Jesus' coming to baptize people with the Spirit in v. 11 which he has taken over from Mk 1:7–8. Comparison with Luke's version of this episode shows that these sayings were also known to Luke and included in this context. Therefore we can conclude that Mt was using material about the Baptist from Q in addition to Mk.

Besides concern for prophetic tradition, the Matthean version of this episode has other themes which will be repeated in the gospel. Compare Mt 3:7 with Lk 3:7. In Lk you will notice that John speaks his words of condemnation to the crowd. In Mt he has a particular target, the Pharisees and Sadducees. As you read through Mt you will find that the Pharisees are often condemned for hypocritical behavior and a practice of the law which makes observing detailed commandments more important than persons and mercy. This attack against the Pharisees seems to be motivated by the circumstances of Mt's time. After the Roman destruction of Jerusalem (A.D. 70), the Pharisees were the ones whose teachings came to dominate Judaism. They may even have had considerable influence on Jewish Christians in Mt's church. But Mt does not think that Christians need to create their own copy of Pharisaism. Jesus has shown them a way to a greater righteousness (Mt 5:20). Right from the beginning, then, Mt makes sure that we are suspicious of the Pharisees. Another theme that Mt will emphasize over and over again is judgment. A different problem in Mt's church may lie behind this emphasis. Mt 7:15–23 warns against persons who are "false prophets," who do not bear good fruit, and some who even think that they will be saved because they have worked miracles in Jesus' name. Mt reminds Christians that they will be judged by their faithfulness to Jesus' teaching.

Now compare Mt's version of the baptism of Jesus with Mk (Mt 3:13–17). This episode shows Mt providing a new perspective on the tradition. There are two major changes. Mt adds a dialogue between Jesus and the Baptist in vv. 14–15. This dialogue makes it clear to the reader that Jesus was not baptized because he needed to repent of sin. Rather Jesus is being baptized as an act of righteousness, to fulfill God's plan. You will also notice another difference. In Mk 1:11 the divine voice speaks only to Jesus (the Greek indicates a second person singular). Mt 3:17 has the voice make a public declaration that Jesus is "beloved Son."

The episode of Jesus' testing in the wilderness is much more extensive than in Mk (Mt 4:1–11). You can recognize some of Mk in its beginning and end (vv. 1,11). Mt's version supplies what the Markan story lacks: a content to the "test" to which Jesus is being subjected. Once again Luke also has a version similar to Mt's, though the "tests" occur in a different order. In this case Mt has used the Q tradition to provide the content of the entire episode.

Finally look at the final episode in the series, Mt 4:12–17. By now you should be familiar with both types of changes that Mt has made. First you can see that Mt has given this episode a longer introduction which describes Jesus' geographical movements and even suggests to the reader that Capernaum rather than Nazareth was now Jesus' home (v. 13). With his interest in Jesus' fulfillment of prophecy, Mt provides another prophetic citation from Isaiah in vv. 15–16. This citation may even be the reason that Mt added the explanation of Jesus' movements. You will also notice that Mt has shortened the words used by Jesus in v. 17 (compare Mk 1:15). He does not have to use the theme of fulfillment, since he has already shown us that Jesus fulfills the prophecy that he has just quoted, so he drops Mk's "the time is fulfilled." Then Mt takes the call to repent to lead off Jesus' words. But Mt also recognizes that to have Jesus speak like a Christian missionary and call people to "believe in the gospel" (Mk 1:15c) is out of place, so he drops that expression as well.

So far we have seen Mt use traditions from Mark, from Q and from the Old Testament. But there is also material in Mt which we only find there. Sometimes this will be designated "M" or "Mt's special tradition" in books about Mt. A quick comparison of Mt's chapter of parables (chapter 13) with Mark 4 will give you an example of this type of tradition. See Chart 13-1. You can see that Mt has included a number of parables in chapter 13 which are not found in Mk (or Lk). Yet variants do turn up in the second century A.D. Gospel of Thomas tradition. Therefore, Mt has probably derived the parables from another source or tradition. The extra interpretations, on the other hand, and the Matthean theme of judgment may be the work of the evangelist.

You will also notice that Mt has taken the hints about Jesus' mode of teaching in Mk and expanded them. He gives prophetic support for the suggestion that the teaching of the parables was in some sense "hidden" from those who heard it. But he also wants the reader to be very sure that Jesus' disciples were not ignorant of Jesus' true meaning. One might draw that conclusion from the sharp reaction Jesus makes to their questioning in Mk. Therefore, Mt has reshaped the whole discourse so that such a confusion could not arise.

Mt's emphasis on Jesus' role as teacher and true interpreter of the will

MT'S REDACTION OF MK 4 *[13–1]*

(a) Introduction: Teaching from a boat (Mk 4:1; Mt 13:1–2)

(b) Parable of the sower (Mk 4:2–9; Mt 13:3–9)

(c) Explanation of why Jesus speaks in parables (Mk 4:10–12; Mt 13:10–11,13 [Mt 13:12 = Mk 4:25]
[Mt 13:14–15, Quotation from Isaiah being fulfilled]
[Mt 13:16–17, Blessing on Jesus' disciples (from Q see Lk 10:23–24)]

(d) Explanation of the parable of the sower (Mk 4:13–20; Mt 13:18–23)

(e) Sayings of Jesus as warnings to disciples about how they hear (Mk 4:21–25: v. 21 see Mt 5:15; v. 22 see Mt 10:26; v. 23 see Mt 13:43 and 11:15; v. 24 see Mt 7:2; v. 25 = Mt 13:12)

(f) Parable of seed growing: in Mk 4:26–29 this is an image of seed growing up "of itself" until harvest, but in Mt 13:24–30 we have a story of a man whose enemy has planted weeds in with his wheat [a version of this parable occurs in Gos. Thom. 57].

(g) Parable of the mustard seed (Mk 4:30–32; Mt 13:31–32) [Mt 13:33, Parable of leaven (also Gos. Thom. 96)]

(h) Jesus speaks to crowds in parables, but explains to disciples in private (Mk 4:33–34; Mt 13:34 = Mk 4:33)
[Mt 13:35, Fulfillment quotation]
[Mt 13:36–43, Jesus explains parable of wheat and tares to his disciples in private]
[Mt 13:44, Parable of treasure (Gos. Thom. 109, has a related story)]
[Mt 13:45–46, Parable of pearl merchant (Gos. Thom. 76)]
[Mt 13:47–48, Parable of fishnet (Gos. Thom. 8)]
[Mt 13:49–50, Explanation of the fishnet]
[Mt 13:51, Jesus' disciples have understood his teaching (see Mk 4:34)]
[Mt 13:52, Saying about the scribe trained for the kingdom of heaven]

of God is evident in the structure of this gospel. At the beginning of Mk
we saw references to Jesus' teaching which spoke of it as manifesting the
same power or authority as his miracles (Mk 1:27). Mt puts the teaching
before the miracles of Jesus. He picks up Mk's reference to Jesus' activity
in Galilee (Mk 1:35–39) and reformulates it to provide a general summary
of Jesus' activity (Mt 4:23–25). You will notice that the geographical range
of Jesus' activities has been increased in Mt's version. Look at a map of
Palestine in Jesus' time. You can see that all the major regions are covered
by the crowds which come to hear Jesus. In addition Mt 4:24 asserts that
Jesus' reputation had even spread into Syria. With the exception of the
reference to the Roman governor in Lk 2:2, this is the only reference to
Syria in the gospels. With its focus on Peter as a leading figure, Mt's gospel
has often been linked with Christianity in the region of Antioch in Syria.
This brief reference may be another "footprint" that points toward Mt's
audience.

Now look at the outline of Mt's gospel. You will see two major changes
in the presentation of Jesus' story. The first change involves expanding the
beginning and end of the story. Mk began with John the Baptist. Mt has
brought together early traditions about Jesus' Davidic heritage in a genealogy (Mt 1:1–17), Jesus' birth as the one who is to save Israel (Mt 1:18–
25), and the persecution by the evil king Herod which drives the family to
repeat the journey of the people of Israel by going down into Egypt and
then being brought back by God (2:1–23). As you read through, you will
notice that Mt has continued to insert quotations from the Old Testament
prophets to show that Jesus is fulfilling God's plan. Mark ended his story
with the women fleeing the empty tomb because they were afraid. We
know from the angel's words in Mk 16:7 that Jesus will fulfill his promise
to meet the disciples again in Galilee, but Mk ends without telling that
part of the story. We also know from Paul that Jesus did appear to groups
of disciples and to Paul himself (1 Cor 15:3–10). Mt's ending includes that
part of the story. The women do not simply run away. Jesus appears to
them and repeats the message that the angel had given. Then at the very
end of the gospel the risen Lord appears to the eleven disciples. They are
told of Jesus' divine authority and of his continued presence with the
church, and they are given a mission to spread Jesus' teaching to all the
nations.

The Sermons: Jesus Instructs the Community

The second major change you could already predict. Jesus is presented throughout the gospel as a teacher. Mt has Jesus deliver five ser-

OUTLINE OF MATTHEW   [13–2]

Infancy narrative (1:1–2:23)

Beginning of Jesus' ministry (3:1–4:25)

Sermon: Sermon on the Mount (5:1–7:29)

Healings and gathering of followers (8:1–9:34)

Sermon: Disciples on mission to Israel (9:35–11:1)

Jesus' teaching in Galilee (11:1–12:50)

Sermon: Parables of the kingdom (13:1–52)

Ministry in Galilee and surrounding areas (13:53–16:12)

Jesus as messiah who will suffer (16:13–17:23)

Instructions for the community (17:24–18:35)
  (a) On paying the temple tax (17:24–27)
  (b) Sermon: Relationships within the community (18:1–35)

Jesus teaches disciples on journey to Jerusalem (19:1–20:34)

Jesus in Jerusalem (21:1–25:46)
  (a) Entry into Jerusalem and cleansing of the temple (21:1–22)
  (b) Controversies with religious authorities (21:23–22:46)
  (c) Denunciation of scribes and Pharisees (23:1–39)
  (d) Sermon: The end of the world and judgment (24:1–26:1)
    (i)   Prediction: Temple will be destroyed (24:1–2)
    (ii) Coming of the end: Always be watchful (24:3–51)
    (iii) Parables of judgment (25:1–46)

Passion of Jesus (26:1–27:66)

Resurrection of Jesus (28:1–20)
  (a) Empty tomb (28:1–8,11–15)
  (b) Jesus appears to the women near the tomb (28:9–10)
  (c) Jesus appears to disciples in Galilee: Go preach to the nations
    (28:16–20)

mons. Each one begins with the people or disciples gathering around Jesus. Each one ends with a reference to the fact that Jesus had finished speaking. We have already seen that Mt is concerned about the theme of judgment. Each one of the five sermons concludes with that theme. Mt often uses parables about judgment to make his point:

(a) Sermon on the Mount: two types of foundation (7:24–27)
(b) Kingdom parables: Interpretation of weeds and wheat (13:36–43)
(c) Community relationships: Parable of the unforgiving servant (18:21–35)
(d) On judgment: Wise and foolish servant girls (25:1–13); talents (25:14–30); sheep and goats, the judgment of the nations (25:31–46)

Each one of these parables concludes with a warning to the audience to be ready for the judgment.

The missionary discourse in Mt 10 concludes with a different kind of reference to judgment. It speaks of the reward that will come to people who treat the disciples well even if those people do not actually become Christians (Mt 10:40–42). In the world of wandering preachers who are completely dependent upon others such help would be crucial to survival. Jesus says that whatever such people have done for his disciples will be treated as though they had done it to God. Perhaps you are already familiar with the parable of the sheep and the goats (Mt 25:31–46). There you will find a similar teaching about judgment. Jesus comes to judge all the nations of the world. But the grounds on which judgment is made turn out to be the way in which persons have treated the poor, oppressed and suffering "little ones" with whom Jesus identifies himself.

Mt does not want you to think that just because God will reward or punish people on the basis of the justice and mercy that they have shown to others there is no real point to being a Christian. Remember that at the end of the gospel the risen Jesus told his disciples to go and teach all the nations what he had taught. Christians have the advantage of knowing Jesus' teaching and having Jesus' help in following it. But Mt is also realistic. We have seen that he knows there are some Christians who think that believing in Jesus is enough. They do not have to be concerned with producing "good fruit." Mt's warnings about judgment are directed to them. Mt also sees that Christianity is a small group of disciples living in a much larger world of Jews and pagans who will not all become Christians. Mt knows that Christians have often been helped by sympathetic outsiders.

He knows that such people can be just and merciful. God will never forget the good which people have done for the poor and suffering even if these people are not believers.

Jesus as Fulfillment of the Law

In Mt 3:15 Jesus says that he is to be baptized by John because "it is fitting for us to fulfill all righteousness." The verb "fulfill" usually appears in Mt as part of the introduction to a quotation from the prophets, which Jesus has fulfilled (e.g. Mt 1:22; 2:15,17; 4:14; 8:17; 12:17). However, in Mt 5:17 we find the affirmation: "Do not think that I have come to destroy the law and the prophets; I have not come to destroy but to fulfill." Mt 5:17–20 affirms the abiding validity of the commandments of the law and asserts that entering the kingdom requires a righteousness "greater than the scribes and Pharisees." Thus, the teaching of Jesus which follows is set in the context of "fulfilling" the law and prophets and presenting a "higher righteousness" than that of the Jewish interpreters of the law.

Mt's preoccupation with the Jewish teachers of the law is evident elsewhere in the gospel. Mt 23:2–3 suggests that one might even "obey" the teaching of the Pharisees but not their conduct. If you compare the controversy stories about the greatest commandment and who is the "Son of David" in Mt 22:34–40,41–46 with their Markan source (Mk 12:28–34,35–37a), you will notice that Mt has changed the focus of the story. Jesus is questioned by a Pharisee (not a scribe as in Mark). Mt omits the exchange of praise (Mk 12:31–34a) which culminates in Jesus saying that the scribe is "not far from the kingdom." Now the story presents Jesus' declaration about the double love command as fulfillment of the law in opposition to the Pharisees. The next episode, the question about the "Son of David," has also been shifted from a general statement from Jesus to the crowd to a question which Jesus puts directly to an assembly of Pharisees. Their inability to answer (v. 46a) demonstrates Jesus' authority as the true interpreter of God's will. The condemnation of the teaching and practice of the scribes and Pharisees which follows in Mt 23 draws together a number of sayings from Q as well as tradition special to Mt.

Compare Mt 23:23–24 with Lk 11:42. Mt has added "scribes" and the epithet "hypocrites" to the "Pharisees" of the saying. He has also shifted the expression of what is neglected from Luke's "justice and the love of God" to "the weightier matters of the law, justice and mercy and faith," and then attached an additional condemnation of the Jewish teachers as "blind guides, straining out a gnat and swallowing a camel." The Sermon on the Mount draws a sharp contrast between the way in which Christians are to give alms, pray and fast and the ostentatious, public display of the "hypocrites" (Mt 6:1–6,16–18).

But Mt's concerns are not simply directed against the growing influence of Pharisaic teaching. His references to "their synagogue" (4:23; 9:35; 10:17; 12:9; 13:54) and "your synagogue" (23:34) suggest that Mt's church has its own assemblies separate from those of Jewish neighbors. Compare Mt 23:34–36 with the Q version of the woe oracle reflected in Lk 11:49–51. In Q God's Wisdom pronounces judgment against the people for killing and persecuting the prophets and messengers sent by God. Mt is attacking the scribes and Pharisees (v. 29) for hypocritical behavior. They consider themselves better than their ancestors who had persecuted the prophets. But their deeds prove otherwise. Identifying Jesus with Wisdom, Mt omits the reference to Wisdom as speaker. Jesus becomes the "I" who sends "prophets, wise people and scribes" who are killed, crucified, and scourged in "your synagogues" and persecuted from town to town. The separation between Judaism and Christianity is not a polite agreement to go separate ways. It has resulted from the hostility with which Christian preachers were treated (also see 5:10–12,44; 10:23).

Mt 23:8–12 warns Christians against copying the behavior attributed to Jewish teachers. They are not to seek titles and positions of honor. Some of the sharp polemic against the "hypocrites" may well be aimed at Mt's own community. Mt also warns against other Christians who are not the "prophets" sent by Jesus but "false prophets" (7:15). Simply claiming Jesus as "Lord" will not gain entry into the kingdom. A person must do the will of God (7:21–23). Mt 24:9b–13 expands the warning about persecution in Mk 13:13 to include evils within the community: (a) betrayal and hatred; (b) false prophets leading people astray; (c) love growing cold and an increase in lawlessness.

Yet Mt does not seek to establish a Christian Pharisaism. His gospel concludes with an affirmation that Jesus' teaching is to be spread to "all the nations." The word *ethne,* "nations," is often used to mean "Gentiles." Mt has even based his gospel on Mark, a work which originated among Gentile Christians. He acknowledges that Christians are engaged in missionary efforts to convert Gentiles (10:17–18) even in the missionary discourse which limits the activity of the disciples to the lost sheep of Israel.

James, the leader of Jewish Christianity in Paul's time, had been martyred ca. A.D. 62, and the Christian community at Jerusalem had been scattered during the Jewish revolt against Rome in A.D. 66–70. Mt's portrayal of Jewish hostility toward Jesus and his followers suggests that by the time he writes there is not much hope for a continued mission to Israel.

His gospel advocates a mission among the Gentiles. But such a mission must have seemed to mean rejecting the strong Jewish Christian heritage of the community. Why, people may have wondered, is such a turn toward the Gentiles not another example of "apostasy" and "lawlessness"? Mt's presentation of Jesus and the law responds to such suspicions.

We have already seen that Jesus is presented as the "fulfillment" of the law and the one whose teaching emphasizes the fundamental elements of the law on which all else depends: love of God and neighbor, justice, mercy. Now take a look at the way in which Mt 15:1–14 handles the controversy with the Pharisees over the custom of ritual washing before meals from Mark 7:1–15. Naturally he omits the explanation of Jewish purification rituals in Mark 7:3–4. He then relocates the argument to show that Pharisaic "traditions" are often ways of rejecting the commandments of God from its Markan position after the Isaiah prophecy to before the prophecy. The reader thus sees that the "traditions" which the Pharisees seek to enforce are the human doctrines and false worship about which Isaiah speaks. Mt adds a brief exchange between Jesus and the disciples about Pharisaic objections to Jesus' teaching (vv. 12–14). They are "blind guides" whose teaching does not come from God and will be destroyed. In the explanation which follows (Mt 15:15–20//Mk 7:17–23) Mt omits Mark's generalizing of the episode to imply that Jesus had also suspended all kosher rules (Mk 7:19b).

Jesus' teaching presents the true commandment of God. It is possible to include Gentiles in the community without abandoning the law as God intended it. Some Jewish customs and traditions can even be done away with in Christian circles, since they do not represent the "word of God" but mere human customs. Traditions which are seen as ways of avoiding the will of God expressed in the commandment should be done away with. In this episode we have the example of declaring some part of one's property "Corban," dedicated to God, and thus avoiding the obligation to support one's parents. The controversy over divorce in Mt 19:3–9 (Mk 10:1–12) presents us with another example of such a distinction. This time a provision of the Mosaic law, granting the divorced woman a certificate of divorce (Deut 24:1), is rejected as an accommodation to human "hardness of heart" but not part of God's will which is exemplified in creation.

You can see that Mt has been careful to make it clear that Jesus does not "annul" the law. Jesus' teaching expresses the will of God which is the norm for all obedience to the law. The way in which Mt links the double love command with the affirmation that Jesus is Son of David in 22:34–46 reminds us that Jesus is more than just another interpreter of the law. Because Jesus is the messianic Son of David, the one who fulfills the proph-

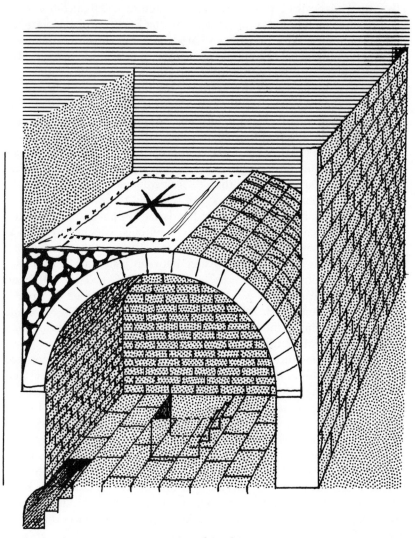

Ritual Bath.

ets, his word about the will of God is more than a human interpretation. It is the renewal of God's own intention in giving the law. Indeed by going beyond the law as the possession of Israel and its Jewish interpreters, the scribes and Pharisees, Mt sees that Jesus' teaching can be preached as God's word to all the nations (28:19).

Discipleship in Matthew

The commission in Mt 28:19 calls upon Jesus' followers to "make disciples" from all the nations. The verb *matheteuein*, to "make a disciple of someone" or to "be a disciple," occurs in Mt 13:52 and 27:57. In the latter it designates Joseph of Arimathea as Jesus' disciple. Mt 13:52 speaks of "every scribe who has been made a disciple for the kingdom." Such a person is able to bring out of his treasure both old things and new things. Many scholars think that this verse is the evangelist's description of himself. We have seen hints that Mt's community needs both "new things" and "old ones" to meet the situation in which it finds itself. Externally disciples must face persecution, opposition from both Jews and Gentiles, and other hardships that went along with preaching the gospel. Internally the community appears to be sharply divided. There are conflicting voices among the teachers and prophets. There is confusion about how the community should proceed in the future. There is confusion about how it should relate to its Jewish Christian heritage.

Even worse than the uncertainty and confusion, we find hints that relationships between Christians are also deteriorating. This problem emerges most clearly in the discourse on relationships within the community in Mt 18. As in the other discourses Mt has gathered together material from Mark, Q and his own tradition and reshaped it. The chapter opens with an affirmation that only one who is willing to be humble, of no importance, like a child is great in the kingdom. Notice how Mt 18:3–4 has reformulated the tradition of Mk 10:15. The issue is no longer "receiving" the kingdom like a child or, as in v. 5, receiving a child in Jesus' name (cp. Mk 9:37). Rather the disciple must become like a child. Remember that in the first century being a child did not have warm, positive feelings associated with it. Being a child was like being a slave, someone of no significance or importance. Mt 18:4 emphasizes that point by speaking of one who "humbles" himself or herself.

Mt 18:6–9 shifts abruptly to a severe warning against persons who cause others to stumble. Mt adds v. 7 to material he has taken over from Mk 9:42–48. Even if it is necessary, part of the evils at the end of the age, that stumbling blocks will come, the person responsible is condemned. From this general warning against leading others to sin, Mt turns to leaders of the community. He uses the parable of the lost sheep from Q (Mt 18:12–13//Lk 15:4–6) to remind them that they must always seek out one of the "little ones" who has gone astray. God wants them to be saved, not to perish.

Several sayings about relationships between Christians follow in vv.

15–21. A simpler Q saying exhorting Christians to forgive one another (cf. Luke 17:3–4) has been expanded to form a set of rules for handling disputes between Christians. Whatever decisions the community reaches in re-solving such conflicts are viewed as binding in heaven (v. 18). Finally this teaching on forgiveness is concluded with the parable of the unforgiving servant (vv. 23–35). Christians are warned that if they do not forgive one another they are liable to judgment. This emphasis upon mutual forgive-ness appears to be Mt's response to the betrayal, hatred and "love growing cold" that afflicts the community. We have seen that Mt constantly warns the reader that Christians must always be prepared for God's judgment. Otherwise they could find themselves excluded like the wedding guests with the wrong attire in Mt 22:11–14.

Mt also has a message of comfort for this troubled church. They can trust in Jesus' eternal presence (Mt 28:20). Mt reworks a sequence of three Markan stories of Jesus and the disciples in a boat to show how the "little faith" of the disciples is strengthened by Jesus. The first is the storm at sea (Mt 8:18,23–27//Mk 4:35–41). Where Mark has Jesus rebuke the disciples for having no faith after he has calmed the storm (Mk 4:40), Mt has Jesus ask why they are afraid, persons of little faith, and then calm the storm. In that way we see Jesus' gesture as one of reassurance. Trust and reassurance for a battered community become the focus of Mt's presentation of the walking on water miracle (Mt 14:22–23//Mk 6:45–52). In Mark the episode concludes with a severe chiding of the disciples for being persons whose hearts are hardened. Mt's version, on the other hand, demonstrates Jesus' ability to save. Not only are the disciples rescued, but even Peter could walk on water if his faith had not failed him. At the end of the story, the disciples acknowledge that Jesus is the Son of God.

The final example shifts from the realm of miracles to that of teaching. The warning about the leaven of the Pharisees (Mk 8:14–21//Mt 16:5–12) again finds the Markan disciples chided for their lack of understanding and hardness of heart. In Mt Jesus refers to the "little faith" of the disciples. He then explains in such a way that the disciples do understand that the "leaven" means the teaching of the Pharisees and Sadducees. Thus Mt suggests that it is not just the presence of Jesus helping the community but also Jesus' teaching which can sustain them during this time of "little faith." Mt also makes it clear that the disciples understood that teaching in 13:51 and 17:13. He omits the elements of fear and misunderstanding from their response to the passion predictions (Mt 20:17–19 contrast Mk 10:32–34).

Of course the Sermon on the Mount provides the basic description of what it means to be a disciple of Jesus. The beatitudes describe the blessings on Jesus' "little ones" who are persecuted for the sake of the kingdom (5:3–12). The sayings about salt and light admonish the disciples never to surrender their mission of witnessing before humanity (5:13–16). Then the "higher righteousness" which Jesus has made possible is described first in a series of antitheses which culminate in love of enemy (5:21–48). Teaching about true almsgiving, fasting and worship again emphasizes the need for forgiveness (6:1–18, see 6:14–15). Disciples must be devoted to the kingdom. Neither desires for earthly possessions nor anxieties about how they are to survive are to deter them (6:19–34). Mt 7 turns to teaching and warning directed at some of the tensions within the community. Once again we are reminded not to judge others (7:1–5). Only "hypocrites" try to take a grain of dirt out of someone else's eye while they have a log in their own. Whatever happens, disciples are not to abandon their confidence in God as the source of "good things" when they turn to ask (7:7–11). But as in the earlier teaching about prayer, the disciple's prayer is complemented by love of others. Here the golden rule summarizes the positive ethical teaching of the Sermon (7:12). These instructions on discipleship conclude with warnings about judgment (7:13–27).

Summary

We have seen that Mt is more than a collection of traditions about Jesus gathered together in the framework of the ministry and passion of Jesus. The evangelist has shaped the traditions about Jesus to address the situation of Christians who must find their way outside the original confines of Judaism. Mt assures them that Jesus and his teaching bring that tradition to its fulfillment. They can go out to the nations with a treasure that embraces both old things and new ones. In the teaching which Jesus gave the disciples Christians have a guide to the true expression of God's will for humanity.

For those who are troubled by the on-going hardships of discipleship and even the internal turmoil which divides the community, Matthew shows the disciples learning to overcome their "little faith" by trusting in Jesus' power to save them. As long as it exists in this age the church will be a mixed community of good and bad. God's judgment will be the time of separation. In the present Christians must remember that discipleship asks them to always be ready for the Lord's return. Their relationships with one another are not to be marked by legalism, judgment or exclusion. They are to be characterized by justice, mercy, forgiveness and a repeated willingness to go out to the "lost." Mt ends with a ringing affirmation of the Lord's presence to the community of "little ones" (28:20b). This presence fulfills the promise given in the naming of Jesus "Emmanuel," "God-with-us," at the beginning of the gospel (1:22–23).

STUDY QUESTIONS

Facts You Should Know

1. List five ways in which Mt has revised material taken over from Mk and give an example of each one.
2. Give three examples of Mt's emphasis on judgment. To whom is the warning about judgment directed in each example?
3. Give three examples of Jesus as "true interpreter of the law" from Mt. How is Jesus contrasted with other teachers in the context from which you have taken your examples?
4. Give three examples in which Mt has shifted Mark's picture of Jesus' disciples away from "misunderstanding" and "fear." What characteristics has Mt given the disciples in his portrayal?
5. How does Mt use the warnings against the "hypocrites" (Pharisees) to address dangers within the Christian community?

Things To Do

1. Using a concordance find the passages in which Mt uses the verb "to fulfill." What do these passages tell the reader of the gospel about Jesus?

2. Using a gospel parallels, study the five sermons in Mt's gospel. How has Mt brought together traditional material in each case? How do the concluding warnings about judgment fit in with the teaching given in each sermon?

Things To Think About

1. Mt addresses a warning about judgment to the Christian community of his day. What failures in Christian discipleship today call for such warnings?

2. Both the sermon on relationships within the community (Mt 18) and the condemnation of the Pharisees (Mt 23) carry lessons about leadership for Christians. How could those lessons be applied today?

Chapter 14

LUKE: JESUS, THE LORD

The Composition of Luke

Luke opens with a prologue which tells the reader that the evangelist follows in a tradition of others who have already given accounts of what has happened among the Christians. Scholars have often pointed out the parallels between the prologues of Luke–Acts and those of Greek authors. The Jewish historian Josephus wrote an apologetic work, *Against Apion*, which is addressed to a distinguished figure and which picks up the account in a second volume (*Against Apion* 1.1 sec. 1–3; 2.1 sec. 1). As a reference to earlier writings, Josephus points to his own history, *Antiquities of the Jews*, which is based on the sacred books of the Jews. He assures his distinguished reader that his book is written to "convict our detractors of opprobrium and deliberate falsehood, to correct the ignorance of others, and to instruct whoever desires to know the truth about the antiquity of our race."

You can see that Luke's preface is similar to this model. The purpose for his composition appears in v. 4b, "may know what assurance (*asphaleia*) you have for the matters about which you have been instructed." Some scholars think that this phrase is another way of phrasing the apologetic concern represented in Josephus. Luke is defending Christianity against false accusations before a sympathetic Roman audience. Luke uses a similar expression "to know the *asphales*," "certainty/truth" in Acts 21:34. There the uproar of the crowd shouting contradictory opinions makes it impossible for the tribune to tell what Paul is being accused of. Paul is taken inside and gives a speech in his own defense. This pattern is repeated in the introduction to Paul's speech before the council in Acts 22:30. When Paul is brought before king Agrippa in Acts 25:26, the Roman procurator says that he has nothing *asphales* to charge Paul with. Again

Paul will give a speech in his own defense. These examples suggest that *asphaleia* means knowing the truth about the Christian message.

Persons who know this truth will recognize that accusations brought against those who preach the message are false. In that sense Luke-Acts can be described as an apologetic work. However, Theophilus is not an outsider like the officials in the trial stories. Luke says that he has already received reports about or perhaps even been instructed in Christian matters. Therefore other scholars have suggested that Luke has more in mind than apologetics. He wishes to assure the reader that what the church is preaching goes back to the kerygma (preaching) of Jesus and the earliest disciples.

Luke's preface has already told us that he is going to use earlier material but set these traditions in a more appropriate order. Like Mt, Luke takes over much of Mark but makes additions from Q and from material unique to Luke ("L"). There are two sections of Mark that are not represented at all in Luke: Mk 6:45–8:26; 9:41–10:12. One of the most striking differences between Mark and Luke is the block of material between Luke 9:51 and 18:14. This new section follows the Lucan versions of the transfiguration, healing of the possessed boy, passion prediction and dispute about greatness (Lk 9:28–50) which are from the Markan teaching on discipleship (Mk 9:2–41). Luke returns to this section of Mark at 18:15–43.

Luke 9:51 is phrased in formal language, much like the Greek Old Testament. Jesus turns toward Jerusalem to fulfill a divine plan by which he will be "taken up" (to heaven) from Jerusalem. Luke turns that journey to Jerusalem into a lengthy period of instruction. Over half of the "L" material in the gospel is found here. This material includes a number of well-known parables of Jesus: good Samaritan (10:29–37); persistent friend (11:5–8); rich fool (12:16–21); fig tree (13:1–9); lost coin (15:8–10); prodigal son (15:11–32); dishonest steward (16:1–8a); rich man and Lazarus (16:19–31); unjust judge (18:1–8); Pharisee and tax collector (18:9–14). The journey section reaches its conclusion when Jesus reaches Jerusalem.

Luke divides the ministry of Jesus in three sections: (a) Galilean ministry (4:14–9:50); (b) journey to Jerusalem (9:51–19:27); (c) ministry in Jerusalem (19:28–21:38). Luke introduces the gospel with an account of the births of John the Baptist and Jesus in fulfillment of God's plan of salvation (1:5–2:52) and the career of the Baptist as preparation for the opening of Jesus' ministry (3:1–4:13). The gospel ends with the passion (22:1–23:56a) and resurrection of Jesus (23:56b–24:53). However, Luke makes it clear that the end of the gospel is not the end of his story. The disciples are told to wait in Jerusalem for the coming of the Spirit; then they will be witnesses of all that has happened to the nations (24:47–49).

Luke also shifts the order of episodes taken over from Mark to provide better narrative continuity. He finishes with the Baptist before Jesus' public ministry begins by mentioning John's imprisonment in the context of his baptismal activity (3:19–20). Jesus' rejection at Nazareth (from Mark 6:1–16) is incorporated into a synagogue scene that inaugurates Jesus' ministry in Luke 4:16–30. There we learn that the Spirit rests on Jesus in fulfillment of the messianic prophecies. But we also see that Jesus will have a double fate. Some will receive the news with joy. Others will reject God's salvation. Luke has also built the same contrast into the infancy narratives. Read Luke 2:24–38. When Jesus is brought to the temple the prophetic figures Simeon and Anna, who represent the pious of Israel, receive him with joy. Anna becomes a "witness," telling others who are looking for the promised redemption about him. Simeon proclaims that God's salvation has come for all people. However, his blessing on Mary warns of opposition. Luke has moved the episode about Jesus' real relatives (Mk 3:31–35) to follow the interpretation of the parable of the sower (8:19–21). There it becomes an example of those who do hear and follow the word of God.

Luke has also built parallel episodes into each of the three sections of the ministry of Jesus. These episodes are another way of contrasting those who welcome Jesus with those who reject him.

We also find another block of special Lucan material in the passion and resurrection accounts of the gospel. The passion includes an appearance before Herod (23:6–12) and explicit declarations of Jesus' innocence

DIVISIONS IN JESUS' MINISTRY			[14–1]
	Galilee	**Journey**	**Jerusalem**
rejection:	Nazareth (4:22–29)	Samaria (9:52–56)	Jerusalem (19:42–48)
sends disciples:	"the 12" (9:1–6)	"the 70" (10:1–20)	"the 12" (22:35–38)
relatives/ women:	true relatives (8:19–21)	mother blessed (11:27–28)	women of Jerusalem (23:26)
true greatness:	receive child (9:46–48)	Jesus' "baptism" (12:50)	one who serves (22:24–27)
Herod:	his opinion (9:7–9)	Jesus warned about (13:31–35)	Jesus appears before (23:6–16)

OUTLINE OF LUKE   *[14–2]*

Prologue (1:1–4)

Infancy narratives: John the Baptist and Jesus (1:5–2:52)

Preparation for Jesus' ministry (3:1–4:13)
  (a) The Baptist's preaching and imprisonment (3:1–20)
  (b) Jesus: Baptism, genealogy and temptation (3:21–4:13)

Jesus' ministry in Galilee (4:14–9:50)
  (a) Proclamation and rejection at Nazareth (4:14–30)
  (b) Healings and calling of Peter (4:31–5:16)
  (c) Controversies with Jewish authorities (5:17–6:11)
  (d) Teaching: Sermon on the Plain (6:12–49)
  (e) Healings: Testimony to Jesus (7:1–50)
  (f) Galilean women disciples (8:1–3)
  (g) Parables: Hearing and doing the word (8:4–21)
  (h) Miracles: Jesus' power (8:22–9:6)
  (i) Jesus' identity, passion prediction and transfiguration (9:7–36)
  (j) Exorcism, passion prediction and instruction of disciples (9:49–50)

Journey to Jerusalem (9:51–19:27)
  (a) Departure: Rejection in Samaria (9:51–56)
  (b) Disciples and their mission (9:57–10:24)
  (c) Parables and sayings of Jesus (10:25–13:21)
  (d) Rejection of Jesus: Warning about Herod, departure from Galilee and lament for Jerusalem (13:22–35)
  (e) Sayings and parables of Jesus (14:1–18:14)
  (f) Conditions of discipleship, passion prediction (18:15–19:27)

Jesus' ministry in Jerusalem (19:28–21:38)
  (a) Entry, lament over Jerusalem and cleansing of the temple (19:28–46)
  (b) Reaction to Jesus: Hostility and acceptance (19:47–48)
  (c) Teaching: Controversies with authorities (20:1–21:4)
  (d) Teaching: Fate of Jerusalem, persecutions, end-time (21:5–38)

Passion of Jesus (22:1–23:56a)

Resurrection of Jesus (23:56b–24:53)
  (a) **The empty tomb (23:56b–24:12)**
  (b) **Appearance on the road to Emmaus (24:13–35)**
  (c) **Appearance commissioning the disciples (24:36–49)**
  (d) **Jesus is taken up into heaven (24:50–53)**

by Pilate (23:4, 14–15, 22). Luke's narrative even makes it appear that Pilate turned Jesus over to the hostile crowd for execution (23:25–26). This emphasis may be apologetic. Luke wishes to make it clear to anyone who reads his narrative that Jesus was not guilty of the charges of rebellion and insurrection that led to his death. Even those involved in his execution knew that he was innocent.

You will also notice that the scene on the cross is quite different in Luke. Instead of praying Psalm 22:2 (see Mk 14:34) Jesus speaks like an exemplary martyr. He forgives his enemies in their ignorance of what they are really doing and prays Psalm 31:6, entrusting his spirit to God (23:24, 46). Even the two criminals crucified with Jesus are divided. One shares the mockery of the crowd, challenging Jesus' claim to be savior (23:39); the other acknowledges his own sinfulness and Jesus' innocence. The repentant criminal is promised the reward of all who believe, eternal life with Jesus (23:40–43). This exchange also shows the reader the value of repentance and faith in Jesus.

Luke's resurrection traditions included appearances of the Lord in the vicinity of Jerusalem as well as the disciples' vision of Jesus being taken up into heaven as had been promised in 9:51. These stories include the famous encounter of Jesus and two disciples on the road to Emmaus (24:13–35) as well as an appearance to the disciples at a meal (24:36–43). The meal story includes a tradition of Jesus' commissioning the disciples to mission (24:44–49) which Mt 28:16–20 has in the context of a Galilee appearance. We saw that in Mt the final commission reflected the concerns of the gospel. Luke's commissioning scene plays a similar role. The message which the disciples carry is one of repentance and forgiveness of sin. They are the witnesses upon whom the faith of the later community depends. Luke also emphasizes a pattern of salvation history in which Jesus fulfills God's promises in his suffering, in his resurrection and in the preaching about him to all the nations. That last episode in the story will be the theme of Luke's second volume, Acts.

You can see from the outline of Luke that the introduction of the journey section has shifted the passion predictions, transfiguration and teaching about suffering discipleship out of the central position that they occupy

in Mark. You can also see that the blocks of teaching are not organized into
identifiable sermons as they are in Mt. Look up the Lucan version of material which Mt has in the Sermon on the Mount (6:17–7:1). You will notice
that the section has a formal ending (7:1) but that its beginning has Jesus
teaching and healing crowds of people. The opening beatitudes appear to
be addressed to those who have come for healing. Within the smaller units
of the gospel we do find Luke linking material together around particular
themes. Read Chapter 15. Verses 1–2 create a setting for the whole: the
accusation that Jesus welcomes tax collectors and sinners and eats with
them. The gospel reader has already met this objection in the story of the
calling of Levi (Lk 5:27–32), which included a feast given by Levi for Jesus.
There Jesus answered the objection by quoting a proverb about the sick
needing a doctor and asserting that his mission is to call sinners to repentance.

Here Jesus does not answer directly but tells three stories which focus
on the finding or return of what has been lost. The first, the lost sheep,
also appears in Mt where it is addressed to community leaders (Mt 18:10–
14). Luke's version of the story suggests that a repentant sinner brings
more joy in heaven than many righteous people (v. 7). Luke pairs the story
of the lost sheep with a story of a woman searching for a lost coin. We
frequently find pairs of stories with male and female characters in Luke.
Again the emphasis is on the joy in heaven that comes from a repentant
sinner (v. 10). In both of these stories the person who finds what is lost also
calls together neighbors to rejoice in finding what is lost. The parable of
the prodigal son picks up this theme in an even more dramatic way. The
father gives a great banquet for his lost son. He also answers the objections
of the dutiful older son. Rejoicing at the return of one who is lost does not
mean that the older son is excluded from his father's love. Of course,
Luke's introduction leads the reader to think of the older son as representative of the complaining Pharisees in vv. 1–2. If they continue to refuse to rejoice in the return of the lost being brought about by Jesus'
ministry, then they will be shut out of the feast.

You can see that these stories begin to provide the reader with an
explanation for the rejection of Jesus. Luke will insist that the charges
against Jesus at his trial were recognized as false. No one should claim that
because Jesus was executed by crucifixion, he was a bad person or had
sought to lead his disciples in revolt. Rather the rejection of Jesus is
grounded in the attitudes exhibited by the religious leaders. Jesus' ministry to the sinners of the people and his table fellowship signifying their
place in God's kingdom led to hostility. Like the older brother in the parable these people were unable to see that God's will makes it "right" to

call what is lost to repentance and to celebrate their return as the sign of
salvation.

The Time of Salvation

Jesus' opening sermon in Luke 4:16–30 proclaims that the scripture's
promise of a time of salvation is fulfilled in Jesus. The repentance and celebrations of joy which are responses to Jesus' preaching in the gospel are
further signs that a new age of salvation is being inaugurated. Another sign
of the "new time" are persons praising and glorifying God. Both Eliza-
beth's blessing upon Mary and Mary's Magnificat speak of the joy of faithful people now that God's promises are being fulfilled (Lk 1:42–45,46–55).
Zechariah blesses God (1:64,68–79). So do the angels in heaven (2:13–14).
The people respond to Jesus' miracles by praising God (5:26; 7:16; 9:43 [are
astonished at the majesty of God]; 13:17; 17:15 [proper response to heal-
ing]; 18:43). Luke's version of the entry to Jerusalem adds praises by a
crowd of disciples for the great works they had seen Jesus perform (19:37).
In Mark the centurion at the cross had recognized the true secret of Jesus'
identity, that he was Son of God (Mk 15:39). In Luke that episode becomes
recognition of Jesus' innocence and praise of God (23:47). And at the very
end of the gospel we see the disciples returning to Jerusalem in joy and
praising God in the temple (24:52–53).

These examples of praise show that the faithful of Israel received Jesus
as the fulfillment of God's promises. Luke thus presents the reader of the
gospel with a pattern of "salvation history." First there were God's promises to Israel and the formation of those pious ones who are waiting for
salvation from the Lord like Simeon and Anna. John the Baptist is the culmination of that part of salvation history. This period is followed by the
time of salvation experienced in Jesus' ministry (16:16). The Spirit had
been at work guiding Israel and shaping its faithful people during the first
period of salvation history (1:15,35,41,67; 2:25–26). It has come to rest on
Jesus and guides his ministry (3:22; 4:1,18).

Salvation history does not move from the ministry of Jesus directly to
the second coming. Luke uses Jesus' parable of the master entrusting servants with money (19:11–24) to caution those who think that the kingdom
is to appear immediately. He also formulates Jesus' predictions about the
fate of Jerusalem so that the destruction of Jerusalem is not a prelude to
the end-time as it is in Mark 13 (21:20–24; cp. Mk 13:14–20). Instead the
destruction of Jerusalem is the prelude to the "times of the Gentiles" (v.
24). They must be fulfilled before the end-time. This shift along with the

commissioning of the disciples (24:44–49) and the continuation of the gospel story into Acts points toward a third epoch in salvation history, the period of the church's mission. Luke 24:49 looks toward another out-pouring of God's Spirit to inaugurate that time of salvation. It comes upon Jesus' Jewish disciples at Pentecost (Acts 2:4) and then upon the first Gentile converts (Acts 10:44–48).

Luke has also set the scene for this time of salvation at several points in the infancy narratives. We have seen that Simeon's prophecy spoke of a salvation for all the peoples (2:31–32). The evangelist also points to the birth of Jesus as an event that belongs to "world history" in 2:1–2. Instead of dating Jesus' birth in terms of Jewish history by using the kingship of Herod as in Luke 1:5 for John the Baptist, Jesus' birth is associated with an event in the Roman history of the province of Judea. The angelic announcement in Lk 2:10–14 also has similar overtones. The "peace" which is linked to the birth of the messiah-lord might well have been compared to the "peace" which the Roman emperor Augustus claimed to have brought to the civilized world. Three times the doors of the temple of Janus open in war time were closed and the great altar to the Augustan peace was constructed in the Campus Martius. We also have inscriptions from the eastern Mediterranean which hailed Augustus as "savior of the whole world" and said of his birthday, "[the birthday] of the god has marked the beginning of the good news through him for the world." Since these themes were repeated on coins and inscriptions throughout the empire, Luke's readers would easily get the message of the angelic announcement: Jesus, not the emperor, is the source of peace and salvation. Lk 19:38 has this theme picked up by the crowds as Jesus enters Jerusalem. You can see that from the point of view of salvation history the story is still incomplete. The gospel only points toward the next phase, the period of the church. The story which still must be told in Acts is the story of how the "good news" was brought from among the faithful of Israel to the Gentiles. Geographically Luke will depict the progress of the gospel outward from Jerusalem (24:47).

Jesus as Universal Savior

Clearly Luke's narrative uses the dynamic movement of a history unfolding according to God's plan to address the question of the place of non-Jews in a salvation that was rooted in Israel. Greco-Roman society was grounded in tradition. Roman piety respected the ancestral religions of conquered peoples. As a form of Judaism, Christianity might well have claimed a legitimate place in the world. But what of a religious movement which is converting Gentiles away from their ancestral traditions? Is this movement really a religion or a malicious superstition which can only disrupt the good order of families and society? The Roman historian Tacitus reports the trial of a Roman noble woman, Pomponia Graecina, on the charge of practicing a "foreign religion" (*Annals* 13.32.3–5). Scholars have suggested that she may have been attached to Judaism or perhaps even a Jewish Christian group in first century Rome. In his account of Nero's persecution of Christians after the great fire, Tacitus describes Christianity as a pernicious superstition:

> Nero . . . inflicted most extreme punishments on those, hateful by reason of their abominations, who were commonly called Christians. Christus, the originator of that name, had been executed by the procurator Pontius Pilate. The pernicious superstition, checked for the moment, was bursting out again not only throughout Judea, the birthplace of the plague, but also throughout the city into which all that is horrible and shameful streams from every quarter and is constantly practiced. Therefore first those who confessed were arrested, then on their information a huge throng was convicted not so much on a charge of arson as because of their hatred of the human race. (*Annals* 15.44.2–8)

Many scholars think that part of the apologetic function of Luke–Acts is to provide a way of answering such charges against Christianity. For Paul the problem had been to defend the inclusion of Gentiles in salvation based on their faith in Christ against objections that were Jewish in origin. Luke's situation appears to be different. He must ground a Gentile movement in its Jewish heritage. In so doing, Luke can show that Christianity is not a pernicious superstition but a religion with an ancient tradition founded on divine revelation.

However Luke must also show that what begins in Israel is appropriately expanded to others. Acts will tell the story of how that expansion comes about in the earliest period, the "rebirth" after the crucifixion to which Tacitus refers. We have seen that the gospel points forward to this project.

Luke's gospel also presents another form of universalism, which is sometimes reflected in the opponents of Christianity who think of Christians primarily as social misfits. Luke depicts Jesus dealing with persons, women and men, from all levels of society. Tax collectors, often wealthy men, are frequently mentioned (5:27,29–30; 7:29,34; 15:1; 18:10–13; 19:2–10). They exemplify the larger class of "sinners" who hear Jesus' message, repent and find salvation (7:36–50, sinful woman; 15:11–32, prodigal son as an example story). Women are explicitly mentioned among Jesus' disciples. Some like the Galilean women (8:1–3) and Martha and Mary (10:38–42) are represented as women who have houses or other financial resources under their own control. But we also meet the poor in the persons of widows (7:11–17; 18:1–8; 21:1–4) and the parable of Lazarus and the rich man (16:20). They are singled out in Jesus' announcement of salvation (4:18; 6:20).

"Seeking and saving what is lost" (19:10) is presented as the mission of Jesus. The sweep of Luke's vision of salvation history recognizes that all persons are to be included. This perspective is expressed in Acts 4:12: "Salvation comes through no one else, for there is no other name under the heavens given to human beings by which we must be saved." Luke suggests that true peace and unity among peoples is not created by the order of the Roman empire but by a common hope for salvation which is open to all people.

Where Paul often speaks of salvation as the future destiny of Christians (Phil 2:12; 3:20), Luke presents it as something which is already achieved. He is the only synoptic author to call Jesus "savior" (2:11; Acts 5:31; 13:23) and frequently speaks of salvation (1:69,71; 19:9; 2:30; 3:6; Acts 4:12; 7:25; 13:26,47; 16:17; 27:34). Christ's role as savior is frequently spoken of as forgiveness of sins. This expression only appears in the other synoptics at Mark 1:4 and Mt 26:28. Jesus forgives sins during his ministry and makes it the focal point of the disciples' mission to the world (24:47). This mission is fulfilled in Acts (2:38; 5:31; 10:43; 13:38; 26:18). Other manifestations of salvation are found in the Lucan use of expressions like "peace," "joy" and "life." Luke even speaks of the resurrection as the way in which Jesus became "the leader of life" (Acts 3:15). Thus, the coming of Jesus has opened up new possibilities of life for all of humanity.

Discipleship in Luke

These new possibilities have to be embodied in a life of discipleship. We have seen that repentance and conversion mark a person's entry into that new life. We have also seen that Luke takes pains to emphasize the diversity of persons who are called to discipleship by Jesus. We meet women and men from all social categories. The calling of Peter in Luke 5:1–11 exemplifies the response required of a disciple. Peter's first response is to confess his sinfulness (v. 8). But he, James and John accept the Lord's call and "leave everything and follow him" (v. 11). Levi the tax collector also responds by "leaving everything" to follow Jesus (5:28). The women disciples in Galilee are following Jesus and providing for Jesus and the disciples (8:1–3). In the story of Mary and Martha, Mary is commended for her single-minded devotion to the word which Jesus teaches (10:38–42). True discipleship is characterized as "hearing and keeping the word of God" (8:19–21). Throughout the gospel, Jesus' mother Mary is pictured as the first disciple for her hearing of the word.

Luke's emphasis on disciples "leaving everything" to follow Jesus draws attention to an important theme in Luke: the danger of wealth and position to the life of discipleship. Luke's version of the beatitudes blesses the poor and condemns the wealthy and important persons who have achieved satisfaction of their desires in this life (Lk 6:20–26). Jesus speaks to the poor directly, promising them the kingdom (6:20). Several of the parables from Luke's special material deal with the traps posed by wealth: the rich fool (Lk 12:13–21), the unjust steward (16:1–8a) and the rich man and Lazarus (16:19–31). The conversion of the rich tax collector Zacchaeus exemplifies the kind of response such a person should make to the message of salvation (19:1–10).

Compare Luke's story of the rich ruler (18:18–30) with the Markan prototype of the rich man (Mk 10:17–31). Luke shifts the "go sell what you have and give to the poor" to emphasize the radical nature of the "selling" to "sell *all* that you have" (v. 22). In Mark the rich man goes away sad and the dialogue about wealth takes place between Jesus and his disciples. Luke omits the reference to the man leaving and makes him the recipient of Jesus' words about the difficulty rich persons have in entering the kingdom.

Luke understands discipleship as a call to following Jesus. His interpretation of the parable of the sower emphasizes the danger that the concerns of daily life will rob people of their enthusiasm for the gospel. Some may fall away because of "testing," perhaps when their faith is challenged by persecution. Others never gain any mature faith because it is choked off by "cares, riches and pleasures of life" (8:11–15). Luke recognizes that true discipleship requires not only hearing the message but holding onto it. It means a whole lifetime of "bearing fruit" which comes from the "good heart" of the faithful disciple.

Luke's model of the "first disciple" is Mary. He uses the episode of Jesus' mother and brothers to show that the true disciple "hears the word of God and does it" (8:19–21). This is the example which Mary set in the infancy narratives at the beginning of the gospel. Representing all of the faithful, pious ones of Israel, she heard and accepted the word of the Lord so that the promises of salvation could become realized through her. The same devotion is held up to all disciples in the gospel.

Summary

Luke makes the reader aware that the gospel stands at the center of a larger story of salvation. Its roots go back into the Old Testament. All of God's promises to the holy people of Israel are being fulfilled in Jesus. Its branches reach into the spread of the gospel throughout the known world by the disciples whom Jesus has selected as his witnesses. Luke will tell that story in his second volume, Acts. But from the beginning Luke reminds the reader that the coming of Jesus is not just an event in Jewish history. It is an event in the history of all humanity. He is careful to link the events of Jesus' birth with the Roman empire. Jesus, not the emperor Augustus, is the real savior of humanity. Jesus is the real source of God's peace.

Luke has also told the story of Jesus in such a way as to answer some of the charges and suspicions which people had about Christians. He emphasizes the fact that there is no evidence for the charges against Jesus. Jesus dies as an innocent person. His last words are a message of forgiveness and salvation. Christianity is not some new, dangerous superstition. It is rooted in the piety of Israel. The founder whom Christians revere is not subversive. He teaches people the way to peace. Christians are the ones who are following along the way which that Jesus set out for them.

STUDY QUESTIONS

Facts You Should Know

1. How do the following themes fit into the picture of Luke as a "defense" of Christianity: (a) the piety of Jesus' family in the infancy narratives; (b) the declarations of innocence at the trial of Jesus; (c) the pattern of acceptance of Jesus by the pious of Israel and his rejection by her leaders?
2. Give three examples of the Lucan theme of repentance and joy. How do these examples show that salvation is open to all?
3. What are the three major divisions in Luke? How does Luke tie the three sections together?
4. How does Luke show the reader that the events he is narrating belong to "world history" and not just the story of the Jewish people?
5. Give three examples in which Luke deals with the theme of wealth and discipleship. What message does he have for the Christian about possessions?

Things To Do

1. Luke often uses pairs of stories in which one has a man and the other has a woman as its central character. Find three examples of such pairs in the gospel.

2. Luke 7:36–50 contains a variant of the tradition of Jesus' anointing (cp. Mk 14:3–9). Find as many similarities as you can between this story and Mk's version. Which themes in the Lucan story are special emphases of the gospel? How is Luke's story related to what comes immediately before and immediately afterward in the gospel?

3. Using a gospel parallels compare Luke's account of Jesus in Gethsemane (Lk 22:39–46) with Mark's (Mk 14:32–42). How is Luke's picture of the relationship between Jesus and the disciples different?

4. Using a concordance find all of the times that Luke mentions prayer. What role does prayer play in the life of Jesus according to Luke?

Things To Think About

1. How can we preach a "time of salvation" for today's world?
2. What is the role that prayer plays in our lives?

Chapter 15

JOHN: JESUS, THE DIVINE SON

The Composition of John

The fourth gospel presents a strikingly different picture of Jesus from that in the synoptics. Read John 1:1–18. You can easily see the allusions to the opening chapter of Genesis: "in the beginning," reference to God's word as a creative power, the creation of light in the darkness and all things, including humans, coming to life through the word. Where the first creation story in Gen ended with God "resting" and making the sabbath holy, John 1:17 contrasts the law of Moses, which included the sabbath, with the "grace and truth" that comes in Jesus. This prologue, probably based on an earlier hymn, presents us with the story of Jesus as the coming of the divine Word to humanity. The Word is rejected by those who should receive it (1:11) but is the source of salvation and rebirth as children of God for those who believe (vv. 12–13). There is no other way to "know" God except through the Word that has come among humanity in Jesus (vv. 14,18).

Familiar elements of the story of Jesus have been incorporated into the prologue. John the Baptist is presented as the one sent to give testimony to the light (vv. 6–8,15). The presentation of the Baptist in John 1:19–37 mixes traditions familiar to those who have read the synoptics with the elements of the Johannine material. "Testimony" or "witness" (Gk. *marturia*) governs the whole story. We find the familiar citation from Is 40:3 used to describe the mission of the Baptist (v. 23; cf. Mk 1:3; Mt 3:1; Lk 3:4). The synoptics have the narrator introduce the quotation as a prophetic text about the Baptist. Here the passage becomes the content of what the Baptist said when questioned about his identity. You will also notice that Jn 1:23 collapses the second two phrases of the passage into one. Instead of "preparing the way" and "making straight his footsteps", we have "making straight the way."

We also find a traditional saying about the relationship between John and Jesus: "One stronger than I is coming after me, the strap of whose sandals I am not worthy to undo" (Mk 1:7; Lk 1:16; Mt 3:11 shifts the final phrase to "carry his sandals"). Jn 1:27 comes closest to the synoptic version of the saying. It is attached to John's testimony that the true prophet-messiah is present but unknown to those who are questioning John's authority: "the one who comes after me, of whom I am not worthy to undo the strap of his sandal." In addition, the evangelist has created "cross-references" to this saying. Jn 1:15 makes the content of the Baptist's testimony: "the one who comes after me ranks before me because he was before me." Jn 1:30 repeats the variant in 1:15.

As you read through the Baptist's testimony, you can see that the evangelist is assuming that the persons reading his gospel already know some version of the story about Jesus. The reader knows that John is engaged in baptizing (v. 25). The "Christological titles" about which the Baptist is questioned by the Jewish authorities are not being used as Jewish titles but as they have become traditional among Christians. Curiously the Baptist even denies being "Elijah." The synoptics know a tradition in which the Baptist was considered to be "Elijah," the forerunner of the messiah (e.g. Mk 9:11–13). While the Q tradition had presented the Baptist preaching a message of judgment and repentance (Lk 3:7–9; Mt 3:7–10 against the Pharisees and Sadducees), in the fourth gospel his message is about Jesus from the beginning. The evangelist has shaped two parallel stories using different groups of leaders from Jerusalem to make the point. Each ends with one of the traditional sayings (vv. 19–23, 24–28). The culmination of the Baptist's testimony comes in episodes set on the next two days. First, the traditional story about Jesus' baptism in which the Spirit descends on Jesus and the divine voice announces that Jesus is God's Son (Mk 1:9–11; Mt 3:13–17; Lk 3:21–22) is no longer a revelation addressed to Jesus. Instead, the Baptist has been given the vision of the Spirit descending on Jesus as a dove and testifies that Jesus is "Son of God." Second, John's witness leads two of his own disciples to become disciples of Jesus (vv. 35–37).

You can see from these examples that the fourth gospel differs from the synoptics in its presentation of individual episodes, in the wording and use of traditional sayings, and even in matters of chronology. You will hardly be surprised to discover that in the Johannine stories about the calling of disciples (1:35–51) those who follow Jesus do so because they recognize his messianic identity. From the outset we are presented with the story of God's Word come from heaven confronting a world in which there will be two reactions, unbelief (remaining in darkness) and belief (achieving salvation as God's children).

You can also see that in the gospel the narrator steps into the story to address the reader and to point out corresponding events. Sometimes we encounter passages in the gospel in which the evangelist appears to be summarizing the message about Jesus but has not marked the shift. Look at Jn 3:31–36, for example. Jn 3:30 has the Baptist testify to the relationship between himself and Jesus. Verses 31–36 summarize the significance of Jesus' mission in terms that recall the prologue of the gospel. Jesus has come from above to speak the words of God. His appearance divides humanity into two groups: believers who receive eternal life and unbelievers. Summary passages like this one give the reader insight into the gospel's understanding of Jesus. Jn 4:1–3 returns to the theme of Jesus and the Baptist.

You will notice that the transition is very awkward. Verse 1 reads "when the Lord [or "Jesus" in some manuscripts] knew that the Pharisees had heard that Jesus . . . ." This awkward transition is an example of a number of puzzles in the gospel. Sometimes we find very carefully crafted discourses patched together with rough transitions or even what appears to be an illogical sequence of events or places. Unlike the synoptics in which Jesus' ministry moves from Galilee to Jerusalem and the crucifixion, the fourth gospel has Jesus alternating between Galilee and Jerusalem as he does here. Sometimes the alternations appear to separate material that seems to belong together. For example, chapter 4 has Jesus leaving Judea for Galilee (v. 3). He meets a Samaritan woman on the way (vv. 4–42) and then arrives in Galilee where the healing of the official's son is set in Cana. But Jn 5:1 shifts back to Jerusalem where a sabbath healing leads to controversy and a lengthy discourse by Jesus. Jn 6:1 does not even mention Jesus' return to Galilee. It seems to presume that Jesus is journeying around Galilee. Jn 7:1a seems to contain the transition to Jesus going about in Galilee because of danger in Judea that would fit the gap at 6:1.

Many scholars think that the gospel passed through more than one edition. At some point chapter 6 might have followed chapter 4. Similarly Jesus' Supper discourses appear to be over at Jn 14:31, but we now have more discourses in chapters 15–17. In addition passages like Jn 16:5 pick up a theme of the earlier discourse "Where is Jesus going?" but contradict the development of the theme there (13:36 where Peter does ask where Jesus is going). The gospel comes to a conclusion in 20:30–31 after resurrection appearances in the vicinity of Jerusalem. Suddenly Jn 21 provides a new story of Jesus' appearance in Galilee in which the disciples seem to have no knowledge of what had happened before. One suggestion is that

the version of the gospel which we possess was edited after the death of
the original evangelist in order to preserve traditions that had been circulating in the Johannine communities.

John and Synoptic Tradition

You will notice that the Johannine Jesus speaks in long discourses
about himself and his mission. The short parables and sayings about the
kingdom of God found in the other gospels are missing here. This shift
makes the Johnnine Jesus sound quite different. Yet there are sayings and
even blocks of tradition which are similar to material found in the synoptics. One of the most striking appears in the story of the feeding of the
multitude in John 6. Chart 15-1 lists the parallels between this section of
John and material in Mark.

JOHN 6 AND MARKAN TRADITION		[15-1]
Episode	**John**	**Mark**
Feeding Crowd	6:1–15	6:30–40 (8:1–10)
Walking on Water	6:16–21	6:45–54
Request for a Sign	6:22–34	8:11–13
Jesus' Parentage	6:41–44	6:1–6
Misunderstanding	6:60–65	8:16–20
Peter's Confession	6:66–69	8:27–30
Passion Prediction	6:70–71	8:31–33

Other links can be drawn between sayings in John and the traditions
of Jesus' sayings preserved in the synoptics. Compare Jn 12:25 and Mt
10:40; Jn 5:9 and Mk 2:11; Jn 12:24 and Mk 3:24. The evangelist also
appears to have reformulated a tradition of Son of Man sayings. Chart
15-2 illustrates parallels between Johannine traditions and the three
types of saying found in Mark: (a) the coming of the Son of Man in glory;
(b) the present authority of the Son of Man; (c) the suffering Son of Man.
In each case the transformations reflect important themes in the fourth
gospel. Jn 1:51 picks up the pattern of ascent/descent that is repeated in
the gospel. The disciple is promised a vision of Jesus' true glory. Jn 5:27
appears in a discourse which has gone beyond the forgiveness of sins
linked to a healing miracle (cf. 5:14) to insist on Jesus' identity with God.
The Son can exercise the functions of the Father, judgment and giving
life. The final example is a passion prediction. But for John the passion

---

**JOHANNINE SON OF MAN SAYINGS AND MARKAN
TRADITION**   *[15–2]*

(a) *coming in glory:*

John 1:51	**Mark 14:62**
Truly, truly I say to you you will see the heaven opened, and the angels of God ascending and descending upon the Son of Man.	You will see the Son of Man seated at the right hand of Power and coming with the clouds of heaven.

(b) *authority of the Son of Man:*

John 5:27	**Mark 2:10**
and has given him authority to execute judgment because he is the Son of Man.	that you may know that the Son of Man has authority on earth to forgive sins.

(c) *Son of Man must suffer:*

John 12:34	**Mark 8:31**
We have heard from the law that the messiah remains forever; how can you say that the Son of Man must be lifted up?	And he began to teach them that the Son of Man must suffer many things . . .

---

is Jesus' return to the Father. It is the hour of Jesus' being "lifted up" or glorified (cf. 3:13–14; 8:28).

Some scholars think that even though John does not appear to depend upon the synoptics as written sources the evangelist may have known of one or more of the synoptics. Others feel that the parallels between John and the other gospels are accounted for by the hypothesis that the Jesus traditions in the Johannine community developed from a variant line of tradition that was related to that which is embodied in the synoptics. In addition John also has its own special material just as each synoptic writer did. The carefully shaped discourses in the gospel appear to have been formed in the preaching of the Johannine community before they were written down as we have them. Some scholars think that their distinctive style and symbolism go back to the "Beloved Disciple" who appears to have founded the Johannine group.

BOOK OF SIGNS: JESUS REVEALS THE FATHER (Chapters 1–12)

Prologue (1:1–18)

Gathering disciples (1:19–4:54)
  (a) Jesus as messiah, Son of God, Son of Man (1:19–51)
  (b) Miracle at Cana: Jesus' glory (2:1–12)
  (c) First Passover: Cleansing of the temple (2:13–25)
  (d) Nicodemus: Rebirth from heaven (3:1–21)
  (e) Judea: Jesus and John the Baptist (3:22–4:3)
  (f) Samaritan woman: Water of life (4:4–42)
  (g) Healing official's son: Second Cana sign (4:43–54)

Disputes: Jesus' True Identity (5:1–12:50)
  (a) Healing cripple: Son is like the Father (5:1–47)
  (b) Feeding five thousand: Son is bread of life (6:1–70)
  (c) Tabernacles discourse: Light of the world (7:1–52)
  (d) Divine I AM: Jesus greater than Abraham (8:12–59)
  (e) Healing blind man: Walk in the true light (9:1–41)
  (f) Jesus' sheep: True shepherd (10:1–42)
  (g) Raising Lazarus: Jesus gives life to the world (11:1–44)
  (h) Officials decide to kill Jesus (11:45–54)
  (i) Mary anoints Jesus (12:1–11)
  (j) Jesus' final public appearances in Jerusalem (12:12–50)

BOOK OF GLORY: JESUS RETURNS TO THE FATHER (Chapters 13–21)

At the Last Supper (13:1–17:26)
  (a) Footwashing: Example of service (13:1–30)
  (b) First discourse: Jesus' presence with disciples (13:31–14:31)
  (c) Second discourse: Remain on the true vine (15:1–16:4a)
  (d) Third discourse: Paraclete to console disciples (16:4b–33)
  (e) Fourth discourse: Jesus' prayer of unity (17:1–26)

Passion of Jesus (18:1–19:42)

Resurrection of Jesus (20:1–21:25)
  (a) Empty tomb (20:1–10)
  (b) Appears to Mary Magdalene (20:11–18)
  (c) Appears to disciples at meals (20:19–29)
  (d) First ending to the gospel (20:30–31)
  (e) Appears by the sea in Galilee (21:1–23)
  (f) Second ending to the gospel (21:24–25)

You can see from the outline that the gospel falls into two major sections. The first presents Jesus' public ministry up to the final rejection of his message in Jerusalem. It is punctuated by a series of miracles which climax in the raising of Lazarus. This miracle demonstrates that Jesus is the source of life even though people are about to put him to death. The second section gives the culmination of Jesus' mission in the return to the Father. The return is Jesus' glorification on the cross. The two divisions fit a pattern that dominates the whole gospel. Jesus is the one who has come from heaven to reveal God to those who believe. Jesus is the one who returns to heaven from the cross. There he lives in the glory of God which he has had since the beginning.

Jesus, the Jews and the World

The sharp division between Jesus, who comes from heaven, and those who belong to this world is reinforced by other dualistic symbols in the gospel. We have already met some of the most important: belief/unbelief; light/darkness; life/death. The separation of the heavenly Jesus and those who follow him from the world is clearly expressed in Jesus' prayer (Jn 17:13–19). Jesus is not "of the world." His disciples are being left "in the world" as witnesses to the words of God which they have received. Like Jesus they now have a mission to the world, but they are also to be made holy. They are to be kept safe from the "world" which John pictures as ruled by "the evil one." Like Jesus they will also have to expect hostility and persecution from a world which remains unwilling to hear the word of God (15:18–26).

The positive side of this separation between believers and the world is an intense unity of love with Jesus, the Father and one another. The gospel even speaks of those who believe as having passed into eternal life already (5:24; 6:51; 8:52). Of course the evangelist knows that believers will die at the end of this life. The gospel includes the traditional Christian view that Jesus will raise the faithful to new life on the last day. But the gospel presents the life-giving power of Jesus as already effective. The story of the raising of Lazarus in Jn 11:1–44 makes this point very dramatically. Martha already believes that her brother will be raised on the last day (11:21–24). Jesus tells her that because he is the "resurrection and the life" she will see something even greater than that: "Whoever lives and believes in me shall never die" (v. 26).

As you read through chapters 5–12 you will notice that the dualism in the gospel takes a very sharp form in disputes between Jesus and Jewish opponents. "The Jews" in these chapters represent the forces of unbelief.

They are constantly plotting to kill Jesus. Jesus accuses them of failing to worship God, failing to understand what Moses taught and even of being "children of Satan" rather than children of Abraham (8:39–47). Unlike the stories in the synoptics where Jesus answers his opponents with clever arguments that they should accept, the Johannine Jesus always answers with an even more difficult or extraordinary statement. Each episode moves from its initial tension toward even greater hostility. In Jn 8:12–59, for example, Jesus finally claims for himself the name of God "I Am." The Jewish charge that Jesus is not from God because he bears witness about himself becomes an angry debate over Jesus' claim to an identity with God which makes him even greater than Abraham.

You have probably guessed arguments like this would not be much good in persuading skeptical Jews to accept Jesus as the messiah. The hostility toward "the Jews" in this section of the gospel goes well beyond anything we find in the other gospels. What could be responsible for this picture? The gospel gives us a hint when it speaks about Jews forcing Christians out of the synagogue community and even putting some to death. Read the story of the healing and conversion of the blind man in Jn 9:1–41. The man is investigated by a group of Pharisees. His parents try to avoid becoming involved in the case. The evangelist tells us that they did this "because they feared the Jews, for the Jews had already agreed that if any one should confess him to be the messiah [Christ], he was to be put out of the synagogue" (v. 22). When the man will not give up his belief that Jesus is "from God," he is called a sinner and thrown out (v. 34).

Jn 12:42–43 returns to the theme of fear: "Many, even among the authorities, believed in him, but for fear of the Pharisees they did not confess it lest they should be put out of the synagogue." Jn 16:1–4a warns Jesus' disciples not to "fall away" when such persecution comes. They will be put out of the synagogues and may even be killed. You can see from these examples that Johannine Christians had lived through a period of severe persecution by Jewish authorities. This persecution had not only led to suffering but had also divided families and cost the community potential converts. The evangelist recognizes that there were Jews who did not share the hostility of the leaders of the persecution. He even gives us a portrait of such a sympathetic, "hidden believer" in the figure of Nicodemus. Nicodemus came to question Jesus, but he does so "at night" (3:1–15). Later he makes an attempt to defend Jesus when the Pharisees are plotting to kill him (7:45–52). Finally he reappears to help Joseph bury Jesus (19:38–42).

Many scholars think that this persecution broke out around A.D. 90. At that time the Jewish authorities at Jamnia inserted into the synagogue benedictions a formula which cursed persons who held false opinions.

Among those condemned in this "benediction" are Christians. The accusations against Jesus in the fourth gospel may well represent those faced by Johannine Christians. Jn 7:47 refers to persons being "led astray," a formal charge against those who were held to be false prophets. You may have noticed in both this chapter and chapter 9 that the "Pharisees and authorities" are pictured as pitting themselves against the crowds who are uncertain about whether or not to believe in Jesus. But the charge which runs throughout the whole gospel is that Jesus is a "blasphemer" because as a human being he is claiming equality with God. Jn 5:9b–18 explains to the reader that the accusations of "sabbath-breaking" are not the real reason for hostility toward Jesus. The real reason is the special relationship between Jesus as "Son" and God as "Father" which makes Jesus equal with God.

Jesus, Revelation of the Father

The equality with God, which is the subject of dispute in the gospel, is linked with another important theme: Jesus is the one who reveals the Father. You may remember that the prologue ended with the assertion that Jesus alone makes God known to humanity. In the last discourses Jesus tells his disciples that having known him they have "known" or "seen" God (14:8–11). The vision of God in Jesus appears in a number of other places in the gospel. The messianic titles collected in chapter 1 end with a promise that like Jacob the disciples will see a vision of Jesus linking heaven and earth (1:51; for Jacob's vision at Bethel see Gen 28:12). Even the patriarch Abraham is said to have "seen" Jesus and rejoiced (8:48–59). You can see from the debate over Jesus' relationship to Abraham that "seeing God" in Jesus is part of the definition of salvation in John. The person who "sees" and believes in Jesus has eternal life.

Another way in which the gospel describes the relationship between Jesus and God is in the use of symbols. These symbols are collected in the great I AM sayings of the gospel. Jesus is identified with great religious symbols: flowing water (4:14, interpreted as the gift of the Spirit in 7:39); bread of life (6:35,41,48,51); life (8:12; 9:5); sheep gate (10:7,9); good shepherd (10:11,14); resurrection and life (11:25); light (8:12; 12:46); way, truth and life (14:6); the vine (15:1,5). You could say that there is no image or hope for salvation which is not fulfilled in Jesus.

As the Abraham episode in 8:48–59 makes clear, Jesus represents the goal of all human hopes for salvation because he is one with God. This unity is expressed in the most striking of the "I Am" sayings, those which do not have some symbol after the verb but simply use "I Am." Any Jewish reader would recognize the divine name of God, which was revealed to Moses at the burning bush (Ex 3:14; 20:4; Is 45:5–6,18,22). The Greek translation of Is 43:10–11 contains a number of parallels to the language used in the gospel:

> You are my witness and I am a witness says the Lord God and the servant whom I have chosen, that you may know and believe and understand that I AM. Before me there was no other God, and after me there will be none. I AM God and no one saves except me.

Notice the importance of "witness" language in Jn 8:13–30. Jn 8:28 affirms that when Jesus is "lifted up" his divine "I Am" will be made known. Belief in the crucified and exalted Jesus is the only source of salvation (cf. Jn 3:14–15). Throughout the gospel Jesus defends his equality with the Father by insisting that he only does what the Father has sent him to do. The words which he speaks are God's words and are recognized as such by those who are truly "children of God." Of course the evangelist knows that many people reacted to these claims about Jesus with outrage. He can only offer some possible reasons for their response. Some might prefer to remain "in darkness" because of their evil deeds (3:16–21). Some are afraid of the human consequences of believing in Jesus (12:42–43). But the evangelist is also aware of the mystery involved in coming to faith. God draws people to Jesus (10:26–30; 17:6). Thus faith is not simply an individual, personal achievement. It is response to a call which comes from God.

Discipleship in John

Reading through the fourth gospel you have probably noticed that the teaching about the rule of God and the ethics of discipleship so evident in the synoptics is missing. As we have just seen the gospel issues a call to faith in Jesus' identity: "I and the Father are one" (Jn 10:30). Humanity is divided by its response. John even speaks of those who fail to believe in Jesus as already judged (3:16–21; 5:19–29). But we have also seen that this belief had concrete consequences. Johannine Christians had been persecuted and thrown out of the synagogues. The episode of the blind man in chapter 9 may have reminded the gospel's first readers of their own experiences. Thus we know that discipleship means a willingness to "bear witness" to one's faith in Jesus in a hostile world.

This impression is strengthened by the farewell discourses and the resurrection stories in the second half of the gospel. Jesus turns to instruct his disciples at the Last Supper. You may have noticed that John's story of Jesus' final meal is different from the other gospels. The formula which designates the bread and wine the body and blood of Christ had been introduced during Jesus' ministry in connection with Jesus' revelation that he is the "bread of life" (Jn 6:51–59). At the supper Jesus makes a striking gesture of humility and service. He performs the "slave-like" act of washing the feet of his disciples (13:1–20). The evangelist reminds us that this gesture is also a sign of how much Jesus, who is about to give his life for us, loves "his own" (13:1; see 10:17). It might be easy to let the emphasis on Jesus' divinity in the gospel make us forget that Jesus' mission was to save humanity by offering his life out of love. The evangelist never forgets the importance of love. When Jesus raises Lazarus, we see how much Jesus loved his friend (11:3,36). We see them repaying Jesus' love with their own when Mary anoints Jesus before his death (12:1–8).

In the Last Supper discourses Jesus draws his disciples into the relationship of love that exists between himself and the Father. They are promised a share in that love if they fulfill Jesus' command to love one another (14:21–24; 16:27). Jesus prays that there will be the same unity among his followers as exists between himself and the Father (17:21–24). The earlier parts of the gospel already hinted at one of the threats to such unity, external persecution.

We have already seen that Mt and Lk understand the resurrection appearances as part of Jesus' commission to his followers. These scenes point forward to what the disciples must do now that Jesus is glorified in heaven. When we look at the fourth gospel, we find a similar pattern. Jesus' first appearance, to Mary Magdalene, warns against clinging to the earthly Jesus. Jesus must return to glory with God, who is Father both to him and to his disciples (Jn 20:11–18). When Jesus appears to the disciples at a meal (20:19–23), he commissions them and gives them the Spirit. They are now "sent" just as Jesus had been sent by God. However you will notice that John has something unique, a second meal appearance to Thomas (20:24–29). The evangelist is very much aware that those who read his gospel no longer belong to the first generation of Christians. Even the disciples who were witnesses to Jesus have apparently died (21:20–23). Jesus prayed for these believers in Jn 17:20–21. Now Thomas is made to represent them. They might feel as though their faith is somehow weaker or inferior to that of the first generation of believers. Thomas shows that even among that group there was disbelief. The episode concludes with a blessing on those who have believed "without seeing" (20:29).

You can see that faith lies at the heart of discipleship in John. Many of the characters in the gospel find it impossible to believe that Jesus really is one with God. But John insists that without believing in God's Son we cannot enter into any relationship with God. The person who does believe has a special relationship of love with God. That relationship is expressed in the life of love and service which those who follow Jesus are commanded to lead (Jn 13:31–36). It is also manifest in willingness to testify to one's belief in Jesus despite hostility from outsiders. Disciples do not simply believe for their own benefit. They also have a mission to be a witness to the world just as Jesus had been.

Summary

Everything which happens in the fourth gospel is a consequence of Jesus' mission from the Father. Jesus is the Word of God sent into the world to summon people to faith and salvation. Jesus' death expresses God's love for the world in sending the Son. But even though Jesus represents God the mystery of human freedom remains. Instead of welcoming the Word some persons turn away from it. Some even react with hostility and seek to kill both Jesus and those who follow him.

Jn 20:30–31 says that the point of the gospel is to bring its reader to faith in Jesus as messiah, Son of God. We have seen that the gospel presumes that we already know something about Jesus. This is not a beginner's gospel. It is addressed to those whose faith may be weak like Thomas' or who may be unsure of how to respond to charges that for Christians to honor Jesus as "one with" God is blasphemy. Only God, the evangelist insists, can do the signs which Jesus does. Only God can offer those who believe eternal life. Those who are unable to believe are blind to the presence of God in Jesus.

STUDY QUESTIONS

Facts You Should Know

1. Explain how John differs from the synoptic gospels (Mt, Mk and Lk) in each of the following areas: (a) chronology of Jesus' ministry; (b) use of messianic titles for Jesus; (c) teachings which Jesus gives; (d) reason given for Jewish hostility against Jesus.
2. Give three examples of Johannine variants of synoptic-like stories which would support the view that the Johannine church must have known traditions about Jesus like those in the synoptic gospels.
3. What imagery does John use to describe Jesus' crucifixion? How is this

imagery appropriate to the relationship between Jesus and God as it is presented in the gospel?

4. What is the symbolic role played by "the Jews" in the Johannine narrative? Why do scholars think that the evangelist cast "the Jews" in the role of "bad guys"?

5. How is Jesus' equality with God demonstrated in the gospel? What arguments does John give in response to Jewish claims that it is blasphemy for a human being to claim such a relationship to God?

6. What are the obligations of discipleship as they are presented in the fourth gospel?

Things To Do

1. Using a concordance trace the images of "life" and "light" from the prologue through the rest of the gospel. What do they show us about Jesus each time they occur?

2. Find all of the I AM sayings in the gospel. What symbols does Jesus identify himself with? How is the relationship between Christians and Jesus as the source of salvation represented in those symbols?

3. Read Jn 9. Trace the stages by which the "blind man" develops faith in who Jesus is. How does the story of the blind man reflect experiences of Christians in the Johannine community?

Things To Think About

1. Jn claims that the disciples are now "sent" to the world as Jesus was. How do we participate in that mission today?

2. How does Jesus reveal God to us?

Chapter 16

ACTS: THE GOSPEL TO THE NATIONS

The Composition of Acts

We have already seen in our study of Luke that Acts picks up the story which is left unfinished by the gospel. Like other multipart writings of its time, the prologue to Acts reminds the reader of the earlier work (1:1–4). You may already have detected a puzzle in these verses. Lk 24:50–51 pictures Jesus blessing the disciples and being carried up into heaven on Easter Day. Acts 1:3–4 paints a different picture. It suggests Jesus appearing to the disciples and teaching them during a forty day period before his ascension.

If you look closely at the other references to Jesus' resurrection, you will notice that the time span of Jesus' appearances does not appear to have been clearly fixed. 1 Cor 15:3–9 suggests a rather lengthy period of such appearances culminating in the conversion of Paul, which may have been as much as two years after Jesus' death. Mark hints at an appearance in Galilee, which would seem to be some time after Easter Day (Mk 14:28; 16:7). Luke knows that "forty" is a significant number in salvation history. Israel remained in the wilderness forty years. Even more important for our story, Jesus was in the wilderness forty days between his baptism and the beginning of his public ministry. Now the period of resurrection appearances establishes the disciples as witnesses to everything about Jesus that will be part of their preaching (by Philip in Acts 8:12; by Paul in Acts 14:22; 19:8; 20:25; 28:23,31). Acts 1:6 has Jesus correct a misunderstanding about the "kingdom of God." One is not to expect the second coming immediately. No one knows what God has established. This correction reminds us of the "time of the Gentiles" in Lk 21:24. You probably noticed that vv. 4–5 also refer back to the gospel. Jesus told the disciples to wait in Jerusalem "for the promise of the Father" in Lk 24:49. Here he interprets what

that promise of "power from on high" will be. It will be the "baptism with
the Holy Spirit" predicted by the Baptist (Lk 3:16).

These passages show us something important about Luke's composition. When Luke repeats an episode, he gives the reader a different version. Usually that version contains new information that is appropriate in
the particular setting in the story. You can see this process at work very
clearly if you look up the three versions of the conversion of Paul (Acts 9:1–
19; 22:4–16, 17–21; 26:12–18). The introductions are very close in the three
versions, though the final version expands the description of the light, suggests that Paul's companions as well as the apostle fell to the ground, spec-
ifies that the communication was in Hebrew and expands the reprimand
(26:13–14). Acts 9:11–19 then focuses on the story of Paul's blindness and
the "miraculous healing" by Ananias that accompanies Paul's formal conversion: reception of the Spirit and baptism. This healing element is shortened in Acts 22:10–13a, which suggests that the blindness was the result
of the intensity of the light. Acts 22:16 seems to reflect the baptismal practice of the Lucan community, since the "washing away of sins" and "calling
on Jesus' name" are part of the process.

Acts 26 reports what was "hidden" from the reader in the earlier version: the words of the commission which the Lord gave to Paul on the road
to Damascus (26:16–18):

> I have appeared to you for this reason: to appoint you for service
> and witness to the things in which you have seen me and in which
> I will appear to you, rescuing you from the people and from the
> Gentiles among whom I am sending you, to open their eyes, that
> they may turn from darkness to light, and from the power of Sa-
> tan to God, and may receive forgiveness of sins and inheritance
> among the saints through faith in me.

Earlier hints of Paul's commission were contained in God's words to Ananias (9:15–16):

> . . . he [Paul] is my chosen instrument to carry my name before
> the Gentiles and kings and children of Israel. I will show him how
> much he must suffer on account of my name.

Perhaps you noticed that this commission is similar to that of the disciples
at the opening of Acts (Acts 1:8):

> You shall be my witnesses in Jerusalem and in all Judea and Sa-
> maria and to the end of the earth.

Ananias refers to God's commission in Acts 22:14–15:

> The God of our fathers appointed you to know his will, to see the
> Just One and to hear sounds from his mouth; for you will be a
> witness for him to all people, of what you have seen and heard.

Acts 22:21 makes Paul's departure from Jerusalem for the Gentile mission
a response to the hatred which his earlier role as persecutor of Christians
had stirred up. Luke assumes that Paul must have been present at the martyrdom of Stephen (8:1; 22:20) though neither Paul himself nor Luke's own
tradition gave Paul an active role in that episode. By the time we come to
the final version of Paul's conversion we know that the apostle has fulfilled
the commission to witness to the Gentiles, before kings and before the
children of Israel. A reader familiar with the story of Paul's life also knows
that Paul is about to be sent as a prisoner to Rome where he will eventually
die as a martyr. You can see from the outline that Acts follows a geographical pattern that moves from Jerusalem to Rome:

OUTLINE OF ACTS   *[16–1]*

Prologue (1:1–5)

Commission and ascension (1:6–11)

Earliest days of the community in Jerusalem (1:12–8:1)
  (a) Successor to Judas chosen (1:12–26)
  (b) Pentecost and Peter's sermon (2:1–13,14–41)
  (c) Life in fellowship (2:42–47)
  (d) Healing and Peter's sermon (3:1–10,11–26)
  (e) Witness before the council (4:1–22)
  (f) Prayer and life in fellowship (4:23–5:16)
  (g) Miraculous escape and witness before the council (5:17–42)
  (h) Appointment of Hellenist leaders as deacons (6:1–7)
  (i) Martyrdom of the deacon Stephen (6:8–8:1)

Christianity spreads in Judea and Samaria (8:2–12:25)
  (a) Philip: Into Samaria and the Ethiopian eunuch (8:4–40)
  (b) Paul's conversion (9:1–31)
  (c) Healings by Peter (9:32–43)
  (d) Conversion of Cornelius: Spirit to Gentiles (10:1–48)
  (e) Peter defends conversion of Gentiles in Jerusalem (11:1–18)

(f)   Church at Antioch (11:19–30)
(g)   James martyred and Peter delivered from prison (12:1–19)
(h)   Death of Herod (12:20–24)

Barnabas and Paul (Saul) sent out by Antioch (12:25–15:40)
  (a)   Cyprus, Pisidian Antioch, Iconium, Lystra (12:25–14:28)
  (b)   Jerusalem council: Conditions for Gentile Christians (15:1–35)
  (c)   Barnabas and Paul separate (15:36–41)

Paul's missionary journeys in Asia Minor and Greece (16:1–20:38)
  (a)   Journey to Macedonia (16:1–15)
  (b)   Philippian imprisonment and danger in Thessalonica (16:16–
        17:15)
  (c)   Paul at Athens (17:16–34)
  (d)   Paul at Corinth (18:1–17)
  (e)   Christianity comes to Ephesus (18:18–19:41)
  (f)   Farewell visits in Asia Minor (20:1–38)

In Jerusalem: Paul's imprisonment and testimony (21:1–26:32)
  (a)   Journey to Jerusalem: Prophecy of Paul's fate (21:1–16)
  (b)   Arrest and defense before the crowd (21:17–22:29)
  (c)   Paul before the council (22:30–23:11)
  (d)   Plot against Paul's life: Paul taken to Roman governor (23:12–35)
  (e)   Paul's defense before Felix (24:1–27)
  (f)   Paul's defense before Festus and appeal to Caesar (25:1–26:32)

Journey to Rome (27:1–28:31)

We might expect Acts to end with the story of Paul's death in Rome.
Instead we last see him preaching (28:23–31). This ending reminds us that
Paul's story is not an exercise in biographical writing. It belongs to the
larger purpose of Acts to describe the spread of the gospel outward from
Jerusalem to the ends of the earth. Peter and the disciples carry the movement of the story in the first half of Acts. Their last active contribution to
the outward spread of the gospel appears when James and the others set
the terms under which Gentiles are to be admitted to the new movement
(Acts 15:1–35). After that the story belongs entirely to Paul as God's "instrument." At this turning point in the narrative, Luke introduces sections
of material which sound like a travelogue. They are told in the first person
plural "we" instead of the third person (16:10–17; 20:5–15; 21:1–18; 27:1–
28:16).

Some scholars think that the shift to the first person plural indicates that Luke had found some form of travel diary by one of Paul's companions. Others point out that there are examples of shifts into first person narrative in both fiction and history writing of Luke's time that do not indicate first-hand knowledge by the author or a source. Scholars also debate the extent to which information in Acts provides sufficiently accurate detail to complement what can be gleaned from Paul's own letters. Though attempts have been made to base a chronology of Paul's life only on the letters, most reconstructions make some use of Acts. Only in Acts do we learn such commonly accepted "facts" about Paul as: he came from Tarsus (e.g. 11:25); he was a Roman citizen (e.g. 16:37); his trade was tent-making or leather-working (e.g. 18:3); he was in Corinth under Gallio (18:12). But some parts of the picture of Paul in Acts seems much different from the Paul of the letters. One can hardly imagine the Paul who wrote that he kept the Jerusalem council from imposing any restrictions on Gentile Christians (Gal 2:1–10) obediently carrying a decree from James which says they must avoid marriages forbidden by Jewish law and non-kosher food as Acts has him doing (15:28–31; 16:4). One can hardly imagine the apostle maligned for weakness by the "super-apostles" (2 Cor 12:7–13) as the powerful miracle-worker of Acts (13:4–12; 14:8–10; 16:16–18; 19;11–20; 20:7–12; 28:3–6,7–10), or the weak, unimpressive speaker of 2 Cor 10:9–10 (also 11:6) as the impressive speaker of Acts (14:12; 17:16–34).

You make also have noticed that none of Paul's favorite theological themes appear in the sermons he gives in Acts (e.g. 13:16–41; 17:22–31; 22:2–21). Scholars have divided the various speeches given in Acts into two categories. Some are "kerygmatic," that is, they set forth the basic message of salvation (e.g. 13:16–41, by Paul and speeches by Peter in 2:14–39; 3:11–26; 4:18–22; 5:29–32; 10:34–43). Others are "apologetic," that is, the apostle is making a defense of Christianity in a "law court" setting (7:2–53, by Stephen, and Paul's speeches in 20:18–35; 22:3–21; 24:10–21; 26:1–23; 28:17–20,25–29). The speech Paul makes in Athens is like an apology, since it is set in the Areopagus, a famous court in ancient Athens, even though Paul is making a plea for belief to the pagan philosophers of Athens (17:22–31).

Ancient historians used to formulate speeches for their characters that reflected what the person ought to have said in a given situation. The kerygmatic speeches in Acts give us glimpses of what Luke thought the first missionary preaching was like. They may well have been based on models that were still used in his own community. These speeches follow a typical outline. Read the most famous, Peter's Pentecost sermon in Acts 2:14–39.

(1) Introduction locates the speech in the narrative (vv. 14–21).

(2) Outline of the message about Jesus using proofs for Jesus' messiahship from the Old Testament (vv. 22–36).

(3) Call for repentance and conversion (vv. 37–39).

You will notice that repentance includes forgiveness of sins, baptism and the gift of the Holy Spirit to new believers (v. 38). Even though the official mission to the Gentiles has not begun by this point, Pentecost points toward the spread of the gospel throughout the earth. Everyone heard the apostles speak in his or her own language (2:5–11; notice how many countries Luke includes). Peter points out that the promise of salvation through Jesus is to all, even those who are far off (v. 39). Luke also insists that all these different believers gathered together in the community life of the church: teaching, fellowship, breaking bread and prayer (v. 42).

The Church in Salvation History

Luke's emphasis on the geographical spread of Christianity is likened to his understanding of the important role of the church in salvation. You have already seen something of this role in the picture of Pentecost with which Acts begins. We have seen the peoples from different nations hearing the good news. We are shown that they joined together in a single fellowship which heard the teaching of the apostles, shared fellowship meals and prayed together. Acts 2:43–47 repeats this picture with two additional elements. First, the community saw signs of God's power in the miracles done by the apostles. Second, members of the community shared all things in common. Each person was provided with whatever he or she needed through the sacrifice of those members who had sold property to provide for the poor.

At the same time, Acts also preserves traditions about the early Jerusalem community which are less than idyllic. Acts 4:32–37 repeats the tradition that Christians sold property to provide for the poor. But the next passage, 5:1–16, tells the story of a couple who lie about the amount received for their property. The result of such an attempt to deceive the Holy Spirit is immediate death. Other examples of divine "punishment" in Acts are the death of Herod (12:20–23), the blinding of the magician Elymas (13:8–11), and the attack of an evil spirit on the sons of Sceva (19:11–16). In short, Christians are not spared divine punishment. Some interpreters think that the temporary blinding of Paul is meant as punishment for his persecution of Christians.

Acts 6:1–7 links the appointment of Stephen and others to be deacons with a quarrel between Hebrew and Greek-speaking Christians. The

"Hellenists" claim that their widows are being neglected. Although this story makes it appear that the role of the deacon was simply to administer the distribution of food among the poor, the most famous of the group, Stephen, is martyred for his preaching of the gospel. Luke reports that the persecution of the Hellenists was responsible for the spread of Christianity outside Jerusalem (8:1–3). Thus the persecution has a providential side. It is part of the realization of God's plan to spread the gospel to the "ends of the earth."

Some readers may be surprised by the extent to which the Holy Spirit intervenes in the story in Acts. Often divine action is required at a critical juncture in the mission. Dreams and visions are often the medium of communication. Ananias is instructed to find Paul in a vision (9:10–16). Visions are responsible for the conversion of the first Gentile, Cornelius (10:1–16). Paul takes the critical step of expanding his ministry into Greece (Macedonia) when summoned by a vision (16:6–10). He is told by the Lord not to fear the opposition aroused by his preaching in Corinth (18:9–10). The Holy Spirit warns him of the coming imprisonment in Jerusalem (20:23). In other cases the words of community prophets serve as guides to future events. Agabus, a prophet from Antioch, is said to have foretold a famine under Claudius (11:28). Community prophets direct the church at Antioch to send Barnabas and Paul on a missionary journey (13:1–3). Agabus prophesies that Paul will be "bound" by the Jews and handed over to the Gentiles (21:11). Many other smaller acts are also attributed to the Holy Spirit.

Modern readers may find this persistent reference to divine guidance either "unreal" or "triumphalistic" as though whatever happens in the history of the church is automatically God's doing. Luke's audience would have recognized these parts of the story as a way of establishing the claim that this history is God's doing. Luke has gone to great pains in both the gospel and Acts to emphasize the connections between the Christian story and the larger world of events in Roman history. His references to various Roman governors in different provinces, to the death of Herod and even to the famine under Claudius are part of this pattern. Roman historians would have argued that their own history was divinely guided, that they had been destined to rule the civilized world. Luke presents the Christian reader with a "counter-history." The Roman world is the larger context within which God's providence is working to spread the news of salvation to all peoples. It is not a "divine event" in itself.

Although Luke emphasizes divine deliverance, joy and harmony among the first Christians, we are never far from another episode of persecution, rioting, arrest or "courtroom defense." Usually the instigators of persecution are "Jews", who reject the preaching about Jesus in their communities. But once the story moves out of Jerusalem they must enlist local magistrates and Roman officials against the apostles. But sometimes the enemies are persons whose financial interests in pagan religious practices are challenged by the gospel (e.g. owners of the possessed girl, 16:14–24; silversmiths at Ephesus, 19:24–41). Often Luke expresses the view that Jewish blindness and refusal to accept the gospel causes the apostles to turn away from them to the Gentiles (e.g. Acts 13:44–47; 18:5–11). It would appear that Luke no longer considers the conversion of Israel part of the missionary effort. On the other hand, he often mentions devout Jews who became believers (e.g. Crispus, 18:8; unnamed Jews in Thessalonica and Borea, 17:4,11–12). Some interpreters have suggested that Luke views this group of believing Jews as the "renewed Israel." The Gentile converts are brought into salvation by being made part of the reconstituted Israel.

Just as Luke's evaluation of the "Jews" is a mixture of negative and positive, so the presentation of magistrates and Roman officials has good and bad elements. Authorities often rescue the apostles from mob actions. Roman authorities have to take Paul into custody outside Jerusalem in order to foil a plot against him (23:12–35). They sometimes provide a sympathetic hearing for apologetic speeches (e.g. 22:30; 24:22–24; 25:13–22). But we also find magistrates accused of beating Paul, though he is a Roman citizen (16:37–39; 22:24–29) and holding him in prison without proven charges against him in hopes of being paid a bribe for his freedom (24:26). Some scholars have suggested that the benign acts of Roman officials are intended to lessen the hostility toward such authorities felt by Christians who have suffered beatings and imprisonments like those of Peter and Paul. Others hold that the imprisonment stories seek to answer the charges which outsiders routinely directed against Christianity. It was a "superstition" which turned people away from the gods of their ancestors and caused civic and social disruption. We find some of these charges mentioned explicitly in the course of the story. Paul is charged with "being a Jew" and advocating customs "unlawful for Romans" (16:20–21). Jews charge him with leading people to worship in a way contrary to their law (18:13–15; 21:21,28). He attacks the pagan gods and goddesses who were protectors of their cities (19:25–26).

Though the reader of Acts always knows that these charges are fabricated by people hostile to the gospel, they persist throughout the story. Luke presents the charges against Paul in Jerusalem as an "inner Jewish" squabble (23:6–10; also evident in the episode before Gallio in 18:13–15). You may have noticed in reading through Acts that the apostles are often freed from imprisonment by some form of divine intervention (e.g. 5:17–26; 12:6–11; 16:19–40). They are not let off through their own efforts. The reader knows that Stephen and James have been martyred. The Lord tells Paul that he will have to "bear witness" not only in Jerusalem but also in Rome (23:11). Thus the defense which Acts gives is not put in terms of human legal judgments. The suffering of the apostles is ultimately seen in light of the divine plan for the spread of the gospel.

The Apostle Heroes: Peter and Paul

Although other figures are mentioned, Acts focuses on Peter and Paul as the "heroes" of its story. Peter dominates the first half of the book which deals with the spread of Christianity from Jerusalem to the surrounding areas. The second half is the story of Paul's missionary activity in Asia Minor and Greece. Then the scene returns to Jerusalem for one last time to describe Paul's arrest and testimony there. As a prisoner Paul makes the trip which brings him to Rome. Luke has shaped both the gospel and Acts so that Jerusalem provides a focal point for the dramatic action. Jerusalem is the city of destiny in the story. But with Paul's imprisonment and appeal to Rome for trial we see that Jerusalem has lost its place. Christianity is now to unfold within the larger world of the Roman empire.

Both Peter and Paul play a central role in the shift from a Jewish messianic movement to a Christianity which presents salvation in Jesus' name to all peoples. Paul is God's chosen instrument for the spread of the movement into the Greek-speaking cities of Asia Minor and Greece. Peter follows God's direction in baptizing Cornelius and his household, the first Gentile converts. Although their various imprisonments already indicate that Peter and Paul will suffer for the gospel, Luke never tells the story of how they died. Yet we have already seen allusions to the fate of Paul in Ephesians (Eph 3:1; 4:1; 6:20) and to Peter's martyrdom in John 21:18–19.

Luke has shaped the stories of the two heroes so that they run along parallel lines as you can see from Chart 16-2. You can see that the extensive parallels between the two sections of Acts make it clear that both apostles are following the plan which has been laid out for them by God.

Luke has shown the divine plan guiding the Christian mission in another way. He has introduced extensive parallels between the gospel account of Jesus' life and the story in Acts. You have probably noticed that the miracles which the apostles do to awaken faith in the crowds are like miracles which Jesus performs. Luke has also patterned Paul's journey to Jerusalem after Jesus' journey there in the gospel. Chart 16-3 shows some of the parallels between Jesus' story and Acts.

PETER AND PAUL: PARALLEL STORIES   *[16–2]*

STRUCTURE OF APOSTLE'S MISSION

	Acts 2–12 [Peter]	Acts 13–38 [Paul]
Witness to risen Christ	1:21–22	23:11; 26:16
Spirit initiates	2:1–40	13:1–40
Heals lame and speech	3:12–26	14:8–17
Persecution (stoning) leads to wider mission	[6:8–8:4, Stephen]	14:19–23
Defends Gentile mission in Jerusalem	ch. 11	ch. 21
Imprisoned at Jewish feast	12:4–7	21:16–28
Conclusion: Success of word of God	12:24	28:30–31

DEEDS OF THE APOSTLE

	Acts 2–12 [Peter]	Acts 13–38 [Paul]
Encounters a magician	8:9–24	13:6–12
Gentiles try to worship him	10:25–26	14:13–15
Raises the dead	9:36–43	20:9–12
Delivered from prison	12:6–11	16:24–26
Laying on hands gives Spirit	8:14–17	19:1–6
Appoints leaders with prayer/laying on hands	6:1–6	14:23
Defended by Pharisees in Sanhedrin	5:34–39	23:9
Accused of acting vs. Moses	[6:13–14, Stephen]	21:20–21; 25:8

JESUS' STORY AND ACTS		[16–3]
	Luke	Acts
OPENING SEQUENCE OF EVENTS:		
Spirit descends in physical form	3:21–22	1:14,24; 2:1–13
Opening sermon: Scripture fulfilled and Jesus rejected	4:16–30	2:14–40
Preaching/healing prove fulfillment of promises; conflict and rejection	4:31–8:56	2:14–12:17
lame healed	5:17–26	3:1–10
vs. leaders	5:29–6:11	4:1–8:3
pious centurion	7:1–10	ch. 10
widow/dead raised	7:11–17	9:36–43
Pharisees criticize	7:36–50	11:1–8
JOURNEY TO JERUSALEM:		
Divine necessity	19:51	19:21
Dangers in Jerusalem	13:33	21:12
Resolved to go	19:11,28	21:15,17
Enthusiastic welcome	19:37	21:17–20a
Enters temple	19:45–48	21:26
Sadducees do not believe in resurrection; support from scribe(s)	20:27–39	23:6–9
Bless/break bread	22:19a	[27:35]
Seized by mob	22:54	21:30

Discipleship in Acts

In the gospels teaching about discipleship is expressed in sayings of Jesus. In the epistles the authors speak directly to particular churches and situations. Acts is different from both the gospels and the epistles. Its sermons repeat the basic themes of salvation history. God's promises have been fulfilled in Jesus. All people are called to believe in Jesus, to repent, receive forgiveness for sin and join the new fellowship of believers. Luke is conscious of the fact that the Christian movement is something new. He uses a distinctive name for the group, "the way" (9:2; 19:9,23; 22:4; 24:14,22). This name appears to be a pre-Lucan term taken from Palestinian traditions. The Essenes spoke of persons who joined their community as "choosing the way." Their community rules were "regulations of the way of the master." Luke may have found this term very appropriate since it picks up on Luke's geographical perspective. As we have seen, one aspect of discipleship for Luke is linked to the journey theme. The disciple is the person who follows Jesus along his journey. The parallels between the story of Jesus and the lives of the apostles are one way in which Luke makes this point.

With Acts we also look back to the stories of the earliest community as examples for discipleship. We have already seen that three themes are particularly strong there. One is the theme of hospitality and sharing with the poor. Luke emphasizes the unity of the first Jerusalem Christians. He insists that they shared things in common. Wealthy Christians sold possessions to provide for the poor. In Acts 16:11–15, Lydia, who apparently was engaged in the business of selling dyed cloth, becomes a benefactor of Paul's mission. (This passage is a parallel to the women who provided for Jesus' mission in Lk 8:1–3.) Luke seems to set this "moderate" sharing of possessions in contrast to the radical attitude toward possessions, a tradition he also preserves. The apostles are without money (Acts 3:6). Members of the Jerusalem community are said to have sold all their possessions (2:44–45; 4:35–37). Acts appears to be looking back on such examples as a past ideal. The present application for Christians appears to be generosity and community concern for the poor. Such efforts may call for rich Christians to make resources available by selling some property as in the ill-fated case of Ananias and Sapphira (Acts 5:2–11) but does not suggest that Christians in Luke's day are adopting a radical poverty.

Another very important theme in Acts is piety. We have already seen that the gospel emphasized Jesus' own roots among the faithful, pious persons of Israel. This tradition is continued in the picture of the earliest Jerusalem community. Its members gather daily in the temple area for prayer. They are also depicted offering prayers in their own house church gatherings. Acts 4:24–30 reports a lengthy prayer in which the community rehearses "salvation history" and asks for boldness in its testimony to Jesus despite persecution. Prayer accompanies important acts of the community. It is part of the appointment of leaders of various sorts (6:6; 13:2–3). The apostles are also shown to pray to the Lord individually (9:11; 10:9). It accompanies healings (9:40). It is clear that both communal and personal prayer is a central feature of the Christian life.

There is another element in the treatment of piety in Acts: rejection of pagan religious practices. Throughout Acts the earliest Christians maintain contact with the piety of Judaism in both the temple at Jerusalem and the synagogues of the various cities. Paul even takes pious vows (18:18; 21:23–26). But we also see the apostles confronted with a spectrum of religious beliefs representative of the pagan world. Magicians, soothsayers and other demon-possessed prophets are decisively defeated (e.g. 8:9–24; 13:8–12; 16:17–19; 19:13–20). Christianity is thus shown to be decisively opposed to demonic and magical practices. In other cases, pagans think that the divine powers shown by the apostles mean that they are "divine" and must be prevented from worshiping them (10:25–26; 14:12–18; 28:3–6). Once again Christianity is established as a form of "piety" and not gross superstition. However, the educated pagan might still be suspicious of the new movement. It does turn people away from worshiping the traditional gods of the city. The riot by the silversmiths at Ephesus in Acts 19:23–41 makes this point clear. Luke insists that the only persons "hurt" by such conversion are dubious types who are making a profit from the famous shrine. The city herself would not be harmed as the magistrate's action in rescuing the apostles shows. Finally Luke speaks to the most "enlightened" form of pagan piety, that schooled by philosophy. Paul's famous speech at Athens insists that those who already know that the divine is a

The Asclepion at Messene.

cosmic, beneficent force, and not resident in magic rites or human temples, should now turn to accept Christianity as salvation from God (17:16–31). Thus Luke answers the objections that Christianity is a base form of mass superstition by showing it to embody only the noblest forms of piety.

A third theme which emerges in the opening scenes of Acts is persecution. We have seen that conflict and persecution dog the steps of the apostles throughout the whole book. We are shown how the first disciples prayed for boldness in proclaiming the gospel despite persecution. The various episodes of persecution have different results. But in every case the apostle never hesitates to make a stirring defense of the gospel. Because he is acting out of "divine necessity," the apostle will never be moved by human orders to cease preaching. Luke insists that only persons who have some motive such as envy, jealousy, or greed create trouble for Christians. All others should recognize that neither they nor their preaching is harmful. Whatever happens, the disciples accept persecution without anger. They rejoice in the salvation which God is bringing to many people through their testimony.

Summary

Acts presents the second half of Luke's story of salvation. The reader sees how God guided the process which brought salvation out from Jerusalem to the whole world. Acts is not "church history" in the way we think of history: a collection of events that happened to Christians in the past. Rather Acts is the story of how God's providence worked through such famous apostles as Peter and Paul to bring into being the church and traditions which Luke and his readers have inherited.

Acts also establishes an important pattern for later generations of Christians. Luke teaches us to look back to the story of the earliest community for a vision of what it means to be followers of Jesus. Paul's farewell speech to the elders of the Ephesian church makes the difference between the time of the apostles and that of Luke's readers very clear. Now that the apostles are gone, those who have charge of the churches are responsible for teaching and admonishing others so that the community does not fall victim to divisions and predatory teaching. The departing apostle holds up his own life as an example. Notice that when Luke looks back on Paul's practice of working to support himself, he does not think of it as a sign of Paul's weakness. Rather he presents it as the way in which Paul not only met his own needs (and showed that he was not preaching for money) but also was able to share what he earned with the weak and unfortunate (20:17–38). This speech directs the message of Acts to all Christians who live in the generations after the apostles.

STUDY QUESTIONS

Facts You Should Know

1. How does the outline of Acts reflect Luke's understanding of salvation history?
2. What are the two kinds of speeches in Acts? Give an example of each type of speech.
3. Give two examples of differences between the picture given of Paul in Acts and the Paul we meet in the apostle's letters.
4. How does the picture of the early Jerusalem community given in Acts serve as a model for Christian discipleship?
5. How are Roman authorities pictured in Acts? Give an example for each of the points you make. What purpose might this picture of the Roman authorities have served in Luke's "apology" for Christianity?
6. Describe Luke's treatment of each of the following themes in Acts: (a) wealth; (b) piety; (c) persecution.

Things To Do

1. Compare Paul's picture of pagan religiousness in Rom 1:18–3:31 with the speech Paul gives in Acts 17:22–31. What common themes are there? How do the two speeches differ?

2. Using a concordance find the references to the "spirit of the Lord" or the "Holy Spirit" in Acts. What roles does the Spirit play in the early community?

3. Read the stories of persecution in Acts. How does Luke show the reader that the apostles are innocent of the charges being brought against them in each story?

Things To Think About

1. How might the picture of the early community serve as a model for Christians today?

2. What role does the guidance of the Holy Spirit play in the life of Christians today?

Chapter 17

HEBREWS: THE HEAVENLY HIGH PRIEST

The Thought World of Hebrews

Although Heb eventually found its way into the New Testament as an epistle of Paul, early Christian writers recognized that Heb is quite different from any of the letters from Paul. The third century Alexandrian exegete Origen noted that the elegant Greek of Heb is quite different from the awkward style of the apostle. He finally concluded that the "thought" of Heb is worthy of apostolic teaching, but that it must have been written by someone else (in Eusebius, *Ecclesiastical History* VI 25). He reports suggestions that Luke had been the author or perhaps the Roman bishop Clement who appears to be citing Heb in a letter addressed to the Corinthian church written in A.D. 96 (cp. 1 Clem 36:2–5//Heb 1:3–12; 1 Clem 17:7//Heb 11:37; 1 Clem 17:5//Heb 3:5). Hebrews is not included among the Pauline letters in the Muratorian canon, a list from the Roman church ca. A.D. 200. Several comments in the work suggest an author from the post-apostolic generation who looks back to the earlier days of the community. He identifies himself and his readers as second generation (2:3). They revere "leaders" whose lives have already ended (13:7). Some scholars have detected a reference to the martyrdom of apostles like Peter and Paul. They even look back on a past time in which they suffered persecution. Now that suffering has ended but they are in danger of letting their first enthusiasm cool (10:32–36).

Although Heb is traditionally called a "letter," the formal structure of a letter is missing. Only the concluding verses (13:19–25) have been shaped to sound like the conclusion of a Pauline letter with a final exhortation, prayers, mention of travel plans, and greetings from the sender to the recipients. Mention of Timothy's release (13:23) made later identification of the sender with Paul possible. Timothy is associated with Paul in

OUTLINE OF HEBREWS   *[17–1]*

Prologue: God has spoken through the Son (1:1–4)

The Son's superiority to the angels (1:5–14)

Exhortation: Do not drift away from such a salvation (2:1–4)

By suffering the Son brings many to salvation (2:5–18)

Jesus is greater than Moses (3:1–6)

Exhortation: Do not fall away like Israel in the wilderness (3:7–4:13)

Jesus is the sympathetic high priest (4:14–5:10)

Exhortation: Do not be immature in faith (5:11–6:12)

God's promises are confirmed by an oath (6:13–20)

Jesus is the high priest in the order of Melchizedek (7:1–10:18)
  (a) Melchizedek symbolizes an eternal priesthood higher than the
       levitical priesthood of the old covenant (7:1–28)
  (b) Christ ministers in the true, heavenly sanctuary which fulfills the
       promise of a new covenant (8:1–13)
  (c) Christ as mediator of the new covenant makes the sacrifices of
       the old covenant unnecessary (9:1–22)
  (d) Christ's sacrifice for sin takes place once for all in the heavenly
       sanctuary (9:23–10:18)

Exhortation: Hold fast to your faith and good works; there is no
sacrifice for the sin of turning away from Christ (10:19–39)

Heroes of faith grasp the reality of heavenly things (11:1–40)

Exhortation: Persevere, remembering Christ's example and those who
went before you (12:1–13:19)

Letter-like closing (13:20–25)

an imprisonment in Phlm 1, and the personal reference in Heb 13:19 could be seen as similar to Phlm 22. Some exegetes find in these details hints that Heb was written to the church at Rome by a second generation Christian. The Italians mentioned in 13:24 would be immigrants from Italy. Roman Christians would have been concerned about Timothy's fate since he had been there when Paul (2 Tim 4:9,11,21) and Peter (1 Pet 5:13) were martyred. But as Origen recognized, only God knows for sure. Heb does not provide enough information to establish either an actual or a "fictive" author.

Heb 13:22 describes the writing as a "word of exhortation." In Acts 13:15 this term refers to a sermon. As you read through Heb you will notice that sections of OT proofs about Christ are followed by words of exhortation to the community. Heb presents Christ as the heavenly high priest who has made sacrifice for sin "once for all" in the heavenly sanctuary. Christians must never waver in their own hope of attaining salvation.

You are familiar with New Testament writers who encourage steadfastness and hope by reminding readers of the coming judgment. Paul speaks of striving for the prize which lies ahead, the transformation of the faithful when the Lord returns (Phil 3:12–21). He reminds his readers that "salvation is nearer now than when we first believed" (Rom 13:11–14). Heb retains the language of judgment. Scripture has revealed that the Lord will judge those who have turned away (10:30–31). The final judgment will be much more traumatic than the worst earthquake, since even the heavens will be shaken (12:25–29). But future judgment is not the dominant image in Heb.

Heb is dominated by a contrast taken from philosophical thought and applied to interpreting the Bible by Jewish exegetes, especially those in Alexandria represented by the first century writer Philo. This philosophic perspective saw that everything connected with the material world is imperfect and changing. Such things eventually pass out of existence altogether. But philosophers who followed the teachings of Plato held that this imperfect, changing material world was just a pale reflection of an unchanging, divine, heavenly world. Human beings had access to the divine world through the mind or reason. The philosopher whose mind was constantly trained on that heavenly realm attained perfection. Such a person was no longer driven by passions or ambition to gain things in this world. Philo of Alexandria applied this type of thought to the Jewish scriptures. God is the unchanging source of all that exists. The journeys of heroes like Abraham and Moses really took place within the soul as it sought and finally came to know God. For such great figures knowledge of God meant a union with the divine brought about through the working of God's word or wisdom within the soul.

Heb uses this contrast throughout the letter. Christ is our access to the heavenly world. Its interpretation of judgment in 12:25–29 even uses the theme there. Heb observes that the "cosmic destruction" associated with the time of judgment is really a purging away of all that is imperfect and earthly. What is true reality, the heavenly realm, cannot be shaken. It remains after the judgment. Heb insists that that is the kingdom which Christians have received (vv. 27–28). A number of other basic Christian categories are given a new interpretation by means of this philosophic understanding of the world. Philo had argued, for example, that the "sabbath rest" which is referred to in the Bible really points to the unchanging nature of God. Moses was able to "soar above to hold fast to God." Thus Moses shared in that "rest." Heb encourages Christians to seek the "rest" through their pilgrimage to a heavenly homeland. The famous definition of "faith" in Heb 11:1–3 speaks of it as our way of knowing the invisible, heavenly realities that lie behind everything that is created.

Another concept which is typical of this philosophic tradition is the idea of an "education" of the soul. Elementary teachings are intended for the immature, who must also come to lead a life of virtue through discipline. As the soul progresses it no longer needs the "milk" of elementary teaching but can understand true teaching. The soul in which God's wisdom has come to dwell no longer experiences virtue as discipline because it has become good. The education theme is part of the exhortation in Heb. Heb 5:11–6:12 exhorts the readers not to remain "sluggish." They should not still be going over elementary school lessons but should be among the "mature" or "perfect." Heb 6:1–3 gives a list of the "beginning doctrines" of Christianity: repentance; faith in God; baptism [washings]; laying on of hands; resurrection and eternal judgment. Heb 6:4–8 points toward one difficulty in the community: persons who had once been Christians are falling away. Heb warns that such persons cannot be restored to the community. Heb also invokes the "education" theme when it tells the readers to accept any of the hardships they might experience as God's discipline. Like a parent disciplining a child, divine discipline is part of the training necessary to become a mature Christian.

Since the application of philosophical insights to scripture was practiced in Alexandria, many interpreters think that Heb must have been written by someone with ties to that city. Apollos, an Alexandrian Jew converted by Prisca and Aquila (Acts 18:24) and later a missionary himself (cf. 1 Cor 3:5–6; 16:12), has sometimes been suggested as the author of the discourse. Another unusual element in Heb, its emphasis upon the cultic liturgy of Judaism, can be seen as part of the same tradition. Philo's writings treat the priestly functions of Moses in the heavenly sanctuary. They contain elaborate allegories for the various vestments worn by the high priest. Heb is unique in the New Testament for its emphasis on Christ as the heavenly high priest. The philosophic scheme which held that the earthly sanctuary is an image of the heavenly one is put to a polemical use in Heb. For Philo the patterning of the earthly cult after the heavenly one meant that persons gained access to heavenly realities when practicing the earthly cult. For Heb the earthly cult of Judaism is an inferior copy which is to be rejected now that Christ has provided the believer with access to the heavenly sanctuary.

Christ as Heavenly High Priest

Heb uses two images of Christ. Christ is the divine Son who is the eternal image of God. Christ is the heavenly high priest who belongs to an eternal order of priesthood that was prefigured in the mysterious Old Testament figure of Melchizedek in Gen 14. The tradition of Christ as image of God has been developed from the early Christological hymns. A fragment of one of those hymns is quoted in the prologue to Heb:

> . . . whom [= the Son] he appointed heir of all things, through whom he created the world. He reflects the glory of God and bears the stamp of his nature, upholding the universe by his word of power, who, having made purification for sins, sat down at the right hand of the majesty on high, having become as much superior to the angels as the name he has obtained is superior to theirs (1:2–4).

This fragment follows a pattern that we find in other hymnic fragments. Christ pre-exists as the creative power of God, creating and upholding the universe. The role of Christ in salvation is then described in terms of earthly activity, frequently an effect of his death, and subsequent ascent to glory at the right hand of God. Phil 2:6–11 described the final exaltation in terms of a "superior name" and subjection of the powers. There the name was "Lord." Heb 1:5–6 makes it clear that the name which marks Christ's superiority to the angelic powers is "Son."

The prologue draws upon liturgical traditions to establish Christ's unique place in the heavenly realm. The description of the effect of Christ's death, "making purification for sins," points toward the metaphors of priesthood and sacrificial offering that will be central to the description of Christ as high priest in the central chapters of the letter. Before turning to that imagery, the author draws out the imagery of "subjection" and exaltation as it applies to Christ. Heb 2:7–9 admits that the subjection of all things to the "Son" is not something which we actually see now. Traditionally that subjection is only evident at the judgment (cf. 1 Cor 15:22–28). But Christians do "see" that the Son who had suffered death is exalted with God. Using the image from the "education" tradition that suffering is a way of perfecting the soul along with the liturgical tradition of purification, Heb then argues that the Son's suffering was the source of perfection for many "brothers and sisters" (2:10–13). The author insists that Christ can only be the source of salvation if he shares the human nature, flesh and blood, suffering and death, as those who are saved. His heavenly place above the angels does not mean that Christ is some sort of angelic or non-human divine figure. He is a real descendant of Abraham (2:14–16). Christ's humanity and "education through suffering" are a fundamental part of his service as a faithful and merciful high priest (2:18–19; 4:14–5:10).

Emphasis on the suffering humanity of the Son modifies one of the presuppositions of the philosophical language Heb uses. In the philosophical tradition "rest," "standing" and "unchangeableness" are all attributes of the divine. Suffering and passions imply imperfection and change. Heb insists that the perfection of Christ is not lessened by "suffering with" humanity or by knowing the temptations to which humans are subject. These experiences are part of the obedience which the Son "learned." Christ's obedience is the basis for the sinlessness which made the self-offering in death a perfect, unrepeatable sacrifice. Heb 10:5–10 uses the prophetic critique of the cult of Israel to show that God did not desire that sort of cultic activity. What God sought was obedience. Such obedience can only be offered by one who has come into a body in this world.

Heb 7:1–10:18 uses the language of cult and sacrifice in a series of arguments aimed at showing that the new order which has come into being with Christ surpasses the old Mosaic covenant and levitical cult. For example, Heb 9:1–14 contrasts the effects of the old sacrifices and that of Christ. The levitical cult established rules for worship in an earthly sanctuary. But such rules could only affect the body. They did not perfect the conscience. The earthly tent symbolizes the present age. Christ's sacrifice does not take place in the earthly tent. It implies entry into the heavenly world. The "blood," superior to all the blood of sheep and goats, is the whole self-offering of Christ (9:14,23–25; 10:4,19–20). The superiority of this offering lies in its ability to cleanse what is inner: conscience. Thus unlike the older cult, Christ's offering takes away sin (9:13–14; 10:4,22).

Comparison with the Platonic tradition in Philo makes this emphasis on cleansing the conscience clearer. Philo says of the earthly cult, which images the heavenly, "It is not possible to express our gratitude by means of buildings, oblations and sacrifices, for even the whole world was not a temple adequate for Him" (*Plant.* 126). True worship of God must take place in the purity of the soul. Hymns, prayer and virtue are ways in which the rational part of the human person serves God, who is incorporeal. Only those with "pure souls" can approach the heavenly altar. Conscience can be described as the divine Word sent into the soul which brings to light its transgressions (*Spec. Leg.* i 272). By making forgiveness possible once and for all, Christ cleanses the conscience of believers.

Discipleship in Hebrews

We have already seen that the theological reflection in Heb serves to support sections of exhortation directed to the readers. We have already seen that the readers are second or third generation Christians who have been Christians for some time. The primary danger envisaged by the author is apostasy. Some may have already turned away from the faith which they once possessed. Even those to whom the author writes must be encouraged to "hold fast" and "endure" (3:6,14; 10:36–39). Instead of progressing to maturity and perfection some have a faith which has not gone beyond the "beginner's stages" (5:11–6:2). The author reminds them that they have to encourage one another in good works. Some are reprimanded for neglecting to meet together (10:23–25). Yet this same community can look back to a past in which its members were willing to endure much suffering. They knew that loss of perishable earthly possessions was nothing compared with the permanent salvation that awaits them (10:32–36).

Throughout the work, Heb emphasizes the certainty and permanence of God's promises (e.g. 10:36–39; 6:13–20). The reader is warned that just as the heavenly salvation received through Christ is much superior to the old covenant, so the penalties for failure to remain faithful are greater (10:28–31). Heb 12:18–29 draws a dramatic comparison between Israel coming to Mount Sinai in the wilderness and the people of the new covenant who belong to the "city of the living God, the heavenly Jerusalem." The terrifying appearance of God on Sinai meant death for any living creature which touched the mountain. But the terrifying appearance associated with the new covenant will be the judgment which will consume all transitory, earthly things. Christians must take care to remain part of the "kingdom which is unshaken."

The philosophic tradition insisted that virtue, cleansing of the soul, was the appropriate worship of God. Christian sacrifice, that appropriate to those who belong to the heavenly city and not the earthly realm, takes the form of praising God, doing good and sharing what one has (13:14–16). Heb 13:1–5 lists some of the obligations of love among Christians: hospitality; care for prisoners and those who are ill-treated; respect for marriage and avoiding adultery; freedom from greed and contentment with what one has. This list follows common patterns of ethical exhortation. The emphasis upon remembering the lives of leaders of the community and avoiding false teaching (13:7–8) reflects the concerns of Christians in the generation after the death of the apostles as we have already seen in Acts.

However the warning against false teaching is followed by polemic against eating sacrifices from the "earthly altar" (13:9–10). Combined with the constant reminders that the Jewish cult has been superseded in Christ, this passage may indicate that there are Christians who expected an earthly replacement for the cult of the Jerusalem temple. We have already seen that Acts presented its readers with a picture of the Jerusalem community gathering in the temple for prayer as well as making private vows and sacrifices there. Some scholars have even wondered if the community to which Heb is addressed included former Essenes or members influenced by other forms of sectarian Judaism with a strong interest in cultic piety. But readers need not have been of Jewish origin to have such interests. Impressive temples with processions and sacrifices to the god or goddess formed part of the civic life of every major city. Christians could not adopt pagan rites without becoming idolators, but they might well have been attracted by the cultic elements in Christianity's Jewish heritage.

If Heb was directed to such a group of Christians at Rome as some scholars suppose, then we can see that its negative portrayal of the levitical cult did not win the day. 1 Clement speaks of the temple cult as a divinely established order in which each group (high priest, priests, levites, laity) has an appropriate place (40:1–5; 41:42). This order is replicated in the Christian sphere where Christ is high priest followed by apostles, bishops and deacons (ch. 42). 1 Clement 44:4 insists that one of the main functions of the bishop is to offer sacrifices. Rather than reject the levitical priesthood as transitory and imperfect in contrast to the heavenly sanctuary of Christ's sacrifice, 1 Clement shows us that Roman Christianity had combined it with the tradition of Christ as high priest. That combination would provide the beginning point for extensive development of a cultic understanding of priesthood within Christianity.

Another point at which the tradition did not follow the lead of the author of Heb concerns forgiveness of sin after baptism. In its sharp warnings against apostasy Heb insists that there can be no forgiveness for the person who has fallen into sin after baptism (6:4–6; 10:26–27). The second century visionary work from the Roman community, *Shepherd of Hermas*, offers forgiveness up to the time of hearing its revelation for those willing to repent with their whole hearts (*Vision* II 2–4; *Similitude* IX 26). However its hearers must hurry to repent of blaspheming or denying the Lord before the period of repentance is past. An even more liberal approach to the problem of forgiveness of post-baptismal sin was taken by Pope Callistus (d. 222 A.D.), though it is not clear that the Roman church of the early third century considered Heb to have canonical authority. By the time Heb is clearly accepted as canonical the possibility of forgiveness for sin committed after baptism even if that sin was apostasy had become an established part of the penitential discipline of the church.

For Heb disciples are on an "exodus" toward the promised land, their share in God's "rest" in the unshakable, heavenly kingdom. Faith is the access we have to those realities which we cannot see. Heb 11 catalogues all the great heroes of faith from the Old Testament. Their faith, the author concludes, was particularly exemplary because they did not receive what was promised. They had to wait until the fulfillment of all God's promises in Christ (11:39–40). Christians who have experienced the promised salvation in Christ and have such witnesses as their heritage should be all the more eager to lay aside sin and perfect their faith (12:1–2).

Summary

The unknown author of Heb has fashioned a discourse which points to future developments in Christian imagery and thought just as much of the work also draws on well-established themes from the past. Its picture of the Christian people as journeying toward the heavenly city set in contrast to the earthly city became an important way of understanding how Christians are to orient themselves in the world with St. Augustine's *City of God*. Adaptation of Platonic philosophy to understanding the biblical message of salvation and the soul's progress toward God became an essential part of Christian spirituality. The definition of faith in Heb 11:1 became a classic definition in the Christian tradition.

Even in those areas where subsequent tradition differed from the position expressed in Heb, evaluation of Jewish cultic imagery and post-baptismal sin, the treatise voices important insights. Heb is correct that the "washing" of baptism can never be repeated. Heb is also right to be horrified that someone who has experienced all the richness of the Christian life would throw all that away. Finding in Christ's sacrifice a forgiveness that could extend even to such people if they repented did not mean that

Christians had decided that such behavior was somehow okay. Even though much of the language of Christian priesthood would be shaped by the Old Testament traditions, Christians did not re-establish multiple sacrifices. The only sacrifice that can be offered by the Christian priest is the eternal sacrifice of Christ.

Though Jesus was not of a priestly family, Heb has recognized his death as the supreme priestly act. Heb finds in the mysterious figure of Melchizedek indication of an eternal order of priesthood that is different from the earthly priesthood based on descent. Consequently it is in Heb that we find the clear affirmation that Christ is the supreme priest. Heb has also given us moving images of the divine humanity of Christ as Son. Jesus genuinely shares the suffering and temptations of human beings even though he is without sin. This "education" of the divine Son should make Christians willing to turn to Christ the high priest for mercy and understanding.

STUDY QUESTIONS

Facts You Should Know

1. What type of writing is Heb? How did it come to be included in the New Testament?
2. What is the philosophical picture of reality used by Heb? How does the letter reinterpret the traditional teaching about judgment?
3. What images does Heb use for Christ? How is Christ the high priest different from all other "high priests"?
4. What is the importance of the suffering of Christ according to Heb?
5. What dangers does Heb see facing its audience? How do the words of exhortation in Heb address those dangers?
6. Why does Heb think that there can be no forgiveness for the sin of apostasy?

Things To Do

1. Trace the theme of journey to the promised "rest" in Heb. How does the author use this theme in his exhortation to remain faithful?

2. List the arguments which Heb gives for the superiority of Christ's sacrifice to those of the old covenant. Why could there never be another sacrifice like that of Christ?

Things To Think About

   1. How do we fall into the danger of letting our initial enthusiasm for Christianity lapse?

   2. Do we make an effort to attain a mature understanding of our faith or do we remain content to simply repeat its elementary doctrines?

Chapter 18

THE PASTORAL EPISTLES:
A PAULINE TRADITION

The Image of Paul in the Pastorals

We have already seen in Acts and Heb that by the end of the first century Christians looked back to the apostles as heroes from the past. We have seen that Christians no longer assumed that the second coming was in their immediate future. Christians must expect the church to go on preaching and living in this world for an indefinite period of time. We have also seen that Christians are concerned with preserving the heritage of apostolic teaching against fragmentation. In Acts we are shown the apostles formally appointing persons to guide the local communities. Paul gives his farewell instructions to one such group, elders from the church at Ephesus (Acts 20:17–35). Heb instructs its readers to remember the example of its past leaders and to obey those who must now guide the community as "leaders" (Heb 13:7–9,17).

The three letters, 1 and 2 Timothy and Titus, we are about to consider make these developments even clearer. These letters were called "pastoral epistles" by St. Thomas Aquinas in the thirteenth century. They are cast as letters from Paul to his two associates Timothy and Titus about how they should conduct their ministry as "elders" of local churches. Unlike the earlier group of writings from disciples of Paul close to the apostle in language and theology (Col, Eph, 2 Thess), the pastorals do not attempt to recapture Paul's language and thought. Like Acts they look back to the apostle as an authority and hero but use the language and tradition of the church at their own time. You already know that during Paul's lifetime Timothy and Titus were traveling missionaries who often had to fill in for the apostle when he could not visit a community. In the pastorals they

281

OUTLINE OF 1 TIMOTHY [18–1]

Greeting (1:1–2)

Timothy's task: Maintain apostolic faith against heretics (1:3–20)
  (a) False teaching and immorality (1:3–11)
  (b) Thanksgiving for Paul's conversion (1:12–17)
  (c) False teachers condemned by the apostle (1:18–20)

Specific instructions on community order (2:1–6:19)
  (a) Prayer for all and proper conduct of men and women (2:1–15)
  (b) Qualifications for bishops and deacons (3:1–13)
  (c) Maintain proper behavior in the "household of God" (3:14–16)
  (d) Reject false teaching: ascetic denial of creation (4:1–4)
  (e) Timothy's good example against false teaching (4:6–16)
  (f) Respect for persons of different ages (5:1–2)
  (g) Rules for enrolling widows (5:3–16)
  (h) Rules for treatment of elders (5:17–22)
  (i) Rules and sayings (5:23–25)
  (j) Behavior of Christian slaves (6:1–2)
  (k) Against disputes about teaching (6:3–5)
  (l) Against greed: Be contented with what you have (6:6–10)
  (m) Persevere in the "good fight of faith" (6:11–16)
  (n) To the rich: Trust in God and do good deeds (6:17–19)

Conclusion: Guard what has been entrusted to you (6:20–21)

OUTLINE OF 2 TIMOTHY [18–2]

Greeting (1:1–2)

Thanksgiving for Timothy's faith (1:3–7)

Remember Paul's faithful testimony to the gospel (1:8–2:13)

Reject heretical teachers: some claim resurrection is past (2:14–26)

People will fall into evil in the last days (3:1–9)

Remember Paul's conduct and your own heritage of faith (3:10–17)

Fulfill your ministry by preaching even to those unwilling to hear (4:1–5)

Paul's life is ending (4:6–18)
   (a) He has faithfully fulfilled his calling (4:6–8)
   (b) Faithful and unfaithful associates (4:9–16)
   (c) The Lord will uphold the apostle (4:17–18)

Final greetings (4:19–22)

OUTLINE OF TITUS [18–3]

Greeting (1:1–3)

Titus' work: order the churches in Crete (1:5–16)
   (a) Qualifications for elder-bishop (1:1–9)
   (b) To counter false teachers: Judaizing mythologies (1:10–16)

Titus' work: teaching sound doctrine (2:1–3:11)
   (a) Proper behavior for men, women and slaves (2:2–10)
   (b) Renounce passions and await the appearing of the savior by leading "godly lives" (2:11–15)
   (c) Rules for obedience, honest work and gentle speech toward all (3:1–2)
   (d) Salvation as regeneration and hope for eternal life (3:3–8)
   (e) Insist on the truth and avoid useless controversies (3:8b–11)

Travel plans for Paul's associates (3:12–14)

Final greetings (3:15)

have become the resident leaders of local communities. The letters contain Paul's instructions as to how they are to fulfill their role.

You can see from the outlines that the pastorals might easily serve as a general handbook for church leaders. The letters give qualifications for persons who are to be appointed "elders" or "bishops" in the churches. They provide a number of rules about proper conduct for Christians. They also make preservation of sound teaching one of the primary responsibilities of those in charge of the local communities.

You can also see from the outlines that the distinctive themes of Paul's theology are absent. The apostle is being presented here as the authoritative source for general rules of community life. These rules are not entirely different from the earlier Pauline tradition. You may remember that in his earliest letter, 1 Thess, Paul exhorted Christians to live in holiness, not dominated by passions, quietly and minding their own affairs, working with their hands so as to be dependent on no one and commanding the respect of outsiders (1 Thess 4:3–11). Paul had established rules for the proper dress of men and women who were prophesying in the assembly (1 Cor 11:2–26). He had given advice to widows (1 Cor 7:7, 8–9,39–40) and to slaves (1 Cor 7:17–24). Paul's disciples had included advice about relationships between husbands and wives, parents and children, masters and slaves in the form of a "household code" in Col and Eph (Col 3:18–4:1; Eph 5:22–6:9). The pastorals understand the Christian community as the "household of God." The collection of rules set forth as grounded in Paul's authority are intended to maintain proper behavior among the members of that household (1 Tim 3:14–16).

You can see from the outlines that the rules for church life are concentrated in 1 Tim and Tit. 2 Tim shares with the other two letters the warning to reject heretical teaching and instructions for the conduct of ministry. However, its focus is on Paul as an example. The letter takes the form of a "farewell discourse" from the apostle to Timothy. In the "farewell discourse" the dying patriarch gathers together his children, admonishes them to live virtuously drawing upon his own past life as an example, and predicts their future. The speech to the Ephesian elders in Acts 20:28–35 is a farewell discourse. 2 Tim provides us with a fascinating glimpse of how Paul was being remembered in churches at the end of the century.

We are not surprised to find that Paul is pictured as a prisoner suffering on behalf of the gospel (e.g. 1:8; 3:10–11; 4:6–8). Paul provides a model for all Christians to follow when they have to bear witness to the gospel that is now being entrusted to them. We have already seen another picture of Paul as the imprisoned witness to the gospel in Acts. But 2 Tim picks up an element of Paul's biography that is not present in Acts, the fact that Paul faced enemies within the Christian movement itself. Notice the references to persons who have deserted the apostle (1:15; 4:9, 14–16). Acts 28:17–31 leaves the reader with the impression that Paul spent his Roman imprisonment preaching the gospel with the support of Christians in that city. 2 Tim 4:6–18 gives us quite a different picture. The apostle is almost completely abandoned. 2 Tim 1:16–18 praises Onesiphorus and his household for not being ashamed of Paul's imprisonment but seeking diligently to find him at Rome. Has Luke omitted the embarrassing facts of the end of Paul's life? Or is the abandonment of the apostle in 2 Tim another way of showing the parallel between the suffering apostle and Christ? We do not know the answer to that question. All we do know is that before his ill-fated trip to Jerusalem Paul wrote Rom, a lengthy exposition of the gospel he had been preaching, and was seeking to gain support in the Roman community. We do know that his fears about the Jerusalem trip included concern that the church there might not accept his collection (Rom 15:31). If the polemic against Jewish cult in Heb addresses a movement among Christians in Rome, then we have some further evidence that there may have been persons there who would be less than enthusiastic about helping the controversial apostle.

True Doctrine in the Pastorals

We have seen that one of the major elements in the pastorals is concern to preserve apostolic teaching. The letters continually warn against those who like to dispute and to devise clever "myths." Paul predicts that deceitful and divisive teaching, teaching suited to what people want to hear, will become common in the last days (e.g. 2 Tim 3:1–9; 4:1–5). The pastorals follow a practice common in disputes between rival schools of philosophy. The opposition is always pictured as divided into numerous factions while the true teaching is unanimously held by its followers. Those who teach such "false doctrines" are also held to be morally corrupt, out to satisfy their own passions or greed. False teachers are also often accused of gaining a hearing by appealing to women who do not have the education or rational self-mastery required to resist their appeal (e.g. 2 Tim 3:6–7).

It is difficult to sort out what is merely polemical rhetoric and what may have been actual false teaching. However three areas seem to be disputed:

(a) an asceticism which rejected marriage (1 Tim 2:15; 4:3; 5:14) and required abstaining from some foods (1 Tim 4:3; 5:23; Tit 1:15)
(b) two persons who taught that the resurrection had "occurred already" (2 Tim 2:18)
(c) some form of speculation behind the references to Jewish myths and genealogies (1 Tim 4–11; Tit 3:9)

Paul himself had to answer questions about asceticism from persons in the Corinthian congregation who seem to have thought they should even break up their marriages in order to practice it (1 Cor 7). Rom 14:1–3 mentions disputes about food among Christians. Although we cannot tell what those who claimed the resurrection had already occurred meant, there was a tradition in Pauline churches of speaking of the Christian as "raised with Christ" (e.g. Col 3:1; Eph 2:5–6) as part of the present experience of Christian life. That tradition could have then been taken to mean that resurrection referred to an experience of spiritual illumination, not to a future transformation of persons. We do not know what form the speculations about Jewish myths and genealogies took. In the second century we have evidence for various movements called "gnostic." They claimed to have secret knowledge about the origins of the heavenly world and the fall of a heavenly being whose offspring is the "evil creator" of this material world. They created genealogies of the various heavenly and demonic powers and interpreted the Old Testament Genesis stories as part of their mythology. Since much of this second century material has links to sectarian Judaism, some scholars think that the pastorals are concerned about early manifestations of gnostic sectarianism.

Since there are no arguments against the views of opponents in the pastorals, we cannot reconstruct those views any further. What is the "true doctrine" which the successors to the apostles are to teach? As you can already see there is no sustained development of particular theological themes in the pastorals. We find out clues to the tradition of faith in the short formulaic expressions which the author uses. The unusual expression *pistos ho logos*, "the word is trustworthy," appears five times (1 Tim 1:15; 3:1; 4:9; 2 Tim 2:11; Tit 3:8). 1 Tim 4:9 adds a parallel expression: "It is worthy of all recognition." This formula marks some of the passages in which such traditional material is being quoted. 1 Tim 1:15 refers to the conviction that Jesus came "to save sinners." 1 Tim 4:9 may refer to the affirmation that Christ is "savior of all people, especially believers" in 4:10. You will notice that in the context this affirmation is directed against heretical teaching which over-emphasized "bodily discipline." Therefore it could also point to the previous verse which affirms that while bodily discipline has some value, the real source of salvation is in "piety." 1 Tim 3:1 is equally ambiguous in its reference.

2 Tim 2:11 introduces a formula which affirms that the faithful Christian will live and reign with the Lord while the unfaithful will be rejected (vv. 12–13). Tit 3:8 refers to what has come before in vv. 4–7. These verses provide a summary of the "story of salvation" that we find in the formulas in the pastorals. Humanity is separated from God through sinfulness. The savior appeared thanks to the mercy of God so that humans could be reborn in baptism and the Spirit. As a consequence believers now have the hope of eternal life. You will notice in this passage that the title "savior" applies both to God and to Jesus Christ. 1 Tim 2:3–6 describes God as savior and Jesus as ransom for us. Tit 1:2–3 speaks of God's promise of eternal life which is manifested in Jesus. 2 Tim 1:10 reminds the reader that the "appearing" of Christ abolished death.

There are also a few cryptic allusions to a story of Jesus' coming in the pastorals, though you will notice that the characteristic Pauline pattern of cross and resurrection is not present. 1 Tim 3:16 comments that the "mystery" of "our piety" is:

> who [= Jesus] was manifested in the flesh; vindicated in the Spirit; preached among the nations; believed in the world; taken up in glory.

1 Tim 6:13 refers to Jesus making "good confession" in his testimony before Pilate. God, for the pastorals, is the invisible creator, king of kings (e.g. 1 Tim 3:15–16) who stands behind the salvation Christians have received.

Church Organization in the Pastorals

As we have read through the New Testament we have found references to many different roles within Christian communities: apostles, prophets, teachers, elders, deacons, overseers ("bishops") and the like. Mt's community may even have had persons who could best be described as Christian "scribes." As long as the communities were small groups and could seek advice from their apostle-founder or his associates, the differing patterns of leadership and community service "inspired by the Spirit" (e.g. 1 Cor 12:28–31; Rom 12:6–8) may have been sufficient. However we already see in Acts a concern to establish more permanent forms of "church office." We have seen that persons are formally installed as leaders and missionary representatives of the community in Acts. Prayer and laying on of hands are part of the ceremony. 2 Tim 1:6 links Timothy's "appointment" in this manner with a "gift of the Spirit" which is to help him fulfill the duties he is undertaking. Without the apostles or their close associates to call on, it would become necessary to find a more "regular" process for appointing leaders in the community.

In the earliest traditions the terms "overseer" (*episkopos*), which is usually translated "bishop," and "elder" (*presbyteros*) seem to have been used in different communities for the person or persons in charge of the community. The term "deacon" was apparently used for those who played a role in assisting them. Thus we find Paul addressing Phil to "all the saints in Christ Jesus at Philippi together with their overseers and deacons" (Phil 1:1). In addition to these leaders we also know that other people served as missionaries in the Philippian community, including the two women whom Paul seeks to have reconciled with one another, Euodia and Syntyche (Phil 4:2). Both "elder" and "overseer/bishop" are rooted in Jewish practice. "Elder" would, as the term suggests, indicate older men who oversaw the affairs of the local community. They might also serve as "judges" when disputes arose between individuals. "Overseer" is paralleled by the Hebrew term *mebaqar* which referred to the head of the Essene community. There the "overseer" had to be a priest. He was in charge of admitting members and other affairs of the sect, though in some cases he may have been assisted by another official. The community also had a ruling council of older members, which some scholars have compared to the way in which the group of "the twelve" functioned in the earliest church at Jerusalem.

In Tit 1:5–9 we have a situation in which the term "bishop" and the term "elder" are used interchangeably for the person who is in charge of the community in a particular town. The man appointed to that office, as well as his wife and children, must be above any reproach morally. He must have a firm grasp on sound teaching so that he can convey it to others and refute those who are propagating false opinions. 1 Tim mentions the qualifications for bishops and deacons in one place (3:1–13) and elders, who are apparently subordinate to the bishop, in another (5:17–22). The bishop might have been an "elder" who had risen to pre-eminence because of his aptitude for teaching. In any event we have the basic elements of the threefold order of pastoral ministry and supervision that would become established practice: bishops, "elders" and deacons. As Christianity assumed the cultic language of the Old Testament the "elders" would be referred to as "priests." According to the pastorals the "bishops/elders" are the successors of the apostles, since it is their responsibility to preserve and to continue apostolic teaching and witness in the Christian communities.

As you can see from the list of qualifications in 1 Tim 3:1–13 the persons appointed to these offices had to be well-established Christians. They also had to be well thought of in the larger community, since it would be part of their responsibility to represent the Christian groups in the larger community. Since the Christian church thought of itself as a "household," the bishop had to be a person who was able to manage his own household well. That ability was part of someone's standing in the local community. You can also see that the situation of the bishop or elder is different from that of a traveling apostle like Paul. This person has to be able to guide a single, local community over a long period of time. In the ancient world only a man who was the head of his own household would enjoy sufficient respect to accomplish that task. Even though women often did manage households independently like Lydia in Acts 16:14–15 they would not have been the respected leaders of a local community. The same considerations would have also excluded a younger (and some not so young) man who was not in charge of his own household but still under the power of his father.

It is not clear that the role of deacon was entirely restricted to men at this period. 1 Tim 3:11 inserts a reference to women into the qualifications for that office: "The women likewise must be serious, not slanderers, but temperate and faithful in all things." The roles which women had played in the early household churches of the Pauline mission may have been understood as diaconal. But as the threefold structure developed further and deacons often went on to become priests and bishops, women were no longer designated deacons. This verse came to be understood simply as a reference to the qualities that the wife of a deacon had to have.

Christian Women in the Pastorals

The model of the church being established in the pastorals is that of a "patriarchal household." The church is like the "households" of the surrounding society in which everyone, younger men, women, children and slaves, had a subordinate role to that of the older male who was head of the family. The bishop had to fill this role for the Christian family. In the ancient world women or young men would only head households in extraordinary circumstances. The rules for the Christian household do not reflect such unusual cases. They seek to make the Christian household an example of what was considered appropriate and correct behavior in society at large.

The social model adopted for church order always considered women inferior to men. Indeed they often had much less education, were much younger than their husbands, and could not assume important roles of public leadership. We have seen that in the earlier period women did prophesy in community worship (1 Cor 11:2–16; also the daughters of Philip in Acts 21:9). However as leadership in the community was shaped by the patriarchal model women could not be designated as leaders of the community. Just as they did not teach or exercise authority over men in the larger society, so they were not permitted to do so in the church (1 Tim 2:12; cf. also 1 Cor 14:33b–36).

1 Tim 2:9–15 expects Christian women to dress and behave as any well-bred matron was expected to do. Such behavior would show her superiority as a woman to the weaknesses which people commonly attributed to women as a group. Indeed because of her piety the Christian woman accomplishes even more. What Eve had had to suffer as a punishment for her transgression, i.e. childbearing, would become for the Christian woman a means of salvation (vv. 14–15).

The most extensive discussion of women's affairs occurs in the treatment of widows in 1 Tim 5:3–15. Because of the dangers of childbearing women as a group lived shorter lives than men. But because most were married in their early teens, many women were widowed. Some might have sufficient resources either of their own or inherited from their husbands to continue to live in their own household. Or an adult son might become the head of the household. Others would be dependent upon their own families if they did not or could not remarry. Paul had said in 1 Cor 7:39–40 that a Christian widow could remarry if she wished, though she should be married to a fellow Christian. However he thought that she, like others who had the calling to it, might be happier to remain unmarried. 1 Tim 5:11–15 limits this latter advice to women who are quite old by ancient standards (over sixty—v. 9). Perhaps drawing upon some unfortunate cases or reflecting common social sentiments about unattached women, the author thinks that younger women without a family to care for and a household to manage become idle or even fall into sinful behavior.

1 Tim 5:4,8,16 also insist that Christians should assist widowed relatives so that they do not become a burden on the resources of the community. When these two groups of persons are excluded, those women who have led exemplary lives as Christian women are given a special role in the church, which will also provide for their support. We have already seen that charges of inequitable distributions to different groups of widows had created difficulties in the Jerusalem community (Acts 6:1). The author of the rules in 1 Tim is concerned with several different abuses in the church's tradition of enrolling and supporting pious widows. You will notice that just as 2 Tim 1:5 speaks of Timothy as the third generation in a family that included a pious Christian mother, Eunice, and grandmother, Lois, so 1 Tim presumes that we are talking about widows who have Christian families. Their relatives, children and grandchildren have an obligation to assist them. 1 Tim also hints that there were a number of other women who sought to be enrolled as widows. Though we cannot be sure, they may even have appealed to Paul's own advice in doing so. Some have later broken the "promise" they made when enrolled to remain "wife of one husband," i.e. a widow for life, and married. Others, those accused of becoming busybodies, may have been targets for the spread of divisive teaching in the community. Their preference for remaining unmarried would certainly provide a receptive audience for the ascetic teaching against marriage which is rejected in 1 Tim 4:3.

In the coming centuries devout Christian women would form households, often in the homes of wealthy widows, in which women might choose to follow a calling to remain unmarried and devote themselves to lives of prayer and good works. Such communities would provide alternatives to the rules about Christian widows made in the pastorals. They would also provide a place for women who would never have marriage and family as part of their Christian life.

Summary

The pastoral epistles met the crisis of creating a community structure which could maintain itself and its tradition long after the apostle founders had passed from the scene. Though many of the specific rules would be dropped or modified, the basic models of installing persons in offices which claim to stand in apostolic tradition and of the church as a hierarchically ordered household community with the bishop as the father-figure responsible for teaching and overseeing all that goes on in the community have continued to this day. Our concerns about divergent teaching in the church are also shaped by the language of the pastorals. We may be very quick to consider those whose teaching challenges common views of the faith to be personally immoral in some way. Or we may think that any differences in teaching and preaching among Christians must be stamped out before they can lead to the quarrelsome divisions and idle speculation condemned in the pastorals.

Of course we face a serious difficulty in interpreting many of the statements in the pastorals. These letters do not provide very many clues about the particular situations in the churches that led the author to formulate the tradition in given rules. Yet the rules are clearly directed at pressing concerns. There is no effort to give a systematic or complete set of rules for ordering Christian communities. Although there are references to prayer and citations of what are clearly liturgical phrases, we are not told anything about celebrations of the Lord's Supper or gatherings for worship, for example. Though we know qualifications for bishops and deacons, we do not know anything about how communities went about selecting them. Consequently even though the pastorals have had a profound influence on our understanding of church and faith as a deposit of apostolic tradition, they have not provided the complete blueprint for how the church must be ordered in order to remain in faithful continuity with the apostles.

STUDY QUESTIONS

Facts You Should Know

1. What are the qualifications for a person to fill each of the following roles in the churches of the pastoral epistles: (a) bishop (*episcopos*); (b) deacon; (c) "enrolled" widow? How do these qualifications relate to the behavior, duties and obligations expected in the Greco-Roman "household"?

2. Give three examples of advice or community rules in the pastoral epistles that expand or develop themes already found in Paul's letters.

3. How do the pastorals describe the "false teachers" whom the bishop is to oppose? How are some of the actual issues raised by the disputes over teaching related to problems that Paul had faced during his ministry in Greece and Asia Minor?

4. How is the term "elder" used in Tit? How is it used in 1 Tim? What do the pastorals show us about the development of the threefold pattern of church offices: bishop, "elder" (later "priest") and deacon?

5. What are the social patterns behind the behavior expected of Christian women in the pastorals?

Things To Do

1. Read through the pastorals, picking out the sections in which we are given glimpses of "Pauline biography." Give a biographical sketch of the apostle based upon these passages.

2. Read through the pastorals and pick out the passages in which Paul gives advice about conduct directly to Timothy or Titus. What are the characteristics of the "ideal" leader that emerge in these passages?

Things To Think About

1. If you had to make a list of qualifications for candidates to be "bishop" or "deacon" today, what would be on your list? How many of those characteristics overlap those in the pastorals? Are there any "new" ones which are derived from the special circumstances of the church today?

2. What virtues might be included in a contemporary version of "appropriate conduct" for Christian women and men such as we find in the pastorals?

Chapter 19

THE CATHOLIC EPISTLES:
AN APOSTOLIC HERITAGE

1 Peter, the "Holy People of God"

1 Pet is one of a group of seven letters known as the "catholic" epistles: 1 and 2 Pet, Jas, Jude, 1, 2 and 3 Jn. They are called "catholic" or "general" letters because they are not addressed to a specific church. Some like 2 and 3 Jn are short, private letters. Others like 1 Jn and Jas are really short treatises. In this chapter we will study 1 and 2 Pet, Jas and Jude. The Johannine epistles will be treated separately in the next chapter.

1 Pet begins and ends as though it were a letter. It even contains the beginning of a thanksgiving in 1:3. But as you read through the letter you will notice that there are none of the personal elements which mark the body of a letter. The author is addressing all of the churches in Asia Minor (1:1). One of Paul's associates, Silvanus, is referred to as the actual writer in 5:12, though one would expect more personal greetings if Silvanus had written the letter, since he was certainly familiar with Christians in this region. The allusion to "Babylon" in 5:13 is a traditional "code name" in Jewish and Christian apocalypses from the end of the first century for Rome. Therefore the writing purports to originate in the Roman church. The author of the letter was presumably a Greek-speaking Christian, unaware of Peter's real name, Simon or the Aramaic form of his nickname, Cephas. Perhaps the designation "fellow elder" in 5:1 (contrast the "apostle" used in 1:1) indicates that the author of the work was an "elder" in the Roman church.

Scholars have pointed out that the region addressed encompassed most of the Pauline mission and that there are a number of thematic parallels between 1 Pet and Rom. Compare the teaching on relationship to

Greeting (1:1–2)

Thanksgiving: Future hope for Christians being tested by suffering now (1:3–9)

Live in purity and holiness as God's chosen people (1:10–2:10)
  (a) The prophets predicted salvation for the Gentiles; the sufferings and glory of Christ (1:10–12)
  (b) Having been reborn and ransomed from your sinful past, live in holiness (1:13–2:3)
  (c) You are the "royal priesthood" offering spiritual sacrifices to God (2:4–10)

Obligations of Christian life (2:11–3:22)
  (a) Maintain good conduct so that "Gentiles" [= non-Christians] who accuse you of wrong-doing will be proven wrong at the judgment (2:11–12)
  (b) Silence your opponents by living in free obedience to all human institutions (2:13–17)
  (c) Slaves follow Christ by accepting even the unjust treatment of harsh masters (2:18–25)
  (d) Wives should be obedient and of exemplary modesty so they need not fear non-believing husbands, and husbands should be considerate of their wives (3:1–7)
  (e) Remain free from evil; love those who abuse and revile you while being ready to give a gentle defense of your faith (3:8–22)

Suffering as the imitation of Christ (4:1–19)
  (a) Suffering shows you have ceased from the sinful ways of your past even to those who abuse you because you no longer join them (4:1–6)
  (b) Remember your gifts of Christian service to one another (4:7–11)
  (c) This ordeal of suffering is a share in Christ's suffering if you suffer because you are a Christian (4:12–19)

Stand fast in humility and you will share Christ's eternal glory (5:1–12)
  (a) Humility in elders caring for the flock and in "younger persons" toward them (5:1–5)
  (b) Resist the devil who would use this suffering to destroy your faith (5:6–12)

Final greetings (5:12–14)

civil government in Rom 13:1–7 and 1 Pet 2:13–17 or the treatment of the brotherly love in 1 Pet 3:8–12 and Rom 12:10–17a. Numerous other parallels can be found which are grounded in the liturgical language of early Christian communities (e.g. the "stone" images from Is in 1 Pet 2:6–8 and Rom 9:33; descriptions of Jesus' resurrection, 1 Pet 1:21//Rom 4:25; 1 Pet 3:21–22//Rom 8:34). Parallels to Pauline language do not suggest that 1 Pet is dependent upon Rom but that it draws upon sources of Christian tradition which were also well-known to Pauline Christians.

You can see from the outline of 1 Pet that the author is concerned with shaping the new reality of Christian life in the face of on-going experiences of persecution. You can also see that listing of Christian duties takes up a significant portion of the work. Even the treatment of "duties" such as the section on the behavior of slaves, wives and husbands in 1 Pet 2:18–3:7 is shaped by the ever-present reality of persecution. Christian slaves may be subject to abusive masters. Christian women may be married to suspicious, non-Christian husbands. In each instance exemplary behavior may also be a strategy for alleviating the tension in the situation.

The Christians addressed in this letter are called "resident aliens" and "visiting strangers" (2:11). These terms are not merely a metaphorical way of saying that the Christian's true home is heavenly, with Christ. They also were political terms for persons who did not belong as citizens to the cities in which they lived. The "resident alien" at least had some status as a "registered" member of the city. The "visiting stranger" was merely a transient visitor who could be expelled at any time.

Not only are these churches drawn from persons whose social and legal status is precarious, they have gained the suspicion of their neighbors by conversion to Christianity. 1 Pet makes it clear that the "new life" they have taken on is evident to outsiders. Much of the abuse and persecution they suffer is the result of their changed behavior (4:1–5). Conversion has meant breaking off past ties and associations (1:3–5,10–12,18,21; 2:4–10) to enter the new familial community of mutual love which is God's holy people (1:17; 2:5,10; 5:9). Though some interpreters have tried to link the suffering referred to in 1 Pet to a specific period, the letter makes it evident that persecution and abuse took a number of forms. It was not the result of any specific legal action against Christians. Some act out of ignorance (2:15) or a certain curiosity to see what these persons will do (3:15). Others may suspect them of wrong-doing (2:12; 4:14–16). Still others are openly hostile to Christians as such (3:13–16; 4:4). 1 Pet takes some pains to emphasize the civic loyalty of Christians (2:13–17).

Whatever its source, suffering will not destroy the faith of the community. Christians can look to the example of Jesus and to that of Peter (5:1) to see how the truly holy one suffered. From the same example they know that their suffering will be rewarded with glory. By writing a general letter to these churches, the "elder" from the Roman church also reminds them that they are part of a worldwide fellowship of brothers and sisters.

OUTLINE OF JAMES   [19–2]

Greeting (1:1)

Perfection through faith and single-hearted steadfastness (1:2–8)

Wealth and those who trust in it fade away (1:9–11)

Temptation is not from God but the enticement of desire (1:12–18)

Doing the word which one hears (1:19–27)

Against partiality toward the rich in the Christian assembly (2:1–13)

Faith without works is dead (2:14–26)

Control the tongue (3:1–12)

Wisdom from above is evident in a life of goodness (3:13–18)

Passions are the root of war (4:1–10)

Do not judge or speak evil of one another (4:11–12)

Human boasts and plans vanish like mist (4:13–17)

Woe against the rich who have lived by injustice (5:1–6)

Christians remain patient (5:7–11)

Against oaths (5:12)

Christian prayer: anointing the sick; confession and forgiveness (5:13–18)

Winning back a sinner brings forgiveness (5:19–20)

OUTLINE OF JUDE   *[19–3]*

Greeting (vv. 1–2)

Struggle for the faith against those who pervert it (vv. 3–4)

Judgment will come upon the ungodly (vv. 5–16)
  (a) Proven by OT examples: wilderness generation, fallen angels,
      Sodom and Gomorrah (vv. 5–8)
  (b) Michael contending with the devil for Moses' body (v. 9)
  (c) So irrational they are like Cain, Balaam, Korah (vv. 10–11)
  (d) They pollute your "love feast" and are driven like waterless
      clouds, dead fruitless trees, wild waves, wandering stars (vv. 12–
      13)
  (e) Enoch prophesied their judgment (vv. 14–16)

Apostles predicted such people would come in the last days (vv. 17–19)

Build up your faith and try to win some back (vv. 20–23)

Final benediction (vv. 24–25)

James and Jude, the Legacy
of Jewish Christianity

The list of Jesus' relatives in Mk 6:3 (Mt 13:55) includes a "James,"
later the leader of the Jerusalem community, and a "Jude" who does not
appear elsewhere. The writings which came into the canon under their
names both reflect Jewish Christian traditions. However Jas is written in
an elegant Greek style which suggests its origins lie in a Greek-speaking
Jewish community. Jude, on the other hand, is a short piece of apocalyptic
tradition directed against unspecified false teachers. You can see from the
outlines that James only has a brief epistolatory introduction. It then continues as a work of exhortation. Jude takes the form of a very brief letter.
Neither of the two letters provides concrete details about its community.
Yet both James (5:19–20) and Jude (vv. 22–23) end with a very concrete
instruction to members of the church: they are to seek to bring back fellow
Christians who have strayed. The content of Jude implies that straying
would mean following the perverted teachers. We cannot tell what the
content of that teaching might have been, since Jude follows the conventional rhetorical pattern of describing the opposition as completely im-

moral. In Jas straying could imply any failure to live up to the teaching about a life of holiness.

You may have noticed in reading Jas that there are passages which come close to sayings of Jesus in the Sermon on the Mount (e.g. 4:11//Mt 7:1–5; 5:12//Mt 5:34–37), yet Jesus is only mentioned in 2:1. He is not the authority for the various sayings about moral conduct that make up the body of the work. This teaching is simply presented as general wisdom by which people should recognize what is pleasing to God.

You may also have noticed the pointed rejection of persons who claim that "faith saves" in Jas 2:14–26. The author even takes one of Paul's favorite passages for the priority of faith (Gen 15:6, see Rom 4:3) and argues that it proves the necessity of works. Jas insists that Abraham's faith was expressed in works when he "believed God" and went to offer Isaac as a sacrifice. Scholars continue to wonder whether or not Jas had Pauline arguments or slogans in mind. Of course the "works" which Jas demands Christians perform—providing charity for the poor brother or sister—are not the "works" of Judaizing by Gentiles against which Paul was arguing. Some interpreters think that just as Paul had to counter sloganizing among the Corinthians, so Jas is dealing with a sloganizing about faith which may have originated in popular reports of Pauline teaching.

Another concrete problem with which Jas deals is that of partiality in the Christian assembly (2:1–13). On the one hand, the warnings about trusting in wealth and the concluding woes against the rich elsewhere suggest that Jas and its readers view the wealthy from the position of outsiders. On the other, they seem to have had sufficient differences of wealth and poverty within the community itself as to lead to preferential treatment for the rich. Jas 2:7 mentions in passing that the rich drag Christians into court simply for being Christians. By honoring a rich person and dishonoring a poor one in their own group Christians become like the unjust judges whom they face.

At the conclusion to the letter we get one final glimpse into the concrete life of the community. We see that they have institutionalized healing in a ritual of anointing and prayer for the sick by the elders of the church (5:13–15). They have also developed some form of mutual confession and prayer for forgiveness. Jas argues against those who might be skeptical that the miracle of Elijah and the rain proves that the prayer of a righteous person is powerful. The unstated conclusion to the argument is that if the prayer of an Elijah can control the weather, then that of the community can effect forgiveness for sin.

Jas 2:8–13 shows that, even with its insistence that faith is not living unless manifested in "works," the vision of "true religion" in Jas cannot be described as legalistic. The "royal law" of Jas 2:8 (also 1:25, "perfect law,

law of liberty") is summed up in the love command. Throughout the work Jas emphasizes not only the "good works" of caring for the poor which are traditionally associated with that command (e.g. 1:27) but also the socially divisive effects of other sins. Several passages warn against anger and other sins of speech (e.g. 3:1–12; 4:11–12). Wealth also divides Christians, not only in the danger that the church will adopt the attitudes of a larger society in showing preference to the wealthy, but also in the false confidence it engenders in its possessors. People can even come to the point of not seeing the obligations of charity and justice (e.g. 2:15–16; 5:3–6). Jas draws upon a wisdom tradition which saw perfection as a single-hearted and humble devotion to God. This Jewish tradition was often linked with a stoic concern for the necessity of a victory over the disruptive effects of passions in the soul in the writings of Greek-speaking Jews (e.g. *Testaments of XII Patriarchs*). Jas employs this type of ethical teaching. Consequently the inner passions which tear at the soul are the ones which ultimately destroy the outer fabric of society in wars (4:1–6). You will also notice that the tradition of ethical preaching found in Jas makes extensive use of nature images to describe the shifting character and deceitfulness of false human reasoning. The images for the steadfast purpose of the morally perfect person are linked with the heavenly perfection of God, who sends the humble wisdom from above (1:5,17; 3:17).

While Jas reflects a Greek-speaking Jewish Christianity that drew on the ethical traditions of Hellenistic Judaism, Jude incorporates some apocryphal material from Jewish apocalyptic. The short piece does not provide any concrete information about the false teachers it opposes. Its exhortation to remember that the apostles foretold the emergence of divisions, evil-doers and deceivers in the last days (v. 17) indicates that the writing belongs to the post-apostolic period. The apocalyptic material provides the author with further evidence that heretics will be condemned. The examples in vv. 5, 7 and 11 are taken from the Old Testament. Stories of the fallen angels tethered in celestial prisons until the judgment (v. 6) are part of the Enoch tradition. The seer in 1 Enoch sees their locations. Jude 14 refers to Enoch as the prophet of divine judgment. Apocalyptic traditions also elaborated on the judgment of Sodom and Gomorrah (v. 7; cf. *Testament of Naphthali* 3,4–5). Finally the legend of Michael and Satan contending over the body of Moses (v. 9) appears in such apocryphal writings as *Assumption of Moses*.

2 Peter, Christian Eschatology

The collection of apocalyptic warnings in Jude had little impact on early Christianity with the exception of 2 Pet. Its author faces a crisis of belief in divine judgment. False teachers reject the traditional teaching about the second coming (3:3–4). They may also have appealed to those philosophers who insisted that the world is eternal to back up their argument. In addition 2 Pet accuses them of supporting their views with false interpretations of Paul's letters (3:15–16). You can see from the outline that 2 Pet is cast as a defense of traditional Christian eschatology. It is put in the mouth of the dying apostle as a "farewell discourse" to the community.

The material from Jude is incorporated into the argument that the false teachers will be judged in 2 Pet 2. However careful comparison of the two writings shows that 2 Pet has not simply taken over arguments from Jude. 2 Pet has reordered the argument to follow what is found in the canonical Old Testament traditions. Apocryphal traditions which have no basis in Scripture, like the contest between Michael and Satan for the body of Moses, have been dropped. This reordering fits with a theological principle that is stated at 2 Pet 1:19–20: we have prophecy, God's own word, to prove the truth of our belief in judgment. People did not invent this teaching. Rather it came through "prophets," that is, human beings moved by the Holy Spirit. The arguments set out in 2 Pet are to be understood as "proof" that the tradition of a divine judgment is grounded in the prophetic word of scripture.

2 Pet clearly has a much more developed sense of the authority of a canon of scripture than we find expressed in the other New Testament writings. 2 Pet 1:14 makes the written testimony of the apostle the medium through which the community is to remember his teaching once he has died. 2 Pet 3:1 refers back to the existence of a previous Petrine letter as part of the community's heritage of true teaching. The explicit use of the transfiguration as an apostolic witness to the truth of a coming parousia (1:17–18) suggests that at least one of the synoptic gospels enjoyed authoritative status as "apostolic testimony." The reference to disputes about the meaning of Paul's letters (2 Pet 3:15–16) suggests that there was a collection of the Pauline epistles with authoritative status as well.

2 Pet thus points toward another important development in meeting the problem of continuity of apostolic tradition: emergence of a Christian canon of authoritative scripture. 2 Pet does not claim that everything in scripture is directly inspired. Rather the prophetic words of scripture are spoken by human beings who have been moved by the Spirit. 2 Pet recognizes that there are difficult passages in scripture which will be the subject of debate. However the solution which this writing explores will become one of the central elements in the theological use of scripture. 2 Pet finds a consistent witness in prophecy, sayings of Jesus and apostolic testimony to the central Christian belief that the world is to be judged. Given that witness, the arguments advanced by the opponents cannot be

OUTLINE OF 2 PETER   *[19–4]*

Greeting (1:1–2)

Remember the apostle's teaching: faith, knowledge and virtue will gain
entry to an eternal kingdom with Christ (1:3–15)

First proof: prophetic word made more certain by the transfiguration
(1:16–21)

Condemnation of false teachers: divine judgment is certain (2:1–22)
  (a) They bring on their own destruction (2:1–3)
  (b) Examples of God's judgment against the evil and rescue of the
      righteous: fallen angels, Noah's generation, Sodom and
      Gomorrah (2:4–10)
  (c) Their irrationality and immorality leads them to follow Balaam
      (2:11–16)
  (d) Once freed from defilement through knowledge of the savior
      Jesus, they are now caught in even worse corruption (2:17–22)

Further arguments that the world will be judged (3:1–10)
  (a) Remember predictions of the prophets and commandments of
      the Lord which you received through the apostles, which spoke
      of "scoffers" in the last days (3:1–3)
  (b) Against arguments from the eternal sameness of the world: God's
      word created the earth out of water, reduced it to water in the
      flood and now upholds the world until the judgment by fire (3:4–
      7)
  (c) Against arguments from the "delay of the parousia":
      (i)   time is not the same with God as in human reckoning (3:8–9a)
      (ii) the "delay" is God's patience giving people time for
            repentance (9bc)
      (iii) the day will come suddenly and the heavens and earth be
            destroyed (3:10)

Since we believe God's promise of a "new heaven and earth" we live in
holiness (3:11–15a)

Paul's letters agree with this teaching, though false teachers twist the
meaning of difficult passages to lead people to destruction (3:15b–17)

Final benediction (3:18)

accepted as legitimate interpretations of Paul's meaning. But 2 Pet does not simply condemn the opposition with the conventional rhetoric taken from Jude. 2 Pet also provides counter-arguments to the claims that they make about the "irrationality" of the traditional belief.

Summary

The four writings we have studied show us different aspects of the preservation of tradition in communities that were not directly part of the Pauline group of churches. Both of the Petrine letters have links with Pauline material. In 1 Pet these ties take the form of common traditions and even some association with members of the Pauline circle, Silvanus and Mark. By the time 2 Pet was written both 1 Pet and a collection of Paul's letters were known and had authoritative status in the churches for which the author is writing. It is also possible that the treatment of faith and works in Jas was directed against the influence of sloganizing Paulinism. Thus some scholars have argued that the influence of the Pauline churches extended beyond their own circles. Paul's use of the letter as a way in which the apostle could be present to the churches became a way of preserving ties with apostolic tradition in churches which traced their roots to other apostles.

We will see that the influence of the apostolic letter appears in Johannine churches as well. Even Rev, a Christian apocalypse, includes letters to major churches in Asia Minor. However, its letters are the word of the exalted Lord to the angelic supervisors of the churches. Thus the letter form is part of a larger pattern of prophetic revelation. We have also seen in 2 Pet the beginning of another way of preserving apostolic tradition: creation of an authoritative collection of writings in which God's word is found. 2 Pet recognizes that the tradition will be handed down to later generations of Christians in writings which have come down from the first century.

STUDY QUESTIONS

Facts You Should Know

1. What are the ties between 1 Pet and Christianity and Rome?
2. What is the situation of the Christians to whom 1 Pet is written? How does 1 Pet advise Christians to react to the hostility they experience?

3. What kinds of Jewish Christian tradition do we find in Jas and Jude?
4. What is the ethical teaching contained in Jas on the following topics: (a) rich and poor Christians; (b) the necessity of "good works"; (c) forgiveness of sin within the Christian community?
5. What views are being opposed in 2 Pet?
6. What does 2 Pet show us about the influence which Paul's letters were having in early Christianity?

Things To Do

1. Read through 1 Pet and pick out the passages in which the author contrasts the "past life" of Christians with the new life they have received in Christ. How has their change led to hostility against Christians?

2. Read through Jas. How does the "love command" play a role in the ethical teaching of the letter? Find the passages which echo the teaching of Jesus.

Things To Think About

1. Conversion and baptism changed the lives of Christians according to 1 Pet. What differences does "being Christian" make to people's lives today?

2. Jas insists that faith without works is dead. What "works" show others a living faith today?

Chapter 20

THE JOHANNINE EPISTLES: A CHURCH DIVIDED

The Story of Johannine Christianity

The three writings which we speak of as "Johannine epistles" do not claim to have been written by the author of the fourth gospel but by an unknown person who calls himself "the elder" (2 Jn 1; 3 Jn 1). Scholars think that there was a "school" of teachers in the Johannine churches. They were disciples of the beloved disciple. The author suggests that he was a member of this group when he refers to a "we" whose testimony to the truth about Jesus the hearers accept (1 Jn 1:1–4). 1 Jn frequently calls to mind the traditions which the audience learned when they became Christians (e.g. 1:5–2:17). In fact, 1 Jn is really a tract or homily on true Johannine tradition. The introduction to 1 Jn (1:1–4) is meant to remind the reader of the prologue to the fourth gospel (Jn 1:1–18). 2 and 3 Jn, on the other hand, are short letters from the elder. 2 Jn directs a church in the Johannine circle to exclude persons who have separated themselves from the community and are enticing others away with their false teaching about Jesus (2 Jn 7–11). These are the same persons whose teaching is attacked in 1 Jn. Some scholars even think that 2 Jn might have been accompanied by a copy of 1 Jn. 3 Jn deals with a different crisis. It is a private letter to a person called Gaius. The elder wants Gaius to provide hospitality for missionaries, since another leading Christian in the region, Diotrephes, has refused to receive persons who come from the elder (3 Jn 5–10).

We have seen that many of the later writings in the New Testament are concerned with the divisive effects of false teaching. But it is only in the Johannine epistles that we have clear evidence that conflicts over teaching had led to the creation of a completely independent group which also claimed to be the heirs to the Johannine tradition. When we studied the gospel, we saw that the Johannine church had been divided before. There persecution from outside, from the Jewish community, had led some to deny their belief in Jesus as God's Son and messiah. We also saw that the Johannine picture of the "ideal community" as it is drawn in chapters 13–17 emphasized the unity in love of believers with one another and with the Father and Son.

Salvation depends upon being part of this unity. Jn 15:1–17 reminds Christians that they must remain attached to Jesus, the true vine. Their unity with Jesus is evident by the love that they have for one another. Johannine Christians are also aware that they would not be part of this community if they had not "been chosen" by the Lord. The love command plays a central role in the catechesis of the Johannine community as 1 Jn shows (e.g. 1 Jn 2:7–11).

When we remember these strong images of love and unity, the shock caused by the division within the Johannine churches becomes evident. 1 Jn 2:18–26 speaks of the "going out" of the dissident group. How could people leave this community in which the Father and Son are present? The author answers first by invoking a view that we have frequently encountered in discussions of false teachers: at the end-time false teachers will come to lead the faithful astray. This image has its roots in apocalyptic traditions. 1 Jn is responsible for coining a new way to refer to the enemy of the end-time, the "antichrist" (2:18; 4:3; 2 Jn 7). The author's second explanation is that such persons could not really have been "of us," that is, chosen by Jesus, or they would have remained in the community (2:19).

Many people are struck by the sharp language of 1 and 2 Jn. Love only applies to those who have remained within the community. The dissidents are agents of the "antichrist" and are treated accordingly. Some interpreters have suggested that this sharp tone indicates that the preaching of the dissidents had been very successful in winning Johannine Christians to its side. 1 Jn 4:5–6 uses a contrast familiar to us from the gospel: "of the world"/"of God." The opponents are "of the world" and are able to gain a hearing there that the group faithful to the tradition taught by the elder cannot win. This symbolism tells the reader not to be taken in by the apparent success of the opponents.

Since the key element in the dissident preaching was denial of the significance of Jesus' humanity (e.g. 2 Jn 7), many scholars think that the Johannine splinter groups formed gnostic sects which believed that Jesus embodied a heavenly divine revealer from a world outside this evil creation. The fourth gospel was popular among second century gnostic heretics. Its popularity there made it suspect among more orthodox Christians. You can tell from reading the gospel that its emphasis on Jesus' divinity and on the pattern of descent from heaven and return there could easily be read without the humanity of Jesus. Scholars credit 1 Jn with insisting that the true Johannine tradition is committed to Jesus' "coming in the flesh." They wonder if the disciples of the Johannine school edited the gospel as we have it to make these connections clearer. Some have proposed that discourses like chapter 15 reflect the crisis of the epistles period. Others point to the division among Jesus' disciples in Jn 6:51–59, where some leave Jesus when he insists that the bread of the Eucharist really is his flesh. Reference to Jesus' death as an offering for sin is strengthened by the insistence on blood and water flowing from the side of Jesus in Jn 19:34–35. This element in the crucifixion scene might well fit with the insistence on the testimony of blood, water and the Spirit in 1 Jn 5:6–8.

If the dissidents became gnostic sectarians, what happened to the Johannine churches which preserved the traditions of the elder? Some scholars have found a clue in Jn 21. Remember that this chapter is added onto the gospel after it has already come to a conclusion. As you read through it you will notice that the story focuses upon Peter even though the beloved disciple is present. Peter is the fisherman who draws in the net with many fish. Peter is also commissioned by Jesus as the one to shepherd the flock (21:15–19). Peter is also the one who asks about the fate of the beloved disciple (21:20–23). We learn from the correction in v. 23 that the beloved disciple had died by the time this chapter was written. If this chapter was added to the gospel as part of the final editing, it may contain a clue to the destiny of Johannine Christians. We saw in the pastoral epistles that an important way of preserving the community against dissident teaching was establishing a succession of apostolic leaders who were charged with true teaching. The Johannine letters do not contain any hints of such emergent organization. Some scholars think that this emphasis on Peter provided a way in which Christians who belonged to the tradition of the beloved disciple could join communities that had an apostolic succession based on Petrine tradition. When they did so, they took the unique emphasis on the divinity of Jesus with them. This emphasis when combined with the infancy stories of Jesus' birth provided the basis for what would become the orthodox doctrine of the incarnation of Jesus.

1 and 2 John, Christian Fellowship
and the Crisis of Division

There is no doubt that the crisis to which the elder is responding was a severe one. The elder argues that the dissidents have violated the fundamental commandment of the Johannine tradition: love one another (2:3–11; 3:10–11; 4:20–21). 2 Jn 7 describes the false teaching of the opponents

OUTLINE OF 1 JOHN   *[20-1]*

Prologue (1:1–4)

Walking in light (1:5–2:17)
  (a) God is light (1:5)
  (b) Freedom from sin (1:6–2:2)
  (c) Keeping the commandments (2:3–11)
  (d) Address to three groups (2:12–14)
  (e) Reject the world (2:15–17)

Reject the antichrists (2:18–29)
  (a) Divisions are a sign of the last hour (2:18–19)
  (b) Anointing preserves the true faith in the hearers (2:20–27)
  (c) Confidence at the judgment (2:28–29)

Love as the mark of God's children (3:1–24)
  (a) God has made us children now (3:1–10)
  (b) We must love one another like Christ, not like Cain (3:11–18)
  (c) Our confidence before God, who is greater than our hearts
       (3:19–24)

Reject the antichrists (4:1–6)
  (a) They do not confess Jesus (4:1–3)
  (b) They have not overcome the world (4:4–6)

God is love (4:7–21)
  (a) Christ has shown God's love (4:7–12)
  (b) We know God's love through the Spirit (4:13–16a)
  (c) Our confidence: abiding in God's love (4:16b–21)

Belief in the Son (5:1–12)
  (a) Faith overcomes the world (5:1–5)
  (b) Testimony: Son came in water and blood (5:6–12)

Conclusion (5:13)

Epilogue: sayings and rules (5:14–21)
  (a) Confidence in prayer: God hears our prayer; prayer for sinners
       (5:14–17)
  (b) Confidence sayings: one born of God does not sin; we know the
       true God and have eternal life (5:18–20)
  (c) Keep from idols (5:21)

OUTLINE OF 2 JOHN   *[20–2]*

Greeting (vv. 1–3)

Thanksgiving: Your children are walking in truth (v. 4)

Body: No fellowship with the dissidents (vv. 5–11)
  (a) Johannine tradition is to love one another (vv. 5–6)
  (b) Deceivers deny Jesus is come in the flesh (v. 7)
  (c) Warning: not abiding in the teaching about Christ could cost
      your fellowship with God (vv. 8–9)
  (d) Anyone who aids or even greets a dissident shares that person's
      wickedness (vv. 10–11)

Plans for a visit (v. 12)

Final greeting (v. 13)

as an error in teaching about Jesus: "Do not confess the coming of Jesus
Christ in the flesh." But if you look at the outline of 1 Jn, you will see that
the author is preoccupied with another topic: freedom from sin. 1 Jn 1:6–
2:2 takes up a series of sayings about sin. Those who argue that they are
free from sin are described as liars. The author insists that the Christian
can only claim to be free from sin because Christ's death has atoned for sin
(1:7). Christians who do sin can turn to Jesus as their heavenly advocate
(2:1–2). You may have recognized that this picture of Jesus' death as atonement for the sin of the world and of the exalted Jesus as the one to whom
Christians are to turn is much like the tradition of Jesus as high priest in
Heb 4:14–16. 1 Jn uses this tradition of the atoning death of Jesus as part
of the argument against those who deny the significance of Jesus' coming
in the flesh. Without Jesus' death on the cross there would have been no
atonement and our sins would not have been forgiven.

But the picture becomes somewhat muddied when we turn to 1 Jn
3:4–10. There we have the clear assertion that those "born of God," that
is, Christians, do not sin (vv. 6,9). How does this view of perfection differ
from the view which was rejected earlier? One answer is to insist that the
dissidents cannot claim to be "children of God" since they have destroyed
the community. They are not living in the sinless unity with God that they
claim. The second answer is based on the picture of Christ as the heavenly
intercessor in 1 Jn 2:1–2. The sayings on prayer which are appended to 1
Jn suggest that the community may have had a formal way of dealing with
sin, since they speak of prayer for the sinful Christian. Only one sin is ex-

cluded, that called "the sin unto death." Although the author does not explain what this sin is, parallels with Jewish legislation would suggest a sin which required that a person be expelled from the community. Comparison with Heb 10:26 suggests that that sin would be apostasy, denial of one's faith in Christ. These rules may have first been formed to deal with those who denied their faith in the face of external persecution. 1 Jn has appended them because the author wants the dissidents excluded from all fellowship with Johannine Christians.

You can also see from the outline that 1 Jn constantly reassures Christians that if they are faithful to its teaching they do not have to worry about the judgment (2:28; 3:2–3,19–21; 4:17–18). 1 Jn 3:14 affirms that the mutual love among Christians is evidence that they have "passed from death to life." The conclusion to 1 Jn emphasizes the fact that the faithful have eternal life. This constant emphasis on the certainty of salvation suggests that the opponents preached a form of perfectionism that made Johannine Christians unsure of their own salvation. 1 Jn insists that the "child of God" is sinless, has eternal life, and through faith has overcome Satan.

3 John, Broken Hospitality

You can see from the outline of 3 Jn that there is no reference to the crisis addressed by 1 and 2 Jn.

OUTLINE OF 3 JOHN   [20–3]

Greeting (v. 1)

Health wish (v. 2)

Thanksgiving: You are following the truth (vv. 3–4)

Body: Rendering hospitality to missionaries is "of God" (vv. 5–11)
  (a) **You do a good thing in aiding traveling missionaries (vv. 5–8)**
  (b) **Diotrephes' refusal to allow anyone to aid missionaries from the elder (vv. 9–10)**
  (c) **Exhortation: Continue to imitate what is good (v. 11)**

Recommendation for Demetrius (v. 12)

Future visit (v. 13)

Final greeting (v. 14)

The elder is writing a private letter to Gaius, a Christian known for showing hospitality to traveling missionaries. His letter follows an episode in which some missionaries bearing the recommendation of the elder were turned away by a certain Diotrephes. The elder does not accuse Diotrephes of siding with the dissidents but of being arrogant, speaking evil of the elder and rejecting his authority. The immediate practical purpose of 3 Jn is to secure hospitality for traveling missionaries. The Demetrius who is recommended at the end of the letter was probably its bearer and a "test case" of Gaius' willingness to undertake these new obligations of hospitality.

Some scholars have tried to connect 3 Jn with the crisis of 1 and 2 Jn by presuming that Diotrephes' actions were motivated by the dissident crisis. After all, his treatment of the elder's emissaries is exactly what the elder called for in 2 Jn 10–11. However, there is nothing in the brief letter itself that makes this connection. 3 Jn 10 suggests that the author still expects to talk the matter out with Diotrephes, something that is clearly beyond possibility in the case of the dissidents. Therefore we may assume that this brief note was preserved because it came from the author of 1–2 Jn, but that it originally referred to a different situation.

Summary

The Johannine epistles present us with the severest crisis to confront the small early Christian communities: schism. The elder makes a strong plea to his readers to remain in communion with the authentic Johannine tradition which they have "heard from the beginning." He also takes drastic action to prevent dissident teaching from gaining any further hearing in Johannine churches. Many people today feel uncomfortable at this policy of branding one's opponents agents of Satan and expelling them from any contact with the community. But we can only view the elder's actions as a reflection of how severe the crisis had become. It seems evident that there is no longer any possibility of winning the dissidents back. There are no hints of a hoped for reconciliation such as we find in the Diotrephes case. If the dissidents were indeed gaining ground among Johannine Christians, then the elder and other teachers in his circle may have seen the very survival of Johannine Christianity at stake. In such a crisis there seems little room for compromise.

STUDY QUESTIONS

Facts You Should Know

1. Describe the crisis in the Johannine churches that is reflected in 1 and 2 Jn. Why was division in the community such a shocking event for Johannine Christians?
2. How does 1 Jn emphasize the importance of the humanity of Jesus?
3. How does the author of 1 Jn understand sin and forgiveness in the Christian community?
4. Describe the situation being addressed in 3 Jn.

Things To Do

1. Pick out all of the passages in 1 Jn which refer to the love command. How is this command to be practiced in the Johannine churches?

2. Pick out all of the passages in 1 Jn which refer to the confidence Christians have in the judgment. What is the basis for this confidence?

Things To Think About

1. What situations do we face today in which church communities have become divided even though they share a common tradition? What lessons could we learn from the Johannine churches to help avoid the sharp break into two hostile groups that we find there?

2. 1 Jn 4 contains the famous definition: "God is love." How is the love of God shown in Christian communities today?

Chapter 21

REVELATION:
CHRISTIANITY AND THE EMPIRE

The Composition of Revelation

The final book in the New Testament continues to be one of the most puzzling in the entire collection. It falls into a literary type which we call an "apocalypse" (from the Greek word for "revelation"). Because Rev presents visions of divine judgment, many people interpret Rev as though it presented a detailed, event-by-event allegory of the end of the world. Such interpretations neglect the imagery which would have been familiar to the first century audience of Rev. You can get some feeling for this tradition by turning to your Old Testament and reading the visionary material in Dan 7–12, Ez 1–9, 26–27, 39–44 and Zech 9–14.

We can find a number of images and familiar story patterns being reused by the seer of Rev. Here are some examples:

(1) The inaugural vision (1:12–20) combines features of the visions in Dan and Ez.

(2) Rev 5 depicts the heavenly assembly of the gods, an ancient mythological motif which the prophets used for the divine council of Yahweh.

(3) Another ancient mythic motif that the Old Testament frequently used for Yahweh was that of a holy war in which the god defeats the forces of chaos. That theme appears in the defeat of the Satanic forces in Rev 19:11–22:5.

(4) The idea that judgment is based on what has been recorded in a book (Rev 20:11–15) is another common theme.

(5) Apocalypses have a sharp contrast between the heavenly realm and the earthly one. Here they are exemplified in two cities (14:8–21; chs. 17–18 and 21).

312

(6) Another mythological theme with parallels in both the Ancient Near East and Greek mythology is that of a struggle with the chaos monster to save the divine child (12:1–14:5; 19:11–20).

(7) Rev 6:1–7:17 reuses traditional material about world cataclysms.

(8) The plagues of the Exodus story are evoked and intensified in Rev 8:1–11:4; 15:5–19:10.

(9) The motif of the winepress of God (Rev 14:9–20; 19:13) has been taken from the prophets (Is 63:3; Jl 4:13).

We are also given three scenes in which the prophet has a commissioning vision (1:12–20; chs. 4–5; 10:1–11). Many of the visions in Rev show the heavenly liturgy. The work is punctuated with antiphonal hymns (4:9–11; 5:9–12; 7:10–12; 11:15b–18; 16:5b–6,7b; 19:1b–3,4b,5b–6b,8a). Unlike the Old Testament prophet who might have a vision of the divine council, heavenly altar and throne and then carry out his commission on earth (as in Is 6) the apocalyptic seer remains in heaven. The seer watches the scenes unfolding on earth from the perspective of heaven.

The Seven Letters

Rev also shows the influence of the "apostolic letter" in early Christianity. The seer's vision opens with letters to the angels of the seven churches in Asia Minor. These letters were composed as a group of seven,

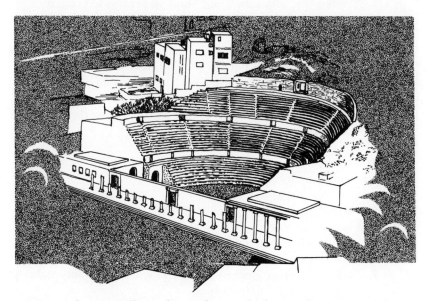

Roman Theatre still standing today, in the heart of Amman, Jordan.

1. Address and command to write:
   (a) To the angel of the church in [i. Ephesus, ii. Smyrna, iii. Pergamum, iv. Thyatira, v. Sardis, vi. Philadelphia, vii. Laodicea]
   (b) write
2. Prophetic messenger formula + description of Jesus:
   (a) the words of . . .
   (b) *description:*
      i. holds the seven stars in his right hand; walks among the seven golden lampstands
      ii. first and the last; died and came to life
      iii. has the sharp two-edged sword
      iv. Son of God; eyes like a flame of fire; feet like burnished bronze
      v. has the seven spirits of God; seven stars
      vi. holy one, true one; has the key of David; opens and no one shall shut; shuts and no one shall open
      vii. the Amen; faithful and true witness; beginning of God's creation
3. I know . . . .
   (a) *the situation:*
      i. works, toil, endurance, not bear evil persons but tested those called apostles but are not; enduring patiently for my name's sake, not grown weary
      ii. tribulation, poverty (though you are rich), slander from those say are Jews but are synagogue of Satan
      iii. dwell where Satan's throne is; did not deny my faith even in days of faithful martyr Antipas
      iv. works, love, faith, service, endurance, latter works greater than the first
      v. works
      vi. works
      vii. works, neither cold nor hot
   (b) *but I have it against you:*
      i. abandoned the love you had at first
      iii. some hold teaching of Balaam: eat food sacrificed to idols and practice immorality; some hold teaching of Nicolaitans
      iv. tolerate false prophetess Jezebel: practice immorality and eat food sacrificed to idols

v. have name of being alive and are dead

vii. would that you were hot or cold; say: rich, prosperous, need nothing but are wretched, pitiable, poor, blind, naked

(c) *admonition to repent:*

i. remember from what you have fallen; do the works you did at first

iii. repent

iv. gave her time, she refuses to repent

v. remember, keep what you have received and heard

vii. buy from me gold refined by fire (rich); white garments (clothing and cover shame of nakedness); salve (heal eyes); those whom I love I reprove

(d) *"behold": prophetic revelatory saying:*

ii. do not fear what about to suffer; devil about to imprison some of you; be tested for "ten days"

iv. will throw her and those who commit adultery with her on sick bed, tribulation; strike her children (disciples) dead; all will know I search mind and heart and give each as they deserve; but those do not follow this teaching and have not learned "deep things of Satan," no other burden

vi. make those of synagogue of Satan, claim be Jews but are not, come and bow at your feet; learn that I have loved you; because you have kept my word of endurance I will keep you from trial coming on the whole world to test those who dwell on earth

vii. I stand at the door and knock

(e) *promise the Lord is coming:*

i. if do not repent, will come and remove lampstand

iii. will come and war against them with the sword of my mouth

v. will come like a thief, you know not what hour

vi. am coming soon

vii. one who hears and opens, I will come and eat together

(f) *exhortation to endure:*

i. this you have, you hate the Nicolaitans

ii. be faithful unto death and I will give you crown of life

iv. to the rest who have not "learned the deep things of Satan," no further burden

vi. still a few not soiled their garments, worthy to walk with me in white

vi. hold to what you have so that no one may seize your crown

4. Eschatological promise to the victors
   (a) *description of victor:*
       i-iii. one who conquers
       iv.   one who conquers and keeps my works until the end
       v-vii. one who conquers
   (b) *the reward:*
       i.   eat of the tree of life, in paradise
       ii.   not hurt by the second death
       iii.   hidden manna, white stone with new name known only to the recipient
       iv.   power to rule over the nations (as I given power from God); the morning star
       v.   white garments; not blot name out of book of life; I will acknowledge before God and angels
       vi.   a pillar in the temple of my God, never go out of it; inscribed: name of my God, name of God's city, the new Jerusalem, my own new name
       vii.   sit with me on my throne (as I on Father's throne)

5. "Let him who has ears to hear, hear what the Spirit says . . ."
   (2:7,11,17,29; 3:6,13,22)

since they follow a standard format (see Chart 21–1). The rewards promised the faithful are picked up again at the end of Rev (e.g. 2:7 and 22:2,14, tree of life; 2:11 and 21:18, second death; 2:17 and 19:12, new name; 3:12 and 21:2, heavenly Jerusalem). Therefore some scholars think that the group of seven letters was composed after the sequence of visions. We meet some familiar themes in these letters. Christians must not be surprised by the persecution they suffer. Others are less endangered by persecution than by loss of their initial enthusiasm. Some are complacent in prosperity. Still other churches are divided by false teaching. Thus the letters easily serve as a general admonition to all churches as the author of the Muratorian canon observed, "John also in the Revelation writes indeed to seven churches, yet speaks to all."

The Vision Cycles

Most of Rev is taken up with the visions which the prophet is shown in heaven. These visions can be divided into cycles of seven, which are punctuated by the contrasting visions of the two great cities: the earthly

OUTLINE OF REVELATION   *[21-2]*

Prologue (1:1–8)
  (a) Preface (1:1–3)
  (b) Greeting to churches in Asia (1:4–6)
  (c) Prophetic sayings (1:7–8)

Call vision (1:9–20)

Letters to the seven churches in Asia (2:1–3:22)

Seven seals (4:1–8:5)
  (a) Vision of God's throne (4:1–11)
  (b) Vision of the enthroned Lamb with the scroll (5:1–14)
  (c) Seals #1–4: Four horsemen (6:1–8)
  (d) Seal #5: Martyrs crying out for judgment (6:9–11)
  (e) Seal #6: Earthquake, proleptic judgment (6:12–17)
  (f) Sealing of servants from the twelve tribes (7:1–17)
  (g) Seal #7: Silence in heaven (8:1–5)
    (i) Silence—preparation of the trumpets (8:1–2)
    (ii) From the altar: heavenward, the incense of prayers to God;
         toward earth, burning coals, thunder, earthquake (8:3–5)

Seven trumpets (8:2,6–11:19)
  (a) Trumpets #1–4: Plagues fall from the heavens (8:6–13)
  (b) Trumpet #5: Falling star opens abyss, locust plague led by angel
       of the abyss (9:1–11)
       [End of first woe, two more to come, v. 12]
  (c) Trumpet #6: Deadly cavalry from Euphrates released (9:13–21)
  (d) Seer eats the little scroll from the hand of angel: commissioning
       to prophesy again (10:1–11)
  (e) Seer measures the temple and the altar (11:1–3)
  (f) Testimony of the two witnesses in Jerusalem; martyred by the
       beast; taken to heaven; deadly earthquake in the city (11:4–13)
       [End of second woe, third to come, v. 14]
  (g) Trumpet #7: Heavenly acclamation of Christ who rules for ever;
       vision of the ark with lightning, voices, thunder, earthquake, hail
       (11:15–19)

Unnumbered visions: Followers of Lamb vs. the beast (12:1–15:4)
  (a) Woman and her offspring vs. the dragon (12:1–17)
  (b) Beast from the sea (13:1–10)

   (c) Beast from the earth (13:11–18)
   (d) On Mount Zion: song of the 144,000 (14:1–7; cf. 7:1–17)
   (e) Angelic heralds: warning and promise to the saints (14:8–13)
   (f) Son of Man and angels harvest the earth (14:14–20)
   (g) Sea of glass: those who have conquered the beast (15:2–4)

Seven bowls of wrath (15:1,5–16:21)
   (a) Introduction: bowls are end of wrath of God (15:1)
   (b) Angels given the seven bowls by throne creature (15:5–8)
   (c) Bowl #1: poured on earth: sores on those worship the beast
        (16:1–2)
   (d) Bowl #2: in sea: becomes like blood, everything in it dies (16:3)
   (e) Bowl #3: rivers and fountains: become blood, just judgment for
        blood of martyrs acclaimed (16:4–7)
   (f) Bowl #4: on sun: it scorches humans, who blaspheme God and
        do not repent (16:8–9)
   (g) Bowl #5: on throne beast: kingdom darkened; humans curse God
        for sores, do not repent (16:10–11)
   (h) Bowl #6: on Euphrates: demonic spirits from mouths of dragon,
        beast and false prophet assemble armies at Armageddon (16:12–
        16; cf. 9:13–21)
   (i) Bowl #7: in air: voice sounds from temple, thunder, quakes,
        cities split, islands and mountains vanish, hail (16:17–21)

Babylon and her destruction (17:1–19:10)
   (a) "Babylon the Great," harlot to the kings of the earth, drunk with
        the blood of the saints (17:1–6)
   (b) Angelic interpretation of the vision: Rome, her rulers, client
        kings and wars (17:7–18)
   (c) Heavenly announcement: the hour of judgment on Babylon has
        come (18:1–8)
   (d) Laments for the fate of Babylon by kings of the earth,
        merchants, captains and sailors (18:9–20)
   (e) Angelic announcement: Babylon and all who dwell in her to be
        thrown down (18:21–24)
   (f) Heavenly praise to God for judgment against Babylon (19:1–4)
   (g) Praise to Lamb: Celebration of divine marriage feast (19:5–10)

Unnumbered visions: Judgment of the earth (19:11–21:8)
   (a) Rider on the white horse (19:11–16)
   (b) Victory feast on bodies of the slain (19:17–21)
   (c) Angel binds Satan for a thousand years (20:1–3)

(d) Victorious martyrs reign with Christ a thousand years (20:4–6)
(e) Fire from heaven consumes the Satanic hosts (20:7–10)
(f) Judgment of all humanity: Book of life (20:11–15)
(g) New heaven and earth: Righteous to dwell with God (21:1–8)

Bride of the Lamb: The heavenly Jerusalem (21:9–22:5)
(a) Jewels which adorn the bride (21:2,9–21)
(b) God's presence in the heavenly city (21:22–27)
(c) River of water, tree of life and God as its light (22:1–5)

Epilogue: Transmission of the prophecy and beatitudes (22:6–21)

Babylon and the heavenly Jerusalem. Some form numbered sets. For others, we have divided the sequence to follow the numerical pattern of seven. There is considerable interlocking between cycles of visions. This technique suggests that the visions do not follow one another in a linear sequence but that they are repetitions of the same pattern raised to another level of intensity. The cycles have also been linked together by internal references to three woes. The final woe is the cycle of seven plagues. The epilogue returns to the opening of the book. Both pronounce blessings on those who heed the words of the prophecy it contains (1:3; 22:7b). Both emphasize that these are things which God's plan has destined to happen soon (1:1; 22:6,12a). Both remind the reader that Jesus, the faithful martyr, is the beginning and end of all things (1:8,17). The beatitudes in the epilogue remind the reader of the promises made to the victorious in the letters. The final blessing in 22:21 may also call to mind the conclusion of the Christian letter form.

The Apocalyptic Imagination

Rev draws its imagery from a rich tradition of mythic and Old Testament imagery. The prophet also reminds the readers of Christian traditions such as the earlier predictions of judgment and exhortations to watchfulness (e.g. Mk 13; Mt 24); the death and resurrection/exaltation of Jesus to God's throne, where Jesus is now "king" over the nations; titles and epithets of Jesus such as Son of Man, Son of God, Son of David and Lamb of God.

Two Jewish apocalypses written at about the same time as Rev, 4 Ezra and 2 Baruch, speak of the suffering and disorientation felt by some Jews after the Romans had destroyed Jerusalem in A.D. 70. Like Rev, they are concerned with the question of why God does not send the messianic age soon and destroy the forces of evil, especially the Roman empire, which all three writings describe in Satanic terms. They both reassure the faithful that the end of the evil age is coming and that faithfulness to God will not be lost or forgotten.

Notice that apocalyptic writings often speak for people who are oppressed, especially by a larger political power that they cannot control. Rev emphasizes the imagery of the faithful martyr. Jesus is the prime example of the martyr. There is even a special thousand-year reign on earth for those Christians who have been martyred. The prophet John tells us that he is suffering exile to the island of Patmos for his preaching (Rev 1:9). The letter to the church at Pergamum mentions the name of a famous martyr, Antipas, who had died in that city. As you can see from the outline there is a major turning point in the book at chapter 12. From chapter 12 on, we are shown the conflict between the children of the heavenly Jerusalem and those who worship the beast. Just before that turning point we are shown a vision of two martyrs in Jerusalem. The vision shows that their fate is like that of the Lord for whom they died. After three days God sweeps them up to heaven (Rev 11:4–13). This manifestation of divine power includes an earthquake, a frequent sign of divine presence. Earthquakes, thunder and signs in the heavens were also a common part of the scenery of the end of the world. Mt 27:51–54 has the apocalyptic signs of earthquake and raising of the dead in Jerusalem associated with the crucifixion. Mt 28:2 introduces another great earthquake and descent of an angel with the opening of Jesus' tomb.

Rev centers its confidence on Christ. By transporting the hearer into the heavenly court where the victory of the Lamb is proclaimed, the prophet shows that Christ is Lord over the kings of the earth. The suffering Christians are swept up into that glorious victory. Throughout Rev we are reminded that Jesus has triumphed over death (e.g. 1:7,8; 2:8; 5:5–6). We are also shown images of the faithful, the holy people ransomed by the Lamb's blood (1:5–6); the 144,000 from the tribes of Israel (7:1–8; 14:1–7); the martyrs clothed in white (6:10–11; 7:13–17) and multitudes from all the nations (7:9–10). These visions of the community of the redeemed provide powerful symbols with which the reader can identify.

Most apocalypses are presented as pseudonymous works from an ancient figure in the past which were hidden until the "end of the age." Rev is quite different. The concluding sayings against tampering with the revelation (22:18–19) also insist that it is not to be sealed up (22:10). Its author does not speak as a voice from the distant past but as a fellow Christian. He gives us his name, John (1:1), and suggests that he belonged to a group of Christian prophets active in the churches of Asia Minor (22:9). Thus the first readers of Rev were receiving a divine message mediated through one of their own prophets. Since the author is in exile because of his preaching, he may have been very well known in the region.

The Political Message of Revelation

We have seen that the symbolism of Rev provides a powerful description of the true divine kingship and its heavenly manifestations. The Christian reader is drawn up into identifying with the holy ones who follow and sing praises to the Lamb. At the same time Rev stands in a tradition which used apocalyptic symbolism to condemn the powerful empires of the ancient world. Dan 7–12 had already established the pattern of using a succession of beasts to describe successive empires. Dan 7 also uses the figure of a Son of Man exalted to God's throne as judge over those empires and as vindication of the suffering martyrs of Israel. Apocalypses written at the same time as Rev use the code name "Babylon" for the Roman empire. No first century semitic reader would have any difficulty figuring out that the number of the beast in 13:18 is the spelling of "Nero Caesar" in a semitic alphabet. Nor would they have had any difficulty recognizing in the laments of the merchants and sea captains a frequent criticism of Rome in the "underground" oracles and apocalypses from the eastern part of the empire. Rome is routinely pictured as raping the provinces of Asia for their wealth. Here are some examples of that perspective taken from the Jewish *Sibylline Oracles:*

> However much wealth Rome received from tribute-bearing Asia, Asia will receive three times that much again from Rome and will repay her deadly arrogance to her. Whatever number from Asia served the house of the Italians [i.e. as slaves], twenty times that number of Italians will be serfs in Asia; in poverty they will be liable to pay ten-thousandfold. (3:350–55)

> Great wealth will come out of Asia, which Rome itself once plundered and deposited in her house of many possessions. She will then pay back twice as much and more to Asia, and then there will be a surfeit of war. (4:145–48)

> . . . the famous, lawless kingdom of the Italians . . . will show many evils to all men and will expend the toils of the men of all the earth . . . the beginning of evils will be the desire for de-

ceitful gold and silver. . . . If the huge earth did not have its throne far from the starry heaven, men would not have equal light, but it would be marketed for gold and would belong to the rich, and God would have prepared another world for beggars. . . . Having abundant gold, [Hadrian] will also gather more silver from his enemies and strip and undo them. . . . [Marcus Aurelius] will control dominions far and wide, a most piteous king, who will shut up and guard all the wealth of the world in his home, so that when the blazing matricidal exile [Nero] returns from the ends of the earth, he will give these things to all and award great wealth to Asia. . . . Woe to you, Italian land, great savage nation. You did not perceive whence you came, naked and unworthy to the light of the sun, so that you might go again naked to the same place and later come to judgment because you judge unjustly. (8:9–11, 17–18, 33–36, 68–72, 95–99)

You can easily see from these examples that the descriptions of the corruption and fall of Rome in Rev 17–18 express a common perception of Roman power in the provinces of Asia Minor. For the *Sibylline Oracles* that power is to be smashed in a political victory, led by the emperor Nero returned to life to lead the armies out of Asia. Rev does not share this type of political hope. The only armies which come from the east are the demonic forces from the Euphrates region. The legend of Nero redivivus is mentioned in 13:3 as the head with a "mortal wound" that heals and then seduces the earth. Nero is no liberator for Asia. Rev 17:15–18 pictures the client kings of Rome (also probably represented by the beast from the earth in 13:11–17) finally revolting and waging a war against her. But the righteous do not participate in any such revolts. Their opposition to the beast consists in refusing to grant the beast "worship" and in continuing as faithful witnesses even at the cost of their own lives.

Honoring the Emperor?

What is implied in these warnings against worshiping the beast (e.g. 13:4, 8, 15)? It is difficult for people today to understand what was involved in cultic and civic honors paid to the emperor. People knew that the emperors were not gods in the sense that the gods and goddesses of pagan mythology and cults were divine. But from the time of Julius Caesar on, Roman art depicted the soul of the deceased emperor being carried up to heaven to join the company of the gods. Temples could be erected and sacrifices offered to the "divine Caesar." From the time of Augustus we have examples of divine honors being paid to the living emperor. Such honors might take the form of temples dedicated to the "genius of the emperor," sacrifices and festal games in his honor, or ceremonial inscriptions describing the emperor as the great benefactor of humanity and savior. Often such honors were voted by a city in hopes that the emperor would respond by bestowing some benefit on the city such as relief from a particular form of taxation.

The emperor does not have to compel people to worship him as a god. You can see that such honors might come from cities as a matter of civic pride or even political calculation. Perhaps you noticed that Rev 13:12–15 speaks of those who received their power from the beast creating a miraculous statue of the mortally wounded head and causing people to worship it. In a well-known incident the emperor Caligula (ca. A.D. 40) had ordered his governor in Syria to see to it that his statue was erected in the Jerusalem temple even if he had to use armed force to do so (see Josephus, *War* 2.185–87; *Antiquities* 18.261–309; Philo, *Embassy to Gaius* 188–348; Tacitus, *Histories* 5.9). Our sources have varying accounts of the details though all agree that the Jewish people were willing to risk death in war

Antonine Altar at Ephesus.

rather than violate the law by putting up such a statue. Philo's account, taken from a work written after he had been part of an embassy of Alexandrian Jews to Gaius, emphasizes the emperor's manic desire to be paid divine honors. While Josephus and Tacitus claim that erection of the statue was only prevented by the emperor's death in A.D. 41, Philo reports that he had relented (after extensive lobbying by his own governor and the Herodian king Agrippa II, then living in Rome). But in doing so he ordered the governor to encourage such dedications of temples and statues in other cities, and such images were forced into synagogues in Alexandria in his name. Failure to pay such honors to the emperor could easily be construed as evidence of subversion and civic disloyalty.

When we look at the cities to which the letters in Rev are addressed, we find that they too were involved in propagating the imperial cult. Ephesus and Smyrna competed with each other in paying such honors at festivals. Pergamum was the regional center of the cult. It had received permission in 29 B.C. to build a temple to "the divine Augustus and the goddess Roma." This famous temple is probably the "throne of Satan" referred to in Rev 3:13. People in Thyatira worshiped the emperor as Apollo incarnate and son of Zeus. In A.D. 26 Sardis was among ten cities competing for the right to build a temple in honor of the emperor but lost to Smyrna. Since Laodicea was the wealthiest city in Phrygia and especially prosperous under the Flavian emperors (Rev was most likely written under Domitian, d. A.D. 96), we would certainly expect some form of emperor cult to be propagated in that city as well.

Such dedications and honors were not only the responsibilities of civic officials. They were also sometimes fostered by particular trade groups. We have already seen that Rev 18 singles out merchants and sea captains as persons who lament the fall of Rome. There is evidence that some mercantile associations might have made offerings in the name of the emperor or erected statues in his honor. Some of these honors were not strictly "worship," that is, they were not sacrifices which solicited benefits as one might from a god. Recent studies have shown that in Macedonia and Greece the distinction between cultic activity directed toward the gods and sacrifices that might be offered on behalf of the well-being of the emperor was carefully maintained. In Asia Minor the distinctions appear to have been more frequently blurred. When they become blurred, then other common practices in which the emperor's name or image was used would appear to be idolatrous. Images of the emperor on coins, for example, might picture the emperor as though he were one of the gods. Local mints put out such coins. Consequently Rev 13:17 remarks that no one could buy or sell unless he had the mark of the beast. The "mark" in question may well be a reference to the images of the emperor on coins. In addition the name of the emperor, with appropriate god-like epithets (the "blasphemous name" of 13:1), would be used on a number of public occasions. Contracts and oaths in court might refer to the emperor; so would the ceremonial libations poured out at public banquets.

As you can see from the Caligula episode, the Jewish community had established limits that it would not transgress in venerating the emperor. As long as the temple was standing in Jerusalem, the priests there did offer daily sacrifices to God for the emperor. But the Jews would not violate the commandments by putting up statues and images of the emperor. Jesus sided with those who were willing to treat the images on imperial coins as unimportant (Mk 12:13–17), though special coins were used within the temple itself. We have seen that in the Pauline tradition (Rom 13:1–10; Acts) and the Petrine tradition (1 Pet 2:13–17) Christians were instructed to honor the emperor. These traditions are shaped by contexts in which the "honor" due the emperor did not exceed the boundaries of what might be considered appropriate respect for one who stood at the top of the social and political order of a great empire. However Rev insists that such accommodation is no longer possible. Christians must resist Satanic divinization of Roman power in all of its forms.

Discipleship in Revelation

You can see from our discussion of martyrdom and refusal to venerate the emperor that Rev calls Christians to a very costly form of discipleship. Rev considers the "mark of the beast" (Rev 13:16–17) to be a parody of the "mark" which the Christian receives (7:1–8). Anyone who has received the "mark of the beast" is destined for eternal punishment (14:9–11; 16:2). This rigorous position would clearly have economic consequences for Christians like those in Laodicea who are condemned for a wealth and prosperity, which apparently derived from the city's extensive textile industry (3:15–18).

The Jewish community was able to retain its policy of non-participation in veneration of the emperor by appealing to its ancestral religion and grants of special privileges to the Jewish community by Roman emperors. When we look at the letters in Rev, we find that there is tension between Christians and "those who claim to be Jews but are not" in the cities of Smyrna (Rev 2:9–10) and Philadelphia (3:9). The message to Smyrna links the "synagogue of Satan" with the coming persecution of Christians. Probably members of the local Jewish community had been involved in bringing charges against Christians before the local magistrates. The city's bishop, Polycarp, would become a martyr as the result of such opposition ca. A.D. 156. The hostile references to Judaism in these passages of Rev reflect the separation of the two communities. Christians claim to be the true heirs to the tradition of Israel. They may also have insisted that they ought to have the same rights as "resident aliens" with their own independent self-government that had been extended to the Jewish community. The Jewish community, on the other hand, may have attempted to deny that this deviant, messianic sect deserved to be considered "Jews."

Another struggle in the churches of Asia Minor was internal. The author attacks a group known as the Nicolaitans, and followers of other Christian teachers who are treated as examples of the false prophets and idolators of the Old Testament, Balaam and Jezebel (2:14–15; 2:20–23). By the second century the Nicolaitans would be a gnostic sect. The prophet claims that the prophetess Jezebel had been given an opportunity to repent (2:21). He may have delivered a prophetic oracle against her teaching at some earlier time. The accusations directed against "Balaam" and "Jezebel" involve "eating food sacrificed to idols and prostitution." The decree of the Jerusalem council reported in Acts 15:28–29 forbids eating food used in idol sacrifices, food slaughtered in violation of kosher laws, and sexual immorality. Clearly Rev expects this ruling to be binding on Christians. We have already met two different positions in the New Testament. Some Christians at Corinth held that whatever Christians did was indifferent. They knew that the food sacrificed to an idol was not offered to a god. Paul rejected their views. He held that Christians had to avoid prostitutes (6:12–20). But he admitted that it was all right to eat idol meat in situations in which it was clear that no worship of the gods was implied. One could eat at home or the house of a friend but not as part of a ritual meal at a pagan temple (e.g. 1 Cor 8:8–10; 10:25–29). This middle ground position kept open the possibility of social and business contacts with non-Christian associates and relatives. The "false prophets" attacked by Rev may even have been advocating more extreme forms of accommodation like those advocated by the "strong" at Corinth.

You can see from these passages that the Christianity advocated by Rev would have to form its own trade associations, burial societies and the like, since it would be very difficult for Christians to participate in groups which included non-Christians. Christians could not engage in any of the associations, clubs or even occupations which would require any form of gesture, word or ritual that might be construed as "worshiping the beast." The martyrs are praised for having practiced virginity (14:4). The author himself may have been an ascetic prophet who had gone from city to city until he was exiled. Though Rev does not suggest that all Christians must refrain from marriage, its ideal of Christianity does suggest sectarian withdrawal from the everyday world of association with non-Christians.

Summary

Anyone who takes the time to study Rev carefully can see that this visionary prophet has a clear and consistent message to the churches of his time and region. He sees the danger that Christians in Asia Minor will be led to accommodate to the structures of the culture with which they are surrounded. Accommodation might be sought by some to avoid persecution. Others appear to have had more secular goals: adaption to the demands of business associates or social relationships. The polemic against other Christian teachers indicates that not all Christians saw the situation in Asia Minor in the same dark tones as the author does.

The dramatic imagery of the beast warring against the offspring of the heavenly Israel makes it clear to the reader that there is no "middle ground" in this situation. For humanity at large, the prophet predicts that no matter how dramatic or severe the divine signs are, people will blaspheme God rather than repent (e.g. 16:8–11). These visions are not to "scare" non-Christians into conversion as some of the Jehovah's Witnesses who ring the doorbell on Saturday morning seem to think. John's message is directed toward his fellow Christians. They can repent and recover their former enthusiasm. They can be encouraged to stand fast when confronted by times of suffering. They can be inspired by its visions of heavenly victory with the Lamb.

STUDY QUESTIONS

Facts You Should Know

1. Give three examples of old "mythic themes" that are used by the author of Rev.
2. What are the basic elements in the letters to the seven churches in Rev? How are the letters linked to the rest of the book?
3. How is the vision section of Rev constructed? What cities represent the earthly and heavenly worlds?
4. According to Rev what is the role of suffering and martyrdom in the life of Christian disciples? Why do Christians find themselves faced with martyrdom?
5. How does the criticism of the Roman empire in Rev compare with other non-Christian writings from this period?
6. Describe what actions might have been considered "worshiping the emperor" in the world of Asia Minor. How had Jews come into conflict

with Roman authorities over "emperor worship"? Why is "worshiping the beast" a danger that Rev warns its readers about?

7. Who was the author of Rev? How does the author of Rev differ from the authors of Jewish apocalypses?

Things To Do

1. Read through the seven letters, making a list of those who are praised and those who are condemned in each letter. What ideal of Christian discipleship emerges from your lists?

2. Read through Rev and pick out each time Jesus is shown as a "faithful martyr" or the Lamb who has triumphed over death. Also pick out each time we are shown the fate of Christian martyrs. How do these images encourage the audience of Rev to remain faithful disciples?

Things To Think About

1. Rev warns Christians against making easy compromises with that culture which surrounds them by showing that some parts of the culture are "Satanic." What warnings would Rev address to Christians today?

2. The visions of plagues show that even with the most terrible devastation of the earth, the nations do not repent. What is the cause of this blindness? How is it evident in our world?

BIBLIOGRAPHY FOR FURTHER STUDY

The bibliography which follows has been limited to recent books in English which can serve as guides to further information about the topics treated in each chapter. An asterisk (*) indicates books which are scholarly reference works.

CHAPTER 1: WHY STUDY THE BIBLE?

Some basic tools for studying the Bible might include:

A Concordance: Lists all the occurrences of a word in the Bible. You have to use a concordance for the particular translation of the Bible you are reading. Pocket concordances are available which are limited to major words and passages.

A Gospel Parallels: Sets out the parallel passages in the gospels side by side or in lines, one above the other, so that it is easier to compare different versions. The most complete gospel parallels, which also includes material from outside the canon, and uses bold face type to indicate words which are repeated in the different versions (based on the RSV translation), is: R. Funk, *New Gospel Parallels. Vol 1: Synoptic Gospels; Vol 2: John and the Other Gospels.* Philadelphia: Fortress, 1985.

Harper's Bible Dictionary, ed. P. Achtemeier. San Francisco: Harper & Row, 1985. Contains articles by leading scholars on all books, places, names and major terms in the Bible as well as topical articles, maps and extensive illustrations.

Commentary series: The quality of a series of commentaries varies with the individual volumes. The volumes in the following series are aimed at the general reader without much background in biblical studies and are generally of excellent quality: Roman Catholic: *New Testament Message Series.* Wilmington: Michael Glazier/Dublin: Veritas; *Collegeville Bible Commentary.* Collegeville: Liturgical Press. Protestant: *New Century Bible Commentary.* Grand Rapids: Eerdmans/ London: Oliphants, then Basingstoke: Marshall, Morgan & Scott; *Interpretation.* Atlanta: John Knox (only some volumes have been completed).

Atlas: J. Rogerson, *Atlas of the Bible.* New York: Facts on File, 1985; *New Atlas of the Bible.* London: Macdonald, 1985; T. Cornell and J. Matthews, *Atlas of the Roman World.* New York: Facts on File, 1982/ Oxford: Phaidon. Both volumes have superb maps; illustrations and articles which deal with the NT world.

Greek language: Basic reference works on the Greek of the NT: W. Arndt & F.W. Gingrich, rev. by F. Danker, *A Greek-English Lexicon of the New Testament.* Chicago: University of Chicago, 1979; F. Blass and A. Debrunner, rev. R. Funk, *A Greek Grammar of the New Testament and Other Early Christian Literature.* Chicago: University of Chicago, 1961.

New Testament apocrypha: Occasionally you will find references to apocryphal writings, that is, early Christian writings which are not part of the NT canon such as the *Gospel of Thomas.* The standard collection of the NT apocrypha is E. Hennecke and W. Schneemelcher, *New Testament Apocrypha,* 2 vols. Philadelphia: Westminster, 1963/London: SCM/Lutterworth, 1963/1965; a useful collection of apocryphal Jewish, Christian and other esoteric literature may be had in W. Barnstone, ed. *The Other Bible. Ancient Esoteric Texts.* San Francisco: Harper & Row, 1984, pbk.

On the methods used in analyzing the NT: for the novice reader: D. Harrington, *Interpreting the New Testament.* Wilmington: Michael Glazier, 1979/Dublin: Veritas 1980; for the seminary level student: R. Collins, *Introduction to the New Testament.* Garden City: Doubleday/London: SCM, 1983.

You may also want to read some of the following studies of the social world and ethics of the NT:

Brown, R. and Meier, J. *Antioch and Rome.* Mahwah: Paulist/London: Geoffrey Chapman, 1983 pbk.
Stambaugh, J. and Balch, D. *The New Testament in Its Social Environment.* Philadelphia: Westminster/London: SPCK, 1986.

Meeks, W.A. *The Moral World of the First Christians*. Philadelphia: Westminster, 1986/London: SPCK, 1987.

Verhey, A. *The Great Reversal. Ethics and the New Testament*. Grand Rapids: Eerdmans, 1984 pbk.

Schüssler Fiorenza, E. *In Memory of Her. A Feminist Reconstruction of Christian Origins*. New York: Crossroad/London: SCM, 1983 pbk.

CHAPTER 2: THE WORLD OF JESUS

Historical studies: Gruen, E.S. *The Hellenistic World and the Coming of Rome*. Berkeley: University of California, 1984 pbk; S. Freyne, *Galilee from Alexander the Great to Hadrian*. Wilmington: Michael Glazier/Notre Dame: University of Notre Dame, 1980; *S. Safrai and M. Stern, *The Jewish People in the First Century. Historical Geography, Political History, Social, Cultural and Religious Life and Institutions*, 2 vols. Philadelphia: Fortress/Assen: Van Gorcum, 1974; *E. Schurer, rev. G. Vermes and F. Millar, *History of the Jewish People in the Age of Jesus Christ*, vols. 1 & 2. Edinburgh: T. & T. Clark, 1973/1979; *E.M. Smallwood, *The Jews Under Roman Rule*. Leiden: E.J. Brill, 1976; E. Hengel, *Jews, Greeks & Barbarians. Aspects of the Hellenization of Judaism in the Pre-Christian Period*. Philadelphia: Fortress/London: SCM, 1980; A.R.C. Leaney, *The Jewish and Christian World 200 B.C. to A.D. 200*. Cambridge: Cambridge University, 1984 pbk; M. Stone, *Scriptures, Sects and Visions. A Profile of Judaism from Ezra to the Jewish Revolts*. Philadelphia: Fortress, 1980, Oxford: Blackwell, 1982.

Archaeology: N. Avigad, *Rediscovering Jerusalem*. Nashville: Nelson, 1980, *Discovering Jerusalem*. Oxford: Blackwell, 1984; B.-D. Meier, *In the Shadow of the Temple. The Discovery of Ancient Jerusalem*. San Francisco: Harper & Row, 1985; E.M. Meyers and J.F. Strange, *Archaeology, the Rabbis and Early Christianity*. Nashville: Abingdon, 1981 pbk.

Sociological studies: R.A. Horsley and J.S. Hanson, *Bandits, Prophets and Messiahs*. San Francisco: Harper & Row, 1985; N. Lewis, *Life in Egypt under Roman Rule*. Oxford: Oxford University, 1985 pbk; S.B. Pomeroy, *Women in Hellenistic Egypt*. New York: Schocken, 1984; G. Theissen, *Sociology of Early Palestinian Christianity*. Philadelphia: Fortress, 1978 pbk.

Jewish literature: J.J. Collins, *The Apocalyptic Imagination*. New York: Crossroad, 1984; G.W.E. Nickelsburg, *Jewish Literature between the*

Bible and the Mishnah. Philadelphia: Fortress/London: SCM, 1981;
*M.E. Stone ed., *Jewish Writings of the Second Temple Period:
Apocrypha, Pseudepigrapha, Qumran, Sectarian Writings, Philo, Josephus.* Philadelphia: Fortress, 1984; *E. Schurer, rev. G. Vermes,
F. Millar and M. Goodman, *History of the Jewish People in the Age
of Jesus Christ, Vol. 3,1.* Edinburgh: T. & T. Clark, 1986; *J.H. Char-
lesworth, ed., *The Old Testament Pseudepigrapha,* 2 vols. London:
Darton, Longman & Todd, 1983–1984/Garden City: Doubleday,
1985; H.F.D. Sparks, *The Apocryphal Old Testament.* Oxford: Oxford University, 1984 pbk; J. Cornfeld, *Josephus. The Jewish War.*
Grand Rapids: Zondervan, 1982/Exeter: Paternoster, 1983 (extensive
archeological and historical information; maps and photographs); G.
Vermes, *The Dead Sea Scrolls in English.* Harmondsworth/Balti-
more: Penguin, 1975 2nd ed, pbk; J. Maier, *The Temple Scroll.* Shef-
field, Eng.: JSOT Press, 1985 pbk; G.W.E. Nickelsburg and M.E.
Stone, eds. *Faith and Piety in Early Judaism. Texts and Documents.*
Philadelphia: Fortress, 1983.

CHAPTER 3: THE LIFE OF JESUS

Reconstructing the life of Jesus: J.D.G. Dunn, *Evidence for Jesus.* Phil-
adelphia: Westminster/London: SCM, 1985 pbk; A.E. Harvey, *Jesus
and the Constraints of History.* Philadelphia: Westminster/London:
Duckworth, 1982.
Special topics: R.E. Brown, *The Birth of the Messiah.* Garden City: Dou-
bleday/London: Geoffrey Chapman, 1977 pbk (infancy narratives); H.
Kee, *Miracle in the Early Christian World.* New Haven: Yale, 1983
pbk; *idem, *Medicine, Miracle and Magic in New Testament Times*
SNTSMS 55; Cambridge: Cambridge University, 1986; M. Hengel,
Crucifixion. Philadelphia: Fortress, 1977 pbk; H. Hendrickx, *The
Passion Narratives of the Synoptic Gospels.* London: Geoffrey Chap-
man, 1984 pbk; F. Matera, *Passion Narratives and Gospel Theolo-
gies.* Mahwah: Paulist, 1986 pbk.

CHAPTER 4: THE PREACHING OF JESUS

Parables: J.D. Crossan, *In Parables.* San Francisco: Harper & Row, 1973
pbk; H. Hendrickx, *The Parables of Jesus.* London: Geoffrey Chap-
man/San Francisco: Harper & Row, 1986 pbk; J. Jeremias, *The Parables of Jesus.* New York: Scribners, 1963/London: SCM, 1972 pbk;

P. Perkins, *Hearing the Parables of Jesus*. Mahwah: Paulist, 1981 pbk; B. Scott, *Jesus, Symbol-Maker for the Kingdom*. Philadelphia: Fortress, 1981; D. Via, *The Parables*. Philadelphia: Fortress, 1967 pbk.

Special topics: G.R. Beasley-Murray, *Jesus and the Kingdom of God*. Grand Rapids: Eerdmans/Exeter: Paternoster, 1986; J. Lambrecht, *The Sermon on the Mount*. Wilmington: Michael Glazier, 1985 pbk; L. Schottroff and W. Stegemann, *Jesus and the Hope of the Poor*. Maryknoll: Orbis, 1986 pbk; *B. Witherington, *Women in the Ministry of Jesus*. Cambridge: Cambridge University, 1984.

CHAPTER 5: THE RESURRECTION OF JESUS

H. Hendrickx, *The Resurrection Narratives of the Synoptic Gospels*. London: Geoffrey Chapman, 1984 pbk.

P. Perkins, *Resurrection. New Testament Witness and Contemporary Reflection*. Garden City: Doubleday, 1984/London: Geoffrey Chapman, 1985.

CHAPTER 6: THE BEGINNINGS OF CHRISTOLOGY

*J.D.G. Dunn, *Christology in the Making*. Philadelphia: Westminster/ London: SCM, 1980 pbk.

J.A. Fitzmyer, *A Christological Catechism. New Testament Answers*. Mahwah: Paulist, 1981 pbk.

R. Fuller and P. Perkins, *Who Is This Christ?* Philadelphia: Fortress, 1983 pbk.

M. Hengel, *The Son of God*. Philadelphia: Fortress, 1976 pbk.

B. Lindars, *Jesus, Son of Man*. Grand Rapids: Eerdmans/London: SPCK, 1983 pbk.

CHAPTER 7: THE WORLD OF PAUL

Jews and Christians in the Roman World: M. Grant, *The World of Rome*. London: Weidenfeld, 1960/New York: New American Library; still the best survey of the Roman world in this period with extensive treatment of religious and philosophical movements); J.J. Collins, *Between Athens and Jerusalem. Jewish Identity in the Hellenistic Diaspora*. New York: Crossroad, 1983 (focuses on writings of diaspora

Judaism); A. Malherbe, *Social Aspects of Early Christianity*. Philadelphia: Fortress, 1983, sec. ed. pbk; W.A. Meeks, *The First Urban Christians. The Social World of the Apostle Paul*. New Haven: Yale, 1983 pbk; B.F. Meyers and E.P. Sanders, *Jewish and Christian Self-Definition. Vol. 3: Self-Definition in the Greco-Roman World*. Philadelphia: Fortress, 1982 (essays on self-definition in religious and philosophical movements that were competing with Christianity); M. Whittaker, *Jews and Christians. Graeco-Roman Views*. Cambridge: Cambridge University, 1984 pbk.

Religious movements: R.M. Grant, *Gods and the One God*. Philadelphia: Westminster/London: SPCK, 1986; R. MacMullen, *Paganism in the Roman Empire*. New Haven: Yale, 1981 pbk; R.M. Grant, *Hellenistic Religion*. Indianapolis: Bobbs Merrill (Library of Liberal Arts), 1953 pbk (selected texts); *H.D. Betz, *The Greek Magical Papyri in Translation*, Vol. 1. Chicago: University of Chicago, 1986; G. Luck, *Arcana Mundi. Magic and the Occult in the Greek and Roman Worlds*. Baltimore: Johns Hopkins, 1985 pbk; A. Malherbe, *The Cynic Epistles*. Atlanta: Scholars Press, 1977 pbk.

Special Topics: K. Greene, *The Archaeology of the Roman Economy*. Berkeley: University of California, 1986; M. Lefkowitz and M. Fant, *Women's Life in Greece and Rome. A Sourcebook in Translation*. Baltimore: Johns Hopkins/London: Duckworth, 1982 pbk; S.K. Stowers, *Letter-Writing in Greco-Roman Antiquity*. Philadelphia: Westminster, 1986.

CHAPTER 8: THE LIFE OF PAUL

Life of Paul: *G. Ludemann, *Paul the Apostle to the Gentiles. Studies in Chronology*. Philadelphia: Fortress/London: SCM, 1984; D.R. Macdonald, *The Legend and the Apostle. The Battle for Paul in Story and Canon*. Philadelphia: Westminster, 1983 pbk.

Pauline Theology: J.C. Beker, *Paul, the Apostle. The Triumph of God in Life and Thought*. Philadelphia: Fortress/Edinburgh: T. & T. Clark, 1980; V.P. Furnish, *The Moral Teaching of Paul. Selected Issues*. Nashville: Abingdon, 1985 2nd ed. pbk; B. Holmberg, *Paul and Power. The Structure of Authority in the Primitive Church as Reflected in the Pauline Epistles*. Philadelphia: Fortress, 1980; H. Ridderbos, *Paul. An Outline of His Theology*. Grand Rapids: Eerdmans, 1975/London: SPCK, 1977.

1 and 2 Thessalonians: E. Best, *The First and Second Epistles to the Thes-*

salonians. New York: Harper & Row/London: A. & C. Black, 1972; F.F.Bruce, *1 and 2 Thessalonians.* Waco: Word, 1982; R. Jewett, *The Thessalonian Correspondence. Pauline Rhetoric and Millenarian Piety.* Philadelphia: Fortress, 1986; I.H. Marshall, *1 and 2 Thessalonians.* Grand Rapids: Eerdmans, 1983.

Philippians: F. Craddock, *Philippians.* Atlanta: John Knox, 1985; R.P. Martin, *Philippians.* Grand Rapids: Eerdmans/London: Oliphants, 1976.

Philemon: N. Petersen, *Rediscovering Paul. Philemon and the Sociology of Paul's Narrative World.* Philadelphia: Fortress, 1985.

CHAPTER 9: CHRISTIANS: JEW AND GENTILE

Righteousness: J. Reumann, *Righteousness in the New Testament.* Mahwah: Paulist/Philadelphia: Fortress, 1982 pbk; E.P. Sanders, *Paul, the Law and the Jewish People.* Philadelphia: Fortress, 1983/London: SCM, 1985.

Galatians: *H.D. Betz, *Galatians.* Philadelphia: Fortress, 1979; F.F. Bruce, *Epistle to the Galatians.* Grand Rapids: Eerdmans/Exeter: Paternoster, 1982.

Romans: P. Achtemeier, *Romans.* Atlanta: John Knox, 1985; *E. Kaesemann, *Commentary on Romans.* Grand Rapids: Eerdmans, 1980/London: SCM, 1982; K. Donfried, ed., *The Romans Debate.* Minneapolis: Augsburg, 1977 pbk.

CHAPTER 10: DIVISIONS IN CORINTH

Ancient Corinth: J. Murphy-O'Connor, *St. Paul's Corinth. Texts and Archaeology.* Wilmington: Michael Glazier, 1983 pbk; G. Theissen, *The Social Setting of Pauline Christianity. Essays on Corinth.* Philadelphia: Fortress/Edinburgh: T. & T. Clark, 1982.

1 Corinthians: C.K. Barrett, *First Epistle to the Corinthians.* New York: Harper & Row, 1968/London: A. & C. Black, 1971; *H. Conzelmann, *1 Corinthians.* Philadelphia: Fortress, 1975; R.P. Martin, *The Spirit in the Congregation. Studies in 1 Cor 12–15.* Grand Rapids: Eerdmans, 1984; J.J. Kilgallen, *First Corinthians.* Mahwah: Paulist, 1987.

2 Corinthians: *V. Furnish, *2 Corinthians.* AncBib 32A. Garden City: Doubleday, 1984; *H.D. Betz, *2 Corinthians 8 and 9.* Philadelphia: Fortress, 1985/London: SCM 1986.

CHAPTER 11: UNIVERSALIZING PAUL'S MESSAGE

*E. Lohse, *Colossians and Philemon*. Philadelphia: Fortress/London: SCM, 1971.

E. Schweizer, *The Letter to the Colossians*. Minneapolis: Augsburg/London: SPCK, 1982 pbk.

C.L. Mitton, *Ephesians*. Grand Rapids: Eerdmans/London: Oliphants, 1976.

CHAPTER 12: MARK: JESUS, SUFFERING MESSIAH

Mark: E. Best, *Mark, The Gospel as Story*. Edinburgh: T. & T. Clark, 1983; E. Schweizer, *The Good News According to Mark*. Atlanta: John Knox/London: SPCK, 1981.

Special Topics: J. D. Kingsbury, *Jesus Christ in Matthew, Mark and Luke*. Philadelphia: Fortress, 1981 pbk; idem, *The Christology of Mark's Gospel*. Philadelphia: Fortress, 1983; E.S. Malbon, *Narrative Space and Mythic Meaning in Mark*. San Francisco: Harper & Row, 1986; D. Via, *The Ethics of Mark's Gospel. In the Middle of Time*. Philadelphia: Fortress, 1985.

CHAPTER 13: MATTHEW: JESUS, TEACHER OF ISRAEL

R.H. Gundry, *Matthew. A Commentary on His Literary and Theological Art*. Grand Rapids: Eerdmans, 1982.

J.D. Kingsbury, *Matthew. Structure, Christology and Kingdom*. Philadelphia: Fortress, 1975.

J.P. Meier, *The Vision of Matthew. Christ, Church and Morality in the First Gospel*. Mahwah: Paulist, 1978.

CHAPTER 14: LUKE: JESUS, THE LORD

*J.A. Fitzmyer, *The Gospel According to Luke I–IX* AncBib 28. Garden City: Doubleday, 1981. (Contains extensive material on Lucan theology which includes material from Acts.)

*Idem, *The Gospel According to Luke X–XXIV* AncBib 28A. Garden City: Doubleday, 1985.

R.C. Tannehill, *The Narrative Unity of Luke-Acts. Vol. 1: The Gospel According to Luke*. Philadelphia: Fortress, 1986.

CHAPTER 15: JOHN: JESUS, THE DIVINE SON

John: *C.K. Barrett, *The Gospel According to St. John*. Philadelphia: Westminster/London: SPCK, 1978 rev. ed.; *R.E. Brown, *The Gospel According to John I–XII* AncBib 29. Garden City: Doubleday, 1966/London: Geoffrey Chapman, 1971; *idem, *The Gospel According to John XIII–XXI* AncBib 29A; Garden City: Doubleday, 1970/ London: Geoffrey Chapman, 1971; *R. Schnackenburg, *The Gospel According to St. John*, 3 vols. New York: Crossroad, 1968/82/London: Burns & Oates/Search, 1980–82.

Special Topics: R.E. Brown, *The Community of the Beloved Disciple*. Mahwah: Paulist/London: Geoffrey Chapman, 1979 pbk; R.A. Culpepper, *Anatomy of the Fourth Gospel. A Study in Literary Design*. Philadelphia: Fortress, 1983; D. Moody-Smith, *Johannine Christianity*. Columbia: University of South Carolina, 1984; G.R. O'Day, *Revelation in the Fourth Gospel*. Philadelphia: Fortress, 1986 pbk; S.S. Smalley, *John. Evangelist and Interpreter*. Nashville: Nelson/ Exeter: Paternoster, 1983 (1978).

CHAPTER 16: ACTS: THE GOSPEL TO THE NATIONS

*E. Haenchen, *Acts of the Apostles*. Philadelphia: Westminster, 1971; Oxford: Blackwell, 1982.

R. Brown, *The Churches the Apostles Left Behind*. Mahwah: Paulist/London: Geoffrey Chapman, 1984 pbk.

*M. Dibelius, *Studies in the Acts of the Apostles*. London: SCM, 1956 pbk.

CHAPTER 17: HEBREWS: THE HEAVENLY HIGH PRIEST

*J.W. Thompson, *The Beginnings of Christian Philosophy*. CBQMS 13. Washington: Catholic Biblical Association, 1982 pbk.

CHAPTER 18: THE PASTORAL EPISTLES: A PAULINE TRADITION

*M. Dibelius and H. Conzelmann, *The Pastoral Epistles*. Philadelphia: Fortress/London: SCM, 1972.

CHAPTER 19: THE CATHOLIC EPISTLES: AN APOSTOLIC HERITAGE

1 Peter: E. Best, *1 Peter*. Grand Rapids: Eerdmans, 1971/Basingstoke: Marshall, Morgan & Scott, 1982; J. Elliott, *A Home for the Homeless. A Sociological Exegesis of 1 Peter*. Philadelphia: Fortress, 1981/London: SCM, 1982; *D. Balch, *Let Wives Be Submissive. The Domestic Code in 1 Peter*, SBLMS 26. Atlanta: Scholars, 1981.

James: *M. Dibelius, rev. H. Greeven, *James*. Philadelphia: Fortress/London: SCM, 1976; S. Laws, *The Epistle of James*. New York: Harper & Row/London: A. & C. Black, 1980.

Jude and 2 Peter: R.J. Bauckham, *Jude, 2 Peter*. Waco: Word, 1983.

CHAPTER 20: THE JOHANNINE EPISTLES: A CHURCH DIVIDED

1,2,3 John: *R.E. Brown, *The Epistles of John*. AncBib 30. Garden City: Doubleday, 1982/London: Geoffrey Chapman, 1983; S.S. Smalley, *1,2,3 John*. Waco: Word, 1984.

Gnosticism: K. Rudolph, *Gnosis*. San Francisco: Harper & Row, 1983/Edinburgh: T. & T. Clark, 1984; W. Foerster, *Gnosis. A Selection of Gnostic Texts*, 2 vols. Oxford: Oxford University, 1972/74; J.M. Robinson ed., *The Nag Hammadi Library in English*. San Francisco: Harper & Row/Leiden: Brill, 1977 pbk.

CHAPTER 21: REVELATION: CHRISTIANITY AND THE EMPIRE

A.Y. Collins, *Crisis and Catharsis. The Power of the Apocalypse*. Philadelphia: Westminster, 1984 pbk.

E. Schüssler Fiorenza, *The Book of Revelation. Justice and Judgment*. Philadelphia: Fortress, 1985 pbk.

SCRIPTURE INDEX

Pseudepigrapha, Dead Sea Scrolls, and Other Ancient Authors

SUBJECT INDEX